MW01074903

THE
SUSTAINABILITY
CLASS

THE
SUSTAINABILITY
CLASS

How to Take Back Our Future from
Lifestyle Environmentalists

VIJAY KOLINJIVADI AND
AARON VANSINTJAN

THE
NEW
PRESS

NEW YORK
LONDON

Requests for permission to reproduce selections from this book should be made through our website: https://thenewpress.com/contact.

[If there are a few lines of text or art permissions, they should go here.]

Published in the United States by The New Press, New York, 2024
Distributed by Two Rivers Distribution

ISBN 978-1-62097-743-9 (hc)
ISBN 978-1-62097-808-5 (ebook)
CIP data is available

The New Press publishes books that promote and enrich public discussion and understanding of the issues vital to our democracy and to a more equitable world. These books are made possible by the enthusiasm of our readers; the support of a committed group of donors, large and small; the collaboration of our many partners in the independent media and the not-for-profit sector; booksellers, who often hand-sell New Press books; librarians; and above all by our authors.

www.thenewpress.com

Composition by Dix Digital Prepress and Design
This book was set in Garamond Premier Pro
Cover design by Impprintz

Printed in the United States of America

10   9   8   7   6   5   4   3   2   1

CONTENTS

Introduction: A Guided Tour of the So-Called
    Sustainable Future   1

1: The Rise of the Sustainability Class   25

2: What Is Ecology?   61

3: Purity   103

4: Innovation   135

5: Efficiency   147

6: The PIE in the Sky   157

7: Exclusively Green   171

8: Taking Back the Future   217

Afterword   267

Notes   275

Index   325

INTRODUCTION:
A GUIDED TOUR OF THE
SO-CALLED SUSTAINABLE FUTURE

On a hot and cloudless day in July we found ourselves poolside at the Beverly Hills Hilton. A man in sunglasses was sunning himself on a neon-pink inflatable flamingo in the hotel's pool. A few women with cocktails in hand were lounging in bikinis. You could hear the occasional clinking of ice from their drinks. The Spinners' "Working My Way Back to You" was playing.

We were sitting across from Chuck, who is on the board of directors of a leading environmental sustainability organization.[1] He was telling us about the next big thing: regenerative agriculture. It would be the path forward to sustainability in the face of a collapsing world.

Chuck used to be a hippie for Jesus, but after a spiritual experience that left him speaking in tongues, he became a yoga teacher. He visited India three times and spent much of his early adulthood with famous yogis in the hills of Los Angeles, who rubbed their shoulders with counterculture gurus like Alan Watts and Timothy Leary.

Dressed now in an unbuttoned blue silk collared shirt, his graying hair combed back, he spoke fervently about the possibilities of regenerative agriculture—a kind of farming that builds up the soil by balancing animal husbandry and biodiversity. While there are aspects of it that are certainly promising, it has also become a buzzword, where no one quite agrees on its exact meaning but

everyone—from Silicon Valley investors to the meat industry—
wants in on the trend.[2]

These were benefits across political lines, said Chuck. Things
that didn't seem to be related at all would start to feel much more
connected for everyone involved. "Farmers are going to start realizing that packaging products and shipping them far away isn't
really regenerative," he told us, "and that they need to sell to local
markets, or that 'Oh, these Mexican Americans working on our
farm are really important to us and we need to start taking good
care of them. They're living beings too.' "

It's "all a bit like that acid trip you took back in the sixties that
opened the world to a million and one possibilities," Chuck informed us. This is where New Age spirituality, respect for Gaia,
Mother Earth, Pachamama, or "whatever you want to call it"
intertwines with the regenerative revolution. These revelations
seemed to have resulted in Chuck doing quite well for himself.

Listening to the golden oldies that must have been on repeat for
the last fifty years ("Thought I could have my cake and eat it, too,"
the Spinners were singing), basking in pool vibes and the glam, we
absorbed the gospel of regenerative agriculture.

We had traveled to Los Angeles because we had been told that
the vision of a sustainable future could be found in California.
That didn't surprise us somehow. After all, this state was the original hippie haven, where young people came in droves during the
heyday of the counterculture to "turn on, tune in, and drop out,"
in Timothy Leary's words.

By the time we met Chuck, we were already well acquainted
with the regenerative revolution on offer in Los Angeles. Only
days before, we had made our way to one of the birthplaces of the
hippie revolution: Venice Beach. It was here, as Jonathan Richman once sang, we could find the "followers of Watts and Leary";
it was "wild and free" and "hip, hip, hip."

Urged on by the teachings of Watts and Leary, we found

ourselves on Abbot Kinney Boulevard, the main street of Venice. Luxury sports cars, purple Hummers, and Uber limos cruised along as the hip, hip, hip dropped in on the vegan restaurants and cafés with names like Neighbor, De Buena Planta, Plant Food and Wine (a favorite haunt of film director James Cameron where we spent over $100 on a tempeh sandwich and a kelp glass noodle dish that left us hungrier than before), and Pudu Pudu (they sold pudding).

Everyone seems to be microdosing on something green. We ogled the impeccably dressed and very fit locals, on their way to get a $25 smoothie or tend to their community garden plot after a workout session at the famous Gold's Gym (where Arnold Schwarzenegger used to train). It felt like all the popular kids from high school had ended up here. It was more hype than the hype itself; it was so visually stimulating, overwhelming even, that its reputation couldn't have prepared us for what we saw.

We passed by Salt & Straw, which offered "handmade ice cream" created with "California's finest seasonal fresh local ingredients." The boutique clothing store Christy Dawn (slogan: "Honoring Mother Earth") promised a "regenerative revolution" in its display window. Grow Venice sold wicker baskets, ceramics, cacti, and fun yard signs that say "Locals Only." GreenLeaf Café, whose tired-looking employees wore shirts with slogans like "Eat well, live well," offered a smashed avocado toast for $16—and we could add a local pasture-raised egg or nitrite-free bacon for another $3.

Just around the corner, on the sidewalk across from renovated cottage houses, gated by tall fences, were planter boxes set up and maintained by an organization called Community Healing Gardens. A sign read "Please Feel Free to Eat Me," but in the boxes there were only spiky agave plants and cacti. Groundwork Coffee advertised "Coffee + Tea + Community, From the Ground Up." When we went in to ask what the community part was all about—do they do live shows, or charity?—the very busy, clearly tired barista told us she had no idea. So we checked their website, which said that, to them, the "thriving" Groundwork community "represents a work ethic unlike anywhere else." Could it just be that, perhaps, the barista wasn't working hard enough to really "get" what community means?

Farm Rio, a Brazilian clothing brand, displayed the slogan "Nature Lovers" in a large, quirky font. We asked one of the models-for-hire outside the store what the nature part was about. She shrugged, went inside, and a few moments later came back to tell us that the company plants one tree for every clothing item you buy. She then gave us a small green paper envelope. It said "Let Joy Grow" and contained "one magic bean seed" with a warning: "This Lima bean seed is not edible." It seems being green in Venice is about cultivating joy, innovative product lines, and the right mindset—sustenance be damned.

Venice wasn't just green and locally minded. It was a community that had social justice on the mind. And everyone wanted to make sure you knew it. Store after store assured us they are LGBTQ+ friendly, hanging the rainbow flag prominently in their shop windows. Intelligentsia Coffee featured Martin Luther King Jr. and Malcolm X posters on its walls. The Cook's Garden, an urban garden that "works with the best and brightest chefs and mixologists" and "supports the growing food revolution," proudly displayed a slight variation on librarian Kristin Garvey's "We Believe" sign that became such a common sight in liberal front yards during the Trump presidency: "In this House Garden, we believe Black rights matter, women's rights are human rights, no human is illegal, science is real, love is love." A "rainbow pedestrian crossing" was sponsored by six local businesses. Faherty, a high-end clothing store just across from the rainbow crossing, had core values that include "Stay authentic" and "Spread good vibes." In March 2021, they commissioned a mural by Indigenous Diné artist Lehi Thundervoice Eagle, with an important message: "From Diné to the Tongva, Still Here."[3] The artist himself also happens to run a clothing company, Thundervoice Hats, offering "the most sustainable hat in the industry" at $800.

Not only does Venice offer a vibrant, sustainable, and woke lifestyle, but it prides itself on being innovative, always chasing the next big thing. They call it Silicon Beach. The area is home to over five hundred technology companies and start-ups, including offices for Google, YouTube, Snapchat, Hulu, Oculus VR, the meditation app Headspace, Tinder, and the game companies Riot Games and Naughty, which created some of the most popular games in the world. Closer to downtown L.A., in the Arts District, the Los Angeles Clean Tech Incubator (LACI) is "a nonprofit organization creating an inclusive green economy" and run "by entrepreneurs, for entrepreneurs." They are also supported by a "community" that includes not only the City of Los Angeles but also BMW, Wells Fargo, United Airlines, and JPMorgan Chase.[4] Across from LACI we were pleased to find Urth Caffé, a high-end chain offering 100 percent organic and locally sourced goods, from turmeric and chai lattes to French pastries and Italian coffee, with branches in other emerging sustainability hubs, like Las Vegas and Riyadh, Saudi Arabia. Sitting alongside its well-to-do clientele, we discovered that it's the kind of place where pioneers of digital real estate get their caffeine fix and scheme about transforming the neighborhood to attract the "right" kind of people. Suffused by the Southern California sun, these companies and nonprofits offer their employees the perfect work atmosphere: a wholesome blend of green living, creativity, and good vibes.

It's that blend of wellness and innovation that has kept California smoothly riding the wave to a green future. In his 1983 autobiography *Flashbacks*, Leary, a psychologist at the forefront of the psychedelic movement in the 1960s, tried to clarify his famous phrase "turn on, tune in, and drop out." "Turn on" meant to become sensitive to differing degrees of consciousness by activating your mind and experiences; to "tune in" meant to interact harmoniously with the world around you, seeing humans and nature as one. "Drop out" meant to be self-made, to discover one's own singularity, to learn to do it yourself and to not let anyone else steal your vibe.[5] In the 1990s, Leary altered the phrase to "turn on, boot up, and jack in" to get the aging counterculture to embrace the interet revolution as a way to sidestep inefficient governments and the inconvenience of having to deal with politics. Like Leary, Venice has booted up, and now it's time to jack in to the sustainable future—no messy politics required.

But where do we jack in? If politics is a dead end, then it's all about lifestyle choices. On one blistering hot afternoon, we were sipping our turmeric lattes on the Astroturf patio of GreenLeaf Café when we met up with Jessica, a vegan influencer and sustainability food blog writer. Jessica told us that she had become interested in veganism because politics and the news depressed her, and making individual choices for herself was the only thing that she could do to change the world. Politicians and companies won't save us from climate change and pandemics, but being a vegan can.

And yet the problem, she said, is when people get preachy and political about veganism. In-your-face veganism scares people away: "It's like the crazy people who don't shave their legs, who make you feel bad for eating meat." To be successful, veganism has to be fashionable, trendy, and easily digestible. Today, she said, so many influential people are bringing veganism to the masses, from NFL players to James Cameron, Jay-Z, and Leonardo DiCaprio. It's about giving veganism a makeover: from shack to chic.

Jessica works at the world-renowned Plant Food and Wine, a restaurant on the leading edge of veganism's chic makeover. The founder, Matthew Kenney, had a lightbulb moment when he started eating raw food: "He was simply glowing with energy and vitality," Jessica told us. Upon dropping meat products, he started Pure Food and Wine in New York, which later became embroiled in scandal and controversy (also the subject of the Netflix series *Bad Vegans*). After a spiritual yoga retreat in Montreal, Canada, Kenney opened a school to teach raw food veganism in Oklahoma

City and soon after started a joint venture with the Saudi royal family, cooking for the vegan Prince Khaled bin Alwaleed at the Four Seasons Hotel. As Kenney told *TimeOut*, "Plant-based food is now on-trend everywhere, and Saudis are always keen to try something new, hyped up, and cool."[6]

It's easy to laugh off the mix of wellness fads and green lifestylism on display in Venice as misguide but harmless. Yet there was something deeper about it that made us very uneasy. Take, for example, Erewhon, a luxury eco-friendly supermarket—its name an anagram of "nowhere" and also the title of Samuel Butler's satiric 1872 novel. Erewhon takes greenwashing to a new, perverse level. As Steve Blum from *Los Angeles Magazine* describes it, you'll find "crowd[s] of ripped men in sweats and twiggy women in yoga athleisure swarm[ing] around a hot food bar that's teeming with yams and brussels sprouts."[7] They've got $30 pints of organic and truly raw nut butter, their own brand of sea moss gel, a numbered catalogue of blindingly bright wellness shots and smoothies—including "Germ Warfare," with colloidal silver and kyolic garlic; traceably sourced adaptogenic hot chocolate; and vegan meal replacement shakes with açai, spirulina, and wheatgrass. And we wouldn't dare to leave out their range of superfood mixes, with their invigorating helping of chaga mushrooms or ashwagandha root. As Blum adds, "It's like stepping foot on an alien planet . . . destabiliz[ing] your idea of what food even is."[8]

Erewhon offers a motley and colorful hodgepodge of ancient traditional practices, combining them like Technicolor potions into fabulous new products that dazzle and awe the seemingly conscientious consumer. We can't help but be reminded of Jonathan Richman once again, when he croons "the ancient world is in my reach, from my rooming house on Venice Beach." Erewhon is making the ancient world from faraway lands hip and bringing it to the masses.

The store's marketing is impeccable, blending chakra balance and alignment with biodynamic, free-range rawness, and frequent mention of sustainability so that the consumer can achieve total wellness. As its vice president, Jason Widener, said to the *New York Times*: "It's a paradox for a health food store to be cool. I don't know if it's cool anymore these days to have a Bud Light jumping off a cliff, you know? It's cool to have a green juice in your hand and jump off a cliff."[9] He also went on to say (with a "Zenned-out, surfer-bro lilt"): "Are there impostors out there who are eating healthy food because it's cool? Probably. But guess what? I don't care. I love it. Fake it 'til you make it."[10]

Even just walking around in the supermarket gives you wholesome lifestyle vibes. The air smelling of patchouli oil and sage—ah, it's the pinnacle of health! It's a return to nature. You are ecological for shopping at Erewhon . . . just by standing in Erewhon. It was almost like a purification ritual, like washing with a special soap in order to scrub away the toxins of an unecological, destructive, and irresponsible Western society forever eating loaves of plastic-wrapped white bread and Spam. It was like doing a purge before inoculating oneself with culturally appropriated practices, knowledges, and foods restored as new glam grub. Instant wellness, instant sustainability. Insta . . . grammable!

The uncomfortable high-end blend of sustainability and cool is the name of the game in Venice. On the fashion brand Farm Rio's website, for example, they confirm that they partner with One Tree Planted, a charity that plants a tree for every dollar donated. Farm Rio has now "donated" one million trees, one for each purchase made. One Tree Planted is part of a new trend of charities, like Trillion Tree Campaign, Trees for the Future, and Plant a Billion Trees, which promise to "offset" climate impacts through tree planting projects worldwide, usually in poor countries—something that seems inherently good. As investigative journalist Fred Pearce notes, "Everybody likes trees. There is no anti-tree lobby."

But the effectiveness of these projects is debatable. Often, the trees planted replace native trees with monoculture plantations, fenced off from locals. In many other cases, researchers find, only a small fraction of trees survive years later—in some instances as little as 2 percent—resulting in "phantom forests" around the world, which then are licensed as "carbon credits" to be sold to corporations to offset their emissions. This is because charities, governments, and companies like Farm Rio measure their success in terms of trees planted, not survival rate or long-term effectiveness. Tree planting, observes Pearce, is often just greenwashing, "aimed at grabbing headlines and promoting an image of governments or corporations as environmentally friendly." [11]

Not only was there greenwashing, but the green dream in Venice was also very exclusive. For example, we learned that the planter boxes on the sidewalks in Venice Beach had initially been started for growing vegetables. But as they fell into disrepair, they were planted with agave and cacti—in the guise of sustainable drought-resistant landscaping—but in fact part of a campaign by local residents to use thorny plants to deter the unhoused from camping on their sidewalks.[12] And there were a lot of unhoused, tucked away in their tents on sidewalks and sleeping in their cars in parking lots. Glaring down from the mural celebrating Indigenous resistance on Abbot Kinney Boulevard, commissioned by Faherty, were three security cameras and signs—placed there by Faherty—which informed us that "loitering, sitting, sleeping, or lying" was prohibited. A security guard patrolled the premises at all times. Given that there is a disproportionately high number of Indigenous people who are without housing, the contrast between the mural and reality was ironic, to say the least.[13]

What's more, Abbot Kinney had been the unofficial border between the more white hippie beach town and Oakwood, a historically Black and, later, Latino community that was, until 2011 at least, still going strong.[14] But when we got there in 2022, it was clear that much of these communities had been obliterated. The heart of the Black community was the Oakwood Recreation Center, which used to be filled with the old and young alike, spending the day in the shade and on the sports field. There was no one there that day, except for a film crew that was shooting in the community center. Extravagant houses with high walls faced the park. The First Baptist Church, which overlooked Oakwood Park and had been an essential part of the community since 1910, had been bought for $11.8 million in 2017 by Jay Penske, a media mogul and owner of *Variety*, and his wife, Elaine Irwin, a former Victoria's Secret model. They turned it into a luxury condo with a rooftop deck and four-car garage. For all its "wokeness," the Venice "community," with its Black Lives Matter signs and rainbow flags, was a living hypocrisy.

The very same morning that we met Chuck to talk about the regenerative revolution, we had been interviewing a community of unhoused people downtown, and a group of housing activists in Los Angeles that supports them. During the interview, we got caught in a confrontation between the staff of Urban Alchemy and the local unhoused community. Urban Alchemy is a nonprofit that pays former convicts (mostly juveniles) minimum wage to get the unhoused off the street—essentially, "ethically sourced" policing of the homeless. As we were chatting with volunteers handing out essential supplies like water and medical equipment, an Urban Alchemy patrol came by and, seeing our cameras, demanded that we stop filming. Rather than try to deescalate, they started shouting at the unhoused leaders, who in turn became very upset, shouting back, "These people are trying to help us, and you're just making our lives worse." The same city that funded the Los Angeles Clean Tech Incubator for a "green" economy was also funding Urban Alchemy—a bigger and even more violent version of the cactus garden beds in Venice. In Los Angeles, like in other cities across the United States and beyond, private security police and tech firms have been teaming up to drive out anyone whose presence puts a blemish on business improvement districts and real estate development projects increasingly branded as climate resilient and sustainable.

The green hipster lifestyle (let's call them greensters) on offer in Venice was clearly not for everyone: it was only for those in the know and, more crucially, those with enough money to be green. And where does that wealth come from? Quite often, the greensters work in the tech industry and invest much of their assets in the same real estate industry that is driving people out of their homes and onto the streets.

For their part, tech overlords like Bill Gates and Elon Musk promise us that innovation will get us out of this mess: a "breakthrough" of technology and engineering, very much dependent on oil and gas, that pushes us beyond the world we live in today.[15] Artificial intelligence technology produced by companies like Apple, Alphabet, and Microsoft is in fact optimizing the efforts of oil companies like ExxonMobil to extract maximal daily output.[16] Without oil and gas, Silicon Valley—and Silicon Beach, for that matter— would be running on empty and failing fast.[17] Like the Saudis, they are funding their visions of a greener future with oil—and when the wind turns slightly, this vision is revealed to be just a smokescreen.

It's not just the tech industry. Around the world, the much-touted shift in renewables is, in fact, underwritten by enormous, growing investments in oil and gas. As Patrick Pouyanné, the CEO of French petroleum company TotalEnergies SE, argued in August 2022, profitability from oil and gas supports more risk-taking in other (greener) parts of the business: "This acceleration of cash flows gives us a lot of comfort" so that they can invest in riskier offshore wind renewables.[18] Record extraction of oil and gas comes even as the world experiences record-breaking temperatures, rainfall, and drought. All in a day's work on Wall Street.

We are being told that all of this is for our own good—it is sustainable. But what does that word even mean anymore? In the Brundtland Commission's 1987 report "Our Common Future," sustainability was defined as "meeting the needs of the present generation without compromising the ability of future generations to meet their needs."[19] This is a commendable aspiration, but it quickly became wide open for interpretation. For instance, it was not immediately clear what *kinds* of needs are worth sustaining. The needs of the wealthy to stay wealthy in the future, for example, can be included in that definition. The vagueness of the concept simply allowed the current system to be maintained.[20]

In 2023, shortly after being picked as the president of the twenty-eighth Conference of the Parties to the UN Framework Convention on Climate Change (COP28), held in the United Arab Emirates, Sultan Ahmed Al Jaber stated that "the common threat to all the problems I am talking about is capital." Did he mean that the pursuit of profits above all else is driving climate change? On the contrary. Al Jaber, who was also the chief executive of the UAE's national oil company, was saying that we need *more* capital investment, rather than burn less oil.[21] "Last year $1.4tn was invested in clean technology globally. We need four times that amount."[22] While COP28 was the first in the UN's series of climate change conferences to explicitly name fossil fuels as causing climate change, the mealy-mouthed declaration only "calls on" a "transition away" from them—making it nonbinding and even leaving room for fossil fuels to continue to be extracted.

Just imagine if, instead of fighting for an end to slavery, abolitionists had "called on" a "transition away" from it. If abolitionists had tried to end chattel slavery by making it voluntary, it would still be with us. Similarly, for oil executives, sustainability is about continuing to do all the things that are wrecking the planet, for as long as possible.

Don't take our word for it, though. In January 2022, Larry Fink, the CEO of BlackRock, the world's biggest investment manager, stated that it was in stockholders' interests to be sustainable. "Stakeholder capitalism is not about politics. It is not a social or ideological agenda. It is not 'woke,' " he wrote. "We focus on sustainability not because we're environmentalists, but because we are capitalists and fiduciaries to our clients."[23] For Fink and Al Jaber, the market is the best tool to solve the problems of climate change, precisely because it is in the market's own interest to sustain itself.

The global market has created the problem of climate change through the development of a fossil-fuel-based economy, and it is the global market that will solve the problem. Through statements like these, Fink and Al Jaber let slip what many in power don't dare to say: that sustainability is not about changing anything significant at all but about fine-tuning and tweaking only what is necessary, so that everything can stay exactly the same.

As an example of how sustainability has become a smokescreen, take a look at what's happening in Saudi Arabia. Forget for a moment that the Saudis are the second-biggest oil producer on the planet (after the United States), willingly sacrificing the world for the sake of personal wealth. Instead, consider Neom, their new sustainable city claiming to be the prototype for the future of humanity. One component of Neom is a project called The Line: a desert megacity enclosed within two parallel buildings originally promised to be 1,640 feet tall, 650 feet wide, and over 100 miles long. Nestled in the Saudi desert between the Gulf of Aqaba and the Red Sea, it would be a city of 9 million people entirely encased in mirrors to minimize its impact and blend like a mirage into the landscape. Surely the migrating birds will learn not to fly into it and accept the way of the future, given time.

According to promotional videos, the city will have zero carbon emissions and no cars or streets. It will be filled with gardens and tree canopies as well as a high-speed rail network that can traverse the length of the city in just twenty minutes. The buildings will house vertical farms growing rows upon rows of lettuce and microgreens, whose massive array of energy-intensive UV lamps will of course be powered by nothing other than green hydrogen—an energy technology that uses low-carbon power sources to charge hydrogen molecules, which can then be transported.

The Line is only part of what Neom has to offer. With an opening date set for 2025 and an estimated cost of $500 billion, Neom is to become 100 percent powered by solar and wind energy and green hydrogen. The Saudi crown prince, Mohammed bin Salman, wants more than your run-of-the-mill green city; he wants it to be filled with robots that serve as workers, caregivers, and police. He also envisions sci-fi fantasies like flying cars, glow-in-the-dark beaches, billions of trees planted in a desert, and a giant artificial moon. It would involve technologies for water sustainability that have never been proven, including desalination powered by renewable energy to serve 1 million residents by 2030.[24]

Support for Neom's carbon-neutral ambitions will come from the likes of Peter Terium, former CEO of RWE, a multinational energy company that operates some of the largest coal-fueled power generating stations in Europe as well as being the continent's largest CO_2 emitter in 2018.[25] Others on the illustrious clean energy team included a former logistics director at Royal Dutch Shell, Frank Birchau, and public relations whiz Andreas Stoerzel, with twenty-plus years of experience at both RWE and British Petroleum. You know, all the companies that have top-notch scores when it comes to ambitious action on climate change. This green marvel also has its detractors: twenty thousand members of the Howeitat tribe from two towns were forcibly removed and relocated without compensation to construct the megacity.[26] Neom's website feels like stepping into a *Black Mirror*–style promotional film on how technology can bring humanity and nature together forever. Glitz and glam are now "eco-friendly," the thousands of evicted people must make way for imported laborers who are going to live in harmony with billionaires, and humanity will be all the better for it. To enhance the efficiency of urban life, your consumption preferences and patterns will be carefully recorded to save you every bit of time to do other things you might enjoy— such as looking for new opportunities to invest your money in. What's free time if it isn't optimized anyway? Hyped, hip, and climate neutral will likely translate to being heavily surveilled in places like The Line.

Never mind the fact that, according to architect Philip Oldfield, the city's construction—requiring unspeakable volumes of glass, steel, and concrete, as well as rare earth minerals—would itself produce up to 2 billion tons of CO_2 emissions, equivalent to more than four years of the current emissions from the United Kingdom.[27] Don't worry about all that: we are informed that when it's built, the ecological footprint of The Line is expected to be forty-six times lower than that of London. "Green" efficiency is the new face of sophistication . . . so fresh, so clean, so upgraded.

It's about blasting out of the present into a weightless, green utopia—like a spaceship ripping through Earth's atmosphere into a cloudless, zero-gravity renewable future. Sustainable cities like The Line will be where the future's at—at least on Earth. There are other plans in store for the Moon and Mars and asteroid belts. Building entirely "smart" urban complexes like Neom will require large amounts of very specialized minerals like cerium, terbium, lanthanum, yttrium, neodymium, praseodymium, and many others.[28] While Earth's reserves of zinc, platinum, copper, and nickel will only last us another forty years or so, it appears the moon has plenty left.[29] Research suggests that regolith (lunar soil) is accessible for mineral extraction and potentially contains hydrogen energy.[30] And since "green hydrogen" is meant to fuel the renewable energy of Neom, what better place than the Moon to find endless quantities of it?

Let the green gold rush begin. Already in the early days of the COVID-19 pandemic, then U.S. president Donald Trump signed an executive order ensuring the rights of U.S. state and private enterprises to mine lunar resources.[31] And the Moon is just the beginning. American companies are now working on rewriting the antiquated 1967 Outer Space Treaty to promote military expansion into space and to prevent competition from the likes of Russia and China. It's the new "wild, wild west" up there. It's also part of our green future. Apparently for senior fellows of the Atlantic Council's Scowcroft Center for Strategy and Security, the space race can have positive impacts for "environmental sustainability."[32] In particular, "only through . . . accelerating space commerce . . . will true security and prosperity be achieved over the next 30 plus years."

But we don't need to go too far from home to dig up a green future. Melting ice is actually making it easier to mine the minerals needed to build the "smart" green future. Some of the richest men in the world, including Bill Gates, Jeff Bezos, and Michael Bloomberg, are financing a California-based mining start-up that has its eyes on Greenland's Disko Island and Nuussuaq Peninsula to tap into the world's largest nickel and cobalt deposits, needed for batteries to store renewable energy and to build electric vehicles.[33] The ice-free summers are making it easier for heavy machinery to extract metals and then for companies to ship them.

Even as climate change offers new opportunities for profit, we are assured that everyone involved has our best interests at heart. Mining will be carried out "sustainably," essentially to make sure that the resource stock remains viable and that the economic benefits of mining will be beneficial for Greenlanders up until the moment the ice melts and the land sinks beneath the rising seas.

Greenland's own entrepreneurs are already ahead of the curve. In 2024, Arctic Ice, a local start-up, began shipping ice from melting glaciers to cocktail bars in the United Arab Emirates. "Helping Greenland in its green transition is actually what I believe I was brought into this world to do," muses Malik V. Rasmussen, the company's co-founder. Indeed, Arctic Ice promises to be fully carbon neutral, using carbon capture and storage technology to suck carbon out of the air and inject it into the ground and compensate for the carbon emissions associated with shipping ice to oil barons so they can release more carbon with less guilt. Greenland will finally live up to its name, becoming one of the world's sacrifice zones for "green" energy. Its melting glaciers—with "the cleanest H_2O on earth," according to Rasmussen—will be served in frozen daiquiris in Neom's cocktail bars.[34]

Another option, as James Cameron—regular patron of Plant

Food and Wine—ventures, would be to mine the deep oceans for those rare minerals. This is even as the European Academies' Science Advisory Council warns that deep-sea mining would lead to "dire consequences" for marine ecosystems.[35] Only 10 percent of the Earth's ocean floor has been mapped—in percentage terms, far less than the surfaces of the Moon, Mars, and Mercury.[36] Despite this, Cameron claims unequivocally of the ocean floor, "What you mostly have is miles and miles of nothing but clay." It seems he has given up on the aspirations of his 1989 blockbuster film *The Abyss*, where (spoiler alert) a heretofore undiscovered super-smart race living on the ocean floor single-handedly solves the problems of the Cold War and ocean pollution. It's just clay and minerals down there . . . might as well start digging!

Meanwhile, wealthy vegans dream of growing vegetables in their hydroponic towers in lunar residential condos—or at least of moving into The Line or a modest $1.5 million cottage in Venice Beach (the average house price in the area). And if most people who live zombified from paycheck to paycheck are unable to even think about, let alone influence, the grand cosmic visions of billionaires concerned about being sustainable, they'll just be left behind—unless they put aside their lack of ambition and their unwillingness to work, shell out more to eat healthy, live up to the wellness hype, and pick themselves up by their bootstraps.[37] Not too in-your-face or preachy, though. It's got to be hip; it's got to be chic. It's got to be marketable; it's got to fulfill a desire. Only then will everyone wake up to the bright new future.

The "breakthrough" on offer by the tech billionaires and the House of Saud is more of the same, but this time a sanitized, "climate-resilient" world reserved for those who profit the most from these industries. They call it "climate adaptation." Much as The Line will depend on the Saudi sovereign wealth fund, generated by profits from being the world's biggest crude oil producer, "green" and sustainability transitions will be underwritten by investments in real estate, industrial agriculture, and oil and gas.

At this point, we should make it clear that there is nothing wrong, in and of itself, with trying to live a lighter and less harmful lifestyle. There is also nothing wrong with wanting to be recognized for trying to make the world a better place. There is nothing wrong with feeling important or valued for being part of a bigger cause. We mean no ill will to the sustainability class, a type that we ourselves—as young urban professionals, two people trying to live ethically in the world—also fall into. We, too, do our best to recycle, bike, and reduce our meat and dairy consumption, and we also feel bad about our carbon footprint when we fly. We, too, were taught to leave a place neater than we found it, to be compassionate to those less fortunate or more marginalized, and try to tread lightly on the planet. Ultimately, many of us—greensters included—seek the same thing: to live according to our values, connection, and belonging. We can see that people like Chuck, Jessica, Matthew Kenney, Bill Gates, and presumably Prince Khaled bin Alwaleed are motivated by very real concerns. Their desire to improve the world may be honestly informed by a concern that there is something seriously wrong here.

We are worried as well. Just like them, we are worried about climate change, the loss of pollinators, the increased risk of antibiotic resistance and viral pandemics, deforestation, desertification, ocean acidification, and mass extinction. The storms, heat waves, floods, droughts, and wildfires. In fact, the climate is changing so fast that even as we write about temperature and weather records being broken, they will be broken once again by the time the book is published. And we have the threat of far-right movements who take advantage of social displacement, economic uncertainty, and health scares to double down on controlling the bodies of women and trans people, of criminalizing immigrants, and limiting the rights of workers.

As of writing, we've already passed 1.0°C of global warming since fossil fuels started being burned at a massive scale during the industrial revolution. Climate scientists say that anything above

1.5°C of warming would be catastrophic, with reduced crop yields, rising sea levels, melting ice sheets, and billions of people exposed to unprecedented, intolerable heat.[38] The summer of 2023 was the warmest on record, and pushed the global thermometer to 1.5°C of warming for much of the year.[39] The year 2024 already started out with the warmest January on record. Climatic changes that have typically taken hundreds of thousands of years have instead occurred over decades, with half of all atmospheric CO_2 increases occurring in the past thirty years.[40] The current rate of CO_2 increase was last observed at the end of the Paleocene, 55 million years ago (humans have been around for only 2 million years). It took the Earth more than a hundred thousand years to recover from the climate changes induced by *lesser* amounts of CO_2 increase than what we are witnessing today.[41] As Scotland's national poet, Kathleen Jamie, writes: "The feeling of being imperiled is now constant: the sense that something is cracking like a parched field, the veneer of our hitherto secure lives. Temperatures climb, the world burns, ice melts, pandemics erupt, and now the seabirds are dying."[42]

In this book, we show how the green dreams promoted by what we call the "sustainability class" won't work even on their own terms. This vision of progress, which imagines a breakthrough moment where holistic living and innovation push us into another realm of reality, a higher plane of existence, is not just accelerating environmental collapse. It is also inherently exclusive, as it depends on the ability to buy into "sustainability." It displaces those who don't have the purchasing power and therefore don't count—except as the workforce for an ever more narrow elite. The new hype to be green, as represented by the greensters and their promises of a high-tech sustainable future, is not green at all. Or rather, it might be painted green, but it's not ecological. Confusing "green" with ecological is fatal, and it is our aim in this book to clarify this distinction.

We use the term "sustainability class" because what unites the smoothie-slurping, incense-lighting "followers of Watts and Leary," the green tech-boosting entrepreneurs, and Prince Khaled bin Alwaleed is their class position: that is, their solutions are—subconsciously or consciously—based on the need to protect their wealth and assets while positioning themselves as the ones who will save the world. In a word, for this class of people the desire to "drop out" has become synonymous with the compulsion to "boot up."

The term "sustainability class," coined by the geographers Kenneth Gould and Tammy Lewis, is a nod to the term "creative class," popularized by Richard Florida in his hugely influential book *The Rise of the Creative Class*, which argued that it was creative types who would drive urban growth in the future.[43] Today, we can see that the creative class is merging with all things "green" and sustainable, a demographic of well-meaning middle- and upper-class people who define themselves as liberal and progressive and are very concerned about ecological issues but can only approach them from their class identity. As a result, everyone from real estate developers to tech companies to automobile makers to oil companies is marketing their products to better appeal to this class.

And yet for the vast majority of people on Earth, the visions of sustainability touted by greensters make no sense. On the basis of resource use and carbon emissions, working-class people are much more environmentally friendly, as they waste less and can't afford to fly all over the world.[44] In New York City, for example, lower-income neighborhoods have, per capita, carbon footprints about one-third those of the rich.[45] Even when the sustainability class moves into dense, bikeable neighborhoods (and displaces working-class people living there), they are still much more polluting than those working-class people.[46] Again, this is because income is still the best predictor of carbon footprint.[47] Globally, the lifestyles of the richest 1 percent are responsible for about half of the world's emissions.[48] When their financial investments are taken into account, a billionaire emits 1 *million* times more CO_2

than the average person.[49] This is not to say that we should measure environmental impact by individual lifestyle choices. In fact, our argument is that measurements like "carbon footprint" and a focus on sustainable lifestyle inherently fail to see the big picture: how extreme wealth inequality—in other words, who owns what, who has a say and who doesn't—actually *drives* the ecological crisis. That said, listing the above figures is still useful, if just to show that, even on its own terms, sustainable lifestyle "choices" cannot live up to their much-touted expectations. These facts alone should make it clear that "green" lifestyles are preposterous nonsolutions. And as we'll see, they can't even be justified by the "well, it's better than doing nothing" argument. They may very well be making things worse.

When we thought back to our trip to Los Angeles, our meeting with Chuck immediately came to mind as a vivid encapsulation of the city's extremes. We chatted in one of the most opulent places in the city about the regenerative revolution under way. That revolution would be a moment of awakening, a breakthrough, propelling our society into yet another era of progress. "Wokeness," wellness, and innovation would become one. Yet that very morning we witnessed how an "ethically sourced" security force patrols the border between progress and its victims. The juxtaposition of the morning's violence against the unhoused with the sun-baked afternoon poolside vibes at the Hilton felt like the perfect summary of what is wrong with the vision of the sustainability class.

We aim to reclaim ecology from greensters (and big tech overlords, oil barons, and real estate tycoons) who promise us all sorts of things like "green growth," a "regenerative revolution," and "smart cities" but end up reserving wealth for themselves, to enrich themselves and sanitize themselves from guilt. How can these new green and smart cities be ecological if people who are lower-income, racialized, or less fortunate or able can't possibly take part?

Our argument is that the sustainability class gravitates to these solutions precisely *because* they do not challenge their security. Worse still, they are non-solutions that worsen the problems they claim to be solving: they accelerate the ecological crisis. And yet, deep down, we've gotten a sense that many among the sustainability class are not satisfied with exclusive sustainability, because it feels superficial and fake. It all just feels like empty branding while the world burns. This isn't a coincidence or a surprise. We argue that, to address the exclusion, ecological destruction, and emptiness, the sustainability class must step outside their class position, reaching their hand out in solidarity with others. This might feel like it would risk their sense of security and fuzzy feel-good vibes. And though it might not seem that way now, the sustainability class themselves will inevitably be left abandoned outside of the "green" fortress already being built by the super-rich. Ecological collapse won't leave anyone with warm fuzzy feelings. Solidarity across class is the only real solution.

The ideology advanced by the sustainability class is not, in fact, sustainable. But then again, the goal should be not to *sustain* the present but to *transform* the present. The solution is not to tell people to be more "mindful," ambitious, and resilient and to just shut up and work harder. It's also not about holing up in fear, anger, and nostalgia for a golden era that, if it ever existed at all, was only for a select few. Rather, the struggle over ecology means coming to terms with change and its inevitability, and paying attention to past relations of power that make up and keep shaping present movements of people and flows of materials and energy around the world. It means being willing to undo class positions, building individual *and* collective well-being. To do all this, the for-profit, virtue-signaling, individualistic, technology-obsessed visions of "going green" should be abandoned, because they are distractions that only worsen the problem. Ecology must be for everyone.

This book is both about the sustainability class and *for* the sustainability class. This is a conscious decision: we believe that, despite its failings, this class can be a crucial node in the ecological transformation we need. With financial means and high education, as well as good intentions, the sustainability class has the potential to contribute to class solidarity rather than deepening the divisions. That's why we chose to speak directly to the members of this class.

To this class, and to everyone else, we put forward the vision of an ecology that is not beholden to sustaining the present. It is a just transition, whose central actors are not the rich but regular, working-class people. Though the sustainability class can take part in this alternative vision, it would ultimately mean the dissolution of that same class. We argue that this is not just possible and desirable but essential if we want to have any hope of pulling the brakes on the ecological train wreck we're heading towards. Let's take back our future from lifestyle environmentalism.

1

THE RISE OF THE
SUSTAINABILITY CLASS

How can there be anything wrong with trying to do good?
The answer may be: when the good is an accomplice to even
greater, if more invisible, harm. In our era that harm is the
concentration of money and power among a small few . . .
and do-gooding pursued by elites tends not only to leave this
concentration untouched, but actually to shore it up.
                                        —Anand Giridharadas[1]

L et's take a short detour to Brooklyn, New York. The Gowanus
Canal is a 1.8-mile-long industrial waterfront, with the unfortunate reputation as one of the nation's most toxic waterways. But
in a city with such alluring returns on investment in real estate,
nothing ever stinks too much. After receiving $1.6 billion of fed-
eral funding, developers planned to dredge and clean the canal,
build public esplanades and shopping areas along the derelict waterfront, and promised a "sustainability themed Whole Foods . . .
a Gotham Greens rooftop greenhouse, electric vehicle charging
stations, wind turbines built into parking lot light poles, and solar
paneled carports."[2]

But there was just one problem: many Brooklyn waterfront
properties are doomed to be under water, or at the very least face
constant flooding, due to sea level rise caused by climate change.
Being highly educated, many of the potential new residents would

be aware of this and might hesitate to buy an apartment in a flood-prone area like the Gowanus Canal. Indeed, in 2012, Hurricane Sandy destroyed housing all along the coast and flooded the Gowanus waterfront.[3] To assuage fears, developers advertised these new waterfront condos as being "climate resilient," building structures that can better resist flooding, including elevated promenades, levees, and seawalls along the shorelines.[4] Obviously, this raised the costs of construction, but these would be covered by the prices the expected residents would be willing to pay to secure prime waterfront property. As you might have guessed, none of this flood mitigation extends to the low-income residential areas surrounding the redeveloped Gowanus Canal. And neither do these lower-income areas get selected for many of the green amenities and parks that the Gowanus Canal residents have.

This story is the centerpiece of the book *Green Gentrification: Urban Sustainability and the Struggle for Environmental Justice*, by sociologists Kenneth A. Gould and Tammy L. Lewis.[5] It is also in this book that they introduce the term "sustainability class," which they define in a later piece as a class that "is well-educated, holds overt sustainability-oriented values, can afford sustainability-themed consumption, and touts their green urbanism (such as living on the waterfront or near green spaces) to brand their lifestyle." This class is a subset of the middle-to-upper-middle classes that is progressive, is environmentally minded, and has disposable income. As Gould and Lewis explain, "Through this dual process of urban greening and structural mitigation of climate change threats, resilience is equated with wealth, and the sustainability class emerges as the new urban elite."[6] Sustainability has become a marker of class distinction, separating the haves from the have-nots.

As Richard Florida himself admitted, his championing of the creative class has unfortunately helped to displace lower-income, working-class people and has contributed to making our cities even more unequal.[7] Starting in the 1980s, developers, investors, and even politicians started to realize that this class represented an immense market opportunity. By redeveloping urban centers, this coalition of elites in cities around the world knew they could begin to attract even more investment. City governments in places like Shanghai, Singapore, São Paulo, and Mumbai started to use similar strategies to attract speculators to fund creative industries, build their brands, and "clean up" unsightly (i.e., poorer) areas.[8] What started as a demographic shift from the suburbs to places like Brooklyn, New York, and Islington, a neighborhood in London, became an immense, global opportunity for capital investment.[9] To give you an idea of how important urban development is to the global market, consider that real estate accounts for about 60 percent of all capital assets globally, in large part because, as anyone who has any savings can attest, it's one of the most stable markets to invest in.[10] And so, for the creative class, the hip urban lifestyle was both an investment in their future and a way to distinguish themselves from others.

American economist and sociologist Thorstein Veblen was the first to coin the idea of conspicuous consumption in his 1899 book *The Theory of the Leisure Class*. Conspicuous consumption refers to how money is spent to display not only wealth and economic power but also moral standing, reputation, and social standing. If someone buys an organic-cotton locally made designer bag, they are saying—whether consciously or subconsciously: "Just so you know, I am more stylish and wealthier, or more morally superior, than you."

When certain lifestyles are prized, anyone who doesn't aspire to live the same way is stigmatized. For example, a farmer in rural America is viewed as backward or quaint. If they want to make a real difference, young people born into farming families would do well to get educated, move to the city, and perhaps learn to code—and then possibly convert their second condo into an Airbnb. Only then can they be part of the in-crowd; only then can they blend in at third-wave coffee bars and rooftop office parties or in studios for edgy design firms. Only then can they get away with saying "innovating creative solutions for the regenerative revolution" in their LinkedIn bio.

The sustainability class is, like the creative class, educated, has access to social and economic capital, and is well-meaning, progressive, and environmentally minded—at least in terms of personal consumption habits. In a study of thirty-seven countries, households with higher levels of education are more likely to buy recycled goods, buy energy-saving products, recycle, and save electricity. In these countries, these people are also significantly more likely to have higher incomes.[11]

Globally, the sustainability class can largely be found in the high-income and upper-middle-income categories, which respectively accounted for 7 percent and 15 percent of the global population in 2020. Being part of the sustainability class isn't limited to residents of wealthy nations; the upper and middle classes in otherwise less wealthy countries can also be members. This is why you can find zero-waste grocery stores, farmers markets, and organic-cotton tote bag vibes in Nairobi as well as in Copenhagen, catering to people of roughly equivalent wealth and aesthetic preferences.

It is this well-educated, high-earning class, of which we ourselves are members, that is largely driving the growth in environmental products—everything from electric vehicles to ethically produced organic fashion to wellness shots. For example, research by industry consulting companies NielsenIQ and McKinsey found that U.S. consumers are not only more and more interested in sustainability but also buying more sustainability-branded products—which accounted for 56 percent of all growth in consumer purchasing between 2015 and 2020. Much of this growth, the study found, was driven by higher-income households, which are more likely to buy green products.[12]

Much of what drives green market growth is the vast sums of money to be obtained from it all. According to a McKinsey report on the business costs and opportunities of transitioning to "Net Zero," environmental and climate action is quite profitable.[13] Banks and asset managers like BlackRock have been generating between $10 billion and $20 billion a year globally since 2010 in "low-carbon" investment, blending public and private funding for new green product lines—ranging from mortgages and building loans to new green commodities like carbon trading and insurance packages.[14] The Glasgow Finance Alliance for Net-Zero comprises 450 firms from across the global financial sector.[15] The International Finance Corporation, a partner of the World Bank, found that there is potential for growth of $29 trillion in environmental goods and services by 2030, largely concentrated in real estate. Of that, $24 trillion would be locked into green buildings, and $1.6 trillion into electric vehicles.[16] Yet, as we'll come to see a bit later, there is zero evidence to suggest that the exorbitant profits from new green commodities has had any role in putting the brakes on ecological breakdown. In fact, the contrary is the case: these strategies, being largely speculative, have only helped diversify stock portfolios and keep the wheel of production going.

The green industry knows very well that the sustainability class, with its expendable income, is its most important customer for new green commodities. For example, in an article for the Network for Business Sustainability titled "To Sell Green Products, Target the Middle Class," Chelsea Hicks-Webster, a sustainability writer and life coach, tells us, without a hint of irony or self-consciousness, why exactly "the middle class is greener." She draws on one study that pointed to the need of this class to either fit in or stand out. People with lower incomes might want to fit in more, but they don't have the money to buy green. At higher income levels, people are more interested in standing out and might be more interested in high-polluting luxury products, such as yachts. The middle class, in contrast, is " 'just right' for green consumption" since standing out is ironically a good way to fit right in. As the author points out, "Having taken care of their basic needs, these consumers have enough money left to splurge on more expensive green products. At the same time, green consumption also signals their education and affluence." [17] Nowhere does the author reflect on whether green consumption translates to being more sustainable; who knows, there might be some research available on that. If you think this sounds a lot like Thorstein Veblen's conspicuous consumption, you're right. In effect, buying green becomes a kind of class distinction, a way to distinguish oneself from others.

It is also in line with research conducted more than thirty years ago by sociologists Denton Morrison and Riley Dunlap. Their goal was to look seriously at accusations, very common at that time already, that environmentalists are elitist and removed from ordinary people. Looking at the data, they found that it is, in general, true that people who care about the environment are from above-average socioeconomic strata. However, it isn't necessarily true that environmentalists hold beliefs that are primarily in their own interest and against the interests of the poor. They found that environmentalists, by far, are strong believers in equity, redistribution, and social justice. And it is also true that, despite tropes of superwealthy scions trying to use their inheritance to save the planet (or, as in science fiction like *12 Monkeys* or *Three-Body Problem*, start a cult to destroy humanity once and for all), environmentalists are rarely from the upper or ultra-rich classes. In fact, at very high income levels, anti-environmental attitudes—more consistent with owning megayachts, mansions, gas-guzzling sports cars, and furs and taking first-class flights—were the norm.

The real question, however, is what you do with your concern for the environment. For the middle class, acting for the planet often comes down to donating to a just cause or buying the right things. That's where the green industry comes in, which promises everything from fair trade coffee to climate-resilient homes to carbon offsets to ease the conscience of this concerned class. But a word of warning: while one's income can inform what one cares about and what one does about those things, it doesn't necessarily determine them. Make no mistake: the middle class is a very broad community, with different views and positions across the political spectrum. Still, the kinds of actions that have come to define sustainability tend to be championed by, and for, the middle class. And, as we have already shown, there are plenty of opportunities today for the ultra-rich to flaunt their green credentials as well.

In this chapter, we introduce three "types" of sustainability class members: the lifestyle environmentalists, the green modernists, and the green administrators. These three types are crude depictions, and there are many overlaps. For example, you might come across someone who is a green modernist and a green administrator, such as when a tech entrepreneur starts to fly around to sustainability conferences, wining and dining with politicians and scientists as they try to sell carbon credits, green gadgets, or the latest hunger-eradicating genetically modified organism. But they all have something in common: they are unwilling to abandon their class comforts.

The Lifestyle Environmentalists

The lifestyle environmentalists—or, as we call them, the greensters—assume that the only way to be green is to have the right kind of lifestyle and buy the right kinds of things. Many of them are well-intentioned and care sincerely about social and environmental issues, but that often gets expressed through aesthetics, vibes, and virtue signaling. Common to their beliefs is that one's individual consumption choices are key to stopping ecological breakdown.

Consumption-oriented beliefs manifest in very subtle ways. They can include proactive and emissions-reducing activities at the individual scale, like deciding not to travel by plane, following the Rainforest Alliance frog when buying coffee and chocolate, buying earth-toned and hemp-based clothing, purchasing an electric car, and using metal straws. It's about "doing your bit to save the planet" and appeasing your conscience as opposed to working together to transform society. Obviously, the latter is considerably harder to do and requires collective organization on an unprecedented scale. But greensters shy away from even going in that direction; for them, such questions are too political and "messy." Individual actions often appear more doable because collective action on a massive scale seems like an impossibility. The irony, as we'll come to see, is that individual actions exacerbate the problems they are meant to address.

When greensters do engage in politics, they often do so in symbolically important but practically impotent ways. Their demands can be quite abstract and far removed from their own lived experiences, revealed through empty statements like "There is no planet B" or simply "Save the environment"—the kinds of slogans often seen at climate demonstrations. They sometimes employ civil disobedience tactics, like taking part in performative acts, as some in the Extinction Rebellion group in the United Kingdom and elsewhere have done. While raising awareness of the seriousness of the issue, the consequences of direct action are often just shy of a slap on the wrist for most, since many are middle-class white people whose privilege protects them from the violence that Black people would be subject to if they were to do the same. While the efforts at protest are laudable, these marches and actions somehow miss the mark and can feel like little more than police-corralled parades and excuses to hang out with friends.

Central to the concept of "green" is the notion of purity. This refers to a return to a kind of original state of being. Being pure is about trying to *become* nature, as though humanity were somehow outside of it and we need to get closer to it to become whole. Here's one example of what we're talking about: a design for a sustainable superyacht, called *Pegasus*. The idea, says yacht designer Jozeph Forakis, is for a yacht that blends into the clouds and the sea, as if it didn't exist at all. Like the mirrored facade of the planned

Saudi city The Line, Forakis's 3D-printed superyacht is described as "virtually invisible" in terms of environmental impact. Its plans include wings with mirrored glass and solar panels that power electrolyzers that extract hydrogen from seawater, convert this to electricity, and store it in lithium-ion battery banks used to power the yacht's operating systems. "I was inspired to create a yacht as close to the sea and nature as possible, made of clouds floating above the waterline," states Forakis. He goes on to say that "now is the time for courageous leaps toward our collective sustainable future," adding that "*Pegasus* is a bold but achievable vision for the near future of the superyacht industry, where man and machine live in harmony with nature rather than competing or compromising it." [18] For a yacht to be sustainable, it simply has to become invisible. *That's* purity.

The concept of "LEED-brain," coined by David Owen, demonstrates the mental backflips that the purity mindset requires. LEED is a design certification system that uses a set of criteria to determine how environmentally friendly a new building is. Owen describes a LEED-certified mansion in ritzy Westchester County, New York, owned by Richard and Maryann Ellenbogen. The house has six bathrooms, a fitness room, a living room the size of a barn, an indoor fountain, and a kitchen with a "warming drawer" (whatever that means) and two dishwashers. Yet this monstrosity of excess also happens to have a wall of solar panels and a geothermal heating and cooling system, a smattering of locally sourced building materials, and other gizmos—and is therefore considered an "ultra-energy-efficient 'smart house.'" Owen quotes Richard Ellenbogen, a plastics magnate by day and green lifestyler by night: "It feels great to go home every night and know that the house is big and beautiful but that it's not detrimental to the environment." [19] That's "LEED-brain" in a nutshell: the delusion that, somehow, a massive mansion for a single family can possibly be sustainable—even if it is marginally more efficient than the neighboring mansion.

The elephant in the room is the mansion itself, the superyacht, the smart city built in the desert. Oil barons and yacht designers dream of cities and superyachts that seamlessly blend into nature. The Ellenbogens vie for a big, beautiful, and weightless lifestyle. The wish for purity is about creating neat and tidy boundaries between things, erasing complexity and context in favor of an idealized facade.[20] Purity involves a certain idea of nature and trying to consume it, trying to *become* natural. It requires a kind of "smoothness," a shiny, frictionless world where nothing is wrong or out of place.[21] This idea of nature is opposed to society, which is too impure and complex to change. Ultimately these desires become ways to distinguish oneself from others—thus creating exclusively green lifestyles.

For many greensters, sustainability as measured by lifestyle choices is a test of a person's inner goodness. Much of this lies in the realm of aesthetics—since the real environmental impact remains for them somewhat abstract. The consumption of "nature" then equates to being "green" or ecologically conscious, while those who can't possibly buy green consumer goods are seen as dirty, lazy, and part of the problem. Wealthy urbanites can live in shimmering condos surrounded by greenery, shielded from impurities, and can then claim that workers, farmers, and migrants are the culprits of environmental breakdown, due to their lack of education, their population growth, their voting habits, you name it.[22]

It is not incidental to the purity mindset that only the rich have the pleasure of being enlightened. When we say "rich," we refer here to people with disposable income, as opposed to those who live paycheck to paycheck or are unemployed. The social and historical conditions that enrich some and impoverish others are so easily ignored in favor of the (ostensibly color- and gender-blind) notion that once a person gets rich and more educated, they can start caring about the environment. There are many who may not realize they follow this logic subconsciously. For example, it's not uncommon to hear justifications such as these: "I bought a hybrid car and a LEED-certified condo because there are many who can't afford to." The Ellenbogens, no doubt, are fully aware of the privilege of being able to have a "smart" mansion. But precisely because they're so lucky, they may believe it's their responsibility to "do their part." If you think about it, however, this kind of thinking implies that the poor don't "do their part," simply because they can't afford it. If someone who grew up in a poor neighborhood like Oakwood—adjacent to Venice Beach and branded for decades as "sketchy"—wanted to give "going green" a go, they'd just have to work harder, get smarter, and get rich first. Only then would they be able to show off their green credentials. In this way, green purity is, from the start, about exclusivity, defining who is "in" and who is "out."

Though green purity is most common among the middle class, those who hold the purse strings—the super-rich—have realized that there are huge profits to be made from this feeling of guilt and desire for distinction. All over the world, developers, politicians, and investors are planning green districts—even entire cities. So where is much of that previously mentioned $24 trillion in green buildings going? In Abu Dhabi, London architectural firm Fosters and Partners started to build Masdar City, an "eco-city" initiated in 2006 and imagined as a carbon-neutral, zero-waste development of fifty thousand residents (and sixty thousand workers who would commute into the city daily). It has a price tag of $18–20 billion. Residents would be zipped around by driverless electric cars and cooled by smart shading and wind towers lining the streets.[23] Today, more than ten years after breaking ground, the city is mostly an expensive showroom surrounded by sand to adorn the public relations pamphlets of some of the world's most destructive companies like weapons manufacturer Lockheed Martin. Despite being billed as carbon neutral, most of its construction was dependent on fossil fuels.[24]

Near Penang, Malaysia, an artificial floating archipelago called

BiodiverCity is being planned by Danish architect Bjarke Ingels and his firm BIG.[25] The city will be the latest and greatest in environmental futurism and high-quality "sustainability living." Besides green roofs, driverless vehicles careening past grassy embankments, and fully walkable streets, the carbon footprint of the planned city of sixteen thousand will be reduced by using energy-intensive 3D-printed prefabricated buildings.[26] But what's more intriguing about BiodiverCity is the proximity and immediacy to "nature" that the city promises. The design of the urbanized floating lily pads is supposed to promote a symbiosis between human, land, and animal. We're left pondering what the Malayan tapirs and sun bears that have been ejected from their habitats because of the country's enormous deforestation for palm oil plantations and certified sustainable timber will think about their new home on floating urban lily pads.

The desire to escape to these green enclaves gets taken to its extreme through the belief in space colonization. The settling of Mars is often proposed as an answer to escape the intractable, complex problems on Earth. Building the infrastructure to colonize Mars is much easier: here is a world that ultimate lifestyle environmentalists like Elon Musk can control, where they can be an architect of a new kind of society and political system, far removed from an overcrowded, warring, and dying planet.[27] Take for example Kim Stanley Robinson's iconic *Mars Trilogy*, where a group of scientists sets out to colonize and terraform the red planet into a green one. Back home on Earth, the world is beset by climate change, famine, and geopolitical tension. The migration to Mars offers humanity a chance to start again, to break away from the dirty past and build a clean and sterile future. The dream of space colonization is peak sustainability class purity: if we can't deal with the complexity of the world, we might as well press the reset button and start afresh. "We," of course, means the select few who can afford it, who are smarter than everyone else, who are ahead of the curve.

The Green Modernists

"Technology must be a violent assault on the forces of the un-known, to force them to bow before man."
—Filippo Tomasso Marinetti
(Italian poet and fascist), quoted by tech
billionaire venture capitalist Marc Andreessen[28]

Those in the second group call themselves "ecomodernists." We hesitate to use that term, because there's very little ecological going on here. In our view, ecology means something quite different from the superficial virtue signaling of "green." So let's use the term "green modernists" instead. Green modernists are the techies, pundits, and elites who make a living pushing technological quick-fix solutions such as carbon capture and storage, cloud seeding, and climate-smart agriculture as strategies to keep business as usual going on a bit longer while they pretend to be doing something about it. They are at the vanguard of sustainability class ideology.

Green modernist thought—exemplified by the San Francisco-based think tank the Breakthrough Institute—is a continuation of what many policy geeks had termed "ecological modernization" back in the 2000s. This group believes society must be totally industrialized and nature has to be tamed to be protected.[29] Ultimately, technological advancement, they say, will pull humanity out of any environmental crisis; there are no limits to growth or expansion as long as the creativity and ingenuity of human mastery prevail over the forces of the universe. For some green modernists, technology will elevate humanity—the worthy (i.e. rich ones) at least—to a posthumanist state, where people can be re-engineered to be like gods, building on the wellness hype of investment in anti-aging and life-extending technologies. They are far more concerned about how many lives could be saved if computers could reboot a few seconds faster than the environmental damage caused by server farms or the hordes of people working in precarious positions along the tech supply chain.[30] Theirs is a vision of the world that depends on an army of artificial intelligence and exploited workers feeding them information, while the eco-conscious (i.e. the worthy ones) float above it all, clicking and swiping their way to the good life. The green modernists are the motor of the sustainability class: they frantically generate ideas and proposals, policies, and technological designs, while the lifestyle environmentalists and the green administrators try to keep up. This is because the ideology of green modernism is shared by elite politicians, IT bosses, technocrats, and the super-rich alike.

Take, for example, Arshi Ayub Zaveri, CEO of the Dubai-based company Oxygenate, who claims that "anything the human eye can see can be made from bamboo."[31] Of course he would say that: Oxygenate's business model is to sell "genetically enhanced" bamboo for carbon sequestration. We were confused about what "genetically enhanced" meant, so we did some research and found out that it just means conventionally crossbred. People like this will spend their days spouting empty sales pitches, rebranded as revolutionary, world-changing green entrepreneurship.

Leading the charge with green modernism are the big tech bigwigs: Alphabet (Google), Microsoft, Amazon, Alibaba, and Meta (Facebook). For Bill Gates, "innovation is the key" to solving climate change. For Robert Bernard, Microsoft's chief environmental officer, the sentiment is stated even more clearly: "We can invent our way out of this problem."[32] For Kate Brandt, Google's sustainability officer, fixing Google's environmental impact takes technological innovation—using machine learning to make their data centers more efficient, switching to 100 percent renewable energy, and urging users to turn on the "energy saving mode" of their Google Calendar.[33] Brandt, in her previous jobs, "helped the Navy, the White House, and the entire federal government become more eco-friendly," and she's well on her way to helping Google build the dream of a light, super-efficient, high-tech economy.[34]

Another feature of the modernist ideology is green urbanism. In the *New York Times* bestseller *Triumph of the City: How Our Greatest Invention Makes Us Richer, Smarter, Greener, Healthier, and Happier,* Edward Glaeser argues that urban living is—you guessed it—actually greener than any other way of modern life. His argument rests in great part on the high density of cities: the closer people can live together, the less energy they need to use to get around.[35] Proponents argue that innovations like LEED-certified architecture, smart urban planning, compact urban living, electric vehicle charging stations, municipal composting, bike-sharing, e-scooters, ride-sharing apps like Uber, and urban agriculture can all work together to make our cities *the* agents in solving our environmental problems. It's not clear, however, how such strategies will serve low-income city dwellers, much less rural people, and how they might slow down the extraction of resources from all corners of the world. As we discuss in Chapter 3, urban lifestyles require enormous amounts of energy and resources regardless of whether more people are huddled together in one place. This isn't to say that they can't be made less polluting. Still, it's a far stretch to claim that we should place our bets on the modern city as the agent of the green future.

Green modernists also claim to be pro-working class, but often in belittling ways—those in the working class just need to level up their skills to join the job market for the green economy. The rationale is that the technology and service sectors—unlike manufacturing—have minimal environmental impact. In the early twentieth century, living in polluted, dirty cities in Europe and North America, you would smell industry in front of you. But now, working on your laptop in a third-wave coffee joint, with your barista blending lattes, it certainly *feels* a lot less resource-intensive than working on the production line at General Motors as your grandfather might have in the 1960s.

This "natural" transition to cleaner and greener is reflected in mainstream economic theories. Foremost economists argue that the richer a country gets, the more people start caring about the environment and the greener that country becomes. Central to this green modernist dream is the belief that we can decouple economic growth from environmental impacts. It's entirely possible, says economist Paul Krugman, that we can create an economy that keeps growing, which creates wealth, but that also increasingly cuts down on its carbon footprint.[36] This idea is taken to its extreme by economist Andrew McAfee in his *New York Times* bestselling book *More from Less: The Surprising Story of How We Learned to Prosper Using Fewer Resources—and What Happens Next.* The title says it all, really, and the key takeaway is that we don't need to radically change what we're doing: "Instead, we need to do more of what we're already doing: growing technologically sophisticated market-based economies around the world." Apparently, we need only look to the United States as the exemplar of a green modern future. Who would have thought? "In America—a large, rich country that accounts for about 25% of the global economy—we're now generally using less of most resources year after year, even as our economy and population continue to grow."[37] No need to wring our hands and worry about the future! Behind our backs, the market is already solving our biggest challenges. We're told that America, the number-one producer of oil in the world, is a paragon of sustainability. Every year, the economy is lighter and more efficient, even as it keeps growing.

Van Jones, a former environmental adviser for the Obama government and later a CNN host and contributor, writes in another *New York Times* bestseller, *The Green Collar Economy*, that switching away from dirty industry and creating lots of green, low-impact jobs is the "one solution" that can fix poverty and climate change while growing the economy.[38] It's also argued that putting people to work in new "green" enterprises provides jobs that boost the economy while simultaneously improving well-being and ecological protection. Jones may be surprised to learn that he shares ideological common ground with Saudi crown prince Mohammed bin Salman, who, in describing his vision for Neom, claims that protecting the economy and preserving the environment are not contradictory.[39] Then again, maybe the crown prince has a *New York Times* subscription, so he is already in the know.

Perhaps the most high-spirited paean to the green modernist dream is Steven Pinker's popular (and—you guessed it—*New York Times* bestselling) 2018 book, *Enlightenment Now: The Case for Reason, Science, Humanism, and Progress*—which Bill Gates called his "new favorite book of all time." In Chapter 10, "The Environment," Pinker attempts to demolish the argument that our environmental crises mean that, in climate writer Naomi Klein's words, we must "change everything." On the contrary, he says, "environmental problems, like other problems, are solvable, given the right knowledge. . . . How to enjoy more calories, lumens, BTUs, bits, and miles with less pollution and land is itself a technological problem, and one that the world is increasingly solving."[40] Putting nuclear energy, carbon capture, geoengineering, and lab-grown meat on the table, he argues that science and technology will solve our environmental problems, just as they solved poverty, eliminated the ignorance of the Dark Ages, freed women from the drudgery of housework, and liberated slaves. The irony: only when the Europeans became "enlightened" did they decide to "free" women and "stop" slavery, and then get the credit for being the moral saviors of the oppressed. We'll get back to this form of gaslighting, which we call "green gaslighting," in the next chapter. Pinker dismisses any criticism of this vision as conservative Luddism and what he calls "eco-pessimism." He argues that, to fight climate change, we don't need to radically change the economy or our way of living; we just have to apply the same old technological know-how in more sophisticated ways.

Incidentally, in January 2020, at the last pre-pandemic World Economic Forum's gathering of economic elites in Davos, Donald

Trump also dismissed "eco-pessimism" as unhelpful for progress and prosperity and voiced his support for a plan to plant 1 trillion trees to save the environment. He added: "I'm a big believer in the environment. The environment is very important to me."[41] Trump's views of the environment are surely not the same as those of Steven Pinker or Bill Gates. But his confidence in human infallibility and ability to tackle the biggest problems with a blend of technology, investment finance, and economic superiority surely makes them bedfellows. Or maybe we shouldn't overthink it: Trump might just really have liked the word "trillion."

What brings all these different pundits, politicians, and experts together is their love of the market. Economic growth, they insist, can keep on going. Not only is growth the best tool to solve the environmental crisis, but it is *already doing so* (despite nearly every indicator suggesting the opposite—as we'll see in Chapter 3).

The ultimate endpoint of the dream of green modernism is something along the lines of the concept of "Half Earth," as proposed by the late biologist and conservationist E. O. Wilson.[42] In the latter part of his life, Wilson's work on ecology and biodiversity conservation led to an idea to turn half of Earth—half of its total landmass and oceans—into one big nature reserve. As Wilson stated, "Only by setting aside half the planet in reserve, or more, can we save the living part of the environment and achieve the stabilization required for our own survival." Let's put aside for a moment Indigenous people who would need to be displaced to make this neat idea a reality.[43] Despite accounting for only 5 percent of the world's population, they are guardians of 25 percent of the world's landmass, which includes 80 percent of the world's biodiversity.[44] Take a moment to imagine this divided utopia of pure "nature" set aside from impure "humans." It would be a civilization of compact high-tech cities powered by renewable technology, filled with virtual-reality social encounters, and fed by lab-grown meat or ultraprocessed energy-intensive vegan "meat" as well as vegetables grown on rooftops or under UV lamps in reclaimed office buildings. This would be the human half. On the natural side of the divide would be wilderness, vast tracts of unspoiled land where gazelles could frolic, elephants roam, dolphins play, and spiders spin their webs. Our human dependencies on anything natural would be officially (and at long last) cut off for good—or so proponents believe. This half would effectively be the largest zoo you could ever imagine, with not a human in sight. Sound fanciful? The United Nations Environment Program pushed ahead with the idea of locking a third of Earth's land and water surface into protected areas with its 30x30 Global Biodiversity Framework, launched at the UN Biodiversity Conference in Montreal in December 2022.

But even if any of this were possible, how would we keep it all in order? We would need to guard the borders of the wilderness from those impure elements (both people and invasive species) that would seek to defile it. Come to think of it, this could provide another great opportunity for profit: we could repurpose the military and the arms industry, which in this era of supposed world peace would have little better to do than harass some "natives" or cheap laborers (almost always dark-skinned) in an effort to guard and protect the forest from people. Just imagine: our military forces, fueled by meatless burgers, trained to become the green police of the future, carefully patrolling the border between the human and the nonhuman. If this feels a bit distant from our present reality, it shouldn't. In 2019, Damien Mander, a white Australian Iraq War veteran, decided to train a private army of all-women, vegan mercenaries in Zimbabwe—sorry, "warriors"—to hunt down evil poachers in the act. Mander's vigilante vegan mercantilism offers us a glimpse of this brave new world.[45]

Does all of this make you feel a bit queasy? Well, if you're not 100 percent on board, maybe you're just a Luddite and a conservative. Or maybe you should consider going back to your romantic and nostalgic version of the past (but even the stores selling restored vintage furniture and deluxe secondhand boutiques on

Abbot Kinney Boulevard in Venice Beach have got those folks covered). For the Steven Pinkers of the world, if you—along with more than fifteen thousand climate scientists[46]—think that we should radically change our way of life, you are a "Marxist ideologue," "misanthropic," or indulging in "ghoulish fantasies of a depopulated planet, and Nazi-like comparisons of human beings to vermin, pathogens, and cancer."[47]

The issue for Pinker and other green modernists is not whether climate change is real. Rather, it is their belief that any claim that climate change and biodiversity collapse demand a fundamental rethinking of modern civilization—a revolution—is against Reason Inc., aka Pinker's version of "enlightened environmentalism." What this amounts to is a steadfast faith in human superiority over nature through technological prowess, which can solve any and every problem. As science fiction author Ted Chiang writes in the *New Yorker*:

> Whenever anyone accuses anyone else of being a Luddite, it's worth asking, is the person being accused of being actually against technology? Or are they in favor of economic justice? We need to be able to criticize harmful uses of technology—and those include uses that benefit shareholders over workers—without being described as opponents of technology.[48]

The Green Administrators

Completely sold by the barrage of schemes peddled by the green modernists, and curious about how their innovations could be implemented? The green administrators have got you covered. These are the scientists, climatologists, development consultants, NGOs, lawyers, diplomats, government officials, and sometimes even the chosen representatives of "youth," "women," and "Indigenous peoples" who attend the circuit of annual climate and biodiversity conferences. Many of these people live in well-heeled urban areas, hold a wealth of knowledge on climate and ecological science, the evolution of multilateral environmental agreements, climate diplomacy, international relations, law, and finance. They know how to navigate the ever-evolving arena of highbrow buzz-words like "nature positive," "sustainability," "nature-based solutions," "climate adaptation," "sustainable development goals," "natural capital," "carbon trading," "biodiversity offsets," "green bonds," "ecosystem services," "land degradation neutrality," and many others. As author and historian Amitav Ghosh jokes, this group likes to use chipper language to conceal the power they wield, like when they use the word "champions" to mean a "small circle of initiates celebrating a rite of passage."[49]

A decade ago, economist Clive Spash called this group "the new environmental pragmatists" because they make concepts, ideas, and science itself marketable and acceptable for political, financial, and business sector elites.[50] The buzzwords that green administrators use have changed over the past few decades, but their tactics haven't. It's about politicking with brandable concepts to exchange vast sums of money among politicians, the private sector, large international NGOs, lending agencies like the World Bank and the Global Environment Facility, and multilateral institutions like the United Nations. The green administrators use their professionalized credo to shape public opinion on what counts as "right" or "wrong" uses of nature, and, in turn, whose experiences and ways of knowing should be discarded. Chief among the "right" ways to use nature are those that prioritize the creation of new markets, while Indigenous and subsistence livelihoods are romanticized at best, and more often cast as irrational.[51] People using subsistence techniques practiced for centuries are environmentally harmful, while very obviously destructive large-scale mining, industrial plantations, and oil and gas developments are not only given a pass but heralded as "rational" environmental saviors for sustainability. As Spash goes on to say, green pragmatists reject anything that does not pander to elites as "impractical" and claim to operate in a "real world" of business and finance, but then in the same breath ignore mounting social inequality and biological evidence of ecological collapse in favor of quick and easy "win-win" solutions. He argues that either the pragmatists share values and ideology with corporate finance or they are simply resigned to siding with money and power to get buy-in and maintain their own jobs.[52]

Green administrators or pragmatists follow the "there is no alternative" logic that has come to characterize the international order following the collapse of the Soviet Union in 1991. One of their favorite activities is to put a dollar value on nature and turn it into a commodity, just like other goods and services we might purchase. They are walking contradictions, supposedly living in a "real" world they have no fundamental interest in changing. Of course, this is because their jobs depend on not changing it. Often, whatever knowledge is generated by these environmental scientists is geared to generate profits rather than address real-world problems. Though they often are funded by industry, that's not necessarily so; in many cases they seem to like doing corporate lobby work for free. As Jérôme Ponrouch of the French bank BNP Paribas stated at a regional climate week conference in preparation for the UN Conference of the Polluters . . . er . . . Parties (COP28) in Dubai, "We need to make a market out of scientific progress." He went on to say that climate innovations for resilience should enhance private sector environment, social, and governance (ESG) portfolios.[53]

Similar to how greensters might opt for industrially produced organic produce or highly processed lab-grown vegan alternatives to meat, the green administrators are big fans of green finance. In recent years, developed nations have pledged $100 billion every year in loans and investment to combat global warming in the Global South. This is a scheme where loans given to poor countries are tied to green projects—that is, infrastructure, farming, or real estate projects that have green labels. Never mind the fact that they have fallen far short of this goal every single year.[54] The real problem is that, very often, these projects have little to do with anything green. For example, a Reuters investigation found that up to $3 billion of that money has gone toward things like an Italian chocolate and gelato chain in Asia, a Marriott hotel in Haiti, a Belgian romance film set in Argentina, a Japanese-funded coal plant in Bangladesh, and an airport in Egypt. Over one-third of the $182 billion given so far was reported in such a vague way that in some cases Reuters investigators couldn't even tell what continent the money went toward. At least $500 million was earmarked for green development projects that never even happened. The real objective with the "green" label is raising funds for developments that very likely would have happened anyway and which just need a bit of marketing. As Mark Joven, who represents the Philippines at UN climate talks, told Reuters, "This is the wild, wild west of finance. Essentially, whatever they call climate finance is climate finance." The beauty of "green" for these green administrators is that there are no legal definitions of what it actually means—and hence no legally enforceable mechanisms for it either.[55]

Part of the "real world" is also knowing how to wine and dine as a networking strategy to save the world. Success is measured with check marks when indicators are met. This group will push for emotional pledges toward "net zero" and make ever more dire warnings of ecological collapse—but their goal is ultimately to keep their funding, grant proposals, two-year projects, published papers, reelections, and pledges flowing. Again, while the heartfelt desire for a better world is evident among this group, the implication of their pragmatism is that they support the very centers of power that are driving us off the cliff in the first place.

With gut-twisting irony, academics who critique the conference-goers also wind up in conference circuits of their own. These academics use their critique of the green administrators to reproduce a parallel world, wining and dining their way up the academic hierarchy. Just because someone is critical of what is going on doesn't mean they are not part of the same process. We would include ourselves in this lot. As academics, many of us adhere to the same kinds of professional and managerial urbanist lifestyles that define the sustainability class. Too often this means gatekeeping knowledge or "firsting"—researchers coining concepts to mark personal research territory, while masking already-existing knowledge on the subject.[56] And while academics do have deep insight on environmental issues, their knowledge is valorized as expertise more than actual lived experience—something that a farmer, nurse, or Indigenous land defender usually has a lot more of. Unfortunately, those voices are too often heard as "research subjects" of academics, who then take the credit for assembling those voices.[57] As Laurie Anderson once sang with bitter irony, "Only an expert can see there's a problem, and only an expert can deal with the problem."[58]

This brings us back to Morrison and Dunlap's analysis of environmental elitism. The green administrators would certainly fit in the category that they call "impact elitism."[59] They describe how, in a kind of self-reinforcing cycle, environmental movements are led by people from wealthy and educated backgrounds, who then steer the focus of those movements to issues that concern elites—like electric cars and conservation of pristine wilderness areas. Concerns coming from poor communities, like toxic groundwater, are systematically overlooked. As a result, resources are sucked away from the people who need them most, and the costs of green action such as buying a Tesla and creating a protected wilderness area are shouldered by the poor—for example, through toxic leaching from cobalt and lithium mines and displacement of Indigenous people. In this way, the green administrators sideline the environmental concerns of the poor, while at the same time claiming to speak for them with that (purified) air of benevolence and confidence that only excessive privilege and world-class education can give you.

Eating the PIE (Purity, Innovation, and Efficiency)

One can be both a green modernist and a green administrator, though sometimes the libertarian green modernist is too impatient to wait for government bureaucracy or Wall Street to catch up with them. Meanwhile, lifestyle environmentalists can be both green modernists and green administrators. But as we mentioned earlier, what they all have in common is an unwillingness to question their class comforts—that cushion of wealth and social capital that separates them from the have-nots.

Each of these groups, in their own way, is also driven by three interconnected ideas of *purity, innovation,* and *efficiency*—or, in other words, the PIE. It's a central part of the sustainability class ideology, which is why we will devote Chapters 3–6 to it. In a nutshell, the PIE refers to consuming a genuine or authentic experience (purity), creating new environmental products and services (innovation), and saving costs so that more new green things can be produced (efficiency). For now, we briefly introduce what we mean by innovation and efficiency after having already introduced the concept of purity.

The onslaught of sustainability products and solutions on offer depends on doing things easily, with a click of a button, or doling out a few extra bucks for some offsets. This requires innovation, creativity, and a mind for profit to keep the operation afloat, of course. The next big thing is always around the corner, riding on the heels (and often the failure) of the last big thing, and ready to disrupt everything that came before it for a bright and glorious future for all. Some have called this phenomenon "failing forward"—the idea that the next big thing emerges on the heels of the last failure, until it itself fails.[60] The process continues ad nauseam to keep the whole charade going a little bit longer.

One example is cryptocurrency, like Bitcoin. The process to validate cryptocurrency requires large amounts of electricity, generated by the burning of fossil fuels. If Bitcoin were a country, by virtue of its annual electricity consumption of more than 121 terawatt-hours per year, it would fall into the top thirty energy users worldwide, rivaling or even surpassing countries like the Netherlands, Greece, and Argentina.[61] An article published in the science journal *Nature* has shown that cryptocurrencies like Bitcoin alone could push the world above 2°C of warming.[62]

And yet, for advocates of the blockchain, what's important is its disruptive potential. Take, for example, the "green" cryptocurrency Rewilder. This organization trades in non-fungible tokens (NFTs), which are essentially original rights to digital artworks that can be bought and sold.[63] In the case of Rewilder, funds from NFT sales are pooled to purchase land around the world for wildlife conservation. One NFT will rewild over one acre of land and cover its future management costs. According to the website, the legal entity that is to act as proxy and new titleholder of lands purchased is a "legacy world non-profit entity 501c3 based in Miami, Florida." [64] It also appears that Rewilder is run by three men, although the future intention is to promote decentralized blockchain-based governance by opening it up to fellow coders and NFT owners.

While all of that might sound fine in theory, imagine the following scenario. One morning, a group of forest-dwelling people in the Amazon wake up to hired security guards, paid by NFT funds, demanding that they leave their home and ancestral territory, as it is now controlled in the name of nature conservation by an unnamed nonprofit company based in Miami. While the families forcibly removed from the land relocate under extreme duress to periurban areas, where they are dependent on wages for a living, the three men and their NFT purchasers and other investors can take pride in knowing they helped "save nature." Perhaps later these same NFT peddlers, clicking away at their computer screens in the comfort of suburban U.S. homes, will cast the blame for environmental problems on overpopulated poor countries whose inhabitants put pressure on the environment by hunting and trapping to make a living—the same people their little scheme helped dispossess from their previous homes in the forest.

Indeed, the number of "save the environment" decentralized autonomous organizations (DAOs)—now branded as "regenerative finance" or ReFi—that have sprung up in the last few years is astounding. It's the latest and greatest in the name of sustainability. There are many initiatives, from the Regen Network's planned eco-credit marketplace for global carbon accounting to the "algorithmic climate protocol" of KlimaDAO to Absurd Arboretum's 3D-printed trees that plant one (yes, one) tree for every NFT "tree" art traded on the blockchain.[65] If you're confused by all these terms and jargon by now, you're supposed to be. It's all about having technical expertise that can put you ahead of the curve—and if you don't know the jargon, you'll be left behind.[66]

There's no limit to what kind of innovation counts as sustainable, with some self-proclaimed environmentalists watching the planet burn from their lifeboat and calling it green. Take, for instance, Pangeos, a turtle-shaped floating city "terayacht"—the next step up from a megayacht and gigayacht—complete with shopping malls, an airport, and hotels fully run on solar power and financed by an NFT-based crowdfunder.[67] Mind . . . blown. A solar-powered and NFT-funded terayacht with hotels, airports, and luxury condos docking at the port of—where else?—Saudi Arabia's Neom. It makes solar power feel like a fashion accessory, a little splash of color on the collar of an otherwise monochrome Armani jacket. Here's an idea: after the great extinction of all large animals on Earth, we could populate the planet with terayachts shaped like tigers, tapirs, sun bears, rhinos—you name it. "Where do you live?" "I'm on pangolin." "I hear that one has a great casino on its lower spine." "Remember the sun bear, which went extinct because of the palm oil plantations? Well, it's memorialized as a yacht!"

The next piece of the puzzle for the sustainability class is to make sure all of this can be optimized to ensure the greatest impact at the lowest cost. Being green means using less and getting more for it. In fact, being green or sustainable has almost become synonymous with efficiency—the sustainability class is obsessed with how efficiently things are produced and how efficiently we use them.

Equating efficiency with greenness can lead to some ridiculous solutions. A particularly astounding example comes from a pair of twenty-three-year-old sophomores from Texas A&M University, Brent Whitehead and Matt Lohstroh, who made $4 million in 2021 by buying a shipping container full of servers and then employing them to mine Bitcoin using power from gas flares generated by offshore oil and gas fields. When oil is drilled, natural gas often escapes as well. That can be captured, but usually producers just burn it off, releasing CO_2 in the process. Whitehead and Lohstroh figured they could "solve" the problem by saving that gas from being burned and using it to generate profit instead, powering Bitcoin mining servers packed into containers.[68] Sure, it's efficient—but it doesn't actually "solve" any problem. All it does is more *efficiently* exploit oil and gas reserves.

Whitehead and Lohstroh's venture is an example of what entrepreneurs and impact investors James Altucher and Douglas R. Sease call "investing through the back door" in their 2011 book *The Wall Street Journal Guide to Investing in the Apocalypse: Making Money by Seeing Opportunity Where Others See Peril*. Back door investing means devising clever ploys to make it appear a company is solving the problems generated by its principal front door activities—say, an oil company investing in renewables. The authors argue that efficient and profitable investments are those that "fade the fear"—that is, reduce anxiety and emotional turmoil—so that traditional investments in things like oil and gas can continue unobstructed. Together, these principles are supposed to neutralize fears of potential threats like climate change and mass extinctions of life on Earth. The inherent uncertainty of climate change is turned into a predictable calculation of risk: we can hedge our bets by continuing to invest in fossil fuels while we avert apocalypse by investing in alternatives to fossil fuels. Apocalypse investment is about being able to control your emotions in the face of the utter calamity resulting from ecological breakdown, while continuing to capture the windfall profits from efficiently exploiting the planet until the last possible yearly dividend rolls in.

The idea of efficiency lies at the root of the lucrative carbon markets, which in 2021 swelled to a record $851 billion.[69] Carbon markets allow companies to trade carbon emission allowances based upon how many carbon credits they have. Rather than mandating hard limits to carbon emissions, which would be the most logical and sane thing to do in a crisis of a scale and magnitude that no human civilization before us has ever experienced, we need to (to borrow Altucher and Sease's catchphrases) "fade the fear" and invest in carbon credits through the "back door" while keeping the front door wide open for fossil fuel investment. As the authors say, apocalypse investing "is both an art and a science, and whether you engage in it at Doug's leisurely pace or with James' intensity, it should be both profitable and, dare we say it, a bit of fun."

Thinking about doing anything environmentally sinful? No problem! Just purchase a carbon credit—a unit of carbon, such as one ton of CO_2, that is taken out of the atmosphere and traded for one ton of CO_2 released elsewhere. Bingo! Your conscience is clear and your impact is neutralized like magic . . . at least in theory. Since the assumption that tons of carbon emitted and tons of carbon sequestered are the same thing, carbon trades can be actual but also hypothetical. In other words, you can promise to buy carbon credits only when investors start buying your product.

Take Rewilder, mentioned above, which claims that any purchase of their NFTs will involve simultaneous investment in carbon offsets, even making your purchase carbon negative. As long as you can offset the damage, there's no incentive to prevent causing the damage in the first place. This is precisely the idea though, as those who stand to gain the most from the status quo have no solution to environmental problems except to move them around like brushing dirt under a rug.[70] Meanwhile, carbon emissions are (if everything goes to plan) neutralized, but net emissions *reductions* remain out of reach, which are what we desperately need.

Within this industry, personalized offsets traded through a largely unregulated and voluntary carbon market (VCM) have become hugely popular and have generated inflated value for already forested land that might never have even been under threat before offsets came onto the scene. Individuals can offset their emissions by buying offsets when they buy something from airlines, cruises, tech companies, oil producers, or other businesses. The VCM has spawned offset retailers like Ecologi—which bills itself as the "Spotify of Sustainability" because of the venture capital it was able to amass, similar to Spotify, Airbnb, and Stripe.[71] Complete with cutesy animations of your own personal forests financed with your offsets, Ecologi lulls you into complacency. Though getting trees planted to cleanse your guilty feelings is made easy and simple, it is a complex operation, with quite a few intermediaries involved. Among these are large clearinghouses or marketplaces like Xpansiv that provide continuous updates on carbon prices and different offset packages, mobilizing hundreds of millions of dollars in real time.[72]

Certifiers like Gold Standard or Verra verify that carbon credits are real, transparent, measurable, and accountable, and that they truly prevented deforestation or some other carbon-emitting activity from happening. But this accounting process is largely based on abstract calculations of threat of forest loss and net carbon gain, rarely if ever considering the historical relations of people to the territory where credits are generated, nor ongoing social disparities and conflicts that the project might cause. The main challenge for certifiers is to generate enough trust that the carbon offset is genuine. Yet this trust is very hard to come by. Much of the carbon market is based on deforestation that is *avoided*—in other words, a company can get credits to pay for a forest to stop being cut down. Basically, if the creditor can claim that a forest is under threat, buying up that forest and displacing the communities that reside in it can become an offset.

For example, in a nine-month investigation of Verra, the world's leading carbon verifier, based in Washington, D.C., it was found that 94 percent of the nearly 100 million carbon credits issued by Verra issued were fraudulent "phantom" credits that do not represent actual carbon reductions. The resulting carbon offsets were then sold to companies like Disney, easyJet, Shell, and the band Pearl Jam, among others, who then passed on to their customers what turned out to be a load of greenwash: that they were at the forefront of the sustainability transition. The threat attributed to forests had been overestimated by roughly 400 percent, disproportionately placing unwarranted blame on people residing in and around these forests. The offsets led to serious human rights violations, home demolitions, and forced evictions of forest-dwelling families. Funny how it's so easy to blame poor families for their impacts on the environment while letting oil and airline companies off the hook, and even applauding them for their public relations chicanery.

There are other perverse examples of offsetting as the efficient solution to addressing climate change. French oil company Total has its sights on an area of carbon-rich tropical forests and wetlands in the Cuvette region of the Republic of Congo for oil drilling.[73] These forests themselves sit atop an enormous carbon-storing peat bog containing upward of 33 billion tons of carbon—equivalent to three years' worth of global carbon emissions. Home to lowland gorillas, endangered forest elephants, and countless other species, the felling of these forests for oil would produce a terrifying multiplier effect of carbon emissions. Yet our conscience should be clear knowing that Total will reforest one hundred thousand acres elsewhere in the Republic of Congo to produce a carbon sink of 40 million trees absorbing more than 5.5 million tons of CO_2 over a thirty-five-year period.[74]

Making things more efficient is sometimes portrayed positively as being disruptive of the status quo. For instance, the blockchain is argued to be less centralized and to greatly accelerate transactions between producers and consumers, cutting out intermediaries and red tape. Fair enough, but how is that in any way disruptive or anti-mainstream? Isn't that what mainstream institutions have sought to do since the deregulations of Reaganomics? Being anti-establishment or even bohemian has become the status quo.

What is common to the purity, innovation, and efficiency mindset is that it appears well-intentioned yet is exclusive by design. Most people can't participate because of the cost, and so "going green" instantly becomes a class issue. The implications of turning sustainability into a class issue couldn't be more dangerous; it too often generates a kind of moral superiority that translates subtly into blaming those who can't afford to buy into "green"—or, even more often, chalking up environmental problems to population growth amid historically unprecedented global inequality in access to basic goods and services. When an average American refrigerator consumes more electricity every year than an average person in Bangladesh does in a year, then it's obvious that class has a lot more to do with our ecological crisis than overpopulation.[75]

Many might realize the green products and services on offer are bogus. Often, the difficulty of achieving real change makes people feel like "it's the best we've got." But the harsh truth welling up in our gut as we hear about the latest flood, heat wave, killer typhoon, or weakening of the Atlantic Gulf Stream is that the best we've got is not just insufficient but, worse, counterproductive.[76]

Prepare for the Greenlash

Malcolm X, the civil rights activist, once compared white conservatives to wolves and white liberals to foxes. Foxes, he said, will pretend that they're friendly and always smile. So, when racialized and oppressed people run away from the snarling wolf, they run straight into the mouth of the smiling fox. The sustainability class is like a fox with a toothy grin: they claim to care about the environment, but their solutions turn out to be non-solutions and disguised forms of the same systems of oppression. When people are told that these solutions will save them, but those strategies end up doing nothing, they will stop believing in the possibility of change. That's why the fox can be more dangerous than the wolf.

We know that it can feel bad to be told that, try as we might, our good intentions aren't accomplishing real change. What we're trying to do with this book is to channel those good intentions away from counterproductive, guilt-laden non-solutions and toward collective change. Together, we have the power to turn our frustrations into collective agency. To do that, it is imperative to understand we're going at it wrong, and to have the courage and vulnerability to be a part of something bigger than what we can achieve individually.

But as the metaphor of the wolf and the fox illustrates so well, it's not just that buying into carbon offsets, climate-resilient luxury real estate, and wellness products is not effective. It's that these approaches are *harmful*: they maintain the status quo, corrode our imagination, waste increasingly limited time for real change, and entrench class divides. Instead of deconstructing barriers between the haves and the have-nots, lifestyle environmentalism, green administration, and green modernism excludes the lowest-income people, whether it is the unhoused in Venice or the laborers in the Democratic Republic of Congo mining cobalt for solar panels and so many others in between. The belief that technology will save us implies that most of us have no role to play in the coming transition to a more ecologically conscious world. Instead, those in power will simply manipulate us into "saving the planet" to serve their own interests.

We're not going to lie: the fact that most of the so-called solutions are just fabulous forms of greenwashing is really depressing. People want to hear good news, but constant critique is a fast way to turn people off from engaging further. Greenwash fatigue is real, and the more greenwash is thrown at us, the more likely green backlash, or greenlash, will happen, fomenting resistance to serious and urgent social and ecological transformation.[77] It's the moment when, not willing to be tricked again by the smiling fox, people turn to the wolf to keep everything in order and protect their way of life.

That would be disastrous. For one thing, we can put off getting eaten by the wolf if we push others to the front. But it is just a matter of time before we're next. And we can't give up at the exact moment we truly need to be acting like it's an emergency—because we are in an emergency situation now. Sadly, the first people to suffer from a greenlash would be those least responsible for causing ecological crises in the first place.

A greenlash is the inevitable outcome of by-design failures of greenwashing strategies like carbon offsets and other public relations exercises, all while ecological breakdown and social inequalities continue to multiply. The wolf, in this case, is a consolidating far-right movement. Right-wing attacks on "ideologically driven" or "woke" investments in ESG portfolios are part of the greenlash. These people argue that fossil fuels are essential to business as usual. They don't even pretend to care about the environment.[78] Perhaps most worrying is the way right-wing talking points against the environment latch on to genuine frustration towards deceptive branding and constant greenwash amid killer heatwaves, flooding, and other kinds of extreme weather. When frustration with all the deception combines with economic woes, inflation, and energy crises from unfolding events like the Russia-Ukraine war, greenlash only gets amplified. Once the greenlash sets in, real action, like investing in publicly owned utilities or mass transit, becomes hard to distinguish from greenwashing. Against cynicism, the will to change anything crumbles, along with a sense of imagination for what's actually possible.

Avoiding the risk of greenlash and mobilizing people for genuine structural change is the only chance we have left. We need to be able to recognize a smiling fox when we see one, even while we continue to stay far away from the wolves. To do this, we need to have a clear head about what kind of ecology we want to fight for, how to identify and cast aside PIE-in-the-sky "solutions," and how to act in ways that do not exclude or discard whole groups of people. Finally, we need to know what solidarity really means in ecological struggle and how it can be built. The remainder of this book will cover these themes and more. The sustainability class faces a choice. Will they bet on being part of the green elite, hidden away in their LEED-certified fortresses, or will they throw in their lot with the dispossessed—whose ranks they and their children will soon join anyway?

2

WHAT IS ECOLOGY?

In the hilly and grassy landscapes of Liwa al-Quds (East Jerusalem), but also further north in Nablus and the Galilee, a plethora of ancient, wild, edible plants grow. This is a landscape where subtle changes in light and temperature have profound effects on vegetation. The landscape is scattered with limestone rocks and green cover—providing excellent habitats for insects, snails, lizards, and gazelles. Among the plants that grow in the picturesque valley, akkoub (*Gundelia tournefortii*)—a spiny thistle-like plant that tastes like a cross between artichoke and asparagus—has been an important food source for millennia. As artist and director Jumana Manna writes, akkoub is a "delicacy" and "culinary obsession" among Palestinians, dating back to Neolithic times. It is a wonder vegetable with many medicinal properties, such as treating diabetes, liver diseases, heart problems, and gastric pain. One needs thick gloves to pick the prickly leaves, covered in thorns. The thicker stems of akkoub are then cooked with olive oil and yogurt sauce.[1]

For many Palestinians, foraging akkoub and other edible legumes in these rocky hills not only provides nutritious food, but also connects people to the land. In Manna's 2022 film *Foragers*, we see that when foragers cut the plant back at the base, they also protect it from wildfire and thus encourage its preservation and replenishment. It is in large part because people forage akkoub that it grows and thrives, that the soil and landscape are protected—highlighting the intimacy between human existence and ecological thriving.

But the film also documents how the lands once belonging to Palestinian villagers who foraged akkoub since time immemorial were confiscated in the 1948 Nakba—the violent displacement and ethnic cleansing of Palestinians from their homeland for the creation of the Israeli state. Since 2005, foraging akkoub has been forbidden by the Israel Nature and Parks Authority, supposedly to preserve the plant from extinction. Ironically, however, the ban on foraging has made the plant more vulnerable to devastating wildfires. The result of the foraging ban has meant less akkoub, not more.

This example begs us to think twice about what ecology is. Is an ecosystem a fenced off wilderness, or is it something that is managed and used, a relationship? In the film, when a group of foragers is arrested by Israeli authorities for foraging akkoub and asked if they knew about the environmental harms of their actions, one replies, saying: "I am nature, okay? I would not hurt myself." [2]

That, in one quote, is a suitable summary of our argument in this chapter: ecology is not something out there, pure and unattainable. Rather, it is a system—and often a conflict between different systems. In the system touted by the sustainability class, problems are "fixed" by making them into consumable products—by fencing them off and, if possible, charging an entrance fee. This is an ecology that promises sustainability, when, in fact, it is all about maintaining the status quo, entrenching it further. It means continuing as before while pretending nothing is actually wrong. It's right there in the word: sustainability has come to mean *sustaining the present order of things.* And this is indeed what the sustainability class may subconsciously desire—to change nothing that will threaten their way of life.

But why should an ecological future look just like the present? In the past half century, archaeologists have collected convincing evidence that the history of humanity looks anything but linear: humans have built up complex hierarchical political and social systems throughout many periods of human history, and just as often intentionally dismantled them, often because people simply decided that this wasn't a great way to do things. From complex forager societies in the Great Plains of North America and the Fertile Crescent of the Levant to the Inuit of the Arctic to civilizations in Amazonia, societies moved fluidly back and forth across social structures with different value systems from one season or generation to the next. Settled agriculture and centralized governments were in many parts of the world conscious experiments, which were then abandoned when foraging and hunting, or decentralized governance, made more sense. As anthropologist David Graeber and archaeologist David Wengrow note when assessing this historical evidence, "with flexibility comes the capacity to step outside the boundaries of any given structure and reflect; to both make and unmake the political worlds we live in."[3]

In contrast to our rich human history of experimentation, sustainability has come to mean *less* flexibility and *greater* discipline to accept one uniform and inescapable future. Sustainable development draws a straight line from the industrial revolution—roughly from Columbus's "discovery" of the Americas—to a future that sustains this way of being in perpetuity.

But there is no "one-way future consisting only of growth," as science fiction writer Ursula K. Le Guin proclaimed.[4] Ecology is contested, both historically and today—from how it is understood scientifically to how it plays out across continents. There are ecologies built on acting together with a whole concert of human beings and non-human life, not on individual action and consumption. These are ecologies of possibility.

Nothing Natural About Nature

Let's start by thinking about the word "nature." What comes to mind when you hear that word? Maybe a forest glen with a waterfall or a coral reef. Maybe a safari with rhinos, elephants, and zebras. Maybe someone doing yoga on a beach at sunrise. Or maybe an overgrown lot in between construction sites. Often nature is considered a space where human beings don't typically reside—a pristine, untamed, and depopulated wilderness. A forest outside of a city is nature. The city itself is unnatural, manmade.

That nature—the kind that you can post to Instagram, the #lifegoals kind—is a hot commodity. According to one report sponsored by National Geographic, "nature" is considered an "underexploited asset" and is a major economic revenue source.[5] That report claims that conservation of 30 percent of Earth's land and waters in protected areas or reserves (a major goal for big corporate environmental NGOs like the World Wildlife Fund) can generate between $64 billion and $454 billion per year by 2050. Peasants and pastoralists will be thrilled to know that their land will now become even more lucrative for nature conservation and tourism industries, and in turn for the airline industry, construction firms for airports, luxury hotels, shopping malls, real estate speculators . . . the works.

Sometimes what we understand as untamed and "protected" nature is a landscape that has been carefully managed for a particular purpose, such as tourism. No different, then, from a busy manicured city park. As geographer David Harvey once quipped, "There is nothing unnatural about New York City."[6] If you think about it, we could go even further: there is nothing natural about nature. Nature is not an established fact; it is managed and mediated by beliefs, culture, technology, and the economy. Nature reserves and wildlife parks aren't just nature protected from humans; they are a created vision of nature imposed by one group of people on others, like the Israel Nature and Parks Authority and Palestinian foragers.

In their book *The Big Conservation Lie*, Kenyan authors John Mbaria and Mordecai Ogada show how nature reserves set up by European colonial powers in large swaths of East Africa damaged the delicate balance between pastoralist cultures and the large African animals we know so well.[7] So, even though the aim was to protect nature, the outcome was more human-wildlife conflicts, overgrazing where pastoralists were forced to become sedentary, drier microclimates, and reduced soil fertility leading to desertification. Unspoiled visions in one place create very spoiled visions in other places, or even in the same place—unbeknownst to the safari tourist.

The centuries-old tradition of kicking peasants, Indigenous peoples, and pastoralists off their land in the name of conservation has both dehumanizing and ecologically damaging impacts. From very early on, British colonizers sought to protect megafauna for hunting and tourism in East Africa, and this strategy inspired the international nature conservation agenda at the turn of the twentieth century.[8] Today in Tanzania, more than seventy thousand Indigenous Maasai are facing eviction from their ancestral pastoral lands in Loliondo by a United Arab Emirates–based conservation company that wants to create a wildlife corridor for trophy hunting and luxury safari tourism.[9] The Maasai are being relocated to a buffer zone near the Ngorongoro Conservation Area designated for both wildlife and people and will join eighty thousand other Maasai who have already been evicted.

Luxury safari tourism is now an export. Take Sharjah Safari Park in Dubai, which touts itself as "the world's largest safari outside Africa." Basically an open-air zoo, it is surrounded by hotel chains, restaurants, and shopping malls that monetize the experience of being in Africa, outside of Africa. As one Google reviewer, Fahad Anooni, said, "I felt like I was actually in Africa." As if a massive continent can be rolled up into a single aesthetic experience. Sharjah Safari Park was so remarkable in its recreation of "Africa" that it even inspired the chief minister of India's Haryana state, near Delhi, to propose another branded version of the African wilderness—bringing cheetahs and lions from the African continent and a massive aquarium to the semi-arid and groundwater-depleted state. And get this: the money to fund this Indian safari park will come as an "eco-compensation" for the deforestation of fifty square miles of primary tropical rainforests and Indigenous territory of the Shompen and Nicobarese, some fifteen thousand miles away on Great Nicobar Island in the Bay of Bengal, which will make way for a new shipping port, international airport, and ecotourism resort.[10] Trading biodiverse forests teeming with life still unknown to science and Indigenous cultures that have resided on Great Nicobar Island for 14,000 years for "low carbon" ecotourism resorts and a reforested safari park with shipped-in cheetahs from Africa in a water-scarce arid climate more than a thousand miles away, all in the name of nature protection? Go figure. We can't help but see similarities between the dispossession of people for "nature" conservation and the way green real estate development gentrifies urban neighborhoods and prices out lower-income residents. All of these strategies commit grave ecological, and often human rights, violations just to refashion the world as a playground for the wealthy and then dare to call it green, sustainable, low-carbon, or eco-conscious—take your pick.

But hold on. Isn't protecting nature—whichever interpretation one might have about it—a good thing? Not necessarily. Being clear about what and whose "nature" we refer to matters because otherwise any billionaire philanthropist can decide what kinds of "nature" he (usually he) wants to protect at the expense of those less powerful and in the absence of any due process of justice. Take, for example, Prince William, the heir to the British throne, who has called for protecting megafauna in Africa but has blamed the continent for being "overpopulated" and hence putting what he called "enormous pressure" on the private conservation reserves that British royalty have historically treated as their personal hunting grounds.[11] For the British crown and conservation game reserves, protecting megafauna is a priority over the people who have lived among them for millennia. For them, "nature" in Africa means untamed wilderness, depopulated of the African peoples who live there.

But others—including Africans—might define nature differently. The ICCA Consortium, an association of 225 Indigenous people's groups and their allies worldwide, does not use the language of nature conservation but instead refers to defending "territories of life." They define these as "territories and areas that Indigenous peoples and local communities collectively conserve and consider at the heart of their identities, cultures, histories and livelihoods." [12] That might not satisfy the need for a clear and concise definition of nature. But they don't need one: the point is that collective ownership, culture, health, living ecosystems, and livelihood are all interconnected. They point to many local terms for such territories, in many languages: *"wilayah adat, himas, agdals, territorios de vida, territorios del buen vivir, tagal, qoroq-e bumi, yerli qorukh, faritra ifempivelomana, qoroq,* ancestral domains, country, community conserved areas, *territorios autonomos comunitarios."* [13] None of these mean anything like "nature," but rather refer to living relationships and governance models. It's clear that nature means different things to different people—and for many, the word itself is rather meaningless.

When people talk about conserving nature or saving the environment, they rarely mean saving them from the economic and political systems that prop up the ultra-wealthy. Instead they often blame working-class people, rural peasants, the urban homeless, and Indigenous people as the culprits of nature's decline. Saving the environment becomes a matter of putting a fence around some piece of land so it can be reserved for Disney-fied safaris and then carving up the rest for intensive agriculture, urban development, and mining. As Ben Goldsmith, a leading advocate for convincing the elite to invest in nature, argued in a philanthropy-funded *Guardian* article, "It's really cheap to fix nature. It recovers itself very quickly if you give it space. It's not like building a hospital brick by brick, machine by machine. No huge investment is required to make things happen with nature." [14] What is left un-spoken is that "fixing" nature requires very little from the rich—they can keep doing as they please as long as they set aside some of their billions to create conservation areas, as if there is an endless world of space to empty of people and refill with trees whenever a new pipeline or mining project is proposed. There *must* be some-thing else that we can do to put a stop to the destruction of bio-diversity, instead of relying on the rich to "fix" it for us, displacing millions of real human beings, and then blaming them (again) as overpopulating Earth when they get displaced elsewhere, all while selling out the rest of life to the highest bidder.

That something else, we believe, means transforming the way we think about nature in the first place: not a thing that is "out there" to be protected, but an *ecology* of living and ever-changing relationships. As a very basic definition, we might think of ecol-ogy as being about dynamic relationships and interconnections. It is a co-evolving process, where species and their surroundings actively shape and are shaped by each other. We can get to this definition by looking at the history of ecology, teasing apart dif-ferent strands and competing visions.

Ecology Is Not Neutral

We are sometimes told the first ecologists were the Greeks. Thinkers like Aristotle, Herodotus, and Hippocrates have left us many texts showing their profound engagement with the natural world—they would spend days cataloguing and describing spe-cies, natural phenomena, and the interactions between them. In-deed, the word "ecology" comes from Ancient Greek, having its root in *oikos* (the home) and *logos* (the study of).

But it is certainly not the ancient Greeks who did this first. The medicinal properties of plants, the way different plants grow well together, the benefit of certain soil types over others, the role of different animals in helping to ward off pests—all this knowledge came about through observation and playful experimentation. If you have a garden yourself, or spent your childhood in one, you know the feeling of spending hours puttering around, poking at things, digging a bit here and there, thinking about what could go where. Millennia of such research and development resulted in perhaps the most groundbreaking inventions ever, no intellectual property or patents needed: most cultivated plant species we eat, from corn and eggplant to barley and potatoes.[15] Indigenous peoples the world over—from Adivasis of the Indian subcontinent, the Seminole, Huron-Wendat, and Iroquois of Turtle Island (North America), the Huli-Wigmen of Papua New Guinea, the Shuar, Mapuche, and Yanomami to name a few—have been practicing (not just thinking about) ecology in this way for millennia.

We now know that for much of human history the line between farming, hunting, gathering, and gardening has been quite blurred. Agriculture as we know it today, as well as all the food we eat, was developed during this period that spanned thousands of years.[16] Still today, research shows that Indigenous people are expert wardens of endangered ecosystems: because of their traditional knowledge and their close connection to the land, their stewardship in most cases outperforms other conservation strategies. The most biodiverse regions of the world have been managed by these cultures for millennia, and removing Indigenous people, pastoralists, and small-scale farmers from them is often followed by ecological collapse.[17]

Ecology is collaborative. The Greek historian Herodotus noticed with delight that crocodiles would leave their great toothy maw open for the sandpiper to peck out the leeches between their teeth. This form of mutual collaboration between species shouldn't be surprising to anyone who spends a long time lying in the grass looking at, say, ants and wasps sharing a meal without fighting, or gazing up at the sky at different bird species warning each other about approaching danger. Despite what is so obviously in front of us, we have taken as a matter of fact the idea, most famously introduced by Charles Darwin, that nature is inherently competitive and hierarchical, that evolution is driven by a mad dash for survival by all species, pitted against each other. It was the anarchist scientist Peter Kropotkin who added to Darwin's theory of evolution by showing how mutual aid is central to the survival of species and has at least as important a role in driving evolution as competition does.[18]

Yet even though ecology is often portrayed as an objective science, there is no single, unified ecological approach. The very *idea* of ecology is contested. Take, for example, Ernst Haeckel, a German zoologist and philosopher, who first coined the word "ecology" (*Ökologie*) in 1866. Known today for his mesmerizing illustrations of nature, especially marine life, he was also a pioneer in species classification and the theory of evolution—being one of Charles Darwin's most influential promoters at the time. Unfortunately, he also believed strongly that human ethnic groups were different species and argued that they should be classified hierarchically (with, of course, Caucasians above all others as a "highly developed and perfect" people whose development would "raise men above the rest of nature").[19] His concerns about racial purity were not separate from his scientific discoveries: evolution, for him, was a hierarchical process wherein a master race would eventually drive progress. Though Haeckel's books were banned in Nazi Germany, his racism was in line with the Nazi worldview of Germanic superiority, which sought to justify itself through the fields of biology, psychology, and eugenics.[20]

There is a long history of biologists and ecologists who have tried to defend racism on ecological and geneticist grounds—claims that are as scientifically unsound as they are reprehensible.[21] E. O. Wilson, a leading proponent of the "Half Earth" conservation strategy mentioned in the previous chapter, was also one of the world's foremost conservationists. But he was preoccupied with genetic purity in a troubling way. For instance, he mused about whether homosexuality, entrepreneurship, war, and "racial variations" could influence a person's genetic fitness. His concerns with nature preservation and genetic determinism fit into a vision of biocentric purity that ran through his work.[22] Still another ecologist, Garrett Hardin, famous for his article "The Tragedy of the Commons"—claiming that any resource that is not privately owned eventually becomes degraded—promoted eugenics and forced sterilization of nonwhite ethnic groups. He also often wrote in far-right journals and engaged with known white supremacists. He is recognized by the civil rights organization Southern Poverty Law Center as an extremist and white supremacist.[23]

Hardin, Wilson, and Haeckel are not alone in how they used ecology to justify white ethnic superiority. In hindsight, much of ecological science was developed in the service of colonial expansion by European powers.[24] Conservationists often advocate taking humans out of the picture: ecosystems are pure and sanitized, and humans add impurity and chaos into the equation. The consequences are not just scientific—they can involve, for example, paramilitary forces hired to threaten and murder land defenders in conservation areas.[25]

Eco-fascist ideas of environmental purity and order can also be used in the service of explicitly supremacist ideas, such as when, in 2019, a gunman in El Paso, Texas, shot and killed twenty-two people, mostly people of color, because he believed that immigration and intercultural marriages would compromise racial purity and lead to the exploitation of pristine nature. Not too far off the mark from E. O. Wilson's "Half Earth" conservation or Garrett Hardin's beliefs. As Kenyan conservationist Mordecai Ogada remarked, the divisions between nature on one side and humans on the other "will not result in the displacement of any white person in the world. For black and brown people, it is blood and tears."[26]

Similarly, as the Indian historian Mukul Sharma writes in the book *Green and Saffron: Hindu Nationalism and Indian*

Environmental Politics, the environmental management of endangered species like tigers has also been a part of the effort to remove certain peoples who did not fit into the idealized vision of a pure Hindu nation—Muslims, Christians, lower-caste, and Adivasi or Indigenous people—from the landscape.[27]

We are not saying we should throw the baby out with the bathwater. There are many redeeming aspects of ecological science, as we show throughout this chapter. But what we are pointing to here is that there is no simple "good" and "bad" ecology, or "objective" or "subjective" claims. Rather, claims about ecology are always in conflict and informed by different, competing perspectives that need careful parsing. We are left with the difficult task of sorting through these perspectives and making up our own mind.

Soil ecology, or the study of how the chemistry and composition of soil encourages fertility and supports different land uses, is a good case study of how ecology can be a site of conflict. This was one of the earliest fields in ecology. Charles Darwin himself was one of its founders: he spent his last years on his knees studying earthworms in his garden, trying to determine whether they were conscious or not. He found that worms are responsible for turning organic matter into soil, and his book on the subject was widely praised.[28] In the nineteenth century, soil science revolutionized farming by advancing our understanding of what quantities of minerals and nutrients, such as nitrogen and phosphate, were needed to induce maximum crop growth. These findings led to huge demands for fertilizer, high in phosphates and nitrogen, to increase crop productivity.

In 1802, pioneering ecologist Alexander von Humboldt investigated guano (the Indigenous Quechua word for dung applied as fertilizer, but usually referring to bird droppings) in Peru.[29] He described how locals harvested guano from islands off the coast—accumulated over millennia—to boost nutrition for their crops. Guano became a highly prized commodity, as it was found that it has high levels of fixed nitrogen and phosphate. A few decades later colonial powers started a mad dash for the resource, with the United States embarking on its first imperial wars to claim guano islands in the Pacific. Available guano deposits were almost entirely exhausted. But in the early twentieth century, a German factory began to produce ammonia with byproducts from coal. This energy-intensive process fixed nitrogen into a product that could be easily applied on the soil, thus marking the end of the guano industry.

But there was still one missing basic ingredient for soil fertility: phosphate. And so began a scramble for phosphate mining, including on the island of Nauru, which, inhabited by Indigenous peoples for over three thousand years, had phosphate-dense rock formations due to fossilized bird droppings. After colonial powers annexed the island, it effectively became one large mine. Eventually 80 percent of the island's surface was strip-mined, resulting in the destruction of Indigenous livelihoods and community. Its economy eviscerated and its people without any form of subsistence, Nauru later signed a deal to host a refugee detention facility in exchange for Australian aid.[30]

The mining of phosphate—80 percent of which ends up as fertilizer—continues its ravaging effects on local communities. For example, in Senegal, the community of Gad sits next to a phosphate mine, which has led to chronic health issues such as miscarriages and infant deaths.[31] Wars are still fought for phosphate: take Bou Craa, a mine in the Western Sahara, a phosphate-rich area that Morocco invaded after the Spanish left in 1976 and has occupied with brute force ever since.[32] All of these knock-on effects started with the drive for maximizing the productivity of soil for agriculture.

To a great extent, soil science was developed in the service of industrial agriculture, with the goal of maximizing yields on European farmland that had been expropriated from peasants by large landowners, or on plantations employing thousands of slaves to produce key crops such as cotton, rubber, and sugarcane in colonial territories.[33] Soil science not only kick-started a world-spanning extractive industry that devastated whole regions and peoples, but it also became a key component of the management of colonized lands by European occupiers. For example, in the early twentieth century, colonial governments imposed soil conservation practices across Africa to mitigate erosion, including through terracing and grazing rotations. Even as they tacitly acknowledged that soil erosion was in large part triggered by the expansion of monoculture and the forced eviction of pastoralist communities from the land they had maintained for millennia, colonial governments became increasingly worried that the potential income from Africa's fertile farmland would be washed away. In the 1940s and 1950s in central Kenya, in a region dominated by the Kikuyu people but where British settlers owned much of the land, the British government made soil erosion control practices mandatory—in great part relying on forced labor of women. These draconian measures, and the grievances against them, triggered the Mau Mau rebellion, the largest uprising in colonial Kenya, which led to the British colonial government killing more than ten thousand people over an eight-year period.[34]

So What Does It Mean to Be Ecological?

Soil science, or ecology more broadly, is of course not inherently colonial. It was also through soil science, in fact, that many came to understand the limits to industrial agricultural production: no matter how much you innovate or mechanize, ecological systems have their limits. At a certain point, squeezing the last drop of profit from the soil will lead to the collapse of its fertility for generations after.[35] Still, this further emphasizes the point that thinking about ecological complexity is not a neutral, objective perspective. You cannot think and act ecologically without engaging in politics of some kind. While ecological insights can be used to further advance the domination and genocide of peoples around the world, they can also be used to show the limits to certain ways of doing things, as well as possible alternatives.

One such positive insight from the science of ecology is that *we humans are ecological*—an insight the forager in Manna's film alluded to. Just as nature is not a static entity separate from us, humans are part of ecosystems and co-create them, as do other species. Evolutionary biologists and ecologists Richard Lewontin and Richard Levins have shown how all animals do not merely live in their environment as though it were some kind of "theatrical stage . . . to play out their lives."[36] Using the example of the phoebe, a songbird, they describe how the bird's ecosystem involves both the building of nests of grass and mud and active patrolling in mixed forests by males in the spring and the arrival of females to a ready-made nest for their brood. Every creature has its constructed environment. "A stone lying in the grass is part of the environment of a snail-eating thrush that uses it as an anvil but is not part of the world of the flycatcher or woodpecker."[37] Likewise, humans don't just live in an environment; we create environments, which overlap with the built environment of other species.

If we are ecological, then *ecology is also social*. Humans are part of their environment, and so are our social and economic institutions. The ecology of human agriculture doesn't just involve the interconnections between specific crop varieties, soils, mycorrhizal fungal networks, nitrogen-fixing bacteria, pathogens, water flows, and climate. It also includes the farmers' labor, cultures of "peace" time and war, and economic pressures that lead to the introduction of new technologies. These social elements tend to be treated separately or ignored altogether, even as they play a central role in the collapse of biodiversity, the excess nitrogen unleashed on ecosystems through industrial farming, water use, and the interactions between humans and zoonotic pathogens leading to increased risks of spillovers and potential pandemics.

Lewontin and Levins highlight this social nature of ecology:

"Every act of consumption is an act of production, and every act of production is an act of consumption."[38] For example, salmon spend most of their lives swimming in the ocean. When they swim upstream to lay their eggs, they die. And so they bring the ocean's nutrients with them and release them when they die. These nutrients feed the soil, plants, mammals, and other fish.

But this does not just apply to the nonhuman world. Think of the production and consumption of any good or service, from organic bananas to tourist resort packages, from insurance schemes to oat-milk lattes, and artificial intelligence. The production of each of these requires resources and human labor from somewhere, and the act of consumption produces waste that has to be treated or disposed of somewhere. When we treat the product as the only thing that matters (the organic bananas versus the non-organic bananas), the reality of how the product came into being and the consequences these relationships generate is simply erased from view. At best, they tend to be relativized (an organic banana is surely better than a non-organic one), putting a blinder on the actual relations of production and consumption and their consequences when carried out on an industrial scale. The point is: there is no endpoint where we can finally say something is "eco-friendly." Yes, we might want to figure out how to develop ecological practices that nourish everyone in the world. But there is no one goal that gets done and dusted; ecologies transform and fold into each other, constantly.

We also now know that *ecosystems always transform*; there is no "pristine" state that they can return to after they are changed. There are no returns to "normal." Ecological systems are not static; they often shift quickly and unpredictably. A single heat wave can force a coral reef to bleach irreversibly. Thus, massive die-offs of corals are not caused by average incremental increases in sea-surface temperatures, but by sudden peaks in temperature.[39] Try as we might to measure ecological impacts like carbon emissions quantitatively, the point at which a threshold like climate system breakdown is crossed is not cumulative or linear. And when change occurs, that change is irreversible, at least in our lifetimes. Just like you can't unburn your toast in the morning, you can't go back to a pure unaltered state after an invasive species is introduced to a forest.

Even the most sophisticated engineering ultimately fails to stop life-forms finding ways to creep in and disrupt the best-laid of plans—take SARS-CoV-2, the coronavirus that caused the Covid-19 pandemic, which fell on a world entirely unprepared for it. At the same time, these ecological chance encounters aren't just a mess of meaninglessness. There is a vague and loose order in the flux of constant change. The direction is what matters: does it stop a diversity of life from flourishing, or does it help this diversity proliferate?

In ecosystems, change happens and is irreversible. At the same time, intervention is possible and even necessary. Emergent relationships can be seized strategically to offer collective hope for a different kind of world.[40] With enough knowledge of what's going on, you can be cautious, be well informed, and make changes here and there, eventually transforming the system as a whole. This doesn't mean that we shouldn't, say, safeguard old-growth forests or prevent the extinction of endangered native species. Rather, it means that while change can be for the worse, it may be *much* more harmful to force a return to a previous state or attempt to preserve an artificial state of stasis—not only because it would be destructive but also because it would be impossible to fully accomplish. The alternative, we think, lies in moving forward to a new system through new, collaborative, relationships.

Another key feature of ecology is that, well, *ecology exists*. Earlier, we said that there is nothing natural about nature. What we meant by this is that the way we see nature is informed by our social systems—for example, an economy that was developed through colonial conquest. This should not be taken to mean that nature doesn't exist, or that there is no objective reality. There are some who argue that, with humanity's transformation of the biosphere, there is no such thing as nature outside of humanity.[41] Though it is true that we have had a significant impact on the biosphere, and indeed even on outer space, this does not mean that there is no nature beyond the human. That would be like saying that once you plant a seed, it is human. In fact, the amazing thing about life is that it appears to have a consciousness of its own, from the biosphere to the microcellular level—a consciousness with which we have a lot in common but which we cannot experience fully as our own.[42] Still, there really is something out there, and we can access it, within the limits of consciousness, through observation and engagement.[43] And though we may have a large impact on ecosystems and have developed impressive scientific tools to study them, that does not mean that we are able to control such systems or know them completely.[44] We're diving deep into the philosophical weeds here, but we're going to be blunt: nature exists, and we can try to understand it, but because it is not us, we cannot grasp it completely.

We should also be clear that ecology by itself *shouldn't necessarily have a "positive" or desirable connotation.* The way terms like "eco-friendly" are employed, one would think ecology is a desirable and positive thing. But no, ecology is about entanglements of beings, defying the idea of an individual, self-contained existence.[45] There is nothing morally "good" about ecology. It just is. For example, if we think about an ecosystem, we might imagine a network of actors, each playing a role in the creation and re-creation of a whole. A forest ecosystem has niches for species across all vertical and horizontal layers of the understory, from the micro-environments of tree bark and the treetops to the leaf litter and going deep below the soil layer. Everyone from the birds of prey above the forest canopy to the dung beetles and mycorrhizal fungi within the soil is cycling and exchanging resources and energy along the food chain.

Similarly, in our globalized economy, different countries find their niche in an economic ecosystem. They produce goods that shape the environments of those places. Israel produces, for instance, a world-class weapons and security industry that it exports around the world, testing their product on Palestinians, who have borne the brunt of casualties since the occupation of 1967.[46] China burns coal, manufactures and exports enormous amounts of goods, and mines important rare earth minerals that are used as inputs for artificial intelligence (AI) technology and other digital marvels like cryptocurrencies. Meanwhile, China's wealthier and AI-powered cities can claim to be green: Liuzhou boasts more than 30 percent electric vehicles, and Hangzhou is nearly 70 percent covered in trees.[47] Italy and Spain produce oranges, kiwis, and other fruit that terraform whole landscapes into monoculture plantations that depend on trafficked and exploited migrant laborers to keep production as economically efficient and large-scale as possible—eerily reminiscent of the slave plantations of sugar and cotton.[48]

While ecology itself is neutral, we want to make the case that thinking and acting ecologically—being ecological—is a good thing. There is an important difference. Ecosystems are clusters of relationships that have their own tendencies, some of which we've outlined in this section. An ecological approach, then, is a way of acting and looking at the world that takes into account these relationships and tendencies before intervening. This is why, in this book, we argue that the sustainability class is not ecological: their well-intended actions portray a misunderstanding of the ecological relations that sustain their way of life—and backfire by further entrenching that particular ecology.

Cancer Cell Ecology

The global orchestration of production and trade is an ecology in its own right. It is what some have called "world ecology," embedded in the web of life and transforming it in the process.[49] It is a global ecosystem of market niches that, in turn, pushes the web of life into irreversible states whose consequences cannot be fully predicted. Seen this way, ecology also describes specialized industrialization and economic development, interconnected to meet demands "just in time," faster and faster around the world with the aid of new technologies, most recently artificial intelligence. It is an ecology because it brings together people and other living creatures into an elaborate ecosystem of industrial production, transforming all aspects of the biosphere in the process. It's a bit like getting sucked up by the Greek mythological whirlpool monster Charybdis.

But this is an ecology of a cancer cell—it reproduces at the expense of the body upon which it needs to survive. Everything gets absorbed into the cancerous growth, and it grows faster and faster. And let's be clear: it's not certain people or population growth in general that should be compared to cancer. No, the cancer is a *system* based, at its root, on profit, which in turn drives the deterioration of life support systems and the widening of wealth disparities. Let us explain.

When profits drive decision-making, things may seem more efficient at first, since putting a price on something can help gauge how much of it there is, how easy it is to make, who wants it, and how badly they want it. But where the natural world is concerned, the whole thing eventually comes crashing down. This is because investors are guided in their decision-making by returns on investment, while natural systems operate on cycles and time scales grossly out of sync with year-end dividends. We already gave the example of soil fertility: once the soil is exhausted from overproduction, its fertility will collapse, leading to loss in productivity, erosion, floods, and droughts. And just like the soil, fertilizer sources like guano, phosphate mines, and coal to make ammonia are eventually exhausted, or the way in which the resources are extracted and processed cause irreparable harm.

Still other examples of mismatches between investor time scales, political election cycles, and ecosystem health abound. Forever chemicals poison our waters and lead to high rates of cancer in both workers and consumers.[50] Industrial fishing has led to the collapse, overexploitation, or full exploitation of 93 percent of the world's fisheries.[51] While efficiency and innovation have doubled or tripled the productivity of these industries throughout history—for example, through the invention of new machines—nature cannot change the rate at which phosphates or coal are produced or toxic chemicals are broken down, or the rate at which fisheries replenish stocks. Nor can for-profit enterprises entirely do away with the risk of pathogens wiping out entire livestock populations or jumping into the human population. In fact, despite the promise of innovation and efficiency, large-scale industrial enterprise—big farms, big fisheries, big pharma, big plastics—tend to *increase* these risks rather than minimize them.[52] Four- or five-year election cycles have little capacity to bridge these divergent temporalities; indeed, they add their own out-of-sync time scale.

And yet it's good to recall that for a large part of human history, people have successfully managed landscapes that regenerated the land and actually made it more fertile over time.[53] Even in Western Europe, soil fertility increased in the Middle Ages in certain regions, mostly due to crop rotation and integrated agriculture. In the last fifty years of industrial agriculture, however, soil erosion—caused by overuse of heavy machinery, heavy application of fertilizer, and monocropping—has caused fertility to tank.[54] Effectively, hundreds if not thousands of years of work to maintain and build up that soil with "traditional" agriculture has been washed down the drain in just half a century of "conventional" agriculture.

How is it possible that this destructive variant of ecology has maintained—or, more appropriately, *sustained*—itself? How do we keep buying into it? The answer is that, despite being extensively integrated and dynamically connected with ecosystems all around the world, it is also very good at hiding its own impacts on those ecosystems—out of sight, out of mind. Let's investigate how this works and why it's so effective at sustaining the status quo.

Green Gaslighting

"Have you ever cheated on your girlfriend?" So asks a man holding promotional leaflets for the company Cheat Neutral on a busy shopping street in Cardiff, Wales. A passerby responds he hasn't: "Certainly not. It would be wrong."

"But what about if I said you could pay £2.50 to our new company if you cheat on your girlfriend, and we'll pay someone else to be faithful?"

This doesn't sound very appealing, so the man rejects the offer. "No, no. I think I like my girlfriend too much."[55]

When the same deal is offered to another couple, the woman remarks it wouldn't work, because "everyone would cheat."

Her boyfriend also thinks it's a terrible idea: "I think we would benefit more from doing a campaign against cheating."

In an interview for the BBC, the budding entrepreneurs try to pitch their business plan. "What we're trying to do is say that cheating isn't something you have to feel bad about anymore; it's just something you have to neutralize or offset. Just make sure the total amount of cheating doesn't go up."

It turns out that this business idea was an elaborate satirical stunt to illustrate the logic behind carbon offsets. Units of carbon released or sequestered are treated like exchangeable tokens in the casino, and like those tokens, they can be traded for money. What's truly remarkable is that these companies have gotten away with convincing us that carbon offsetting is the ethical thing to do, when most people immediately see that offsets for cheating, which would work exactly the same way, are blatantly immoral. As one perturbed passerby said in the video, in a remark that could just as easily apply to carbon offsets, "That's not balancing anything.

That's just doing one thing, and then doing something else that's totally different. I don't see the link, except in our minds."

The act of buying carbon offsets is meant to soothe a desperate desire for rough-and-ready solutions to complex problems. Offsets can be purchased and procured at will; they just require money, and there's plenty of that for the wealthy. Your purchase is couched in a sentiment of care but ends up being deceitful when it's used to cover your tracks and, like the service Cheat Neutral offers, move on as though nothing ever happened.

We might be tempted to commend those who buy offsets, whether of the carbon or cheating variety. At the very least, they are acknowledging there is a problem with their behavior, that they are part of a global system in which they are having a negative impact. But when we think about it, is that really any better than doing nothing at all? This has all the hallmarks of an abusive relationship: confessing to everything you did wrong, apologizing, buying something nice to show you care, and then continuing the very behavior that you apologized for. It's a bit like performative statements that recognize that territory we stand on was stolen from Indigenous people, only to go on stealing more land and making life miserable for Indigenous people around the world.[56]

Despite its obvious moral failings, carbon offsetting has made going "green" simpler than ever. You can pollute as much as you want if you plant the equivalent number of carbon-sequestering trees in a "barren wasteland" somewhere far away. And if you wanted to be green *and* socially minded, you can pay off the small-scale family farmers who live on these wastelands to go live somewhere else, offering them jobs to get them started toward the "American dream" so they can finally improve their lot. Or you could set up a green tourism company that hires locals to maintain the rainforests you bought to ease your conscience. If those locals were members of Indigenous tribes, then you can help them save their cultural practices by putting them to work *to perform their own* culture for paying tourists. And with one fell swoop, it's possible to both save nature and alleviate poverty . . . *ta-da*!

The carbon offset business, like the green lifestyle on offer in hip neighborhoods and in-flight magazines, promises us instant gratification. This green lifestyle is presented to us as through a catalogue of products we can purchase, a plethora of endless choices that we can pick from to curate an identity tailored to our own self-image. And like any successful commodity, the green brand is designed to make us crave more: we try to erase our guilt through consumption. Being green just becomes about signaling our virtue, which, in our more reflective moments, just doesn't feel right. The high is then closely followed by the emptiness in knowing that it is never enough—a deep-down realization that it is all just a performance. We desire fulfilling connections and relationships, we want to feel like we're making a difference, but we only get a fleeting and ephemeral good "vibe," leaving us wanting to consume it again (and again).

The commonality between carbon offsetting, cheating offsets, and the green lifestyle brand is that they leverage our feeling that something is very wrong, offer a quick solution, and end up hiding the root of the problem, pretending it doesn't exist. In this way, many "greening" strategies are really just gaslighting. Gaslighting is when one person makes another question their own reality. The gaslighter does so by coming up with a "rational" explanation for a problem, often blaming the victim harmed by the problem, and then ideally taking the credit for having solved the problem—completely obscuring the fact that they were the cause of the problem in the first place. Often all of that happens in rapid succession, so fast that you don't even realize you've been gaslit. Similarly, corporate public relations campaigns have deliberately persuaded us that we can leave fossil fuel companies in charge of greening themselves and the economy, that they are taking the lead in the sustainable transition. Isn't this like leaving that grinning fox with blood staining its fur to take care of a henhouse? You're made to feel like an idiot by corporate oligarchs and the pundits who parrot them, ridiculed with a thousand and one names from "socialist" to "Luddite," or mocked as just plain backward because you doubt that corporate elites might not address the problems they have generated. This despite every bit of evidence suggesting that not only have their efforts repeatedly failed, but the consequences of their interventions have merely reinforced the problems.[57]

Green gaslighting is not a recent phenomenon. Indian historian V. M. Ravi Kumar, for instance, described through archival data how the colonial British Raj displaced local people to decimate forests across South India for shipbuilding, and then turned around to blame the locals for decimating the forests they depended on. They then planted monoculture tree plantations to replenish stocks of timber and patted themselves on the back for being ecological "civilizers" working to green the landscape, as opposed to the lazy and destructive locals supposedly responsible for degrading the landscape.[58] As in an abusive relationship, the gaslighting comes right after one partner has inflicted serious harm. As historian Vijay Prashad notes, Western philosophers like John Stuart Mill claim to be bastions of human rights and civil liberties even as they owned other human beings as slaves. Even as many colonial empires "were behaving like barbarians," they were calling the people they were brutalizing barbarians. He goes on to say that in order for colonizers to stand morally superior and all high and mighty (and we would add "sustainable"), a river of blood had to flow beneath their feet. To quote the character Kurtz in Joseph Conrad's *Heart of Darkness*, convinced he was sent to Africa to civilize the natives: "exterminate all the brutes!"[59]

Let's return to the example of East Africa, where colonial administrators created conservation areas for large "game," supposedly to protect them from local poachers. Real history, as it turns out, is much more horrifying—and a prime example of green gaslighting in action.

In the nineteenth century, colonialism decimated the herds of

large African mammals like elephants, rhinos, buffalos, and giraffes. This was in great part due to sports hunting by elite and
upper-class Westerners, but also due to the ivory and pelt trade,
which Europeans initiated, and to clear the savannah for cattle
grazing—all seen as more lucrative economic activities. But the introduction of cattle to the East African savannah had unforeseen
knock-on effects. It started when, in the late nineteenth century,
rinderpest, an infectious viral disease among cattle that had long
been present in Egypt, ripped through both cattle and ungulate
populations like giraffes and buffalo. Historian Corey Ross notes
that "while traveling in Kenya in 1890, British colonial army cap-
tain Frederick Lugard saw entire plains covered in buffalo car-
casses and estimated that in some areas at least 90 per cent of the
cattle had perished."[60] East African pastoralist groups like the
Maasai were devastated—about two-thirds of their population
died in the famine that followed. Horrible as it was, it proved a
boon for the colonizers, who were better able to extend their control over the region. Ross quotes Lugard again, who mused that
"in some respects it [the cattle die-off] has favored our enterprise.
Powerful and warlike as the pastoral tribes are, their pride has
been humbled and our progress facilitated by this awful visitation.
The advent of the white man had else not been so peaceful."[61]

Colonial administrators like Lugard could not have predicted
what came next. Without large herbivores and pastoralists to
manage them, brush gained ground over grassland. Populations of
elephants, wildebeest, hippopotamuses, and rhinos bounced back.
The tsetse fly found a natural habitat, and sleeping sickness rav-
aged whole regions in sub-Saharan Africa—leading to the death
of over half a million people in Central Africa alone. Unaware of
how sleeping sickness spreads, colonial regimes like the French
and Belgians quarantined thousands of people into *cordons sani-
taires* ("sanitary zones") that turned out to be death camps (a
stark reminder that concentration camps were not invented by the
Nazis but were an outgrowth of colonialism),[62] while the British

forcibly resettled whole villages and the Germans evacuated rural populations from entire regions. What started with game hunting and the imposition of cattle ranching turned into wholesale ecological and social collapse.

These cascading effects were so blatantly obvious that natural scientists, epidemiologists, and even some European administrators couldn't avoid seeing the colonial regime as the cause of the problem. But rather than reverse colonial control, their solution was to establish large game reserves in no-go zones where the tsetse fly reigned supreme, with these reserves acting as buffer zones against the incursion of the tsetse fly into regions to be "civilized" for intensive agriculture. The further separation of "human" from "nature" was seen as the most efficacious, and moral, solution to the problem. Once again, the cause of the problem gets proposed as the solution, and the hole to pull ourselves out of gets deeper. In one handbook published in 1937 (yes, this is all very recent) advising colonial powers on how to reverse soil erosion worldwide, it was even suggested that the explosion of the tsetse fly in sub-Saharan Africa had actually helped the cause of conservationists, and the authors dubbed the fly a "trustee of the land for future generations."[63] It reminds us a little bit of Crown Prince William claiming that trophy hunting of big game in nature reserves has been a boon for nature—the subtext being that white hunters protect nature better than Africans do.

Added to this was the role of the European hunting lobby, which in fact also acted as a conservation lobby, since they advocated to set up game reserves to preserve wildlife—which they could later shoot. While trophy hunting was legalized, African hunters, who had depended on game meat for millennia, were singled out as poachers and criminalized. Hunting quotas were set up and guns (reserved for Europeans, of course) were classified as humane ways of killing animals, as opposed to African hunting techniques involving spears, snares, or fire that were claimed to be cruel, unsportsmanlike, and unsustainable. The creation of wildlife reserves, then, had a triple benefit: to protect wildlife from poaching, to create areas for legally sanctioned sports hunting, and, later, to protect people and productive agricultural land from the tsetse fly. All of this was wrapped in language framing wildlife conservation as part of the civilizing mission to protect nature and characterize Indigenous practices as dangerous and needing tight restriction. This was next-level gaslighting: conservation became the tool to solve the problems colonialism caused, and colonial governments took the credit, while the blame for ecological collapse was put at the feet of people who for thousands of years had co-constructed those very same ecosystems that colonists were trying to preserve.

This is not just something that happened in Africa in the 1930s. Today, we see how green gaslighting takes form by literally lighting gas to "protect the environment," as illustrated by our example from the previous chapter of two entrepreneurs from Texas. Mining bitcoin with servers powered by natural gas flares from offshore oil projects can solve the climate problem, right? The public is both literally and figuratively gaslit. That oil drilling should have stopped ten years ago, given our climate emergency, doesn't figure at all in the logic.

Whether we are talking about marauding colonizers across the African savannas or absurd climate solutions like mining bitcoin off gas flares, a pattern of green gaslighting emerges in which the perpetrators of ecological degradation take the green credit while they make the victims of development appear to be the culprits, the stupid and backward ones. In this sense, it's far more insidious than greenwashing—where one can polish one's reputation with a few potted plants or a solar panel or two. Green gaslighting is about being able to displace, violate, or abuse others under the guise of being sustainable and progressive—all while questioning the sanity of those abused.

Green gaslighting also repackages the violence of more contemporary colonization as morally progressive and "eco-friendly," while subverting and hijacking victimhood.[64] When Israel was declared a state in May 1948, native trees like oaks, carobs, and hawthorns as well as agricultural crops like olives, figs, and almonds were destroyed during the forced removal of five hundred villages and towns of historical Palestine. In place of the unique biodiversity and cultural connections that had characterized these settled environments for thousands of years, the new settlers planted monocultures of European pine trees. These monocultures made soils more acidic, reduced undergrowth, and enhanced the likelihood of fires, which have further devastated regional ecologies.[65] This is all justified with the slogan "Let the desert bloom." The idea is that local Palestinians have mismanaged the desert and only settlers can make it green.

Over decades, Israel has deprived Palestinians of a livable environment through total ecological destruction. Palestinians in Gaza have long struggled to access clean water, with 96 percent of the territory's freshwater resources contaminated.[66] The situation became exponentially worse after Hamas' murderous attack on October 7, 2023, and the Israeli Defense Forces' subsequent assault on Gaza. Satellite imagery shows the destruction of almost 50 percent of farmland and tree cover, including food-growing olive groves and orchards, exacerbating an imposed famine against Palestinians in Gaza.[67] Soils have been drained of their life-sustaining potential through the destruction of trees, continuous carpet bombing, aerial spraying of chemical herbicides, use of chemical warfare, and the release of hazardous materials, including heavy metals.[68] Meanwhile, Palestinians are arrested, interrogated, tortured, injured, and murdered merely for harvesting herbs, for obtaining firewood from the remaining trees for basic survival, for crossing into conservation areas that were their cattle grazing grounds, or for practicing livelihoods that made the land fertile and lush.[69]

Some might argue that these ecological impacts are just the "natural" outcome of war. But now, after more than seventy-six years of ongoing occupation and dehumanization of Palestinians, Israel is aiming for "green" credentials by violently confiscating additional land in occupied Palestinian territory for so-called eco-friendly reasons, like wind and solar energy generation to combat climate change and mass tree planting, even as these further deplete water supplies for Palestinians, Jordanians, and ecosystems.[70] Yet, while Palestinian's per capita carbon emissions are about 0.8 tons per year, Israelis emit about twelve times that amount, at just under 10 tons per year per capita.[71] Despite having burned the equivalent of 150,000 tons of coal within just the first sixty days of its unprecedented bombardment of Gaza—surpassing the annual emissions of whole countries like Belize—Israel still shows up to United Nations conferences touting its action on climate change.[72]

In all these cases of gaslighting, those who've had to live through some of the worst kinds of abuse, and now are faced with the holier-than-thou attitude of their abusers, are very likely to question their own sense of reality. Green gaslighting is a kind of psychological torture, but it is extremely effective in justifying the "sustainability" of the status quo, aka doing nothing or making things worse while pretending they are the heroes of the day.

Ecology That Reveals Relationships

What if we built an ecology that is not based on hiding the impacts of what we're doing, justifying it with false solutions, and entrenching the very same problems again and again? What would an ecology look like that reveals the many relations we are part of, that is able to transform these relationships into ones that are liberating and affirming?

Let's begin with an anecdote. In the essay "A Mother's Work," the biologist Robin Wall Kimmerer had just moved into a new house with her two daughters. "The deed described a deep spring-fed pond, and a hundred years ago it might have been exactly that." Being a good mother, she wanted her daughters to be able to swim in the pond, but "it was so choked with green that you could not tell where weeds left off and water began." The algae is so thick, in fact, that one day she watches as a gosling gets caught in it; finally it frees itself and starts walking on the mat of algae. "That," she says, "was a moment of resolve for me. You should not be able to walk on a pond." So she set to work to start cleaning out the pond.[73]

Kimmerer approaches this task with the determination of a loving mother, the training of a biologist, and the knowledge passed down to her by her Indigenous forebears—being a member of the Citizen Potawatomi Nation. "The likelihood of making the pond swimmable, even for geese, seemed remote at best. But I am an ecologist, so I was confident that I could at least improve the situation. The word *ecology* is derived from the Greek *oikos*, the word for home. I could use ecology to make a good home for goslings and girls."

And so Kimmerer proceeded by analyzing the system that she intended to intervene in. She studied pond restoration, put the algae under a microscope to find out what she was dealing with, and investigated the trees, birds, and bugs that use the system. The pond, she determined, had become eutrophic—so enriched with algae that the decomposition of those organisms was depriving the pond of oxygen, killing all other life in it. But eutrophication is not in itself bad: its Greek root, after all, means "becoming well fed." The pond suffered from too much good stuff—too much nitrogen, too much phosphorus, all too delicious for the algae that had made the pond their home.

The first thing she had to do, she realized, was to take out the overabundance of nutrients in the pond. Biomass—trees, algae, weeds—fixes these nutrients in their bodies. Animals then feed on those nutrients, and their waste starts the cycle going again. To stop the cycle, she would need to take out the fixed nutrients, in the form of all the algal biomass that had accumulated.

But that's easier said than done. On the weekends she would walk the hill to the pond, her dog capering behind her. She would then spend hours standing waist-deep raking algae from the pond. Eventually, she realized that the willow trees nearby were also living off the pond. She would cart masses of algae and willow branches out to her garden to compost, and the algae were "reborn as carrots." She would introduce different fish and grasses to provoke slight changes in the system. "The job is never over," she muses; "it simply changes from one task to the next. What I'm looking for, I suppose, is balance, and that is a moving target. Balance is not a passive resting place—it takes work, balancing the giving and the taking, the raking out and the putting in."

Hours turned into days, which turned into years. Before long, her dog would saunter slowly behind her up the hill; a few years later, and the dog was buried in the garden.

Twelve years passed, and the pond was now finally in a state where her daughters could swim in it. But it was too late: her youngest was just about to leave for college. Or was it? Kimmerer, observing her work, reflects on the sadness of time passing by, resisting a feeling of futility:

> What I do here matters. Everybody lives downstream. My pond drains to the brook, to the creek, to a great and needful lake. The water net connects us all. I have shed tears into that flow when I thought that motherhood would end. But the pond has shown me that being a good mother doesn't end with creating a home where just my children can flourish. A good mother grows into a richly eutrophic old woman, knowing that her work doesn't end until she creates a home where all of life's beings can flourish.

Kimmerer's eutrophied pond is a small example, at the level of the everyday, of what we mean by the ecological. It is an effort that proceeds cautiously and is in tune with all kinds of relations. One observation—a gosling painstakingly freeing itself from an algal mat—unveils a whole web of past and future relationships, from the growth of the willows by the pond to the future carrots to be grown out of the compost made from the algae and willow branches. The point here is that when a problem is observed, the future can be altered through strategic intervention. The pond does not need to be choked by algae for an eternity, nor is the objective simply to clear the pond of algae and move on to the next thing. In between the two extremes is a process involving many different actors, emotions, sensitivities, contradictions, compromises, and yearnings that influence what takes place in reality. Ecology is not an individual practice—so many actors were involved in the transformation of this pond.

But what if only one relation was selected from Kimmerer's eutrophied pond? Let's say algae production was for storing carbon, the way that large tree plantations for offsets are meant to do. The result would be a dying pond, devoid of life, and held in a static ecological state with the express purpose of maximizing carbon storage potential. The same way that mining sites discard all other ecological relations to maximize the production of one thing—gold or lithium—carbon farming does the same. Similarly, if Kimmerer selected only for the goslings, preventing her daughters from swimming and then later charging users to come visit the geese like visitors to a museum or national park, she wouldn't be a very nice mother to her daughters who want to swim in it. She is not selecting for one relation and freezing it in time, discarding the rest, and turning an ecosystem into a factory for that single relationship. She is developing an ecology where all kinds of relationships thrive, evolving as conditions change.

What would happen if we scaled up Kimmerer's ecological approach to the level of a city? Imagine a city the size of New York whose residents have taken the principles Robin Wall Kimmerer experimented with and scaled them up to their entire sewage treatment system. In fact, this city exists. Kolkata in India (formerly known as Calcutta) has, for much of the past century, treated its own sewage using fishponds.[74] Bluntly put, sewage goes into canals, is left to sit for a few weeks, and then is fed to fish—mostly carp. The fish are then harvested and supply about 40 percent of the city's fish consumption.[75]

To many readers this may sound both gross and unsanitary. But, in fact, it's a technology that is not only proven to be safe but also recommended by some of the most well-respected water treatment scientists as an alternative to modern methods of sewage treatment—which are expensive to run and use a lot of energy.[76]

To understand why this is actually a good way of going about processing our sewage, we have to rewind very briefly to look at how waste works. The standard way we understand waste is basically this: keep it as far away from us as possible. Sewage treatment plants are usually designed to follow this assumption: pump it into ponds fenced off from the public, let it sit for a while, and then dilute it enough to pump it into a river or the ocean. That is, when there is sewage treatment at all—many municipalities just pump it into large water bodies as far away from them as possible. The idea is that sewage is bad, and we should by no means bring it close to society.

But as we already saw with the example of salmon, in ecosystems there isn't really such a thing as "bad" waste. Everything gets used and reused. Producers become consumers. Urine and feces are pure wealth from an ecological point of view. This is because they contain phosphorous, carbon, and fixed nitrogen—necessary ingredients for life on Earth. These nutrients are so valuable that when they appear in high concentrations in water ecosystems, plants and bacteria do so well that their populations explode, leading to a lack of oxygen, killing other forms of life. The problem with the nutrients in our effluent is not that they themselves are poisonous or toxic to us, but that they are so highly concentrated that they become a bonanza for certain life-forms like algae and bacteria, causing rapid growth and eventually leading to collapse of that particular system.[77] Kimmerer solved the problem of her pond being too "well fed" by slowly, over time, taking out the fixed carbon, phosphorous, and nitrogen—in the form of algae and weeds—and distributing it throughout her garden, feeding it, and in turn feeding her family. This principle is taken to a metropolitan scale in Kolkata's sewage-fed fishponds.

So, in standard sewage treatment facilities, we are basically washing some of the most valuable nutrients down the drain, rather than creating a system where they cycle back to grow the garden of life that we maintain and which feeds us. One study even showed that on any given day in the year 2000, India flushed $2 million worth of valuable life-giving nutrients down the toilet.[78] In contrast, the Kolkata system depends on a web of life: algae that grow rapidly from the sewage water, fish that eat the algae, plants like water hyacinth that grow on the hyperfertile water, and are then used as fodder for cattle, and farmers who manage the ecosystem—and all of these elements are able to capture those nutrients and use them effectively.

Other relationships abound in Kolkata's fishpond sewage treatment system. Letting the water sit for two weeks kills harmful pathogens. When fish are introduced, they eat mosquito larvae. Ducks eat snails that may carry potential pathogens. Water hyacinths and other plants are fed to livestock. And at the end of it all, the fishponds are drained and the sludge at the bottom is applied to fertilize fields. All of these techniques have been innovated by farmers over decades, developing an ecosystem that treats most of the sewage of a city of over 15 million, generating a cycle in which the city's effluent becomes reintroduced into the system—turning upside down our conception of what is waste and what is wealth. In a sense, these farmers have created their own "blue infrastructure"—as researcher Jenia Mukherjee calls it—over time, through observation of ecosystem relationships and local ingenuity.[79]

Kolkata's fishponds are just one of many examples of how

people change the landscape and make living environments that are rich and biodiverse with a myriad of ecological relationships. In Japan, at the intersection of mountain foothills and flat arable plains, centuries of small-scale agriculture, village settlements, and forested areas have formed a mosaic of what is called a *satoyama* landscape. Grasslands, ponds, streams, rice paddies, hay or thatch fields, backyard gardens, and mixed community forests of bamboo and laurel crisscross the landscape in hodgepodge style. Each land use generates microhabitats and ecological niche spaces, intertwining species, climates, and biomes.[80]

Satoyama did not emerge as pristine and untouched landscapes; people are very much a part of them. They have allowed migrating wildlife to move easily between and through the landscape. One thing you won't find on *satoyama* landscapes are monocultures, either a monoculture of crops or a monoculture of protected or untouched forest. The diversity that thrives in these landscapes is the result of the incredible array of habitats and efforts to prevent any one type of landscape dominating others. These fluid interconnections across such diverse landscapes also serve as a kind of prophylaxis against pathogens or pests that might otherwise decimate whole crops.

Along with Japan's aging population and accelerating agricultural industrialization, younger farmers have become less dependent on firewood and charcoal and more dependent on petroleum products and chemical fertilizers for both heating and food production. People now rely less on forest gardens, which have also deteriorated due to urban development and leisure projects like golf courses. The result has been the gradual disappearance of these centuries-old landscapes. Their loss has led to the introduction of diseases like pine wilt and the disappearance of species that had come to thrive only in these rich and diverse mosaics of people and nature.

Forest gardens have flourished in parts of South Asia for centuries. In the hills around Kandy in central Sri Lanka, "home gardens" have ensured food security for thousands of years.[81] These areas just outside homes, like *satoyama* landscapes, blend agriculture, forestry, and animal husbandry in intertwined assemblages shaped by topography and soil conditions. They generate a diversity of microhabitats and climates for both people and animals through mixed cropping of trees for timber, trees for fuel wood, fruits, nuts, spices, medicines, vegetables, and meat and dairy. Often these gardens exist within forested landscapes, with food crops as well as ornamental and medicinal plants grown across varying canopy depths to optimize sunlight, soil type, and drainage requirements for different species. Together, home gardens provide people with food as well as autonomy over their own health and food production, without having to depend on insufficient wages, volatile markets and supply chains, toxic pesticides, and expensive fertilizers. These gardens employ very simple technology and have very low input costs, relying on composted manure and the collective labor of extended family and neighbors sharing garden spaces between households. During the 2020 pandemic lockdowns, home gardens in Sri Lanka became lifelines for families given the rice and vegetable shortages that occurred because of bottlenecks in supply chains and subsequent economic crises.[82]

Elsewhere, Vietnamese farmers have developed a marvelous system of agriculture over centuries that mimics and in some ways improves on ecosystem cycles. This system is often referred to as VAC—which stands for *vườn* (garden or orchard), *ao* (pond), and *chuồng* (livestock). It is a system that became more prominent when North Vietnam's leader, Ho Chi Minh, encouraged scientifically managed, low-input, high-yield agriculture to fight "the hunger enemy" during the war against the French colonizers, and later the American invaders.[83] Here is a classic example: Rice paddies are encircled by banks lined with fruit trees—often mulberry trees, on which silkworms feast. The trees hold the banks together and prevent erosion. In between the trees, farmers grow leafy greens, squash, eggplant, and other vegetables. Ducks and water buffalo graze under the trees, keeping the grass short and eating pests. Their droppings fertilize the soil, giving essential nutrients to crops. These are interspersed with fishponds, fed by manure—both human and nonhuman. Fishponds absorb excess rainwater during storms and supply water to rice paddies in periods of drought. Today, it is threatened due to the increasing use of pesticides and chemical fertilizers, as well as the growing pressure on farmers to produce cash crops for export—developments that began when Vietnam opened its economy to international markets in the 1980s.[84]

Whether it's *satoyama*, home gardens, or *vườn ao chuồng*, they are all a kind of agroecology—defined as the application of ecological principles to design and manage agro-ecosystems.[85] Agroecology encourages a rich and thriving biodiversity of all kinds of creatures, and soils that are rejuvenated with organic matter (the gooey, moist, smelly glue made of decomposed leaves, living organisms, and decaying material) that also captures carbon dioxide from the atmosphere. But agroecology isn't just an agricultural practice informed by the study of ecosystems. Agroecology also takes place in the halls of power—and therefore its practice includes things like reforming land ownership and valuing agricultural labor. As filmmaker and author Raj Patel notes, "Agroecology is a way of understanding how to grow things, but also understanding that agriculture doesn't just happen in fields."[86] Agroecological practices do not try to separate people from a "pristine" world of nature.

At the same time, these landscapes are not relics of a quaint and idyllic past populated by "noble" Indigenous people with romanticized "traditional ecological knowledge." They are living landscapes of ordinary people thriving in caring and attentive coordination with each other for generations, with other species, and with constantly changing landscapes. They are dynamic experimental systems that treat food production methods not as a rigid formula but as an opportunity for adaptation, creativity, and sharing of good practices. Their methods are not codified, controlled, bought, or sold (with seeds treated as private property, like precious jewels to be stored in a vault) but are kept purposely diverse and undisciplined, so as to produce a broad range of foods in times of rapid change. It's a myth that it takes a scientific "expert" or scads of education to know how to be ecological. You don't need a degree in life sciences or to be a self-proclaimed nature lover—in other words, you don't need to be an environmentalist—to pay attention to the relationships in your environment. You don't need to be a social media influencer either.

The Ecological Imagination

Nestled in the heart of Los Angeles' Koreatown, about three miles west of downtown, and surrounded by mega-highways, strip malls, industrial parks, and concrete everywhere you look, is another world in the making: the Los Angeles EcoVillage. A few miles from Erewhon, climate-resilient condos, and the cactus xeriscaping being weaponized to shoo away the unhoused is an intentional community in which people try their best to be attentive to the needs of their neighbors, in the process reenchanting a living environment. We admit that we were a bit skeptical at first. Intentional communities can become easily co-opted by a powerful cult-like figure or get mired in internal conflicts. But we quickly found that the Los Angeles EcoVillage isn't just about escaping into a comfy commune of like-minded people; it's about reimagining the whole city of Los Angeles.

Lois Arkin, who is eighty-five years old and a co-founder of the EcoVillage, was giving us a tour of her home. We were standing in an asphalt-paved alley full of potholes between a strip mall and an auto shop in the blistering heat. We thought we couldn't be further away from ecological consciousness. But the sunlight glinted in Lois's eyes as she looked around her.

She had brought us to the alley because she wanted us to get a sense of the future she envisioned. Her dream was to rip out the asphalt to turn the alley into a "promenade" of wheelchair-accessible food gardens, lined with international newsstands, leading to a healing arts and nutrition center, and garages as live-work spaces. Just down the street, she pointed to an auto repair shop whose parking lot, she informed us, had been paved on top of a hot spring. In her vision, the EcoVillage would buy up the garage and rip out the concrete to build a community spa, and a giant public swimming pool in the middle of the street would be surrounded by vegetation. Kids from local schools and attendees of a nearby drug and alcohol rehab center would go to the EcoVillage to meet friends and get involved in cool stuff. It all sounded fantastical, but as we stood in that hot alley and saw the playful look in Lois' eyes, the trees teeming with ripe fruit and catching a slight afternoon breeze, it was almost tangible.

The L.A. EcoVillage began in 1993 when two city blocks were purchased and developed into forty-five units of permanently affordable cooperative housing and put under the ownership of the Beverly-Vermont Community Land Trust. In its lifetime, the L.A. EcoVillage has brought together democracy, economic production, and the meeting of people's day-to-day needs. They make housing affordable and accessible to low-income residents, ensuring that housing as a basic human right is not influenced by the vagaries of the market. Its residents meet in weekly assemblies and are significantly involved in municipal politics. The EcoVillage houses an organic food café, a bicycle workshop, a tool shop, a bulk food cooperative, a plant nursery, and a hostel. And the residents reduce their ecological impact with solar water heaters, permaculture, bicycle workshops, edible gardens, orchards, beekeeping, animal husbandry, gray water recycling, the use of local building materials, and the rehabilitation of contaminated soils.

"The politics of saving this block has been ongoing for forty years," Lois tells us. Saving the block meant transforming it, and at age eighty-five, Lois isn't afraid of imagining how it could continue to be transformed far into the future, long after she's gone. The EcoVillage has survived in the most hostile of settings, and in that process built up a true oasis in a concrete desert.

Walking away from the EcoVillage, we felt our jaded cynicism melt away. We realized that so much of what the EcoVillage had accomplished, and what animated Lois, was a sense of imagination. Where others saw only concrete, the members of the Eco-Village saw food forests. They had turned their garages into carpentry workshops and a gym. They had turned a lobby into an art gallery. And they had turned expensive, exclusive housing into truly affordable apartments. All of that took imagination. It's not a perverse kind of imagination based on selfishness, scarcity, fear, narcissism, and sociopathy. It uses technology—like the myco-rehabilitation of soils, bike repair, and solar-powered ovens—to generate abundance for everyone.

The L.A. EcoVillage wasn't someone's blueprint or policy initiative. It wasn't framed according to the UN's Sustainable Development Goals. It wasn't an offset to compensate for the concrete around it. While it generates return on investment to lenders through its small-scale cooperative businesses, it also embodies an ethos of sufficiency for a good life for all who live in and around the village.

Sure, there has been a lot of conflict, and keeping the Eco-Village going wasn't always easy. Finding financing was hard, and it remains a challenge to keep people involved in the long term in a democratic way. And despite her infectious imagination, Lois isn't very hopeful about the future. She believes the world will get worse before it gets better. "But don't dwell on that," she tells us. "It doesn't mean that we won't fight for the world we want. Someday we're going to break the back of real estate speculation in this city. We will do that through our actions every day . . . not just in thinking and researching about it."

Despite it all, members of the L.A. EcoVillage had the vision to create something new. They prioritize relationships that replenish depleted or lifeless environments and infuse creativity and imagination in ways that everyone can take part in. This approach contrasts with "green" consumption that peddles scarce products reserved for a privileged few, that depends on hiding away the real relationships that sustain us while thriving off empty, superficial vibes that leave you feeling hollowed out.

As Lois showed us, the crises we are facing demand that we pay attention to our surroundings and the relationships required to maintain them. This kind of ecology is about being responsive to relationships between the human and the nonhuman. And it's about doing all that out of care, not out of obligation or because it's the "right thing to do." Furthermore, this can't be an individual affair; it can't even be a series of individual affairs in aggregate. It has to be an ecology for all, like weeds expanding the cracks in the concrete to dismantle the status quo. This can only happen in the collective, where, like in *satoyama* landscapes or the L.A. Eco-Village, relationships fluidly intersect and transform landscapes intentionally over time.

We can build an ecology that reveals more than it hides. This means intervening in the environment and transforming it. But we have to be careful about what such interventions may look like. For people like Elon Musk, Bill Gates, Steven Pinker, and advocates of the "eco-modernist" manifesto, for instance, ecological interventions can be quick and easy technical fixes like energy-intensive carbon capture and storage machines to suck carbon from the air or rolling out enormous tree plantations.[87] As we will discuss in the next chapter, maintaining any system depends on energy and materials, which results in the generation of waste. But the actual ecological question of how these systems produce waste or depend upon energy and material is ignored by the so-called thought leaders of the sustainability class.

3

PURITY

M ike Pearl, a local Venice Beach journalist, had an office next to the luxe "green" supermarket chain Erewhon. Despite the name's anagram, "nowhere," Pearl learned about the supermarket's very real material existence the hard way when he discovered that the high-powered exhaust system from their wood-fired grill was being fed straight into his office: "They were blowing huge quantities of hydrocarbons right into my face, basically all day." [1]

If a brick-and-mortar Erewhon is spewing its wood-fired oven's exhaust—a small but symbolic source of greenhouse gases and other harmful air particles—out onto the streets of Venice, there's even more to say about its bespoke supply chains and curated products, complete with mile-long ingredient lists, crisscrossing the planet just in time (from "nowhere" to "now here") to appear on someone's morning Instagram post. What about that 100 percent sustainable salmon traveling nearly five thousand miles from the Faroe Islands, $10 "zero waste" soap bars, and net-zero-emissions bottled water (one tree planted for every bottle you buy)?

You can walk the aisles of Erewhon and imagine yourself both everywhere and nowhere. The desire for net zero or zero waste is about achieving some illusory state of no impact. In this sense, sustainability means invisibility. Don't mind us with our $25 kelp smoothies and minimalist gated community living.

Erewhon's appeal to the desire to be nowhere reminds us of another fad: no-impact living. In 2009, author Colin Beavan wrote a book called *No Impact Man: The Adventures of a Guilty Liberal*

Who Attempts to Save the Planet, and the Discoveries He Makes About Himself and Our Way of Life in the Process.[2] The award-winning book follows his family—living in a ninth-floor Greenwich Village apartment—trying to save the planet by voluntarily and temporarily changing their consumption patterns to have zero environmental impact. No carbon, no waste, no pollution, no resources. But as Elizabeth Kolbert wrote in the *New Yorker*, Beavan's so-called neutrality only *seemed* neutral in comparison to the lifestyle he had gotten used to. The very people who propped up his lifestyle already had far less impact than him:

> Even during the year that Beavan spent drinking out of a Mason jar, more than two billion people were, quite inadvertently, living lives of lower impact than his. Most of them were struggling to get by in the slums of Delhi and Rio or scratching out a living in rural Africa or South America. A few were sleeping in cardboard boxes on the street not far from Beavan's Fifth Avenue apartment.[3]

No-Impact Man's fantasy that he could live at the top of the world, in an apartment in Manhattan, and cancel out his impact on the world is a bit like thinking you can play Jenga forever—you know, the game where you remove blocks from the bottom of the tower and place them at the top. The tower keeps growing, and it seems like you're making the tower taller even as nothing is actually added and you in fact destabilize the entire structure with each turn.[4] It's the "no impact" part that implies that you can just keep stacking those blocks forever, as though nothing were ever lost. No-Impact Man stands on the tower, continuously gambling away crucial life support systems with fake equivalencies and feeling good about himself.

The reality is that something changes when each Jenga block is taken from the bottom and placed on the top of the tower, and it's not about what's added or subtracted. It's about what transforms *irreversibly.* The planet is transforming on a scale unseen for millennia. Systems that have sustained life for millions of years are being

No-Impact Man, standing on top of the Jenga tower, holding his PIE. *Illustration by Eric Bent.*

ripped apart in half a century. Changes in water temperature and ocean acidity are altering jet stream patterns, making whole regions of the world hotter than they have been for thousands of years.[5] Groundwater aquifers are being depleted at rates many times their rate of natural recharge.[6] The effect is so great that it's actually shifting Earth's axis as the planet spins around the sun.[7] While these changes are taking place in a period of years to decades, the impacts on the Earth's system will likely be felt over hundreds if not thousands of years. There's no going back to "normal" once the damage is done—at least not in our lifetimes or our children's lifetimes.

Just like you can't negotiate your need to breathe or defecate, you can't negotiate with the physics of taking out blocks from the base of a Jenga tower and stacking them on top. The tower will crumble whether you dream of it getting taller or not.

In ecological economics—a branch of economics concerned with understanding the way the economy interacts with ecological systems—this is called metabolism. Every creature metabolizes, from single-celled organisms to complex mammals like human beings. We take energy and nutrients from our environment, process and transform them in our bodies to grow and survive, and then discard the waste products. No living organism can escape this.

When humans congregate in societies, organized by norms of behavior, work, eating, and leisure, we also metabolize (en masse). This "social metabolism" involves resources, energy, and labor to extract resources, process and add value to them, and finally discard the waste products. Regardless of whether our aim is to get energy and resources from outer space or just ordinary niobium and tantalum extracted in the Democratic Republic of Congo for smart devices, the point is that nothing comes out of thin air. Human bodies are needed to extract resources, by hand or to operate heavy machinery, or to code and train the algorithms that run the artificial intelligence programs. The extraction, processing, manufacturing, transport, and consumption of resources also generate waste, and it's very difficult to fully recycle that waste.[8] It's also waste that takes different forms, ranging from human and livestock feces to electronic e-waste to planet-heating greenhouse gas emissions. It too has to go somewhere and be dealt with, and this also requires energy and labor.

Social metabolism is the way that society (and particularly our economy) uses energy and resources, transforms them into goods or services, and then releases wastes. Social metabolism is the material reality of our ecological conundrum. As we'll see, our social metabolism is at present way out of step with what Earth can possibly regenerate (on the input side) or absorb (on the output side). It is also extremely unequal across the world: whole regions have become both a resource extraction site and a dumping ground, while the goods and profits are funneled to other regions of the world. Cobalt and coltan to Silicon Valley, Ivorian and Ghanaian cacao to Belgium and Switzerland, Ethiopian and Guatemalan coffee to Italy.

As we mentioned earlier, the sustainability class is driven by a craving for the PIE—a worldview of purity, innovation, and efficiency. In the next four chapters, we aim to encourage all of us middle-class and progressive-minded folks—who might do things like listen to NPR, worry about the state of the planet for our children, and so aspire to "do our bit" for a better world—to step away from the hype of PIE-in-the-sky visions of sustainability. We bring things back down to earth by examining the *material* implications of these hopes. As we'll see, the sustainability class only looks pure, innovative, and efficient if we look at the numbers with blinders on. It just doesn't add up.

Pure Vibes

Is it possible to live without eating? Breatharians think so. Breatharianism is a pseudoscience claiming that people can survive by just breathing and absorbing *prana*, the vital life force according to Hindu philosophy. While some followers of breatharianism have sadly expired (pun intended), others seem to be doing very well. Some, like power couple Akahi Ricardo and Camila Castilo, charge upward of $1,000 per person for their three-day retreats. Others, like Wiley Brooks, the founder of the Breatharian Institute of America, was known to have charged over $100,000 per session. Breatharianism is the distillation of purity. As journalist Breena Kerr says in *GQ*, it "promises wellness, mental and physical, for less than you're doing, less than you're eating, less than you're paying now—after the initial investment, at least."[9]

That's as good as a summary of the purity mindset of the sustainability class as anything. Purity, we noted, is about the desire to have an authentic experience and return to a natural, pristine, and unblemished state. Like with breatharianism, the idea is that we can transform our selves and our economy with individual or collective fasting—as long as we pay up.

The fantasy takes different forms, from the purity of No-Impact Man who lives in midtown Manhattan to the hope that nuclear energy will finally let us live in a squeaky-clean *Star Trek* future, to the belief that the rich are greener—because they can pay for it.[10] As we've seen, cities play a starring role in the sustainability class scripts. They are often lauded as the vanguard of sustainability, especially by green modernists, who claim that the population density that comes with high-rise living "spares" land for nature and is more efficient. And yet, despite being hotspots for green lifestyles, creativity, and efficiency, cities are, in effect, vortices that suck up mined materials and (mostly) fossil fuel energy and spit them back out as skyscrapers, roads, commercial buildings, big box stores, computers, concrete sidewalks, power lines, rice cookers, and pretty much whatever else makes up the edifice of modernity. Cities are like Erewhon belching out wood smoke to its neighbors—but on a much bigger scale. Yet, they effectively hide their impacts through strategies like false sustainability awards, competitions, and green branding that make them appear far more ecological than they actually are—swindling even the highly educated green modernists in the process.

Underlying this strategy of generating new and creative ways to make it *appear* as though one's impacts are invisible is to claim that the rich are, or can be, more sustainable than the poor. Or, put another way, you can be green only if you have enough purchasing power. It sounds extreme when it's phrased like this, but this is exactly the argument that green modernists have been advancing for decades now. This has come in the form of an argument known as the "environmental Kuznets curve." Named after economist Simon Kuznets, famous for infusing demographics, statistics, and quantitative measurement into the discipline of economics, it is the hypothesis that as an economy grows and becomes richer, it also has the capacity to become ecologically lighter. That's because more income can be spent on green goods and infrastructure, and the economy is no longer dependent on heavy, polluting industries.[11] This same ideology inspires the sustainability class, where it's assumed that because the rich have more money to spend, they can make more sustainable choices. So you can only become sustainable if you're wealthy. Mimosas on a carbon-neutral solar-powered 3D-printed yacht, anyone? We're saving the world!

But let's look at this claim more carefully. As we will see, the only way that this theory holds is if you look at the numbers with blinders on, which makes them appear a lot better. Once we take off the blinders, we see that rich countries, green cities, and the sustainability class itself are far more polluting than anyone else.

Territorial and Consumption-based Accounting

Let's start with the big question: do green choices really matter? Does it make a difference if we abandon our cars, buy that LEED-certified climate-resilient condo, and start biking to work? One important survey based in Germany showed that good intentions only go so far. Of 1,012 respondents, those who self-identified as being environmentally conscious were also the ones most likely to have a green lifestyle. Sounds good, right? But the problem is that having a green lifestyle has little to do with your actual environmental impacts. As the authors state:

> The most important predictor [for energy use and carbon footprint] proved to be income . . . followed by homeownership. In other words, participants with higher incomes and those owning homes tended to consume more energy and displayed bigger carbon footprints than participants with lower incomes and those who rent. . . . Rather than using less energy, people high in environmental self-identity in our sample used slightly more energy

and had a slightly bigger carbon footprint than those indicating less environmental awareness.[12]

So, people who identify as green are more likely to have a bigger carbon footprint. Still, this study is a cross-section of the whole population, but what about people who live in cities? Aren't *they* more environmentally friendly? According to some green modernist pundits, Manhattan is the greenest place you could possibly be.[13] Again, research consistently finds that the best predictor for having a high environmental impact is your income. For example, one study looked at people "choosing to live near public transit, on bike- and pedestrian-friendly streets, and in higher-density mixed-use areas." They find, once again, that these new residents are very likely to have higher carbon footprints.[14]

Why is this the case? The authors explain that, typically, urban planners use "territory-based accounting," which calculates the emissions only in that area—for example, through car use, or heating buildings.[15] So if it's an area with high walkability and well-insulated apartment buildings, then it is claimed to have lower impact. But a more holistic approach would include "consumption-based accounting," which also incorporates the embedded impacts of the goods people buy, such as food, clothing, appliances, and flights. When consumption is considered, emissions of high-density, walkable urban areas are up to twice as high. At the neighborhood level, the reduced emissions from being high-density is mostly offset by consumption. Citing the study's authors once again:

> In New York City, for example, models of per capita, zip-code-based emissions flowing from consumption find that residents of Manhattan's residentially dense neighborhoods have carbon footprints comparable to those of residents in wealthy cities countrywide, despite Manhattan's density. It is in the relatively dense, low- or mixed-income and transit-rich areas of New York's outer

boroughs—especially Brooklyn, Queens and the Bronx—where density and low GHG emissions are found together.[16]

The same holds for entire economic sectors like countries or regions. We've been told that wealthy countries are more sustainable because they no longer have dirty industries. If we continue to replace all kinds of dirty industries (manufacturing, agriculture) with growth-friendly, eco-friendly information technology (IT) and service industries, we've achieved sustainability. At least, so say pundits like Thomas Friedman, Van Jones, Steven Pinker, and Andrew McAfee, introduced in Chapter 1. But here again, these calculations look only at the specific territorial impacts of those industries. Per unit of economic output, the service sector supposedly has a lower environmental impact—especially the "knowledge economy," which includes Silicon Valley.[17] It seems credible at first glance. But if you start taking consumption into account, the picture changes. In one study, researchers decided to include the consumption of laborers in these industries. Since tech industry workers have higher incomes than manufacturing workers, they tend to spend more on consumer goods.[18] As the authors note:

> We found that services like tech industries were as damaging to global climate, land, and water as agriculture and manufacturing when household consumption was included in the accounting. This is because tech is labor-intensive, and its numerous workers tend to be affluent consumers, whose habits cause large environmental impacts. By contrast, sectors typically seen as "dirty," like farming and manufacturing, generate less affluence, and thus encourage less consumption and environmental damage.[19]

This shouldn't be too surprising. The largest and most comprehensive study of global climate inequality has made it glaringly obvious that the people with the most money are also the highest emitters. When counting consumption, the "polluter elite," aka the richest 1 percent, are responsible for 16 percent of all carbon emissions—more than the emissions generated by 66 percent of all people (5 billion humans). It would take 99 percent of humanity 1,500 years to generate as much carbon as the 1 percent does in just a single year.[20] The top 10 percent—which includes the middle class in rich countries as well as in so-called developing countries—accounted for 52 percent of all emissions. These disparities are also startling within so-called developing countries: the top 10 percent in places like China, India, South Africa, and Brazil generate thirty to forty times the emissions of the bottom 10 percent. Emissions embodied in the production and transport of consumer goods like electronics and furniture are between 20 and 50 percent higher for the top 10 percent—the very same class who claims sustainability values and aspirations.[21] These studies, and many others, show clearly that someone's wealth is a far better indicator of their emissions than the country they live in or their concern for the environment.[22] As the authors of another study point out, "Since the level of consumption determines total impacts, affluence needs to be addressed by reducing consumption, not just greening it."[23]

This isn't to say that, because the rich live everywhere, every country is equally responsible. In fact, statistics show that those countries that industrialized early carry most of the responsibility for the pickle that we're in, even if more recently industrializing countries like China, Brazil, and India look like they are starting to catch up. One 2020 study, for example, calculated the "fair share" of each country's emissions to maintain a safe global carbon budget, and how much they overshot them. It was found that the United States was responsible for 40 percent of excess global CO_2 emissions, while the European Union was responsible for 29 percent. China, in comparison, *undershot* its carbon budget by 11 percent. When grouped according to the categories of "Global North" and "Global South," the Global North (which includes the United States, Canada, Europe, Israel, New Zealand, Australia, and Japan) was responsible for 92 percent of national overshoots, while the Global South was responsible for only 8 percent of carbon budget overshoots.[24] Thus, consumption over time matters a great deal, not just wealth disparity. This shows a much starker image of climate injustice than we are often shown.

In short, when you measure not just a person's or country's production emissions but also emissions related to consumption

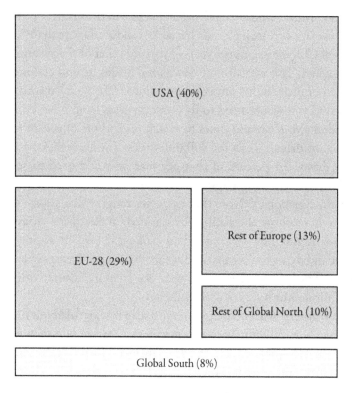

Responsibility for excess emissions. Here, "Global North" refers to the United States, Canada, Europe, Israel, Australia, New Zealand, and Japan, whereas the term "Global South" refers to the rest of the world: Latin America, Africa, the Middle East, and Asia. *Source: J. Hickel, "Quantifying National Responsibility for Climate Breakdown: An Equality-Based Attribution Approach for Carbon Dioxide Emissions in Excess of the Planetary Boundary,"* Lancet Planetary Health *4, no. 9 (2020): e399–e404.*

over time, the picture changes. Basically, the wealthier you are, the more you end up spending on things like vacation, appliances, clothes, and food, and the higher your ecological impacts. The energy and material efficiency of the products you consume has little overall effect on this picture, simply because of the scale on which you consume. All that positive stuff about living in dense, walkable neighborhoods, working low-impact jobs, and dumping your car gets negated.

Elon Musk, whose wealth is comparable to the GDP of Greece, still uses his private jet so much that he produced more than 2,750 tons of CO_2 emissions per year—fifty times that of the average US household. This was after he downsized his house and claimed to get rid of many of his physical possessions.[25] To put that into perspective, you would need to fly economy class from New York to London two thousand times to match his carbon emissions from flying, or drive a Tesla for 900,000 miles. The average American only drives 0.1 percent of that per year, so you'd need to spend 186 lifetimes driving a Tesla before you can catch up with Musk's carbon emissions.[26] Note that these are rough calculations—the point is to show the futility of the carbon footprint measurements. Lightening our individual ecological load by eating less meat and flying less means diddly-squat when you have people like Musk who will wipe away all your eco-friendly efforts within a few minutes or hours of their lifestyles.

We should warn here that we must also be careful about focusing on these individualized measurements. Yes, they do show that, even on their own terms, lifestyle changes are futile unless you address inequality—that is to say, class. But still, we need to be moving away from measuring sustainability according to individual impact—whether it's Elon Musk's or our own.

One frequently touted way to address these inequalities in wealth and emissions is through carbon taxes. A 1 percent tax on Musk's wealth, for instance, would increase global adaptation funding for the most vulnerable populations by 10 percent.[27] At the same time,

focusing entirely on a solution like carbon taxes isn't very consider-
ate to most people, who shouldn't have to cope with additional burdens amid inflation, stagnating wages, and the dismantling of public
services. Poorly designed and communicated environmental policies
that do too little to reverse existing inequalities, like Canada's once-
lauded but now bemoaned carbon tax policy led by Prime Minister
Justin Trudeau, can actually turn people off from thinking or acting
ecologically. Carbon tax policy needs to ensure that payouts from
taxes on polluters go back into the hands of low- and middle-income
people if it is to generate socially distributive and environmental
outcomes and avoid the greenlash discussed earlier.[28] When the
top 10 percent can easily absorb the taxes (or, more likely, not even
notice the increased cost) while growing their wealth, then transformative change just won't happen. What all of this tells us is that
dismantling today's wild and unprecedented class divisions is a more
important step toward an ecological future than the aspiration for
an eco-friendly lifestyle. Environmentalism that doesn't take class
relations or global inequalities into account isn't really environmentalism at all—or rather, it isn't ecological.

Investment-based Accounting

Placing our hope in the spending habits of the rich is clearly self-
defeating. But, as a thought experiment, let's keep thinking along
these lines for a moment, to see where the evidence leads us. If
we wanted to measure the sustainability of the rich, wouldn't
we also need to look at their investments? Members of the sustainability class have assets like real estate, stocks, and bonds, as
well as money sitting in the bank. Those investments have their
own impacts. The thing is, researching the impacts of people's investments is hard—mostly because people don't tend to disclose
them to the public. But as one study demonstrates, when investments are considered on a national level, many of the supposedly

postindustrial countries are still profiting from carbon-intensive economic activities. These investments should be accounted for in the calculations of who is responsible for emissions. The study also found that "the majority of emissions in the world may support capital accumulation in countries other than where the emissions occurred." In other words, when investments and profits were considered, the regions where most carbon emissions occur did not see the profits from production. Those profits were captured by investors abroad, mostly in the United States and Europe.[29]

In a more recent study, which looked at the carbon emissions associated with the investment holdings of billionaires, it was found that the 125 richest people's investments are responsible for carbon emissions *1 million* times that of the poorest 50 percent of humanity. As the study authors note, "To put that into perspective, each of these billionaires would have to circumnavigate the world almost 16 million times in a private jet to create the same emissions."[30] Elon Musk's investments account for a whopping 87,000 tons of carbon emissions per year. Unlike the rest of us, who largely have little choice in what we do with our money—for example, we will take the cheapest apartment we find and can't control its heating or insulation—these billionaires *do* have a choice of where they invest their money.

Even millionaire lifestyles are simply incompatible with keeping climate change within the critical threshold of 1.5°C. In other recent studies, authors find that "the share of millionaires in the world will grow from 0.7% today (2023) to 3.3% in 2050 and cause accumulated emissions of 286Gt CO_2, even as average incomes will fall by almost one-fifth by year 2050 as a result of extreme rainfall, heatwaves and intense storms causing $38 trillion in damage.[31] The additional emissions produced by the relatively tiny (yet growing) share of these millionaires is equivalent to 72% of the remaining carbon budget."[32] If we add up all the assets of much of the sustainability class, which would include real estate, cars, art, and stocks, they are often millionaires themselves. If these investments were considered, the sustainability class's footprint would be much higher still. And if the share of millionaires grows ever so slightly even as average incomes fall—as they likely will about 20 percent by 2050 if temperatures are limited to 2°C—the economy will continue to grow as an ever-tinier minority of ultrarich continue to skim off more and more of gross domestic product (GDP) for themselves, siphoning wealth away from the rest of us, emitting ever more carbon into the atmosphere.[33]

And it's not just individuals or countries, either. Companies also have assets, and these assets are, in turn, invested in fossil fuels and carbon-intensive production. For example, Google claims that its carbon footprint is now zero because it has bought "high quality carbon offsets," compensating for all the carbon it has ever emitted.[34] Even so, its parent company, Alphabet, has $136 billion in the bank—money that, in turn, banks invest in the fossil fuel industry, for example. In one report, the impact of major tech companies' assets was calculated, and the authors found that Alphabet's carbon emissions more than doubled when its "financial footprint" was taken into account.[35] And let's not forget that companies like Alphabet, Uber, Doordash, Slack, Meta, Amazon, X (formerly Twitter), and Reddit are in great part owned and bankrolled by oil-producing nations like Saudi Arabia—whose profits in turn are then reinvested into more oil extraction and green gaslighting schemes like Neom.[36]

Decoupling

Again and again, the picture changes: calculate consumption- and investment-related emissions, and things look a lot more unsustainable. One response to the data showing that the rich are responsible for the vast majority of carbon emissions might be that they can also *choose* to invest in technology that turns a carbon-intensive energy system into a no-impact, sustainable one. Elon

Musk, for example, is turning his investments and private jet use into an opportunity for sustainable growth by making Tesla cars. In other words, because of their position of power, the rich have the greatest potential to change the direction of the economy.

This is the claim behind "decoupling": the idea that it is possible to detach economic growth from environmental impacts through the right *kind* of investments. While it might seem obscure to most people, this concept has taken central stage in the debate about climate change and what to do about it. For several decades, economists and environmental scientists have shown that carbon emissions, and many other environmental impacts, are tightly linked to GDP.[37]

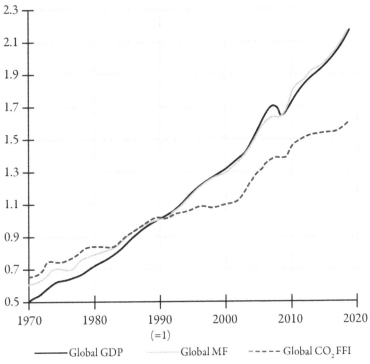

Global trends of GDP, material footprint, and carbon emissions. The figure shows how these are tightly coupled. *Source: Thomas Wiedmann et al., "Scientists' Warning on Affluence,"* Nature Communications *11, no. 1 (2020): 1–10.*

This is worrying for green modernists, who argue that economic growth—and the innovation and investment potential that comes from it—will help us address climate change. As a result, many have tried to prove the "decoupling" of GDP growth from the rate of increase in carbon emissions around the world, arguing that periods of economic growth, combined with lower carbon emissions in specific countries, show that it is possible for the economy to grow while becoming greener. Their argument rests on a few case studies—snapshots in time and place—and much of this research has not yet been peer reviewed. Move the timeframe of each study a few years over, extend the boundaries a couple of miles, and you might get a very different picture.

Take, for example, an article on the liberal news outlet Vox that states rather definitively that "one chart" proves we can grow the economy while slashing carbon emissions.[38] The chart in question shows how twenty-five countries have accomplished this feat between 2005 and 2019. Importantly, these calculations *also* include carbon emissions "imported" from other countries through consumption. Through technological innovation and regulations like those for air pollution, these countries have reduced "the greenhouse gas intensity of their economy—the amount of carbon embedded in each economic buck." It would *seem* as though we're on the right path to a pure breatharian economy.

There's nothing wrong with this picture per se. From basically any perspective, it should be considered a good thing that countries are becoming less dependent on fossil fuels in their economy. That's not the issue here. There is a more basic issue with the argument for decoupling. The literature certainly demonstrates that decoupling is occurring in certain countries over specific periods of time. But the real question is whether *global* emissions are decreasing *at a fast enough rate to stop catastrophic climate breakdown.* According to the UN's Paris Agreement for Climate Change, we need to lower emissions by 45 percent by the year 2030 and reach zero emissions by 2050 to keep the global mean temperature

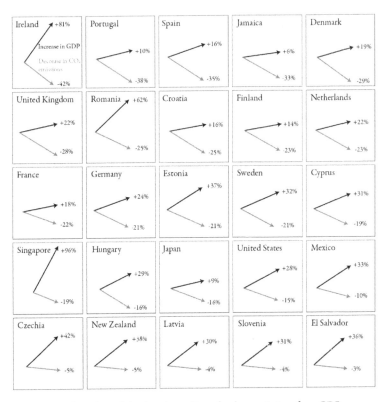

25 countries that achieved absolute decoupling of carbon emissions from GDP between 2005-2019. Emissions are adjusted for trade, meaning that they include emissions resulting from imported goods, while emissions from exported goods are subtracted. Data is sourced from Global Carbon Project and the World Bank. *Source: M. Roser, June 1, 2021. "The argument for a carbon price." Our World in Data. https://ourworldindata.org/carbon-price*

increase below 1.5°C—considered by the International Panel on Climate Change to be the "safe upper boundary" of a liveable planet.[39] Unfortunately, these studies do not show that the rate of carbon emissions is declining nearly fast enough to reach even these countries' stated climate targets, nor is the rate of global emissions going down fast enough.[40] And it's not just missing the mark by a small margin. A 2023 study published in *The Lancet* found that for those countries that claim to be experiencing decoupling, it would take them 220 years to reduce their emissions by the necessary 95 percent, and over that period, they would still emit twenty-seven times what they would need to emit as their fair share for the planet to stay within 1.5°C. As the authors note, "To meet their 1.5°C fair-shares alongside continued economic growth, decoupling rates would on average need to increase by a factor of 10 by 2025."[41] In other words, we need decoupling that not only considers consumption and investments but is also *global* and *permanent*. As the authors of a systematic review of 835 peer-reviewed articles on decoupling note quite conclusively, "Large rapid absolute reductions of resource use and GHG [greenhouse gas] emissions cannot be achieved through observed decoupling rates."[42]

While decoupling CO_2 from GDP growth is theoretically possible, the issue goes beyond the rate at which this is purportedly happening. The real question is whether GDP growth itself (or, in other words, profits) is the right tool for the job. The problem is that any profits made from a green industry can quickly be reinvested in another, more polluting industry or country. As economist Jason Hickel put it, relying on growth to decarbonize an economy is like running down an upwardly accelerating escalator: growth will dominate efficiency gains in the long term, since investors move their money to places where there are fewer environmental regulations.[43] The evidence suggests that economic growth is woefully inadequate for lightening the ecological load of the economy. Indeed, in one survey, a clear majority of climate policy researchers—73 percent—have become critical of the idea that growth can be made green.[44]

Planetary Boundaries

These studies underline how and why an ecological perspective is essential for understanding the challenges we face. What we mean by this is that we need to understand holistically the relationships between carbon emissions, growth, and ecological degradation. Even if economic growth became less linked to carbon emissions, through stronger regulations or innovative technologies, it would still drive many other environmental impacts. For example, if industrial agriculture emitted less carbon, it would still be causing massive soil erosion, water use, and biodiversity loss. Climate change caused by carbon emissions is just one of the many interconnected planetary boundaries (limits that must not be exceeded in order to keep warming at a non-apocalyptic level), all of which are still dramatically linked to economic growth.

Ten years ago, scientists identified nine planetary boundaries, including carbon emissions, soil erosion, land use, nitrogen and phosphorus use, and ocean acidification. Of all nine, six have since been exceeded, and two are close to being breached. These boundaries are all linked—both the overuse of nitrogen and biodiversity loss, for example, are mostly driven by industrial agriculture. They will also affect us in multiple and overlapping ways: increased rainfall and heat due to climate change, together with soil erosion due to industrial agriculture and the timber industry, is already contributing to extreme flooding and forest fires.[45]

This is not to say that these boundaries are static or fixed. The last two hundred years have shown that boundaries can be shifted, such as when the collapse of soil fertility was temporarily addressed by the invention of the Haber-Bosch process, wherein fossil fuels were burned to create synthetic fertilizers. The science of ecology itself has shown us that boundaries shift constantly. And boundaries become malleable as new technologies are introduced and production is "revolutionized." The issue is not quite that we are crossing a few boundaries that are unnegotiable, it's that the boundaries are rapidly proliferating, increasingly connected, and unmanageable.

Try to imagine a net with many hooks, which catch on to each other and to the surroundings. Think of the economy as that net:

through human labor and ingenuity, we might weave and expand that net, allowing investors to catch more profits. But ecological time and space—through the systems that sustain us, such as the carbon cycle, nitrogen cycle, and soil fertility—extend well beyond fiscal years and investment portfolios. When profits guide the decision-making of most of the economy, the risk that these fluctuating, malleable boundaries are snagged and drag down the whole net increases—simply because their time scales and spatial relationships just don't match up with those of economic growth forecasts and election cycles. If Antarctica's Larsen C ice shelf collapses (as it did in 2017), exposing the area's marine life to light for the first time in over a hundred thousand years, then we're talking about time scales that truly do resemble hard boundaries in the scale of any human lifetime. There's no going back to "normal" even in your great-grandchild's life.[46] The failure of one system drags the others down, such as when the overreliance on fertilizer to improve already depleted soils and the use of heavy machinery designed to replace expensive labor costs lead to even more soil erosion, flooding, and eutrophication. We are ensnared in a net that can't get unhooked fast enough.

A note of caution. Pointing out that there are ecological dynamics that can drag down the economy is neither doom-mongering nor Malthusian. Doom-and-gloom apocalypse talk often looms large when someone starts talking about the environment. But we're not talking about some kind of collapse in the distant future: we're talking about deterioration and breakdown of an unprecedented scale happening *right now*. Before our eyes, we are seeing the collapse of fisheries and of bird and insect populations, the rapid oxidation of oceans, the loss of soil, droughts and flooding and fires.

By saying this, we are not being Malthusian—an outlook named after eighteenth-century English priest Thomas Malthus, who feared that overpopulation of the poor would lead to disaster. Malthus believed that moral limits on procreation by the poor working class in Europe was the only way to keep the economy growing. For Malthus, economic growth should be protected for the rich, while the poor were seen as a threat.[47] Think about it: isn't advocating "green," "sustainable" living for the very wealthy to keep the poor at bay and protect the economy far more in line with Malthus's ideas? It is the economy that needs to change, and especially because the poor are the least responsible for ecological breakdown.

We also have to look at the international and historical relationships that support an economy. For instance, while Sweden's carbon emissions might look good on paper, the country's economy still depends on the wealth and profit that flow from investments in mining, real estate development, and industrial agriculture in the Global South. All in all, we can't ignore the connections between one sector of the economy and others. We have to come to grips with the fact that our world—and the way profits are made—is increasingly interconnected. If we were to take that seriously, we'd see that there's something deeply wrong with the claim that those twenty-five countries have decoupled their economic growth from environmental impact somewhere in the world. What we are looking at is rather twenty-five snapshots in time, which completely obscures an entire history of responsibility for climate breakdown that stretches back decades, if not centuries. There's a whole history here: the wealth of countries like Sweden was made from highly carbon-intensive industry. As the authors of the review of decoupling literature say, "Current trajectories of material and energy use, whether suggesting decoupling of resource use from economic growth or not, cannot be correctly interpreted without considering past material and energy flows on which they are also based."[48]

In other words, current evidence of decoupling is little more than a flash in the pan. Whenever it's claimed that sparse and piecemeal evidence for decoupling shows that economic growth can fix climate change, it's another example of green gaslighting.

It's a bit like choosing a photo where an elderly married couple looks happy and claiming, on that basis, that they've solved all their marital problems—when, in fact, their whole family knows that their relationship was dominated by decades of abuse.

Carbon Tunnel Vision

Granted, green modernists will be the first to say that, of course, a lot more needs to be done about climate change. This is why they are betting everything on nuclear energy: with its high electricity output, stability, and small land and material requirements, it seems ideally positioned to successfully decouple the economy from its carbon impacts once and for all. The most prominent among them, including Breakthrough Institute researchers Michael Shellenberger, Ted Norhaus, and Steven Pinker, are trying to convince governments to invest large amounts of capital and research funding to switch their energy systems to nuclear.[49] When you read their work, it's as if nuclear is the answer to everything. It allows us to keep doing what we're doing while switching the energy system to a purer, cleaner source.

Let's be clear: it's certainly necessary to weigh the benefits and drawbacks of nuclear energy. But while the urgency of the climate crisis should make us seriously consider the technologies we have available to us, there are many things we need to think about when it comes to nuclear.

One issue is its exorbitant and constantly ballooning costs—and even as we're told that new technologies like small nuclear reactors and fusion are just around the corner if governments would only invest a little more, none of these exist at scale, and we're still mostly stuck with the same reactors from fifty years ago.

Another issue is the supply chain. Uranium mining is often done in unsafe conditions that affect local communities, and there is no permanent safe disposal of nuclear waste. As journalist

David Thorpe notes, just the 27.5 tons of uranium fuel needed to operate a nuclear reactor for a year requires over 660,000 tons of waste rock and milled tailings, which are toxic and have contaminated water supplies in Brazil, United States, Australia, and Namibia. As Thorpe underlines, "It takes a lot of—almost certainly fossil-fuelled—energy to move that amount of rock and process the ore. But the carbon cost is often not in the country where the fuel is consumed."[50]

Consider, too, the instability of these supplies, which are rocked by war, coups, and geopolitics. For example, Russia happens to be the world's largest supplier of enriched uranium, at roughly one-third of global supply—leading to France having to make uncomfortable choices when it imposed sanctions on Russia for its invasion of Ukraine even as it advocated nuclear energy as a means to decrease dependence on Russian gas.[51] Or, take another example: the coup in Niger in 2023. This country exports significant amounts of uranium to its former colonizer, France. The coup destabilized global uranium supplies even more, and sent France panicking to find alternatives.[52] Then there's the insecurity of the climate crisis, which will most certainly include sudden weather-related disasters and even more unpredictable geopolitical conflicts. In the summers of 2022 and 2023, France had to take up to half of its nuclear power plants offline when a drought meant they could no longer depend on rivers and lakes for thermal cooling.[53]

These examples should make us think twice about relying on a technology that so greatly depends on secure supply chains, large bodies of water that don't run out during periods of drought, political stability, long-term centralized planning, and the capacity to store nuclear waste for millennia—none of which is in abundant supply in today's geopolitical quagmire, not to mention a future of growing climate chaos.[54] As climate justice activist Masayoshi Iyoda notes, "The climate crisis is not just about CO_2 emissions. It is about a whole range of environmental justice and democracy issues that need to be considered. And nuclear energy does not have a stellar record in this regard."[55]

There may indeed be a role for nuclear energy in a climate changed future—we are not discounting that. At issue is what this conversation distracts from—and it's related to the point above about looking at the ecological crisis holistically. The focus on nuclear energy rests on what scientists at the Stockholm Environment Institute—the same research center that came up with the concept of planetary boundaries—are now calling "carbon tunnel vision"—that is, aiming for net-zero emissions while ignoring other environmental and social problems.[56] If nuclear energy is indeed what will save us from climate change, as so many green modernists believe, then what about all its other impacts and problems, and what about all our *other* planetary boundaries?

To illustrate this, let's say we do find some kind of no-impact energy source that could provide us with endless amounts of energy. What would we do with it? Let's imagine that impossible scenario that nuclear energy *was* a perfect, lightweight, conflict-free, easily scalable source of energy. We'd live in a world where everything from car ownership to space travel, heating to air-conditioning, and hydroponic farming to industrial farming would become cheap and easy. It'd be like *Star Trek*: infinite energy for us to go "where no one has gone before."

But to manufacture all those things, we'd need mines, we'd need factories, we'd need landfills. More energy means more material resources needed to maintain the production of that energy source and, in turn, more unintended environmental impacts that disproportionately affect some people over others. We aren't solving any of the structural problems that cause ecological collapse and social injustice by just shifting to another energy source and producing more of the same.

We need to think differently about the *process* of production. Consider for a moment the amount of stuff we use today. In 2020, human-made or human-dependent organic matter (or anthropogenic mass), such as concrete, farms, livestock, and asphalt, exceeded the total biomass of the planet.[57] At the current rate of growth (about 3 percent), anthropogenic mass will be triple the planet's biomass by 2040. And again, we are already nearing or exceeding the limits of many different life-supporting systems, including in phosphorus and nitrogen use, soil erosion, biodiversity loss, ozone depletion, and ocean acidification.[58] Rather than slowing down, we are experiencing a "great acceleration" by almost any metric.[59]

We're not saying that a clean source of energy, if it were available, couldn't sustain GDP growth. What we're saying is that even if it did exist, we wouldn't even have confronted the largest problem of all: the collapse of many crucial life support systems on Earth. The ecological crisis isn't just about how and where we get our energy to power the future utopias dreamed up by the 1 percent; it's about the fallout everywhere you look.

Dematerialization

When presented with evidence of the large-scale, multisystem collapse of the living world, green modernists tend to respond by once again falling back on the ideology of purity. Here we are thinking of the idea of "dematerialization," which describes how rich countries are seemingly decreasing the quantity of materials they are using. Dematerialization is like decoupling, but with a different spin: it is the argument that rich economies are using less stuff in absolute terms, while decoupling describes the connection between ecological impacts and economic growth.

Like decoupling, dematerialization appears to be intuitive but is deceptive on further investigation. For example, in his book *More from Less: The Surprising Story of How We Learned to Prosper Using Fewer Resources—and What Happens Next*, Andrew McAfee argues that "we have at last learned to increase human prosperity while treading more lightly on our planet. . . . [W]e don't need to make radical changes."[60] To make his case, McAfee focuses on the United States and argues that its consumption of several key resources, such as stone, cement, sand, timber, and paper, has been decreasing since the mid-2000s while its economy continued to grow during the same period. This, he argues, is due to the other components of PIE: innovation and efficiency. He argues developed countries are dematerializing because the "intensity" of their use of certain materials has gone down—that is, because of efficiency gains, it now costs less to make the same thing.

Unfortunately, these claims have been seriously put into question in the scientific literature—to such an extent that it's surprising McAfee could still defend them in 2019. To begin with, a first gloss of global data shows quite conclusively that material extraction has accelerated, and even more so since 2000. As the authors of one authoritative 2018 study note:

The global results show a massive increase in materials extraction from 22 billion tonnes (Bt) in 1970 to 70 Bt in 2010, and an acceleration in material extraction since 2000. This acceleration has occurred at a time when global population growth has slowed and global economic growth has stalled. The global surge in material extraction has been driven by growing wealth and consumption and accelerating trade.[61]

Yet, McAfee's argument rests entirely on domestic material consumption—that is, what is used within the borders of the country. When we start looking at *material footprint*, which includes imported consumption, we see that the United States' consumption has been growing faster than its GDP since the 1990s.[62] In fact, research now shows that, globally, material footprints have been increasing since about 2000 because of what scientist Heinz Schandl and co-authors identify as a "shift of global production from very material-efficient economies to less-efficient ones."[63] This is in large part due to the industrialization and urbanization of the Global South, which then exports its resources, goods, and wealth to the Global North—erasing marginal reductions in material consumption, since material use ultimately increases in the aggregate. Once again, looking at aggregate, or global, material consumption is important because of those global economic interconnections—such as how wealthy countries import materially intensive products from poorer countries. If we ignore those, we're just like horses with blinders on.

Finally, it's also been conclusively proven that as far as rich countries go, the moments in time when economies did start decreasing their material footprint were often linked to reduced economic growth. In other words, dematerialization came from economic stagnation, and material footprint shot back up when growth restarted—highlighting again how economic growth and material use remain interconnected.[64] The point is, dematerializing never happened—the costs of economic growth just got shifted to poorer and more vulnerable populations and regions of the world. It's a vicious and predatory relationship, one that hasn't changed since colonialism.

The Circular Economy

One other proposed solution that we want to mention here is the often-heralded concept of the "circular economy." This is the idea that we can switch to an economy of 100 percent recyclable materials. It is intuitively appealing: we all know there is too much plastic, too much garbage, so why not try to at least recycle it all? In theory, if we succeed, we'd end up with an economy that has little environmental impact because we wouldn't have to keep extracting more resources—and so we could grow indefinitely. Many cities in the world are jumping onto the "circular economy" bandwagon—including lifestyle environmentalist hubs like Vancouver, San Francisco, and Amsterdam.[65]

Let's first look at plastics as one example of why the idea of circularity makes no sense. As plastics researcher Tallash Kantai claims, the time it takes plastics to degrade lies between 400 and 1,500 years—this means that every bit of plastic produced today will outlive more than twenty generations.[66] And over 9 billion tons of plastic have already been produced, of which about 7 billion tons have been discarded as waste in landfills, been washed or dumped into the oceans, or have made their way into our food and water supply and bodies.[67] Most plastic production is for single-use products and packaging, and it is far cheaper to produce plastic for its malleability and durability than to recycle it. As long as it remains cheaper and easier to turn new plastics into waste faster than the time it took to produce them, there is no amount of circular production that can stop the accelerating plastic production pipeline.

Beyond plastics alone, the vast majority of the things we use can't even be recycled. Every day we have to choose countless times whether to put something in the trash or in the recycling bin. And so, it's tempting to think that we could just be a bit better at the recycling part. But the things we consumers throw away on a daily basis represent only 15 percent of the total material footprint. The rest is made up of fossil fuels, biomass for fuel, waste from the mining sector, and infrastructure and buildings.[68] Even if we could recycle consumer goods fully, this would scarcely address the economy's total material footprint.

But even only half of the 15 percent of material we do throw away can be feasibly recycled, given current technologies. It's just hard to recycle the things we make. For instance, only 30 percent of the Fair Phone, branded as the most sustainable phone in the world, can be recycled.[69] And many of the things that we can recycle, such as plastics, become less useful over time. Recycling plastics will always result in a poorer-grade plastic, and each time we recycle plastic, it accumulates and then releases carcinogenic toxins and endocrine disruptors, including styrene, benzene, bisphenol A, heavy metals, formaldehyde, and phthalates.[70] For example, in a recent paper, researchers found that of thirty-nine different brands of recyclable or biodegradable straws, almost all "recyclable" or "biodegradable" ones contained significant amounts of PFAS, "forever chemicals" that are not, at a human timescale, biodegradable and have been found to be harmful to both human health and ecosystems.[71] The part of the economy that the "circular economy" focuses on is only a tiny fraction of the total—and even makes things worse by spreading the myth that recycling everything will save us.

The biggest problem with all this comes down to how the whole idea of the circular economy is conceived. Every time you recycle something, you need to use energy, and you need to build places to process the recyclable materials and store them. Constantly recycling is enormously energy intensive.[72] Recycling requires more resources and more extraction. Increasingly, the dirty work of dealing with the recycling waste of so-called green and smart-aspiring cities like Montreal, Melbourne, and Manchester gets shipped overseas to China, Malaysia, and the Philippines—countries that are now no longer willing to accept this waste.[73] In effect, to recycle everything all the time, you would need constant input of more energy and more materials. This means that an economy that recycles everything but doesn't decrease how much it produces would paradoxically depend on increasing and even accelerating material and energy use. The circular economy is like taking a detox pill and hoping that it will fix a collapsing lung.

Sneaky Snacking

What's really at issue here is that ideas like the circular economy, dematerialization, and decoupling propose to fix the problem of our outsized material footprint while not doing anything about the structural reasons why the economy's social metabolism is accelerating in the first place—and leading to ecological breakdown. Perhaps most perverse is how they are framed as state-of-the-art science but are just a different way to describe the status quo strategy of getting a return on investment. Tariq Basmair of the Saudi-based Circular Economy Company, for instance, claims that enhancing the lifecycle of oil can promote circularity and "create a pathway to sustainability."[74] We're told nothing radical has to happen; we just need to do more of the same. What comes around goes around with the circular economy, so we'd better not get thrown for a loop.

While we're spinning in circles, we might as well return to the Breatharians for a moment. Are there perhaps some people who live off air, water, and light . . . like orchids? It's possible, but unlikely. Dig a bit deeper, and you'll find that many who claim this title have been caught eating on the sly. For example, Wiley Brooks, that most famous Breatharian guru, was once caught at a 7-Eleven convenience store with a Slurpee, hot dog, and Twinkies. Similarly, Akahi Ricardo and Camila Castilo, the Breatharian couple, admit that they actually do eat quite a bit—including during their retreats—but away from their clients' hungry eyes. As the journalist Breena Kerr notes, "They often fuel rumors that they don't eat by omitting the fact that they do eat, if not much."[75] Likewise, once you dig deeper into the purity worldview, you'll find that there's a lot of sneaky snacking going on.

4

INNOVATION

Say you have a bathtub that's about to overflow. Would you put some buckets on the floor to catch the overflow or would you turn off the tap? For many, innovation is just about adding more buckets. We spend our lives devising more ingenious ways to keep the whole charade going. Innovation has come to be about devising expert policies that often generate unintended problems that are worse than the original problem. The British attempt to criminalize pastoralists and protect big game for sport hunters in the East African savannahs, mentioned in Chapter 2, is one example. Ultimately, their shortsighted vision of getting large charismatic animals to hunt and later protect in game reserves created the conditions for the spread of sleeping sickness. Innovation often seems like a good idea on paper.

"Disrupting" the market with a new technology, and therefore creating new markets for investment, is seen as a key tool for achieving sustainability, regardless of whether the technology solves the problem or not. Instead of addressing a problem, the intent is to reinvent the problem with a new solution designed to keep the problem going. That way, innovative solutions can be brainstormed forever, all while keeping investors and shareholders happy and creating niches for NGOs to collect tax-deductible donations to "solve" a problem that continues in perpetuity.

One can cut down primary, old-growth forests and grow monocultures elsewhere and call it innovation. One can turn communal land into tree plantations and call it carbon offsets, which companies like Google can buy to claim net zero status. One can even get carbon credits from investing in breastfeeding, as it is less carbon intensive than milk formula.[1] Rather than halting deforestation or stopping carbon emissions, the innovation lies in tradable and financialized credits to compensate for damage and to permit companies to go on deforesting or emitting carbon as before. The implicit understanding is that the economy needs to keep growing—this is ultimately non-negotiable. Reducing carbon emissions or stopping deforestation was never actually the goal, because doing so would threaten existing markets and end the opportunity to create new ones.

Offsetting is a bit like chopping off your arm with the expectation that you'll just get a bionic equivalent, all while providing jobs to medical staff and stimulating innovation in the medical industry. A win-win! The quality of your original arm versus a bionic arm is irrelevant; the innovation lies in making sure nothing was lost. After all, you still have an arm, and an arm is an arm. Even if budget cuts and austerity eventually mean replacing bionic arms with hooks, don't fret—you'll still be assured an arm. Meh, stop complaining and just be happy you have an arm, even if it's just a hook!

The belief in innovation depends on the hubris that a human-made solution to any existential ecological problem will inevitably be found—it's just a matter of time. This expectation is also known as hype, and it's crucial to inflating economic growth. Just as the economy depends on hype to ensure investment and venture capital to keep shareholders happy, promises to become net zero in carbon emissions by the year 2050 allay fears of inaction through lofty and largely unachievable targets. It matters little if the outcomes aren't achieved, because the challenge lies in the innovations—including the metrics and indicators—that make it appear as though progress is being made.

The problem-solving hype becomes a boon for entrepreneurs

who obsess over the technologies of expectation, deploying gadgets like blockchains and highfalutin geoengineering projects like cloud seeding. Too often, these entrepreneurs are wealthy men inspired by science fiction and searching for something to do. Take Luke Iseman, CEO of Make Sunsets—a firm committed to cooling the climate by injecting sulfur aerosol particles into the stratosphere to drop global temperatures. He got his idea from Neal Stephenson's science fiction novel *Terminator Shock*, in which a Texas oil billionaire shoots sulfur into the air with a giant gun. Companies can purchase "cooling credits" to pay for each injection of sulfur dioxide into the atmosphere and wipe away their guilt. When we only look at a small part of the problem in our attempt to solve it, we're those horses with blinders on again. But when the people wearing the blinders are billionaires, it feels like there's not much we can do but watch them trample all over the planet with their "brilliant" ideas.

Fossil Fuel Plus

The graph below is a great illustration of what innovation does do. There's a lot of hoopla about a sustainable energy transition from fossil fuels toward renewable solar and wind energy. Renewable energy advocates are always quick to point out its spectacular growth rate. For example, almost every year the International Energy Agency releases a report on the "massive" and accelerating growth rate of renewables.[2] The reality is that even though the use of renewable energy is increasing, it is still vastly outpaced by the use of oil and coal.

What this graph shows is that total energy consumption has increased, with renewables from wind, water, solar, and biomass simply serving as a kind of "top-up" to meet growing energy demands. Over the time period shown, renewables have simply

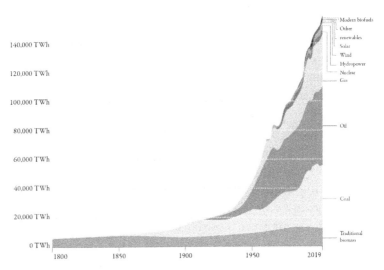

Global direct primary energy consumption. Note that even though renewables have increased exponentially, they are just a "top-up" of existing fossil-fuel-based energy sources. *Source: Vaclav Smil,* Energy Transitions: Global and National Perspectives *(Santa Barbara, CA: Praeger, 2017); BP Statistical Review of World Energy; Our World in Data, ourworldindata.org/ grapher/global-primary-energy.*

added to energy consumption, rather than substituting for fossil fuels.[3] None of it even begins to challenge the supremacy of big oil, who have been seeing record profits in the last few years.[4] Despite the hype around renewables, the harsh reality remains that sources like solar, wind, hydrogen, and nuclear energy are ultimately energy additions to already existing fossil fuel reserves, rather than the energy substitutions they were meant to be. All of this serves to preserve the way of life of rich countries and wealthy enclaves at the expense of an energy system for all.

Now, let's be very clear: civilization thrives on fossil fuels. We are swimming in the stuff. It's only because of fossil fuels that places like Erewhon can sell thirty-ingredient organic shampoos and sustainably farmed seafood from five thousand miles away. A glut of readily available energy allows for all kinds of innovations, including anything from cryptocurrency mining, machine learning, and walkable "smart" cities to TikTok videos and threads on X, as well as the military forces that secure access to resources and wage wars to secure geopolitical supremacy. There is no doubt that over the past 40 years, consumer trends and technological advances stem from a *deepening*, not a lessening, of carbon culture.[5] What all of this means is that there is still little evidence of an energy transition taking place, despite the hype. We just have renewable energy additions topping up traditional fossil fuels. Some have called renewable energy "fossil fuel plus."[6]

Fighting Fire with Flamethrowers

Here's another example: carbon capture and storage (CCS). This technology sucks in carbon and stores it underground or turns it into fuel by, for instance, combining it with hydrogen—itself an energy-intensive process. Investment has skyrocketed in recent years: in 2022, investment doubled from the previous year to $6.4 billion. The Biden administration in the United States and the Liberals under Trudeau in Canada, so-called progressives, have offered incentives to fossil fuel companies like Shell, Exxon-Mobil, and Chevron to encourage them to get involved in carbon capture.[7] Oil and gas companies, as well as the Gulf nations, have been big advocates of carbon capture at the UN's global climate conferences in recent years.[8] Despite the bad actors supporting carbon capture, you might think that capturing at least *some* of that carbon is good, right?

To answer that question, we'd have to look at how much carbon is ultimately stored versus how much gets emitted. Climate analyst Ketan Joshi has done just that in his analysis of this technology. Joshi finds that the proportion of total emissions captured and stored as compared to CO_2 emitted was only somewhere between 0.01 percent and 0.2 percent, very generously calculated.[9] He writes:

[Carbon capture and storage] struggles to exist, and when it does, it struggles to function. When it manages both, all it does is capture a tiny fraction of a high-emitting process, supplying or burning fossil fuels, and the carbon it captures gets sent straight back to work worsening the climate crisis. On top of all of this, it serves a rhetorical function; worsening the climate problem through the empty promise it provides.[10]

It seems that carbon capture and storage is more hype than solution. Joshi thus describes carbon capture promoters as doctors selling cigarettes to patients or firefighters fighting fire with flamethrowers. As he says, "When a solution relies on the continued worsening of a problem, it stops being a solution and becomes the problem."[11] While CCS appears to be a climate innovation, he argues that it is actually *fueling* climate catastrophe—"it causes the problem it fails to solve."

And yet this kind of innovation needs hype: get "green" credentials appealing to ESG (Environment, Social, and Governance) criteria by marketing the next best thing and then use financing from annual global climate meetings or progressive governments to pump up climate-destructive businesses. Even if we assume the promoters of carbon capture are genuinely well intentioned, the technology translates into a barely noticeable reduction in greenhouse gas emissions and is immediately overwhelmed by expanding fossil fuel production. If carbon capture is capturing anything, it's the subsidies and the "green" financing they receive, financing that could be used to help whole nations adapt to inevitable climate crises. Its promoters have also benefited from the "conflict profits" from Russia's ongoing invasion of Ukraine, which has inflated oil and gas prices and opened up new oil and gas projects like those mushrooming along the already fragile U.S. Gulf Coast, and which together far exceed what Russia was ever providing.[12] Meanwhile, amid the inflation and energy crisis, oil and gas companies scored a record $134 billion in excess profit from the fallout of the energy shortages that followed the breakout of war.[13] Joshi further adds: "[Carbon capture and storage] serves its function before it ever needs to actually exist. The promise of its future presence is the core service, not the seizure of carbon dioxide. Just a drop. That's all you need."[14]

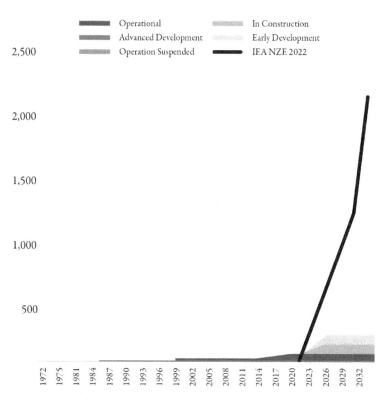

A comparison of carbon capture and storage (CCS) projects and the assumptions by the International Energy Agency of CCS that would be available by 2030, measured in megatonnes of carbon dioxide (each metric megatonne is 1.1 million tons). IEA NZE 2022 refers to the International Energy Agency's Net-Zero Emissions roadmap from 2022. Note that the only CCS that is in operation represents the darkest line close to 0. *Source: Adapted from K. Joshi, "The Technical Hitch," in* The Climate Book: The Facts and the Solutions, *ed. G. Thunberg (New York: Penguin Random House, 2022); K. Joshi,"CCS Causes the Problem It Fails to Solve," Nov. 15, 2022, ketanjoshi.co/2022/11/15 /ccs-causes-the-problem-it-fails-to-solve.*

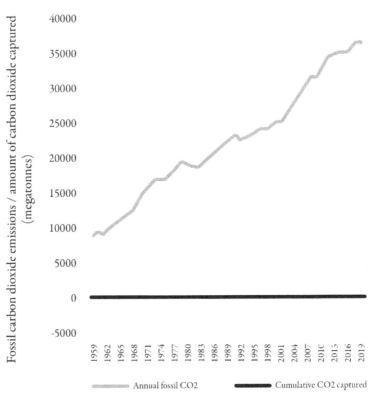

The amount of CO_2 that has been successfully captured versus the amount of CO_2 that has been released. Note that the straight line depicting cumulative CO_2 captured is in the same place as in the darkest line in the previous figure; it's just very hard to see any discernible difference because the difference is so small. *Source: Chart by Ketan Joshi, based on J. Morris, "Electric Vehicles Are Not Zero Emissions—But They Are Much Greener than Fossil Fuel and Hydrogen,"* Forbes, *Oct. 23, 2021, www.forbes.com/sites /jamesmorris/2021/10/23/electric-vehicles-are-not-zero-emissionsbut-they-are-much -greener-than-fossil-fuel-and-hydrogen.*

Innovation is also about developing new technologies that supposedly help us break free from oil, but turn out to be public relations spins by fossil fuel producers. Let's return to the Saudi desert. In addition to The Line, another city in the Neom mega-plex is being built. This city, Oxagon, is "a new paradigm where people, industries and technology come together in harmony with nature." [15] Like the 3D-printed superyacht *Pegasus*, described in Chapter 1, part of that "harmony with nature" is that it is powered by "green" hydrogen, with Oxagon itself a hub of "green" hydrogen production.[16] Hydrogen as an energy source is produced by using electricity to split water into its components, hydrogen and oxygen. But not all hydrogen is created equal—there is a full rainbow spectrum of hydrogen types. There are "green" varieties produced through the electrolysis of water using renewable energy rather than fossil fuels; there are "blue" varieties that are made with fossil fuels, but the CO_2 that is released is then captured and stored; and there is a "gray" variety that depends on fossil-fuel based natural gas. What is left out here is that an enormous amount of energy is required to produce hydrogen in the first place, and this is often created through carbon-emitting energy sources like oil, gas and coal! One study finds that greenhouse gas emissions from the production of certain types of "renewable" hydrogen are more than 20 percent greater than simply burning natural gas or coal, especially when CCS is deployed. [17] Joshi thus calls "blue" hydrogen by its more appropriate name, "fossil hydrogen." [18] And when renewable energy infrastructure is built to make green hydrogen, like the Saudis have promised to do, there are also significant carbon emissions involved in manufacturing and maintaining it. Calling green and blue hydrogen environmentally friendly is like calling a burger vegan because you added some tofu to the beef in the patty.

Speaking of burgers, it's not just CCS and hydrogen. The biotech sector is now hyping lab meat replacements and gene-editing technologies to increase rates of photosynthesis in food crops that both sequester carbon and produce greater yields. These are yet more examples of innovations that are powered by the very problems they seek to address.[19] Increasing the photosynthesis of plants through genetic modification, for instance, also increases demands for nitrogen fertilizers to sustain growth—leading to more greenhouse gas emissions.[20] Lab meat replacements seem to discourage a resource-intensive industrial livestock industry, but they are highly energy intensive, heavily dependent on plastic bioreactor containers for production, and, as Max Ajl and Rob Wallace argue, contain "an unlabeled witch's brew of glucose, amino acids, vitamins, and minerals from industrial monocrop inputs . . . serving as the next dumping ground for many of the very inputs industrial meat now absorbs."[21] All of this feels a lot like the pages from the script of Altucher and Sease's "back door" strategy for investing in the apocalypse. When a few crumbs of hope can jack up the hype, all the effort (and the dollars that back it up) can be redirected through the "front door," or business as usual.

As we've seen, what innovation most often looks like is quick-fix technology funded by venture capital and pushy shareholders whose main goal is to get rich. This is all about making green values perfectly compatible with profit-making: a win-win! The question becomes: can we develop a machine that sucks out carbon from the atmosphere and make the value of that carbon comparable to that of, say, caviar or luxury shoes? Only then can ecological relationships be traded off like any other good or service and aligned to markets and financial speculation. What matters is the creation of new markets, not whether ecological problems are addressed or not. And with each of these so-called solutions, ecological collapse gathers steam. It's pretty much lose-lose.

Convivial Technology

Innovation itself is not the problem. Innovation, properly understood, should be about devising solutions that do not generate new problems, which are well-integrated into our interdependent world.[22] It can be the outcome of dreams for mutual solidarity, care, and reciprocity. We're going to need technologies like renewable energy, low-impact construction materials, and more effective forms of recycling. These *can* be produced with close attention to their social and ecological impacts. This is what has been called "convivial technology"—where the social, ecological, and cultural dimensions of technology are prioritized when a technology's impact is assessed. Designing convivial technology is about paying attention to its impacts from inception to production, transport, actual use, and the end of its productive life.[23]

One example of convivial technology is the practice of tissue culture of matooke (plantain bananas), which make up 35 percent of all calorie uptake for Ugandans. This relatively new technique involves growing plantain bananas from parts of the plant in sterile conditions and then planting them in the field. It's a simple and relatively low-tech innovation that many farmers in the region have taken up enthusiastically and with great success since the 1990s. A study of banana tissue culture in Kenya revealed that when combined with improved crop management, household and farm incomes went up, as did household food security.[24] Key to tissue culture technology is that it does not narrow the variety of the crop base and it promotes stability of the crop yield, in contrast to technologies that focus only on the expansion of a single crop—a monoculture plastered across the landscape that often leads to more problems down the road.[25] It thus has the potential to improve food security in places like Uganda, reduce multiple dimensions of poverty, enhance the quality and nutritional value of food, and encourage and proliferate biodiversity on the farm.

Compare this to the "climate-smart agriculture" advanced by the Bill and Melinda Gates Foundation, which prioritizes genetically modified monocultures for crops like matooke, as well as digital surveillance over farmer practices. The gene editing technology promoted by the Gates targets a single high-yielding variety, which ultimately becomes susceptible to evolving pests and diseases, and destroys other life through monoculture plantations. If the Gates Foundation's version of sustainability means anything, it is to sustain the colonial enterprise of transforming traditional agricultural practices into monocultures that degrade ecosystems and ultimately the food system itself. In contrast, tissue culture promotes a kind of experimental micro-propagation that diversifies matooke cultivars, enhances food security, and improves resilience to changing weather and soil conditions. It promotes genetic diversity rather than undermining it. Like other agroecological solutions described in Chapter 2, tissue culture joins intercropping, agroforestry techniques, and crop rotation as techniques that farmers have practiced for generations in providing thriving food cultures.[26]

Technological innovation and being ecological do not have to be opposed to each other. We need innovation—a kind of innovation that focuses on needs, not profit. Technology can be designed in a way that keeps in mind its impacts at different geographic and temporal scales. It can also be accessible, adaptable, and appropriate for the task at hand or for specific needs. Finally, and perhaps most importantly, what makes technology convivial is the democratic capacity for people to decide if they even want or need it in the first place.

Society needs innovation—in mass transport, affordable housing, secure and affordable energy, lifesaving drugs. For this to happen, we need public investment, not private-sector-led or public-private partnerships often rebranded as "blended finance" and disguised as being for the people. The aim is serving social needs, not novel technologies that can generate more profit by optimizing fossil fuel use or forcing people to purchase new technologies through planned obsolescence.[27] Innovation does not need to be hyped for new markets.

5

EFFICIENCY

"We'll go down in history as the first society that wouldn't save itself because it wasn't cost-effective."
—Kurt Vonnegut

Many projects that claim sustainability justify themselves by saying they are more efficient. India's Barefoot Resorts is a good example. Attracting high-profile guests like actress Kate Winslet, Barefoot opened up a resort in 2009 barely five hundred meters from the Indigenous territory of the Jarawa on the Andaman Islands in the Bay of Bengal.[1] Despite legislation to protect the Jarawa, who remain largely uncontacted and extremely vulnerable to the introduction of diseases by outsiders, Barefoot advertised proximity to the Jarawa reserve as an authentic Andaman Islands experience. Yet to woo ecologically minded customers, Barefoot also focuses on how minimally lit its resorts are, how it harvests rainwater, and how it replaces concrete with gravel and stone for its walkways between huts. While these things are certainly better than not doing them, how Barefoot puts Indigenous people at risk is the elephant in the room, while it hides itself behind all things green and sustainable. Do we really need an efficient luxury resort if it means that the likes of Kate Winslet will fly across the world to go there and if it threatens to destroy the culture of an uncontacted people who have been protecting the land for centuries? Wouldn't it be more efficient . . . not to have the resort at all?

Efficiency is about how effectively resources are used. Depending on the context, this can be a good thing. But, like the Barefoot Resorts, we often assume that efficiency is good in itself: a low-flow showerhead uses less water, a hybrid car uses less gasoline, LED lightbulbs save electricity, a heat pump reduces energy bills for heating and cooling. Making one aspect of product design efficient might reduce the amount of resources it immediately needs. But, paradoxically, it could also increase how much is used in the long run. For instance, windows with low-emissivity glass are thermally more efficient, but also reduce natural light, making rooms darker and leading residents to turn their lights on more often—and so use more energy.[2] This chapter's argument is simple, but has big implications: efficiency isn't inherently good. In fact, sometimes it can even make things worse.

Let Nothing Be Underutilized!

Efficiency is important when the overall aim is to reduce material and energy consumption. But if efficiency just creates new products on the market to consume, then it is bad news. As researcher Sam Bliss explains, the notion that efficiency automatically reduces environmental damage is just plain wrong.[3] The problem is that efficiency not only makes production and consumption cheaper but also gives the product that is becoming more efficient more value. Let us explain, with teakettles.

Bliss uses the example of a hypothetical copper teakettle factory that perfects a technology to make manufacturing kettles more efficient. It can now produce one more kettle with less raw copper. This means either that more kettles can be produced with the same amount of copper or that the same number of kettles can be produced with less copper. As more kettle-producing companies start using the same technology, kettle production gets cheaper, since the companies can afford to lower their prices to attract more customers. As kettles get cheaper, more people buy them. As more people buy the kettles, one of two things might happen: either copper mining becomes more profitable because the demand for copper kettles has increased *or* copper becomes cheaper and thus more profitable for use in other commodities—including photovoltaic panels that collect, store, and distribute solar energy for "green" living. What is key here is that efficiency creates new value for cheap copper. This in turn results in the *increased* use of copper. While this might extend some low-paid and often unregulated work for a bit longer (branded as jobs for a "green" economy), you've also just increased the material footprint of the economy.[4]

Why is this? The answer is that any improvement to efficiency in a growing economy gets harnessed toward more growth. The problem that efficiency gains may increase total output is called the Jevons paradox. English economist William Stanley Jevons noted in 1865 that every improvement to the steam engine was making coal cheaper, leading to the increased use of coal. Nothing sits idle in a growing economy; it's always reinvested in growth.[5] To use a favorite word of the World Bank, nothing should be left "underutilized."[6]

We are impelled to use every bit of money, every square inch of space, and every second of our waking life producing goods and services, and those efficiency gains will supposedly save the planet. Think of your house. Why keep a room empty when you can rent it out? It doesn't matter if "sharing" your house for short-term vacation rentals ends up inflating real-estate values in your neighborhood and affecting people who can't afford to have their rents rise. The increasing rate of economic production through technology creates a greater throughput, or turnover of resource extraction, energy use, and waste production. Even as everything is supposedly getting more efficient, Earth is being forced into an ever faster metabolism.

And while there is an obsession with optimizing time, space, and money in the name of efficiency, so much of what is produced and then subsequently wasted is grotesquely inefficient. For instance, despite frequently advocating for optimizing energy and fertilizer inputs to maximize food production with minimal cost through so-called climate-smart agriculture, industrial agriculture is anything but efficient. The amount of food waste produced is startling and completely tolerated within supposedly "efficient" intensive food production systems. Annually, 2.5 billion tons of food, or over one-third of all food produced, is lost or wasted in the production process or as expired surplus on supermarket shelves in wealthy enclaves and regions of the world, even as, in 2023, more than thirty million children under five years old suffered from acute malnutrition.[7]

If we want to stop ecological destruction, rampant waste generation, and ensure everyone is well nourished, we have to redistribute the surplus savings and then slow down, and rewire, production, not ramp it back up again. Reducing the amount of copper in kettle production *requires stopping more copper production* if efficiency is to translate into sustainability, as it is touted as doing. As Bliss reminds us, we've done this before with things like mercury, ozone-depleting chlorofluorocarbons (CFCs), and asbestos. We've actually limited them.

The endless compulsion toward efficiency and optimization also affects us on a more personal level. There's a myth that efficiency will save us time to do all the things we love to do. Why waste time walking to the corner store to get a toothbrush when you can order it online or on an app and have it delivered? You can now use that efficiency gain to get to work earlier. The efficiency gains from having your boss on Whatsapp or Telegram means you can send that reply while sitting on the toilet. That's an efficiency gain! The efficiency gains from these innovations reinvest the time savings made from the innovation into new opportunities for productive work. This is what philosopher Hartmut Rosa calls social acceleration.[8] Does it sometimes feel to you like time is speeding up, and you end up having little time left to do the things you actually want to do? That's because greater efficiency ends up generating more work. It's like running on a treadmill that keeps speeding up, testing your stamina until you break. Is it any wonder everyone is so burned out all the time? And all of this ultimately results in enhanced overall material and energy use.

Efficiency Gains in a World of Competition

Efficiency is so dominant in the narrative that we quickly reach for it as the solution to some of our biggest problems. The role of agriculture in crossing planetary boundaries is undisputed: around the world, intensive industrial agriculture, especially factory farming, is one of the key drivers of greenhouse emissions, biodiversity loss, soil erosion, and excess nitrogen in our waterways and oceans. To solve this, green modernists propose "land sparing"—the idea that land can be saved from development and preserved for nature conservation by intensifying agricultural production elsewhere. This is also called sustainable intensification. It includes a range of proposals with names like "climate-smart agriculture," "precision agriculture," and "vertical farming."[9] Though it may sound quite technical, the debate over land sparing has important repercussions globally, and clearly illustrates the fallacy of thinking that efficiency is inherently good.

At first sight, the reasoning behind proposals like these appears sound. We need more food. Nature isn't doing well. We have the technology to make agriculture a lot more efficient and productive. So if we intensify land use over here, then we can set aside land for nature over there. Without a doubt, the global transformation of land around the world for grazing livestock and crops to feed them is causing enormous ecological harm. But this cannot be solved by making farming more efficient. Food systems scientist Adam Calo provides a useful example to think with. Say a big agribusiness, like Bayer, develops a new breeding program that makes cattle more efficient by fattening them without increasing the amount of land needed.[10] Like copper, the cattle become cheaper per acre because there is more production of their meat per unit of expenditure that went into the process. In a society driven by profit, a farmer is encouraged to increase the number of acres for more cattle. Neighbors then see these benefits and buy into the same breeding program, clearing more forest in the process to allow their cattle to graze. As a result, producing beef becomes more efficient than before, but at the expense of the landscape. Calo writes:

> Efficiency gains in a world of competition fall off quickly, placing farmers on a treadmill of production where the next move is to degrade more land to receive the same profits, or to seek another efficiency package—starting the process over again.[11]

Green modernists often assume that efficiency gains in agriculture automatically result in land sparing, but research quite clearly shows that the opposite is true. For example, one study looked at the effects of improving efficiency in food production in 122 countries in the tropics and quite conclusively found that greater yield led to deforestation and expansion of agriculture in most regions, not less. As Adam Calo stresses, "Increasing agricultural yield in no way guarantees the conservation of some land elsewhere."[12]

What is the alternative, then? If efficiency in agriculture doesn't mean less land is used for agriculture, what should we be doing? In a study published in *Frontiers in Sustainable Food Systems*, Calo and his co-authors show how farmers who try to practice sustainable agriculture can't get a foothold in the market because powerful landlords largely control it—from owning the land to using farmland as a speculative investment. For example, in Canada, the last half century has seen land ownership become concentrated among a few corporations, and independent farmers, who face increasingly tight profit margins and debt, start "tilling native grasslands, filling in wetlands, and deforesting their land."[13] In other words, it would be far more impactful to change land ownership structures to benefit sustainable farmers than to tinker at improving the efficiency of an already ecologically disastrous cash-crop-oriented farming system. Indeed, small family farmers around the world, led by La Via Campesina, have been calling for land *reform* for decades, arguing that highly unequal land ownership is the primary barrier to farmers when it comes to practicing more sustainable agriculture.[14]

The supposed link between further intensifying production and then saving land for nature is based on an ignorance of real-world problems facing farmers, which have a lot more to do with who has access to land, who doesn't, and what the historical drivers of land and soil degradation are. As Calo says, "When some agriculture produces more yield per hectare, what is the rationale that connects more calories made to less land cleared? There is no good answer to this question unless you believe in an oversimplified microeconomic version of the food system where food is produced in perfect lock step for demands of human consumption."[15] Actually, food is produced in lockstep with profit; if food were produced in lockstep with human needs, we wouldn't have starving babies, and we would probably not have $25 smoothies, or any overpriced health and wellness food stores at all for that matter.

Integrated, Not Separated

This brings us to another important issue, which is that notions like "land sparing" falsely conceive of nature as existing separately from the economy. Effectively blending the ideology of purity with that of efficiency, agriculture is seen as most efficient when farming is done as intensively as possible outside of an untouched nature.[16] There are many problems with this approach, not least its roots in colonial-era thinking where colonized lands were imagined as both a vast, pristine wilderness to be protected and empty space to clear for vast monocultural plantations of sugar, cotton, and other cash crops.[17] As we stressed in Chapter 2, this "humans here, nature there" mentality has helped to sever humanity's living, intertwined relationship with the planet.[18]

What would be the alternative to the obsession with efficiency and the "humans here, nature there" approach? First, research shows that protecting both biodiversity and food production is best accomplished when nature and agriculture are *integrated*, not separated. This involves stopping the use of pesticides and instead using organic fertilizers, establishing biodiversity corridors between farmlands, intercropping, using lighter machinery to protect against soil erosion, and many other techniques that fit under the rubric of agroecology.[19] These techniques must be implemented outside of monoculture industrial production, not added to it.

Second, there is an alternative to protecting nature by walling it off—which isn't just more efficient, but also avoids playing in to corporate greenwashing. For example, directly inspired by E. O. Wilson's "Half Earth" proposal, the conservation industry through the UN's 2022 Global Biodiversity Framework has been demanding an annual allocation of $140 billion to turn 30 percent of the earth's surface into protected areas. The result would mean displacing upward of 300 million people from the land, with untold ecological and social consequences. Two of the largest environmental NGOs that are leading this charge, the World Wildlife Fund for Nature (WWF) and the World Conservation Society (WCS), either are being funded or have direct professional links to a nexus of some of the world's biggest polluters and extractive industries, including British Airways, GM, Nestlé, DeBeers, and Coca-Cola—helping these companies greenwash their images. And yet the human rights organization Survival International has found that giving land autonomy and cultural sovereignty to Indigenous people through full territorial rights would carry a one-shot cost of $3 billion—which would go much further in stopping species going extinct and protecting biodiversity.[21] Now *that's* efficient.

Sufficiency

Efficiency by itself should never be the goal. By looking at a problem only through a technical lens—how to increase productivity to "feed the world"—the efficiency ideology elides the historical and political roots of the problem, such as who has access to the land. If we were to begin opening that box, however, we would have to begin asking some difficult questions, like about the role of unequal land ownership in driving inequality the world over—from Venice Beach to the Andaman Islands in the Bay of Bengal. It's more of the same: the sustainability class is unable to step outside their class perspective, and therefore can only come up with solutions that don't challenge their own secure class position.

Now, once again, don't get us wrong. Efficiency isn't an absurd idea in itself. Why would you stop in Seattle when you were planning on going from Denver to Phoenix? Why would you want your potatoes grown in the Netherlands only to then have them transported to Argentina to be packaged and then sold at a retailer in the United Kingdom, with the leftover packaging then sent to Malaysia as waste? Efficiency can make life simpler. But there is a difference between efficiency and *sufficiency*. The first focuses only on a certain context. Anything can be efficient if you look at it in isolation from everything else. You can have efficient private jets, efficient casinos, efficient cruise ships, efficient golf courses, efficient indoor ski resorts in the desert, efficient gold mines, efficient crypto mining, efficient yachts, efficient tax havens, efficient ethnic cleansing. You can even have "greener," cleaner, more efficient killing forces—witness the U.S. military's plans to slash its emissions by half by 2030 through electrifying its vehicles, or the Israeli Defense Forces offering its soldiers vegan meals and leather-free boots.[22] These contradictions lead us to ask: what do we really want, how much is enough, and where do we draw the line? Strangely, in the middle of ecological breakdown threatening the very basis of human life to thrive on this planet, the production of superyachts, the development of more waterfront properties or luxury ecotourism resorts, and billions of dollars in military aid are just not up for public debate. Without sufficiency, efficiency is used to justify completely irrational, unjust, and utterly catastrophic decisions.

Ultimately, efficiency improvements in cars, trains, heating, agriculture, and energy use are all important if we're going to have even a glimmer of a chance at avoiding more than 1.5°C of warming, but this must be accompanied by overall reductions in material and energy use, especially in wealthy nations in Western Europe, North America, and Oceania. Sure, electric vehicles are more efficient than conventional oil-guzzling cars—but their benefit applies only if the overall use of personal cars drops. When efficient vehicles are accompanied by urban re-planning for mass public transport that serves people's mobility needs first and not the speculative dreams of property developers or the automobile lobby, we might be getting somewhere.

6

THE PIE IN THE SKY

The PIE is held up by No-Impact Man standing on a planet he treats as a Jenga tower of equivalent and replaceable units of monetary value. So what makes the PIE appear weightless, yet able to nourish No-Impact Man's vision of sustainability?

If the upper middle classes are more likely to be "green" because they've followed the Kuznets curve, dematerialized, and successfully decoupled economic growth from environmental impact, it's the unsexy lower classes and unlucrative nature (where elephants, lions, or pandas don't live) that are charged with carrying the burden of all that supposedly no-impact sustainable living. These others, be they human, plant, or animal, prop up the sustainability class. They are the blocks that allow No-Impact Man to climb ever higher.

Cost-shifting Successes

In economics, the heavy burden carried by everyone and everything but the wealthy is called an "externality." It's a harmless enough word: whatever we have dumped is now external to the market, out there somewhere. In outer space, in the sky. But we know by now that there is no outside: wherever you dump a slag heap, there are people living, there are vital ecosystems. In his ahead-of-its-time book *The Social Costs of Private Enterprise*, published in 1950, the economist Karl William Kapp came up with another word for an externality: a cost-shifting success.[1] A cost-shifting success is when the costs of producing something are successfully shifted to other people and places, while the company that makes it keeps the profits.[2] Cost shifting is when it's easier to dump toxic waste into a river, making people—often Black and Brown—pay downstream, in another jurisdiction or country. On a planetary scale, cost shifting happens when whole regions are turned into sacrifice zones for polluting industries, when a company sells products that contain "forever chemicals" that poison our bodies and groundwater, or when oil companies see massive profits even as society and Earth's life support systems pay for climate change caused by the burning of fossil fuels.[3] It's called a cost-shifting success because so-called externalities cannot meaningfully be internalized. The poor have little power in a market-based economy because they don't have money that they could use to, say, lobby politicians, become shareholders, or pay for lawyers. So while polluters cash in, the poor pay with their lives, their health, their homeland.[4]

Cost-shifting successes can be painted green. A new 1 million-square-foot "sustainable" headquarters for France's largest bank, BNP Paribas Fortis, in Brussels has been adorned with a massive green roof and innumerable photovoltaic panels as well as four Olympic-sized swimming pools' worth of stored water to warm the building in winter.[5] But not only has this bank been one of the world's major investors in the deforestation of the Brazilian Amazon for €5 billion soy and palm oil deals with major agribusinesses (chiefly Cargill), but its "green" makeover of its headquarters demands specialized mineral extraction for rare earths like neodymium, tellurium and gallium as well as lithium, copper, and nickel. Mysteriously, the labor conditions that directly result in the construction of this so-called green building are not considered in the advertising material. This includes the labor of (especially migrant) workers in Belgium as well as the labor of the supply chains well beyond Europe's borders that are required to extract raw materials, process them, manufacture them, transport them, and assemble them.

Uneven Trade

None of this is new, even if it has been recast with "green" whistles and bells. Since Columbus set sail for the "New World" in 1492, European powers started a process of slavery and Indigenous genocide on a global scale unprecedented in human history. The transatlantic slave trade involved the exportation of labor to power the economies of the countries where they were forced, on pain of death, to work.[6] Insatiable European appetites needed cheap (dark-skinned) hands and vast plantations designed by the same logic that underlies the PIE to provide the raw materials for subsequent stages of industrialization.[7] Nothing, not even humiliating peanuts for wages, has ever been paid back in return for this stolen labor value.

Today, labor and nature continue to be stolen systematically. One study calculated that 25 percent of total consumption in the United States, Canada, and Western Europe is provided *for free* from countries in Africa, Latin America, and Asia. By free, the authors mean that it is not compensated in terms of equivalent trade. In the year 2015 alone, wealthy countries in Europe and North America grabbed 13.2 billion tons of raw materials, over 2 billion acres of land, 3.4 billion barrels of oil, and 392 billion hours of work (or 188 million person-years of labor) from Latin America, Asia, and Africa. The scale of resources and hours grabbed continues year after year and is growing over time.[8] This is so great that traditional development aid is absolutely meaningless; for every $1 richer countries give to poorer ones, they receive $80 in return, while for every $1 that poor countries receive, they lose $30 in land, labor, and resources.[9] Either this can be understood as downright theft or it can be understood as a conscious gift to Western Europe and North America. But when Elon Musk states—in referring to the lithium needed for "green" electric vehicles from countries like Bolivia—"We can coup whoever we want! Deal with it," we know we're not talking about gifts.[10]

And the labor stolen isn't just between rich and less-rich countries. It happens even within the population of a single country. In the United States, $47 trillion was obtained from 90 percent of the population of working people between 1980 and 2018 and channeled to the top 10 percent.[11] If that $47 trillion were distributed equally to the whole population, every American would get $140,000 extra in their bank account. This is money obtained, or rather stolen, from all of our work hours. If this money wasn't being used to build someone's fifth (LEED-certified) mansion, we might be able to imagine future generations living on this planet.

Economists call the unequal distribution of labor and resources "uneven trade." Uneven trade is a kickback from the colonial empires of the nineteenth and twentieth centuries—except now the United States, Canada, Australia, Japan, New Zealand, Israel, and Singapore are in on it, too—as well as a handful of elites in every other country. China is rapidly emerging as an alternative creditor with its Belt and Road Initiative, deploying the same perverse and exploitative tactics, but with notably less overt military interventionism.

What is perhaps most striking is the way labor is treated. Why, for instance, should labor in Canada, the United States, Australia, or Western Europe receive higher wages than the same labor carried out in Mexico, Nigeria, Sri Lanka, Indonesia, Vietnam, or Peru? Manual labor, processing, engineering, transport, and logistics tend to characterize labor demands in these countries, while end-of-chain labor (e.g., design, advertising, retail, delivery) often falls to the richer countries.[12] In both cases, labor productivity is generally the same, so why the wage disparity between these regions? You might point to the cost of living, but this doesn't come out of a vacuum. How, for instance, has a happy, warm-and-fuzzy (through indoor heating, not because of climate), and eco-friendly—yet expensive—life in places like Vienna, Zurich, Seattle, Osaka, Toronto, or Copenhagen been the *deliberate* outcome of resource and labor exploitation elsewhere?

The implications of this question are crucial to understanding ecological breakdown. Unfair labor arrangements mean that workers across Asia, Africa, and Latin America see highly precarious work without adequate safety or environmental standards. They also mean that workers in Europe and North America see their jobs moved overseas, their communities abandoned, and their sense of meaning and purpose lost. The only ones who gain from all of this are the transnational creative professional and managerial service sector workers in cities (many of whom belong to the sustainability class) across the world, who may not recognize how their high wages come at the expense of manufacturing workers or cheapened laborers in the darker-skinned nations of the world.[13] Rather than writing statements about diversity, equity, and inclusion, it would make better sense to build an international anti-racist coalition that supports *all* workers.

The stolen goods and life energies also extend to carbon emissions. For example, more than half of all emissions in the year 2004 indirectly supported investments in Western Europe, the United States, and Canada. Western Europe required an import of 72 percent more emissions than what is emitted within Western Europe itself, while the Middle East exported 58 percent of emissions for consumption in other regions (namely, Europe and North America).[14] Overall, the economic investments in richer regions are underwritten by emissions in poorer places, with China's emissions being central to maintain living standards in the West.

Ecological Debt

So, while many ex-colonies are in endless debt to their financial creditors in North America and Europe, these same ex-colonies are also burdened with the responsibility of dealing with climate change and ecological collapse as well as being most vulnerable to its impacts. This "ecological debt" caused by the emissions from manufacturing, raw material production, and industrial agriculture, which accrues largely to consumers in the richer countries, is not being paid—it's hardly even being recognized.

Many emerging wealthy nations impose their way into poorer regions and grab resources—adopting the same forms of resource imperialism that the United States carries out in Latin America and other parts of the world, and not dissimilar to the playbook of the European colonizers' "scramble for Africa." For instance, the United Arab Emirates, one of the world's richest petrostates, has recently acquired nearly 20 percent of Zimbabwe's land surface as reserve land for carbon credits that companies can purchase to offset their climate-breakdown-inducing activities. The Dubai-based company Blue Carbon acquired forest land across five African countries totaling nearly the landmass of the United Kingdom for carbon offsets that continue to allow climate criminals to burn more fossil fuels.[15] This gross public relations exercise by countries and investors largely responsible for planetary climate collapse has led to skyrocketing land values for forested regions across the continent, all while displacing and evicting the very communities who know best how to steward their forests. The displacement of communities across the continent, in turn, contributes to conditions leading to periurban informal settlements and precarious migration across the Mediterranean and the U.S.-Mexico border. This also leads to rising xenophobia and labor exploitation in the wealthier nations, whose so-called solutions don't get us out of ecological collapse but just dig us into deeper holes.

Ecological drain doesn't just occur between countries. Sometimes it travels around the world only to manifest in the same city it started in. For instance, the gated enclave of Talatona in Luanda, Angola, looks like a replica of an upscale Houston suburb, complete with backyard swimming pools, lawns, and cul-de-sacs housing American oil executives and their families.[16] All of this is smack dab in the middle of the open sewers and tin-roofed shantytowns in a country that consistently scores among the very lowest on the Human Development Index. Recalling the Kuznets curve and the fact that "green" living isn't too far removed from investments in fossil fuels, it's also not too great a stretch to imagine a Talatona family deciding to purchase an electric car or hybrid SUV to combat the guilt and anxiety every time they travel from their enclave home to the airport and back.

As we explored in these last chapters, when the consumption of the urban professional and managerial workers is taken into account, the cloth-bag-toting, vegan, wellness-oriented urbanite might be considered among the most highly polluting individuals on the planet—though perhaps unknowingly. It is also no coincidence that the sustainability class tends to be concentrated in high-income nations in North America, Western Europe, Scandinavia, and Australia. Consumption and lifestyles in these regions are sustained by unpaid or uncompensated appropriation of land and labor in Latin America, Africa, and southern and Southeast Asia. These are terms of trade that are extensions of the plunder from colonial empires.

The point is that the "no impact" Breatharian sustainability vibes—with hanging plants, fair-trade lattes, and neon-pink non sequiturs under the LED track lights inside hotel lobbies, airport terminals, or cafés in Los Angeles and so many other places—wouldn't have a leg to stand on if it wasn't for all the appropriated life energy from the rest of the world. As we've argued, without oil and gas, none of it would hold up, either.

Imagine if all that land, energy, material, and labor could be redirected to meet the needs of the people who need them—instead of going toward speculative real estate investments baked into deeply unequal and unfair international trade agreements. The 2 billion acres of stolen land mentioned above (a total area twice the size of India), for instance, could be used to provide varied and nutritious food grown with ecological sensitivity to the needs of the land for up to 6 billion people, grown with ecological sensitivity to the needs of the land.[17]

Making the Material Political

The sustainability class of green modernists, jet-setting participants in climate conferences, and professional classes buying property in eco-friendly neighborhoods is not taking us anywhere . . .
except off a cliff. Ecological breakdown and worker exploitation
go hand in hand. It harms everyone—steelworkers in West Vir-
ginia, undocumented Guatemalan farm workers in the United
States and Canada, Congolese and Nigerian child laborers who
mine coltan for Wi-Fi-enabled stovetops or make a living refur-
bishing electronic e-waste dumped in their backyards.

Some of the world's most polluting industries have even admitted that they are gaslighting the public with their "sustainable
this" and "sustainable that" solutions. At a U.S. congressional
hearing in 2022, leaked emails and memos were revealed showing how ExxonMobil, Chevron, Shell, and BP have all cleverly deceived the public about their commitments to addressing climate
change, even as Shell and ExxonMobil reported record quarterly
profits in 2022.[18] At the same time, they are mocking climate activists, with one Shell communications representative emailing in
2019 that he wished "bedbugs" on the youth-led Sunrise Movement. In response, Sunrise activist Varshini Prakash stated: "First
they ignore you, then they laugh at you, then they wish bedbugs
on you, then you win." [19]

We have the power to not be continuously deceived by climate
criminals condemning billions of people to a deadly future. To do
so, we need to do the opposite of what the sustainability class has
been doing: recognize that we live somewhere (instead of nowhere)
and that our lives have impacts—which eco-friendly consumption
choices and branding do absolutely nothing to address. We can't
ignore social metabolism, hoping it will go away. The key is to
make the material political. What does it mean to make something
political? It means making it something to work on, together, as a

society. Just as we can play down material reality by making it an individual problem, a problem of lifestyle, of what you buy, we can also make it our everyday social and political reality.

Climate Reparations

Let's look at one major strategy for making the material political: climate reparations. For at least a decade, social movements and governments in the Global South have been pushing for the West to redress historical harm caused by the pollution they are largely responsible for.[20] For example, at the 2010 World People's Conference on Climate Change and the Rights of Mother Earth, in Cochabamba, Bolivia, over 35,000 people from 140 countries, comprising Indigenous peoples, labor unions, and social movements for climate justice, agrarian reform, and women's rights, gathered to draw up a declaration that asserted the need for repaying climate debt: "Developed countries, as the main cause of climate change, in assuming their historical responsibility, must recognize and honor their climate debt in all of its dimensions as the basis for a just, effective, and scientific solution to climate change."[21]

Reparations are direct transfers of resources that can repair historical and ongoing damage to people whose ways of knowing about the world have been erased. In this way, they are an attempt to repair relationships marred by centuries of harm. They seek to restore the "freedom dreams" of people whose pasts have been marred by colonial pillaging and whose futures are being compromised by financial speculation dependent on cheap Black and Brown labor.[22] It's key that these reparations, as philosopher Olúfẹ́mi Táíwò notes, "make tangible differences in the material conditions of people's lives"—including through secure housing, accessible food, and drinkable water.[23]

Yet it's not enough to frame reparations as being about a better distribution of resources; it is also about correcting past atrocities and the ways these continue into the present and future. It is about acknowledging, and redressing, abusive behavior and gaslighting. This means not only transferring resources but also, and perhaps more fundamentally, ceding power and staying silent (for a change) by giving no-strings-attached decision-making power and autonomy to those who have been and continue to be robbed of their territories and their own bodies (as enslaved, indentured, and exploited workers), and who are subjected to climate change's impacts (like sea level rise)—which they did not cause. But very concretely, it means preventing people like Bill Gates and other land investors from interfering in decisions that affect historically disadvantaged groups, so that these groups can make decisions over their own lives on their own land, rather than listening to a (too often, white) savior from outside telling them how to best run things. As Táíwò states: "A refusal to take reparative steps when one has injured another can signal that the injured party morally deserved their injury or need not be regarded as a moral equal."[24] Reparations are particularly important for Indigenous people, whose autonomous land-use practices not only have a record of being more compatible with stewardship and sustenance, but who have also been subject to some of the most extreme kinds of violence, condescension, and patronization.

In October 2022, in response to a UN Human Rights Council draft resolution asking former colonial and slave-trading nations to pay reparations proportional to harms committed, the countries that refused included the Netherlands, Germany, the United Kingdom, France, and the United States.[25] The United Kingdom, for instance, rejected the notion of reparations, stating that the slave trade and colonialism "were not, at the time, violations of international law" and argued that reparations were diverting "focus away from the pressing challenges of tackling contemporary racism and global inequality."[26] By refusing to be held accountable and then gaslighting the world, these nations are implying that those who suffered and continue to suffer from colonialism deserved it. But "implying" is perhaps too light a word; the reality is they are conveying something like a thinly veiled contempt. Past attempts to implement reparations, for instance, have been thoroughly and heinously co-opted, such as when in 1833, British slave owners were handsomely compensated for giving up their rights to human property as part of agreements to abolish slavery.[27]

A so-called loss and damage fund was agreed upon by world governments at the 2022 climate conference in Sharm-el-Sheikh, Egypt. A year later, in time for the next climate conference in Dubai, a special UN committee proposed the World Bank as interim trustee and host of the fund. At Dubai, countries' pledges for the fund totaled only $700 million, which covers less than 0.2 percent of what one NGO estimated was needed *per year*.

Hosting the fund at an institute notorious for funneling wealth to wealthy Northern creditors and corporate interests hardly bodes well for addressing the historical legacy of exploitation that created climate crises in the first place.[28] And a fund whose purse strings are held principally by North American and Western European nations does not bode well for ceding power to poorer countries and regions that urgently need to develop without depending on richer nations. Wealthy and ex-colonial nations like Belgium, France, and the United Kingdom have yet to repair historical damage to the societies they exploited, causing unthinkable violence. Others, like the United States, do not even acknowledge, let alone attempt to repair, debt-driven foreign policies and deadly dictatorships they installed and propped up in places like Indonesia, Angola, and many parts of Latin America to keep resources flowing in their direction.[29] In this context, a "loss and damage" fund that supposedly accounts for the historical responsibility of climate breakdown and is framed as climate reparations has a much greater risk of reproducing the same patterns, especially if those who manage the funds are the perpetrators of previous and ongoing wrongdoing. Strings-attached development aid, especially from Europe and North America, but increasingly from China and India, has entrenched poverty, keeping the conditions intact for cost-shifting exploitative labor practices and degraded environments to places where most people can't afford to complain without risking imprisonment or worse.[30] Climate reparations mean climate justice to undo historical wrongs. They can't mean reproducing the same cycle of debt-driven loans, the stripping of public assets, an excuse to grab resources or find a cheap location to dump wastes.

A recent study has quantified what reparations would imply for countries that historically have been responsible for climate change. Taking as a baseline the year 1960 (a very generous baseline, given centuries of colonial pillaging) and assuming a collective goal of keeping global warming at 1.5°C, the study's authors found that places like the United Kingdom, the United States, and the European Union have exceeded their fair share of carbon emissions 2.5 times over. The authors show that if all countries were to reduce their emissions to zero by 2050, the over-emitters in the wealthy countries of Europe and North America will still overshoot by nearly three times the amount of greenhouse gases that can be safely emitted to stay within 1.5°C of warming. This would also take up half of poorer countries' emissions budgets and force them to mitigate their impacts faster. According to these authors, the climate reparations owed to countries who suffer the most from climate breakdown would amount to a total of $192 trillion by the year 2050. The over-appropriation of the carbon budget by the United States alone would require reparations of $80 trillion.[31]

Down to Earth

Other than climate reparations, there are many other examples of movements that make the material political. Smallholder farmer movements, represented by La Via Campesina, a global coalition of farmworkers that represents 200 million farmers across the world, have been calling for land reform and an accounting of the true costs of industrial agriculture. They have been joined by the global Shack Dwellers International and the Landless Workers' Movement (Movimento dos Trabalhadores Rurais sem Terra) in pushing for a recognition of and reparations for the "ecological debt" carried by the world's poor. The Indian Farmers' Movement of 2021–2022, *Kisan Andolan*, built broad-based alliances across urban and rural divides and demanded action to protect small-scale farming livelihoods, and they did this even amid a global pandemic and despite an authoritarian and increasingly undemocratic government. We could also mention here movements like the Yellow Vests in France, who in 2018 took to the streets and set up people's councils across the country in protest against a carbon tax that would ultimately have a greater impact on working-class people than on climate change.[32]

Social metabolism can be made political in many more ways. Our point is that this is very different from pretending that the material doesn't exist at all. And as we describe in the next chapter, making the material political means solidarity with the people organizing for a better kind of world—a real somewhere, not a nowhere pie in the sky. This means coming "down to earth," so to speak, to take back our future and reclaim ecological balance for everyone. We have to take our eyes off the PIE and focus on the class aspects of our ecological dilemma. It's time to delve into exactly *how* greening has become an excuse to exclude people considered not worthy enough to join an elite and enlightened club— and what can be done about it.

7

EXCLUSIVELY GREEN

Mynah birds screeched all around as I (Vijay) walked along the dirt path, past spectacular banyan trees and blazing magenta bougainvilleas. I was in the eco-utopia of Auroville, the "city that Earth needs," in the southern Indian state of Tamil Nadu. I was walking toward a house nestled in the city's "greenbelt" of forested homesteads and agricultural plots.

Upon my arrival in the outdoor bamboo kitchen, Hans, a long-time Auroville resident, offered me a homemade drink of organic lemon and passionfruit pulp mixed with water purified through reverse osmosis, as is common in Auroville. His son was squatting on the earth in the yard poking a hole into an old plastic jug, reusing it to plant some seedlings. Originally from the Netherlands, Hans and his family are happy here. They return to Europe very occasionally to visit family and friends, but do so in eco-conscious ways that require crossing over land and sea rather than flying.

As Hans spoke to me about his life in Auroville, I looked around at the lush forest, fostering the conditions for rich micro-organisms to thrive in the soil and refill the underground aquifers. Over the fifty-five years of Auroville's existence, significant emphasis has been given to the reforestation and rehabilitation of the tropical dry evergreen forests and to the conservation of the soil and water through the construction of swales, bunds, and catchment retention ponds. There are dozens of Auroville homesteads and communities that grow organic food to support the resident population. Nearly three thousand acres of land have been reforested with more than 3 million shade, fruit, and fuelwood trees. Energy to power the eco-utopia comes primarily from small-scale solar PV panels for electricity, windmills that pump groundwater, and biogas systems that process animal and vegetable compost. Residents of Auroville receive a monthly fixed "maintenance" income of nearly $220 in exchange for community service or other income-generating activities. They receive free schooling for kids until age eighteen, medical insurance (including dental), and access to groceries and meals at reduced costs. There is even a housing care facility for aging Aurovillians. The city is self-sufficient in dairy production and is able to produce nearly 50 percent of all of its vegetables and pulses.[1] Could it be a sustainable haven on Earth?

According to its 1965 mission statement, Auroville was designed to be a utopia, a "universal city where men and women of all countries are able to live in peace and progressive harmony above all creeds, all politics, and all nationalities" and "realize human unity." It was meant to be a city that belonged to no one, where private property was forbidden, and where money would have no power.

Auroville was the vision of Mirra Alfassa, a French woman and a tourist to India also known as "The Mother." Alfassa was deeply inspired by, and a close disciple and friend to, Sri Aurobindo, an Indian freedom fighter and spiritualist who was involved in the struggle against British colonization. Her close ties with Sri Aurobindo commanded her much respect and prestige among the outgoing colonists and other elites, and she commissioned French architect Roger Anger to oversee the physical development of the city she envisioned. According to Anger's design, Auroville would look like a galaxy, spirals of roads and settlements converging on its spiritual center.[2]

Auroville was eventually founded on February 28, 1968. On that day, a group of people from all over the world came together on a twenty-acre plot of land in between Tamil Nadu and

Puducherry (previously known as Pondicherry). They called it "the cradle of a new man" and estimated it would eventually be home to fifty thousand people. The children present brought soil from 124 countries and collected it into a marble urn, symbolizing unity in diversity. Today, Auroville is home to over 3,200 residents, with people from fifty-nine countries living there, just less than half of them Indian nationals.

Auroville seems like the paragon of an ecological alternative: a tiny oasis in what feels like a global desert of extraction, imposed scarcity, and a rat race of endless production. Combining humanism and ethics, environmentalism and peaceful coexistence, the utopian project could be said to be what ecology is all about. And while there are some extremely inspiring examples of alternative economies and ways of development taking shape here, there are certain aspects of this dream that are disturbing—particularly in terms of how the city was created and sustained, and more recently, co-opted. Auroville is what happens to ecological visions and projects that start out claiming to be "beyond politics."

As Puducherry historian Jessica Namakkal writes, The Mother was driven by the need for connection that she could not find in her homeland: "The Mother wanted to transform her identity as a white bourgeois French woman into that of a dedicated Eastern spiritualist, removed from the emptiness of contemporary European life."[3] To settle Auroville, thousands of local Tamils were displaced from the land and later became the laborers who performed much of the backbreaking work under the brutal sun to build and maintain the city. "Liberal ideologies of universal equality, the basis of the Aurovillian model of utopia," notes Namakkal, "depended on the exclusions of other 'non-believers' to isolate their community."[4]

What started with the search for connection and ecological living became a branded, and, in many ways, exclusive destination built on erasure of the past. For instance, the Auroville Foundation, which governs the city, was never able to fully purchase all of the land, and so Aurovillians are still negotiating with Tamils and engaged in land litigation in courts to secure the land needed to realize Anger's galaxy-shaped model. Despite the fact that Tamils have resided on the land since well before Auroville was conceived, Auroville's original (mostly European) settlers are still working to fulfill The Mother's vision of separation from locals. The Mother had urged Aurovillians to convince the Tamils to sell their lands to Auroville, that it would be better for them if they did so, and that the land would be "given back to all after their and our [spiritual] transformation."[5] These views are now also held by Indian settlers in Auroville and by those in the central government keen on creating what amounts to a Disney-fied national attraction, premised on religious intolerance and oppressing dissent.[6]

Auroville exhibits some of the same trappings of the sustainability class. As we'll see in greater detail in this chapter, exclusivity was built into its very design from inception. The failure to reckon with the exclusion of Tamil people threatens to reinforce division, with serious ecological and social consequences. For example, Hans told me about how the central governing body of Auroville was quietly being taken over by far-right Hindu nationalists of the ruling Bharatiya Janata Party (BJP), under prime minister Narendra Modi. He told me about how they want to infuse their own brand of Hindutva ideology with that of the spiritual teachings of Indian freedom fighter Sri Aurobindo. He warned of the arrival of Silicon Valley tech-obsessed green modernists and architects, some even making claims that mechanical trees can sequester carbon more efficiently than real trees can, and the desire of some of these interests to cut down Auroville's well-tended forests to fulfill The Mother's vision. The arrival of these groups in Auroville is not an accident, but baked into its design.

Auroville represents many of the pitfalls found in the sustainability class's vision. In the previous chapter, we discussed the actual environmental impacts of the sustainability class. But how does this process happen? Why, exactly, must their green dream lead to more of the same? In this chapter, we shift our gaze from the environmental impacts of the sustainability class toward its social impacts. As has happened in Auroville, we show how a desire for authenticity motivates the sustainability class, but what they desire ends up being destroyed. We focus on five themes: conviviality, branding, speculation, exclusion, and finally solidarity. It is not that we need to strive for immediate perfection—every effort toward progress is riddled with contradictions. Messily muddling through things is the only way to know what works and what doesn't. But we can't build our alternatives on apolitical purity—they need solidarity as a foundation.

Conviviality

Yes, we suffer pain, we become ill, we die. But we also hope, laugh, celebrate; we know the joy of caring for one another; often we are healed and we recover by many means. We do not have to pursue the flattening-out of human experience.
—Ivan Illich[7]

Sometimes, when we're walking in a forest, cooking together with friends, dancing, or at a protest, we might feel a certain kind of interconnectedness, where our bodies intermingle with and become animated by our surroundings. Colombian anthropologist Arturo Escobar describes this interconnectedness through the example of a mangrove forest, a continuously transforming web of living relations in which both people and nonpeople participate:

The mangrove-world is enacted minute by minute, day by day, through an infinite set of practices carried out by a multiplicity of beings and life forms, involving complex weavings of water, minerals, degrees of salinity, forms of energy (sun, tides, moon), human activity, spiritual beings, and so forth. There is a rhizome-like logic to these entanglements, very difficult to map and measure, if at all; this logic reveals an altogether different way of being and becoming in territory and place . . . things and beings are their relations; they do not exist prior to them.[8]

The environment we live in is constantly tended to by the myriad relations, both human and nonhuman, that sustain it. This tending to is an endless collaboration that knows no boundaries between human and nonhuman, nor along the lines of gender, race, or class.

Throughout history, artists, writers, poets, and musicians have painstakingly tried to articulate this interconnectedness. Sometimes they get close to the essence of it all. Sometimes—because this constantly forming interconnectivity is always out of reach: a sensation, or a feeling—it crystalizes in a shared and collective moment left beautifully unspoken. It is the sublime, if fleeting, moment of feeling connected to everything in the universe. We can call this connectedness conviviality: *living with.* Conviviality is not something that can be produced at will; it is a state of unconditional liberation in which people and non-people interact and weave a world in common. It knows no space and time constraints. It just unfolds.

The search for conviviality is what drives many of us to transform our own lives. It is also what drives much of the sustainability class. When Namakkal interviewed some of the early Aurovillians, she found that its first settlers came to the project propelled by a desire for belonging and connection and by a sense of alienation from Western life. For example, Verne, an American, was on a quest "to discover [his] soul" and "unravel the mysteries of life" and had come to Auroville after receiving a postcard from an American woman there that said, "This is the place I've been searching for my entire life." [9]

This is the same kind of desire that led young hippies to move to the famous Venice Canals neighborhood in Los Angeles. Sociologist Andrew Deener quotes Gina, who moved to the Canals from the San Bernardino Valley, a vast middle-class suburb, in the early 1970s, as saying:

> I was trapped in a sense in the Valley, in a kind of traditional marriage, in a traditional setting, and I really wanted to get out of it. And Venice was a great place to come for that. . . . It was just a lovely sense of belonging. And lots of young people, and most of the people were vegetarians. There was a common consciousness. [10]

Gina felt alienated by suburban life in the Valley and found Venice's countercultural spirit—which included regular political protests, occupations of public land to create community parks, and active tenant organizing against negligent landlords—compelling.

A similar kind of search for connection drives the sustainability class today. Just outside of Hanoi, Vietnam, the large new development Ecopark opened its golden gates in 2020. Promising a "perfect harmony of humans and nature," this $10 billion project of 110,000 residential units offers a green and clean lifestyle within commuting distance from the dirty, smoggy city center. It won several International Property Awards for its "careful planning and sustainable development strategy." [11] Though Ecopark is still partly under construction, the developers boast that it will include the "tallest vertical garden in the world" and involve the planting of 1 million trees. [12] Beyond its green appeal, what attracts the class of young urban professionals moving in is the communal life on offer: walkable streets, plazas, and a sense of neighborliness. As the developers describe, the project boasts "various open areas where you and your family can go for a walk or simply sit under the shade of a tree for a picnic and enjoy nature at its best."[13] Eco-park's website is full of soothing words that encapsulate the sustainability class to its core: "the need to live green, live in luxury in the middle of nature, enjoy high quality utilities to live healthy, live happily and truly experience a 'full life' . . . the Ecopark class, creating an elite life for residents." It's even proclaimed that Eco-park induces an emotional value that generates a "green soul," with the luxury developers claiming that "ecology is a human value."[14]

Hoàng Thị Thùy, a teacher and poet, moved to Ecopark for two years when she wanted to live closer to her family and friends in Hanoi. "In Hanoi, I couldn't find a bit of nature. I thought Ecopark would be the alternative. It would give me a bit of nature and closeness to friends." So she rented an apartment and started teaching the children of new residents there. She got to know the families really well: "I was a teacher, a baker, a nanny, a maid, and their psychologist." Remarking on the kinds of people that moved there, she noted:

> A lot of middle- and upper-class people bought a villa there with a garden. It does give you a feeling of owning freedom and peace. There are people there who look for a sense of community, a sense of connection. The very first families that moved there tried to build something together.

From Auroville to the Venice Canals and Ecopark, people are looking for connection, a life of conviviality and community. But it is precisely this desire for authenticity that gets quickly turned into a brand that only some are able to buy in to, and others are excluded from—often violently.

Branding

In the eco-utopia of Auroville, attaining divine consciousness is the ultimate act of purification; it is a requirement for ascending to a more "perfect" state of humanity. At the center of the utopia's innermost "Peace" area, for instance, lies the Matrimandir—a massive geodesic structure covered in glistening gold-plated discs of stainless steel and surrounded by immaculately manicured gardens where one must walk in complete silence.

Inside the Matrimandir's inner chamber, you have to wear white socks to avoid dirtying the tightly woven white carpeting made from the finest merino wool imported from New Zealand. It has white marble walls and twelve steel pillars, painted white and each weighing eighteen hundred pounds.[15] At the very center is the world's largest optically perfect glass globe, known as "the crystal." A heliostat tracks the sun and projects a single ray of sunlight onto the center of the crystal, which refracts perfectly to light the inner chamber without any need for artificial lighting. Here, at the center of "the cradle of a new man," there are no rough edges; everything is smooth, white, and pure.

Experiencing the white inner chamber of the Matrimandir is a kind of purification rite. It is a metaphor for what happens when conviviality becomes distilled into a representation of itself—a spectacle, a brand. Before the authentic experience can be turned into a product, its imperfections and roughness have to be cleaned up, smoothed out.

How this process happens is very visible in the world of real estate. During our time in Los Angeles, we spoke to Eduardo, a property developer who makes a hefty living flipping houses. Focusing on trendy, gentrifying neighborhoods, he buys what he called "ugly" homes that are dated and take up too much space, demolishes them, and builds new homes that sell for much more than the original was purchased for. Rather than getting a bank loan to purchase the house, Eduardo and his real estate investor friends convince landlords to ask long-standing tenants to give up their lease for a sum of, say, $50,000. In what has been called "cash for keys," tenants are uprooted and the house is seized with the landlord's approval. All parties (except the tenants, of course) expect a good return on their investment for the cash handout in the newly flipped property.

After demolishing the house, Eduardo designs delightfully "curated" upgrades that reflect what sustainability- and wellness-minded people want: multi-unit housing, alcoves for indoor plants, and energy-efficient fridges. The possibility that his flipping a house with the expectation of a sixfold return might be inflating land prices didn't seem to have occurred to him. "The most environmentally friendly and equitable solution is to get four or five families living in a single building. It's more desirable and encourages walkability," he said. He also pointed to the fact that his houses often have design accents like large windows that overlook landscaped gardens and are positioned to allow neighbors to see each other in ways that facilitate "community."

Eduardo's observation is a perfect example of how conviviality gets turned into a representation of itself. You can connect with others, but only through a window, which frames the interaction and turns it into an image. While this attempt at conviviality is driven by the desire for authenticity and connection, it becomes devoid of actual engagement—the other is only viewed from a safe distance, with a pane of glass in between you and them. It's about as convivial as a zoo. Meanwhile, while you stare out your window longing for conviviality, you shut out the thought that you had anything to do with the erasure of people who lived here before and are now looking for an affordable home with increasing desperation, as that $50,000 won't last long in today's rental market.

Deener uncovers a similar logic taking place in the Venice Canals neighborhood in the 1980s. Even though Gina was attracted to the Canals by its free-spirited community and its political, rebellious nature, another resident, Jason, had little intention of participating in its counterculture; rather, he wanted to "tame" it. "It was a great time and a very vibrant community. . . . We were the young adventurous ones and we basically came in and sort of tamed the neighborhood. . . . I mean, I bought my first house for $42,000." [16] Another resident, Don, justified his decision to buy a home in the area: "It's one thing if people move in with the idea of being carpetbaggers, and another thing if they move in with the intent to live." [17] These homeowners were attracted to the counter-culture vibes of the area, the sense of belonging that they couldn't find in the Valley or Beverly Hills. Yet, unlike the activists that preceded them, their aim was simply to live there, not to partici-pate in the rebellion. In other words, they were into the *vibe* of the place without doing anything to actively contribute.

This desire to dwell in the vibe continues to have serious social and ecological consequences. By the early 1990s, property values in Venice rose beyond what even these middle-class residents could af-ford. As Deener notes, over the span of three decades, Venice came to have a "stylized, rather than politicized, public culture. . . . There is no struggle involved . . . no celebration of a subversive lifestyle." [18] When we walked through Venice Canals in 2022, we were indeed stunned at just how stylized it had become—and by the absence of any conviviality. In fact, we felt deeply alienated: every house was a fortress, garages were stuffed with SUVs and sports cars, no one talked to each other, no one was in their garden or boating on the canals, and there were signs everywhere telling us what we couldn't do. Private security patrolled the streets. Even the small park that residents had fought hard for, decades ago, intending it for commu-nity use, was now behind a fence, with a sectioned-off area where only ducks were allowed to go.

Yes, there was a park for kids to play and the streets were walk-able. But kids had to play behind a gate, you weren't allowed to bike, local residents only went around in their cars, and the ducks, well, they weren't allowed near any people. And yet busloads of tourists come every day to gawk at the neighborhood, known for its unique character and countercultural aura. On the boardwalk nearby, you could buy T-shirts and fridge magnets featuring the Canals. Owning a cottage there has become synonymous with distinction and a certain hippie attitude—despite the prohibitive price tag (up to $7 million).

The Venice Canals neighborhood was, in fact, worse than the Valley. It had become a zoo. But unlike most zoos, in this one, its inhabitants pay to put themselves behind cages. That organic, shared experience had been transformed into a consumer spectacle and then a marketable brand. As Deener notes, Venice Canals has turned into "a scene to be looked at," which "required the elimination of competing symbolic codes"—namely the rabble, the hippies, the dirty community gardens, and the ducks pooping in places they're not supposed to.[19]

In Ecopark, too, the desire for community and authentic connection got ambushed by branding. As Thùy told us, "The people who first moved here are not around anymore. She described it as a ghost town: on weekdays it was quiet, since very few people actually lived there. The few people she saw were often real estate agents giving tours to potential buyers. "Ecopark is now like Ciputra [a gated community largely for foreigners] but with more trees and real estate agents." The dream of community that animated the first residents was gone: "It's a place for a transition of dreams that did not come true. . . . This whole Ecopark thing became a concrete location to give shelter to these businesspeople. But there's none of the real stuff happening there. No community, no support. The people living there, it's not real life that they feel with their heart. It's just bodies walking around looking for something." So Thùy decided to move back to downtown Hanoi, where she could at least be near her family and friends.

Ecopark is just one example of green urban developments that have turned into dead space. South Korea's Songdo City was branded as a city that would "banish the problems created by modern life," with over 20 million square feet of LEED-certified space, water recycling, and significant green space. And yet people are lonely, the streets feel empty, lifestyles remain luxurious, everything is sanitized, and nothing seems transformative—as it was claimed to be.[20]

Branded neighborhoods like Venice, Ecopark, and Songdo City are not the only things that become spectacles of themselves. From the moment we wake up, we are encouraged to transform our experiences, our thoughts, and our connections into images, posts, and tweets to be forever inscribed into a database of raw material for more fake consumable vibes. Yesterday's posts don't matter—content must be continuously created. Authenticity is bound up with purifying the brand, rather than reflecting the actual reality of ecological collapse.[21]

For French philosopher Guy Debord, the problem with the spectacle, and why it is ultimately so dissatisfying, is that it can only be looked at or consumed. He wrote that "this has culminated in a world of autonomized and endless production of representations for consumption, where even the deceivers are deceived. The spectacle is a concrete inversion of life. . . . Its essential character reveals it to be a visible negation of life."[22] The problem, for Debord, is that conviviality can't ever fully be reduced to spectacle, no matter how immersive or sophisticated the attempt. The spectacle can only turn interconnectedness into representations of ideas and values, emotions and feelings, which get plastered onto overly broad categories like "nature" or "vibrancy." The spectacle is not connection; it is a vapid aesthetic—and a deception. It is life-sucking. It is anti-ecological. What started out as a desire or yearning to access the interconnections that make us all alive and keep us generating life has ended up as the very opposite—more alienation. The supposedly smooth world that is presented to us is actually full of potholes and blemishes once you look a bit closer. As writer Kate Wagner (known for coining the term "McMansion"—describing mansions that are enormous, cookie-cutter, and ugly) writes for *The Nation*:

We find ourselves subject to a relentless drive toward optimized, frictionless happiness, enabled by an endless array of apps and tools devoted to the task of getting someone to do your grocery shopping or find you a date. The contemporary urban end goal is a utopian world without conflict, but one that never confronts the fact that the social order that enables this utopia of commodified pleasure centers is itself produced by a lot of conflict.[23]

Speculation

In previous chapters, we showed how green lifestyles are unfortunately not sustainable—in fact, they just make things worse. But this does not explain why they are so appealing, why we seem to get stuck in the choices we're presented with. This is the real problem: that even when we try to be sustainable and make the world a better place, we have so few options available, options that, on deeper reflection, are entirely unsatisfying. Why does this keep happening?

At the heart of the matter is a financial system that feeds off that yearning and turns it into a commodity. Our economy depends on this repackaging and rebranding: it offers new and endless opportunities for investment. It's not even that people are blindly following the mantra of speculative finance. Many of us are simply trying to ensure our own security in a system that forces all of us to make more money from what we have—or lose everything. Our very pension funds are dependent on speculative finance, which in turn involves investing in everything from fossil fuels to genocidal drones, and real estate projects that evict the elderly.[24] Just think: so much of what is fueling ecological breakdown is driven by people just wanting some security in their old age. If they can do so under the promise that what they are investing in is "green," it alleviates some of the guilt. We have to come to grips with the fact that at the root of the sustainability class lifestyle—its green brands, its gentrification of whole neighbor-hoods, its jet-setting UN conference-goers, its wellness fads, its electric cars and luxury farmers markets—is a massive financial infrastructure, driven by a globe-spanning glut of cold hard cash.

To illustrate what we mean, let's return to Neom, that pinnacle of green engineering nestled in the Saudi desert. Scroll through its website and promotional materials, and you'll find that they've thought of everything.[25] Want a livable neighborhood? "Unlike traditional cities," Neom will prioritize "health and wellbeing," it won't have cars, and all services will be walkable within five minutes—meaning that "residents see family and friends often through spontaneous encounters." It advertises "clean air for everyone," "more time to spend with loved ones," and "a perfect climate all-year round."

Worried about nature? Neom presents "a new model for protection, preservation, and regeneration," with 95 percent of the land "committed to the natural world" through its "regreening and rewilding model." Want a top-of-the-line, high-tech lifestyle? Don't worry: "automated services will be powered by artificial intelligence," it will run on 100 percent renewable energy, its port city will also include the largest floating structure in the world (making it resilient to climate disaster), and it will be "a cognitive city that predicts and reacts to what we need, not the other way around."

But what if you get tired of always running into your family and friends through spontaneous encounters? Don't worry, Neom has you covered: the mountain resort Trojena offers everything from a wellness summit and alternative medicine to paragliding, music festivals, art fairs, and year-round skiing.

Want to be part of the global elite, planning the next green revolution? No sweat: Neom is also right across the Gulf of Aqaba from Egypt's luxury walled town of Sharm El-Sheikh, the setting for biodiversity and climate conferences, conveniently far away and secure from anyone protesting elite lifestyles and centralized control by the ruling class.[26] Neom is carefully designed to appeal to the sustainability class, from the green modernists to the wellness gurus. Neom is green, progressive, liberal, high-tech, healthy, futuristic, regenerative . . . whatever you like, that's what Neom is.

But why does this seem so dissatisfying? So empty? It all comes across as a distillation of the life we hope to live, but, like an advertisement for antidepressants, it feels too packaged, too warm and fuzzy.

The reason it feels like an advertisement is that it is nothing more than an advertisement, a greenwashing exercise by the Saudi royal family. Let's put Neom in context for a moment. Saudi Arabia rakes in an estimated $1 billion in oil exports *per day*, making it one of the world's fastest-growing economies.[27] These profits, which are mostly pocketed by the royal family, are then funneled into speculative investments ranging from real estate to technology, infrastructure, art, and tourism. It is estimated that the House of Saud has a net worth of $1.6 trillion—sixteen times the British royal family's net worth and seven times the net worth of Elon Musk, the richest man in the world. They have gold-plated cars and a $450 million painting in a megayacht.[28] Saudi Aramco, the country's primary oil company, also run by the royal family, is valued at $2 trillion.[29] The Saudi government's investment portfolio—which is basically synonymous with the fortune of its royal family—includes significant shares in companies such as Uber, Tesla, Twitter, Lyft, Snapchat, General Motors, and even Jared Kushner's investment firm.[30]

There's an Arabic saying, "Money begets money." It means that when you have money, you invest it in more money, and that lets you make more money. It is here that Neom comes in. In 2016, Deputy Crown Prince Mohammad bin Salman Al Saud (or MBS, as he is affectionately called) announced that he would consolidate the country's holdings into a $2 trillion sovereign wealth fund, half of which would be invested in domestic infrastructure and the other half of which would be invested outside of the country in safe investments that would themselves generate money. In July 2022, MBS dedicated $80 billion to Neom, with the hope that other investors would buy stock in the project for a total of $500 billion invested.[31] It's possibly the most expensive, focus-grouped advertisement ever, aimed at changing the Saudi royal family's global image in order to help them diversify their investment portfolio.

Whether it will actually be built is an open question—even doubtful, considering the track record of projects like these. And indeed, as this book was in its last editing stages, it was announced that, regrettably, The Line would no longer stretch for 170 kilometers in the desert, but would be cut a little short to 2.5 kilometers. That's a reduction of 98.6 percent.[32] But that's not important. What's important is the extent to which investors around the world can be convinced the project is worth putting money into, just long enough for the Saudis to sell shares of it. In the meantime, the House of Saud gets a progressive and green makeover, and Saudi Arabia improves its reputation as a place to invest with low risk. The $80 billion price tag is spare change considering Neom's long-lasting benefits to the kingdom.

Neom is just one egregious example of a global process, where real estate investments get packaged with green wrapping and sold to the highest bidder. Ecopark (Vietnam), Amaravati (India), Sidewalk City (Toronto), Masdar City (Abu Dhabi, UAE), Bicentenary City (Peru), Songdo City (South Korea), Forest City and BiodiverCity (Malaysia), Eko Atlantic (Nigeria), Nusuranta (Indonesia's future capital city), Telosa (potentially in Nevada, United States; featuring an "equity skyscraper" decked with solar panels and aeroponic farms), Toyota's Woven City (Japan)—the list of smart and green cities just goes on and on.[33] They are typically clusters of skyscrapers that claim to be "self-sufficient," with recycled water, tons of trees, and renewable energy, all protected by sea walls—that is, if they're not in the desert.

We have to come to grips with the fact that these projects exist for one reason: speculation. They are largely the products of consortia of private companies, banks, architectural firms, and city governments, and offer an opportunity to shell out billions of dollars to construction companies to build outlandish infrastructure from scratch. Some—like Eko Atlantic, billed as "an investment opportunity on an unprecedented scale" near Lagos, Nigeria—exist to boost already surging land values while creating financialized economies for the ultra-wealthy to set up shop, completely out of touch with what ordinary people need right now, not to mention what the planet needs.[34] Most of them become laboratories for police surveillance, automated technologies, and privatizing what remains of public goods and services in order to solve the problems caused by privatizing public goods and services. They are not just greenwashing— they are social and ecological disasters.

These cities are rarely ever fully built; some of them are, but they end up looking nothing like what was pictured on the box. To attract investors, they draw on the currency of images that appeal to the sustainability class (green, creative, modern, hip, healthy, serene, spiritual) and package them into a product that you can safely park your assets in. As Sarah Moser, a researcher on planned cities at McGill University, said about the proponents of these cities, "It's so seductive to say, 'I'll start over,' rather than just pay my taxes. Then they present themselves as this beacon of hope for humanity."[35]

On a smaller scale, neighborhoods like Venice in Los Angeles are laboratories for the same kind of branding. Their convivial vibes are fixed in time and turned into a spectacle by real estate brokers and business owners, who advertise them and sell them as products to investors. Meanwhile, the conviviality that they represent also becomes currency: the urban village, the creative arts district. These images were molded in the crucible of once-convivial neighborhoods and solidified into brands. Once successfully translated into a representation of itself, they then enter the world of global commodity markets.

All of this has to be understood in a wider context: how the global financial system works. Doing this topic the kind of justice it needs would take a lot more space than we have here—and others have described it much better than we can. But we do need to explain three big problems in the global market that are at the root of what we are talking about in this book.

First, the way money works has a large role in driving the so-called green economy. Say you want to buy your next green home, with all its sustainable bells and whistles. To do so, you'd go to the bank, and they'll assess how much money you have, your future income, and the value of the home. Then, if all goes well, they give you a loan, and the amount of your mortgage and the interest rate will depend on how well you scored.

But that money didn't come from the bank's vaults. In fact, banks *create* money when they give loans. In other words, someone clicks a button and money is made out of thin air, which goes into your account so you can buy your home.[36] At any given time, most banks in the United States create more money than the money they have, roughly at a ratio of $10 for every $1 they have in their customers' accounts.

That's why, if you zoom out and look at the global economy, there is a vast amount more debt than there is actual money—the Institute of International Finance calculated that in 2021 global debt was 300 percent of global GDP.[37] Think about that for a second: it means that unless the economy sees some big changes, all the world's debt will never be repaid. A world with more debt than real money means that investors are always playing musical chairs, running faster and faster to buy and sell assets—hoping not to be left without a chair when the next crash hits, wiping out trillions in investments and leaving the planet and its creatures in utter ruin. But, in the short term, investors can always get cheap loans as long as they show that they already have good investments. Because of this, there is actually very little risk involved for investors: if you have lots of money, you can make much more money, as the values of your assets are always increasing.[38] Money begets money.

The second big problem is that there's so much concentrated wealth that the rich barely know what to do with it. Extreme wealth is becoming more and more obscene: between 1995 and 2021, the top 1 percent captured 38 percent of all wealth globally, while the bottom 50 percent only saw 2 percent of global wealth. Interestingly, the share of wealth of that top 1 percent is growing faster than the wealth of the top 10 percent, which includes the middle class of rich countries. The ultra-rich are making money faster than the middle class—who are still only a very small fraction of the world population. Compare this now to the period between 1945 and 1980, when inequality was actually shrinking around the world.[39]

We can point to a few reasons for this growing inequality. One is that governments tax the rich less than they used to, and it's become easier for the wealthy to park their money in untaxed assets—like art objects, NFTs, or real estate. Governments have also loosened regulations for investment in real estate and lowered interest rates, to spur an industry that is increasingly taking a larger share of the economy. Another reason is that these assets are increasing in their value—mostly because the rich keep buying them, and banks keep giving them cheap loans to do so. And so wealth once again creates more wealth. Lastly, actual productivity of the biggest economies has been steadily declining since at least the 1970s.[40] Even as there is more and more money going around, resources like oil and minerals are becoming more expensive, while employment, wages, and the production of goods are stagnating. As an example, in 2021, investment in real estate in Canada for the first time surpassed investment in businesses— signaling a recognition by investors that returns on investment in the housing market were more trustworthy than investment in jobs, factories, or natural resources. Indeed, in the same year, real estate accounted for a whopping 10 percent of Canada's GDP, and roughly one out of four homes in the province of Ontario was bought by an investor, not by a household.[41] The result of all this is that the vast majority of all capital globally, about 60 percent, is held in real estate—the safest, most stable investment with the highest potential returns.[42] This doesn't just pertain to homes; it also involves speculation on farmland.[43] Bill Gates, for example, is now the largest private owner of farmland in the United States. He owns upward of 242,000 acres, worth nearly $700 million—and yet it's possible that he has never once grown a tomato for himself.[44] Just 1 percent of the world's landowners control 70 percent of the world's farmlands, while 84 percent of the world's farmers own 5 acres of land or less and farm only 12 percent of all farmland.[45] In short, real estate has become the pressure relief valve for an economy swimming in cash, and governments, having recognized that financial assets are becoming a key source of economic growth going forward, have made it still easier for investors to speculate on it.

The third big problem, caused by the second, is that we are now in what's being called an "asset economy."[46] Assets are the stuff you buy—like a house, stocks, or an NFT—that can potentially be worth more money in the future. As pensions, child benefits, healthcare, and social assistance programs continue to see cuts by governments, many households increasingly rely on their assets for future security. Essentially, this means that if you own a home, you can use it as an asset to get a cheap loan for a second home, and either rent that second home out or sell it in a few years. There's more to it, too: when you buy a home, the money you make either from renters or from the sale tends to be taxed far less than wages. In other words, rich people can just buy assets and then get taxed less than working people do. In fact, most wealthy people in the United States make their money not from their wages but from the assets they hold.[47]

So if you already have some money, you'd be wise to spend it all on some assets, so that you can make more money. But it also means that if you don't have any assets to start with, you're a loser: you'll be forever shut out of the economy and a future worth living. We already mentioned the Arabic saying "Money begets money." Though less well known, there's a second part of the saying, too: "Lice beget lice."[48]

It's here that the sustainability class comes in. Being largely in the upper middle class, they constitute the lucky segment of the population who have some assets. They might have enough savings for a down payment on a home, or their parents can lend them some money to buy a condo. Some may themselves be under financial pressure and see buying their first home as an investment for the future—one that is becoming more and more unaffordable and insecure. They don't want to get left behind. At the same time, many want to do good in the world: they want to spend their money in ways that change the world. They value things like protecting nature, exploring their spirituality, satisfying their travel bug itch, donating to good causes, living healthy lives, and having a community.

It's this class that has become a big market for investors, developers, real estate brokers, crypto scammers, wellness and spiritual gurus, and entrepreneurs of all stripes. As every good entrepreneur knows, to sell your product, you have to create a need. And so the values of the sustainability class—environment, health, community—have become repackaged and branded into green, wellness, vibrancy.[49] These are big business because they can be replicated from the coast of California to Saudi Arabia, they can travel around the world, and they offer a stable return on investment.

It all comes down to this: the dream of the sustainability class is made possible by a glut in speculative finance. The sustainability class is looking for a sense of connection in a world that feels increasingly alienating, unfulfilling, and ecologically destructive. But for investors, whether it's really ecological doesn't matter: the promise of "green" is gift-wrapping, it's trendy. What matters is whether it sells, and how fast. And they are selling the planet off as fast as possible before a crash happens.

Though many members of the sustainability class mean well and have a legitimate desire to live lightly on Earth, their class position has allowed sustainability to be framed as a vision that ultimately only serves to line the pockets of investors, real estate moguls, entrepreneurs, developers, and all the paper pushers who prop them up. There's so much "sustainability" noise that people are distracted from the kinds of system transformation that we need. That noise is by design, not by accident.

Exclusion

Leaning against the marble wall of the utterly white luminous inner chamber of the Matrimandir, it was impossible to disregard the enormous amount of material and human labor that went into this gargantuan spectacle of purity. While others escaped into their heads in search of higher consciousness, I (Vijay) tried to resist the alienation of being obliged to focus only on myself and not on the many invisible others (the rocks, the water, the insects, the soil, the people) that were and are continually put to work to maintain the purity of this space. I sat recalling Jessica Namakkal's description of the self-entitled Aurovillian attitudes toward the workers who built the gigantic orb I found myself in.

From its inception, the gold-plated spiritual orb symbolized a world free of material concerns, even though the orb itself would need plenty of materials to be constructed. According to Auroville's own website, the Matrimandir was built in 1971 "with some Aurovillians and a number of other workers who undertook to build [it] without paid labor, putting their heart into it."[50] Who were these mysterious laborers who volunteered to realize the dream of Auroville's spiritual and ecological utopia? The answer to this mystery will bring us just a bit closer to understanding why

Auroville, and green lifestylism in general, is really a story of class segregation.

Auroville's location was chosen in large part because of The Mother's French connections. Pondicherry had, in fact, been a French colony until 1962 (achieving independence nearly twenty years after the rest of the country became independent from Britain). After ceding its territory in India, the French embassy took particular interest in promoting the Auroville project. When, in 1968, Auroville's founders described their project in a progress report to UNESCO, they claimed that before its settlement the area was a "bare wasteland," "sparsely populated" with much land "uncultivated"—and the construction of a new city would cause "minimum disturbance to the local population." [51] And yet Namakkal shows how the population of Tamils in the area had numbered in the thousands—more than, it should be noted, the population of Auroville today, standing at 3,200 residents.[52] The Mother, who was often called a "pioneer" by her mostly European supporters, claimed that local Tamils had "spiritual superiority" and, like all Indians, were spiritually in tune with Auroville's ideals. "Auroville belongs to nobody in particular," she said, "but to humanity as a whole." It was taken for granted, then, that the local population would support the project and *naturally* would want to be a part of it.

Interviews with locals tell a very different story. Namakkal quotes villagers at the time expressing skepticism and bitterness about the project. One villager stated: "It may be slavery again, as before, because they find us black, ugly and poor." [53] Another villager had sold his land to the project: "I don't care much [about Auroville], but I need 2000 rupees for my marriage so let them buy my one-acre. Then I can marry and get work in Auroville." [54] As Namakkal states, "impoverished local farmers who needed money sold their land to Auroville, only to find themselves unemployed and landless." [55]

This became the base of labor needed by Auroville's pioneers.

As one early Auroville settler, Roy Chyat, reflected, "You couldn't do anything without help from the village people. So everything was basically them. In those days, you would hire a laborer who would work all day for three rupees twenty. Which is really like nothing. Even in those days."[56] Today, the green utopia depends on roughly four times as many laborers from the surrounding villages as there are Auroville residents (incidentally, that's also roughly the same ratio of workers to customers as on a cruise ship). On closer examination, it turns out that the people who showed up to build the Matrimandir were not volunteers there out of goodwill. Poor and desperate locals had accepted extremely low pay to build the utopian town's central spiritual orb. As Francis, another Auroville pioneer, recalls, "They hired themselves out as a full village to dig . . . it was amazing to watch because it was just like ants on the move."[57]

This was a far cry from the myth Auroville spun of itself, as a little utopia free from material concerns. It's easy not to concern yourself with the material world when you can pay your landless neighbors next to nothing to do your work for you. These attitudes paved the way for a hierarchy of human relations, placing Aurovillians as more important than non-Aurovillian Tamils whose land and labor were and continue to be needed for the utopian project of building a community capable of realizing divine consciousness.

Faced with the reality that the local people were not interested in the project, except as a means for employment, Aurovillians began to see themselves as responsible for educating the villagers, making life easier for them and informing them that they too could become Aurovillians if they cooperated and saw the utopians as their "benefactors."[58] So The Mother instructed her followers—all Europeans, who knew not a word of Tamil—to enter the surrounding villages and recruit locals, hoping that as construction progressed, locals would become more supportive of the project.

All this is not to say that Aurovillians did not honestly attempt to build positive relationships with the surrounding villagers, or that they didn't engage in admirable ecological practices like forest gardens, accessible health and education initiatives, alternative economic systems, and low-impact housing. It's also not to only point fingers at Aurovillians, who surely had good intentions to build an inclusive vision of a global humanity in ecological harmony. And it's clear that there were many settlers who did end up building positive relationships with villagers—though these would always continue to be uneven, given the class differences between them.

Indeed, despite all its best intentions, Auroville has not been able to bridge the divide. The consequences of this are dire. The failure to recognize and reconcile this troubling history has led to more than fifty years of complacency among many rather self-entitled expats who call Auroville home (at least when it's not too hot for them to stay). Ecology without social justice isn't ecology; it's just lush landscaping.[59]

The failure to address the colonial roots of Auroville is now moving in new and very disturbing directions. Let's look into how and why this is happening. In recent years, some Aurovillians have become fed up with the slow pace of collective deliberation. Others, who are more hardline devotees of The Mother, are upset by deviations from The Mother's and Roger Anger's master plan. Meanwhile, amid the power struggle to define and concretize the vision of Auroville, land prices have shot up as tourists, especially domestic tourists with growing middle-class wealth, continue to arrive to partake in the spiritual learning experience and witness the hippie-looking *vellaikaran* (Tamil for white folk) living "eco-consciously" in India. Many private actors have been gobbling up nearby land, keen to take advantage of the tourism industry and the speculative potential of owning real estate in an area of such great international interest. Then, the government-appointed secretary of Auroville's governing bodies, Jayanti Ravi, took it upon herself to reappropriate power over the Auroville project. Aurovillians complained about a lack of consultation with the Residents' Assembly and even complete rejection of their democratically determined suggestions and proposals.[60]

One night in early December 2021, the Auroville youth center and hundreds of trees were bulldozed with no warning.[61] These trees had been carefully planted and tended to by Auroville residents, and were crucial to ensuring groundwater replenishment. Hired hands from the surrounding villages joined the destruction. Not all Aurovillians were against the destruction, as it meant the fulfillment of Anger's galaxy model and the completion of the Crown Road. The conflict even became a national item of discussion, a controversy at the center of India's recent rightward nationalist push. For the ruling BJP, Auroville represents an important showcase of the ecological vision of its Hindu modernist project, which they felt had fallen prey to foreign and "anti-national" interests. For instance, pro-BJP public policy analyst Satheesh Namasivayam wrote about Auroville that "India has been generously hosting an international experiment, but it cannot be a bystander to foreign residents' rebellion against Indian authorities."[62] The so-called rebellion was a series of protests by Aurovillians against the bulldozing. In response, the Indian government incited public anger at the "foreigners" of Auroville by accusing them of undermining Indian laws.

The government has also enrolled locals in an effort to take over Auroville's governance institutions, and invoked an "emergency ordinance" to reclaim territory in dispute. Worried about the deeper implications of the Hindu authoritarian project, Indian ecologist and writer Ashish Kothari explains how Auroville is riddled with unfair divisions based partly on class and race divides between Aurovillians (the spiritually enlightened) and the outside villagers (the spiritually *un*enlightened) the city depends upon as day laborers.[63] Yet these divisions, Kothari argues, cannot exonerate the government's strategic instrumentalization of villagers' anger and its destructive power grab.

Since its inception, Auroville has generated exclusions. The adherence to a lifestyle centered around the teachings of Sri Aurobindo and The Mother alienated and excluded the surrounding communities who no longer had access to their land and who became day laborers for a community of settlers. These exclusions had class consequences. Almost overnight, a working class was created outside of the morally superior "eco" enclave. Two groups of people were created: the worthy (the Aurovillians) and the unworthy (the laborers working for Auroville). The divide between the worthy and the unworthy took on a new dimension when the central government tried to redefine the ecological science and spirituality behind the utopia in order to envision a Hindu fundamentalist alternative. Exclusionary Hindu nationalism is a vision that seeks to instill a pure Hindutva society, in contradistinction to what are considered "polluting" lower castes and non-Hindu religions, especially Islam.[64] As Indian fiction and climate writer Amitav Ghosh writes, upper caste Hindus have conceptions of sacredness that are highly susceptible to manipulating the "language of green activism with upper caste ideas of diet, purity, and sacred spaces." He goes on to say that environmentalism in India is being appropriated "in a classically eco-fascistic fashion" to forward the interests of elites and upper caste groups.[65]

In Auroville, this has meant weaponizing decades long non-Aurovillian discontent among local Tamils to further an agenda that is ultimately about marginalizing lower caste people and Muslims. Meanwhile, Aurovillians, and particularly those who dissent from central government interpretations of The Mother's and Sri Aurobindo's philosophies, are being recast as "foreign" interests seeking to trouble Hindu purity.

Unlike many of the green development projects we discuss in this book, Auroville is not meant to be a vehicle for speculation, since private property is not allowed—nor do its residents fit neatly within the picture of the sustainability class as we've so far described it. They aren't necessarily green modernists or administrators/conference groupies or even greensters. And there are many redeeming aspects of Auroville—from its ecological forestry practices and soil rehabilitation to its innovative architecture and its honest attempt at making its residents' lives more spiritual and fulfilling.

But digging deeper, we can start to see how the desire for authenticity so easily becomes co-opted and made exclusive, and how this co-optation and exclusion have evolved over time under changing political circumstances and in relation to growing authoritarianism in India and increasing interest in Auroville by tourists and the real-estate industry. If Aurovillians are aghast at the current power grab and top-down direction by the central government, they must also ask themselves how a bourgeois French woman, The Mother, could have commanded the supreme authority and cult-like status to build such a city in the first place. When asked in 1966 what the political organization of Auroville would be like, The Mother responded: "There will be no politics."[66] The current situation is a consequence of ecological projects that avoid responding to concrete everyday politics in pursuit of abstract higher-level consciousness (a consciousness that is perhaps more self-absorbed than all-knowing).

Auroville is a fascinating example of how ecological connection gets manufactured, purified through devotion, and made exclusionary to keep out those who cannot adhere—all the while being branded as a global community for all of humanity. Ultimately, it was the lack of attention to politics, power, positionality, and the purpose of the brand of "human unity"—and the exclusions that sustained it over the past half century—that allowed it to be co-opted once again by the BJP in their effort to rebrand Hindutva nationalism as ecological.

What about other green utopias like Ecopark and Neom? In contrast to Auroville, Ecopark in Vietnam is a for-profit, speculative project. But like Auroville, its construction involved the displacement of local farmers—though even more violently. To clear the more than twelve hundred acres needed for the project, the local government forced the removal of four thousand families from their land. Of these, two thousand families refused the compensation money, which they said was far too low considering they would entirely lose their livelihoods. When these villagers protested in 2012, police attacked them with tear gas, leading to some of the most severe conflict between authorities and civilians in Vietnam in recent memory. Later, a thousand villagers set up camp to guard their land against the second phase of the development. In April 2012, three thousand police and soldiers descended on the camp, arrested dozens of villagers, and beat journalists documenting the attack.[67] In February 2014, the developer sent armed men to the site who shot at several farmers, injuring five.[68]

Ironically, it was in May of the same year that Ecopark won its International Property Awards—which, as we have seen, touted its "careful planning and sustainable development strategy."[69] This is especially ironic considering that the farmers likely have a fraction of the carbon footprint of the members of the sustainability class moving into the project. The large-scale bulldozing of farmland, pouring of concrete in floodplains, installation of sewage systems, and excessive pesticide use for landscaping have also had serious impacts on the biodiversity and resilience of the land, risking increased flooding and pollution of waterways. When the developers say Ecopark offers the "perfect harmony of humans and nature," they may in fact just mean the perfect harmony of having your guilty conscience soothed by public relations.

Neom has also had to deal with its share of pesky locals. Roughly twenty thousand members of the Howeitat tribe are being evicted to make way for the project. To date, 150 dissenting members of the tribe have been arrested, and many more harassed and intimidated. One tribesman, Abdul Rahim al-Huwaiti, had openly declared that he would defy the eviction order. He was later killed in what Saudi security forces say was an open attack on them and for which they were forced to retaliate—but which eyewitnesses reported as an extrajudicial execution.[70] To combat criticism, MBS hired U.S. public relations firm Ruder Finn for $1.7 million. In October 2022, three brothers of the man who was killed were sentenced to death, while two other members of the family were sentenced to fifty years in prison.[71] And lest we forget, journalist Jamal Khashoggi expressed criticism of the project shortly before he was killed.[72] The irony is that these tribespeople are far more ecological than the residents of Neom ever will be—if there ever are any people living there, that is. As journalist Robert F. Worth writes in the *New York Times Magazine*, "There are already thousands of people living in harmony with nature in the same area: a tribal community that has been there for centuries and is now being replaced by the project."[73]

Exclusions aren't just limited to green urban development projects. Green infrastructure such as solar and wind farms, carbon offsetting, hydropower, and biofuel projects all generate their own losers. Large-scale solar power farms in India, for instance, were branded as an ecological solution, which in turn justified the reclassification of public lands as "wasteland" in need of improvement.[74] These solar parks have become well-funded zones of economic exclusion, leading to the removal of small family farmers from fertile soils, leaving them without jobs or homes. The land has now been turned into giant solar panel farms that worsen water scarcity in an already dry and warming climate.

At the 2021 COP 26 in Glasgow, $1 trillion for solar financing was sought for the rollout of similar parks all across tropical regions of the world—regions that are, by and large, the least responsible for climate change, and which also are inhabited by many tribal and Indigenous peoples, who are increasingly at risk of eviction from their land because of the "green economy."[75] The Environmental Justice Atlas has catalogued forty-nine conflicts in the Americas alone related to mining for minerals needed for the "green transition," such as lithium, copper, nickel, platinum, and manganese.[76] These conflicts involve murders of Indigenous and environmental activists, rape, dispossession of land, contamination of water systems, and incursion into protected habitats.

There are plenty of examples of these kinds of "green sacrifice zones."[77] Here are just a few: Fires on Indonesian palm oil plantations (palm oil is sometimes touted as a "green" biofuel) caused upward of a hundred thousand premature deaths in 2015 alone.[78] Wind turbines in Oaxaca, Mexico, have forced local residents to flee their lands, while turbines deplete groundwater, leak oil, and worsen erosion.[79] The generated energy is then used by companies like Walmart, allowing them to rebrand themselves as sustainable.[80] In 2020, the United States halted funding of over $12 million to the environmental NGO WWF after a bipartisan investigation found that the NGO was responsible for human rights abuses by anti-poaching guards, involving murder, severe torture, and rape. These occurred against the Baka, who live deep in the rainforests of the Republic of Congo, where a protected area was being set up with money from the UN Development Programme, the WWF, the European Commission, the UN's Global Environment Facility, and the U.S. and Congolese governments. At the same time, the CEO of WWF is on the list of the highest-paid charity CEOs, earning over $1 million in 2021.[81]

What is important in these examples is not simply to add renewable energy and conservation to a laundry list of failed sustainability solutions. This is too reductionist. Instead, it shows that being ecological means asking the more difficult question of whether anything fundamentally changed within the broader dynamics of economic production that keep steering the world toward ever more pure, efficient, and innovative technologies, goods, and services.

Those discarded by this vision are predominantly the people who can't possibly play the game because they just don't have the money to buy into it. These include anyone who isn't adept at generating a spectacle, who isn't tapped into the "vibe." They deserve all the blame for the mess left behind, as they still haven't figured out how to optimize their productivity. And boy, are there *a lot* of discarded people. Exclusion is not an unintentional side effect of the green brand. It's baked into the whole thing.

The sustainability class are those (perhaps unknowingly) contributing to this exclusion. As we showed in Chapters 3 through 6, the whims and fancies of the sustainability class are always dependent on resources and produce wastes that are sourced from and exported to faraway places. The faraway-ness, both temporally and spatially, is an instant devaluation, and results in violence toward other people and other generations. It is a place and a time that are less important, less human, less desired, or perhaps just "not our problem." Through this dynamic, environments are constantly made (for the rich) and unmade (for the poor). Making anew requires turning what might already exist into something more palatable for worthy kinds of people. As Jessica the vegan influencer told us, veganism for dirty hippies isn't attractive; it's when football players, celebrities, and the Saudi crown prince get on board with it that it starts to feel like something a little more "sustainable"—something that will shape the future.

And yet most people don't actually want this. The sustainability class works to constantly keep up appearances of being ethical consumers, but a lot of that also has to do with shoring up a fear of falling behind the curve, of ultimately being discarded like the rest—ending up on the other side of the wall. Members of the sustainability class want a convivial future. We want to feel like we belong. And we use the assets we have to buy a stake in that future. But when we get there, either we realize that it was all just empty, that we too were just seen as an asset by the investors, or we remain oblivious and drink the Kool-Aid by always seeking new "green" consumption.

Breaking Out from Branding, Speculation, and Exclusion

As we've detailed, it all begins with our personal desires—entirely normal and justified—to have convivial, fulfilling lives. But through the process of branding, these desires are subsumed into the vast machinations of an economy based on speculation, which then unmakes people's lives. The things we desire are pitted against the desires of the working class, and those excluded from the economy altogether.

We should note that our aim here isn't to point fingers and blame members of the sustainability class for this exclusive economic system. There are bigger forces that reshape whole environments before a single vegan bistro, cereal café, boutique beard trimmer, tattoo artist, or third-wave coffee shop opens its doors.[82] These chic establishments may attract the sustainability class (and everyone else's ire), but behind the scenes, it's the investor class— the 1 percent, not the 10 percent—that holds the keys to the neighborhood's future. As Willy Staley writes in the *New York Times Magazine*, "Investors could buy and sell every building on your block without your ever noticing, but the coffee shop where the staff is mean to everybody is right in front of you."[83]

How do we break out of this cycle of yearning, speculation, and exclusion? There are two ways people from privileged backgrounds often go about it. The first is by using their privilege to improve the lives of the excluded through charity, philanthropy, volunteering, or even more ethical lifestyle choices. But this is ultimately unsatisfactory. These actions just replicate the same kind of logic of branding that duped the sustainability class in the first place. Donating to a charity—even if that charity does good work— becomes just another brand, an ethical consumption choice that makes us feel good about ourselves but doesn't challenge our own class position in the first place. It's just virtue signaling. Think of the pioneer settlers of Auroville who thought they could help the displaced villagers by educating them about ecological practices and their spiritual mission, and by providing them with much-needed employment. It's just more posturing to appease their guilt, because, in all honesty, the Aurovillians were never going to change the vision of *their* utopia to be more inclusive—they just wanted to feel better about it. And so the class divisions were never actually resolved, deepening into feelings of alienation and resentment among settlers and Indian nationals alike over time, sowing the seeds for new forms of violence and co-optation.

A second approach is to cast blame on the sustainability class—often by members of that class itself. These people, it is argued, will always side with their class interests, and any solution they propose will just be stuck in the same ideology that got us here. But this is also unsatisfactory, because it merely permits new powerful actors to reassert the same kinds of exclusion under a different branding—just as the BJP is currently doing in its effort to reclaim Auroville under a Hindu nationalist frame. It also casts the sustainability class as a monolithic group unable to transcend its own position, a self-proclaimed "woke" elite always at odds with "what working-class people need." Ultimately, this kind of reasoning leads members of the sustainability class to see no other option but to disavow their privilege, to pretend to be something they're not. We all know the type: perhaps a greenster urbanite dressed in "working-class" clothes and talking about how poor they are. They know very well that they are privileged, but they identify with the working class, and so they try to be like them. But this kind of performance, as convincing as it may be, won't actually help anyone, least of all themselves.

Either way, assigning blame doesn't really help us do much about the problem, which is ultimately that we're all being played against each other. In her book *Nickel and Dimed*, the late Barbara Ehrenreich went undercover to guide middle-class readers into the world of minimum-wage jobs.[84] She showed that essential workers are, in fact, the greatest philanthropists of our society, giving up a large part of themselves to make us happy. For Ehrenreich, however, it wasn't enough for members of what she called the "professional managerial class" to drop everything and become cleaners themselves—"slumming it," as it's often called.[85] Instead, she argued, we have to accept certain contradictions—that perhaps members of this professional class have a relationship that is complementary to that of the working class without wishing away the important distinctions. For Ehrenreich, we can't just assign blame, nor can we assume people are helpless in their class position. It's about *breaking* class divisions.[86] This means getting angry: angry enough to stop projecting our dissatisfaction with our lives onto others, to look at ourselves and see how our own choices, contradictions, and compromises for personal comfort have led us to take others for granted, including our own neighbors, and turn our backs on them.

As we'll argue next, the only way out of this dynamic is to break out of these doomed class divisions, to build relationships across class. This is called solidarity. It's a different kind of individual choice, distinct from "green" lifestyles, virtue signaling, or performative class disavowal. Breaking class divisions requires acting in unity without squashing the many important differences between us—across class, race, gender, age, ability, or sexual orientation. Solidarity won't come about by meditating in isolation, remaining stuck in your head. It requires active engagement, knowing that all relationships are political. It also goes back to that initial desire for conviviality. Either we can act on these desires by enrolling ourselves in the speculative market, or we can step out of that cycle and reconfigure those desires toward building a different kind of world.

Solidarity

On August 29, 2022, 180,000 residents of Mississippi's capital, Jackson, no longer had access to drinking water. An unprecedented flood the previous week had caused the primary water treatment plant to fail, leading residents' taps to either go dry or spit out sludge-colored water.[87] Eighty-five percent of Jackson's population is Black, in a state whose ruling Republican Party is predominantly white. The city has been plagued by disinvestment in much of its infrastructure. Chokwe Antar Lumumba, the city's mayor, had been warning for months that the water system needed a serious upgrade—but his warnings fell on deaf ears.[88] In recent years, the city's water system had seen high levels of lead, bacterial contamination, and storm damage. But the flood, coming during a summer of forest fires, storms, and droughts, was the final nail in the coffin for the city's beleaguered water treatment plant—and so it failed. Within hours, locals started filling cars and minivans with bottled water, setting up distribution sites across the city. At the center of the effort was Cooperation Jackson, a local organization whose goal is to "replace the current socio-economic system of exploitation, exclusion and the destruction of the environment with a proven democratic alternative."[89] Members of the organization rallied volunteers, raised funds, and helped to coordinate the relief effort, making sure that tens of thousands of residents got access to drinkable water in the middle of the crisis.

Cooperation Jackson didn't come out of nowhere. In the early 1970s, activist Chokwe Lumumba (Chokwe Antar Lumumba's father) and hundreds of Black freedom activists moved to Mississippi to start an agricultural community based on a cooperative economics. They were stopped by "a phalanx of local police, state police, the FBI and the Klu Klux Klan."[90] Their story has some similarities to that of Auroville, but, as we will see, in other aspects it is completely different.

After serious police repression, the elder Lumumba moved back to Detroit to pursue a law degree. Ten years later, he was back in Mississippi. This time he moved to Jackson and, with a growing group of committed individuals, started organizing in the city. In 2005, when Hurricane Katrina hit the state, they organized the Mississippi Disaster Relief Coalition. By 2010, the coalition had transformed into the three-hundred-member Jackson People's Assembly, which, according to Cooperation Jackson member Makani Themba-Nixon, was a "forum [. . .] for mass engagement to address the issues that affect a community's life."[91] A few hundred members might not seem like much, but in a city where voter turnout is typically 25,000 people, it was significant. The assembly campaigned for the elder Lumumba to run for city council in 2009 and for mayor in 2013—and he won both posts. Sadly, Lumumba died of a heart attack in 2014, seven months into his term as mayor. In 2017, his son Chokwe Antar Lumumba ran for mayor, promising to run on his father's platform—and that of the People's Assembly—winning with 93 percent of the vote.

In the meantime, the organization Cooperation Jackson was founded and started buying up land in the city. As author Pete Dolack writes, the tactic of buying up land to turn it into cooperatives is part of the group's wider strategy of fighting gentrification through building an ecological community:

> The neighborhood where Cooperation Jackson is based has large amounts of vacant lots and abandoned buildings, but because it is near downtown, real estate developers and the city capitalist elite are hungrily eyeing the area. The backers of Cooperation Jackson are buying land to create an "eco village" that is intended to include quality, "deeply affordable" cooperative housing, a grocery and the other coop projects, all powered by solar energy. The larger goal is for the city of Jackson to become self-sustaining

through comprehensive recycling, composting, local food production, links to regional organic farms, a city solar-power system
and zero-emission public transportation.[92]

And all of that land was pulled out of the urban real estate
market, out of the endless branding and speculation loop that is
destroying our planet. The goal is nothing other than a democratically run city—and that means not just a more democratic municipal government but a democratic, ecological economy as well. The
actions of Cooperation Jackson form what Amitav Ghosh calls
"livelihood environmentalism," focused on everyday political organizing intimately associated with the vitality of the land.[93] This
is very different from the *lifestyle* environmentalism of vibing out
in new branded merchandise and virtue-signaled wellness ploys.

Flash forward to 2022. During the pandemic Cooperation
Jackson had spent much of its limited energy building community
networks of support. Cooperation Jackson's dream projects have
struggled with setbacks such as contaminated soil, lack of stable
financing, and key activists being hired by Lumumba's municipal
government, leaching their scarce energy and resources.

And yet when the water crisis finally hit the impoverished city,
Cooperation Jackson was the first respondent. They helped start
Justice for Jackson, a coalition of community groups whose principal demands were for the state and federal government to fund the
"complete overhaul of the Jackson water treatment and delivery
systems," which should be "within the democratic control of the
city of Jackson" and be "ecologically designed" and built by local
contractors from the majority Black community.[94] Rather than
waiting for the state, which was dragging its heels, Cooperation
Jackson started raising funds and calling for volunteers to develop
a network of water catchment, treatment, and delivery systems in
community centers across the city. Cooperation Jackson calls this
double strategy "build and fight": on the one hand, they pressure
those in power and hold them accountable, while on the other,

they build the alternatives their community needs in the here and now.[95]

From Black freedom activists marching to settle farmland in the U.S. South in 1971 to being a key player in city politics today, the story of Cooperation Jackson is almost the reverse of Auroville. While both initiatives shared a utopian vision, Aurovillians tried to set up their utopia by parachuting into a place full of meaning and significance for the people who already lived there. Very little thought was put into how they would not just educate the locals but build community *with* them too. The Auroville utopia was also born out of a kind of mourning of the colonial project, an attempt to reclaim it so that the founder (The Mother) could continue feeling "Indian."[96] Its version of ecology comes from a rather naive dream of peace and salvation through aloof spiritual discipline, which does little to address class division.

In contrast, for Cooperation Jackson and its predecessors in the Black freedom movement, their vision of economic and political democracy meant raising up the community for what they call "self-determination": the ability to have collective ownership of their own future. Cooperation Jackson might not have the hippie or divine-spirituality branding of Auroville, nor the blessings of UNESCO, the United Nations organization that endorsed the creation of the global village on newly liberated Indian territory. And like any such project, the successes of Cooperation Jackson come up against just as many challenges and failures. But after decades of being in the community, they have built strong relationships and earned the trust of the local people, who turned to them first when their taps were cut off. Cooperation Jackson is an example of livelihood, rather than lifestyle, environmentalism. It is also an example of solidarity.

What do we mean by solidarity? First, *solidarity is not charity.* Charity implies a one-way relationship: someone who is better off gives time, food, or money to someone who is worse off. A relationship of power is evident, and the power sits squarely with the person giving the charity. It is assumed that the reverse—that the poor can't help the rich—isn't true. Solidarity is instead a two-way relationship: through building a connection, both people change each other.[97] It is reciprocal, but not tit for tat. When they distribute water, members of Cooperation Jackson aren't just doing so out of goodwill; they are doing it out of love, wanting recipients to become participants. To quote Zapatista activist Gioconda Belli, "Solidarity is the tenderness of the people."[98]

Second, *solidarity is not the same as voting*. Often we are told that if we want real change, we need to convince enough people to vote for us or the candidate we believe in. For many, politics stops and ends with "getting out the vote." Not only does this limit politics to a single action, but it also saps much-needed energy from the kind of sustained and constant relationship-building that solidarity depends on. And it directs the energy of what should be relationships between many people toward a single person, held upon the shoulders of an assembled cult of personality. That person is then either a hero or a scapegoat to dump all your problems on, turning all the concerns of society that require collective action into an issue for individuals to deal with. When they fail (which they inevitably will), the political pendulum swings to an even worse option.

When political action is limited to voting, elected officials become actors, circus performers even. We watch them juggle and walk on tightropes, and we judge them based on how charismatic (or not) they are—distracting us from what's going on and what we can do about it. But unlike with a circus, we're not just spectators who have nothing to gain or lose from the outcomes of the performance.[99]

While Cooperation Jackson has had success getting its candidates elected, many in the movement believe that this effort channeled too many resources to fighting for elections every year, when in fact they needed to put that into keeping the People's Assembly going and using the little funds they had to buy up land for more cooperative businesses and housing—which would, in turn, create an even larger movement. They argued that they needed to build alternatives first, so that once they did participate in local elections, they'd have a big enough movement to hold those elected officials accountable and restrain the cult of personality that often develops.[100]

Third, *solidarity is also not representation*. Notions like diversity, equity, and inclusion risk becoming a social equivalent to "greenwashing," and can often worsen class tensions, to the detriment of convivial and collective solidarity. Just as perfecting the vibe of a particular aesthetic causes both social exclusion and ecological harm, making sure that diverse people are represented is not the same as respecting diverse people and their diverse backgrounds and knowledges. There are plenty of instances, from presidents to chiefs of police forces, to CEOs, when greater representation has only meant replacing white figureheads with nonwhite ones, or replacing men with women, just keeping things as they are—now with a new face! Making an organization more diverse and equitable might in fact involve completely changing its core strategy and goals—what an organization actually does. It isn't an add-on.

While solidarity requires building relationships across difference, it also means that *everyone has something to contribute*. Not only do the members of Cooperation Jackson have an important goal they want to achieve, they also know that they can't achieve it without the support of the wider community, and without creating space for people, and particularly often less heard voices of women, the disabled, and young people, to change the organization itself from within.

Fourth, *solidarity is not a career*. Often when we are faced with an issue—say, racial profiling or environmental pollution—we are tempted to think the best thing to do is to find the people who work on this issue and donate money to them, assuming that they know best. What this does, however, is create a class of professionalized activists, a cadre of external "experts" who proclaim to know a lot about a problem but are often far removed from everyday experiences of it. It also props up an ecosystem of nonprofit organizations who spend much of their energy on endless funding drives, branding, and outreach. NGO staff are often hired on one-year contracts, funded by single-issue grants and fickle philanthropists.[101] When the funding dries up, nonprofits are forced to move to new, more fashionable projects. Then there are "critical" academic researchers who want to hear pain stories about environmental and social injustices so they can write about them to boost their careers.[102] Mind you, many nonprofits and researchers are doing excellent work. And it's only fair that activists seek steady income to keep doing what they love. But the issue here is that donating to these nonprofits or following the academic career path within the university's ivory tower can't replace solidarity.

Solidarity requires that we do more than just give our money or create new jobs for anything that actually requires systemic, structural change. It means more than just spending our time publishing paywalled journal articles, making CEOs in swivel chairs laugh gleefully at all the "radical" academic publications that lead to massive profit margins. We have to step outside of our careers and the class structures that keep us perpetuating an endless stream of #content, grant applications, and quantified measures of our worth.

In addition, both academics and nonprofits are well known for parachuting into conflicts, taking the steam out of local movements, appropriating them for their own cause, depoliticizing key issues, and then claiming to be experts on them.[103] Again, Co-operation Jackson offers an alternative model: go to their (rather poorly designed, non-grant-funded) website and you'll immediately see that they're not in the business of fundraising or branding but are working steadily toward their transformative vision, optics be damned. They aren't an organization as much as a movement of *people power*.

Being Convivial

As the water crisis rages in Jackson, Mississippi, and continuously gets ignored by the media, Cooperation Jackson is slowly
and steadily working to foster the kinds of relationships that meet
people's needs where the government and the market have so blatantly (and arguably *deliberately*) failed. But few of these relationships are recognized by the UN's Sustainable Development Goals,
"eco-friendly" consumption patterns, or green branding firms. It
isn't easy, but it gives meaning and purpose to people's lives and
brings about another way to imagine living together, transforming the environment where people live in the process. It's the real
deal.

There's a good case to be made that at the heart of Cooperation Jackson's strategy is conviviality. Building relationships over
time has gained them the trust of the local community. It's these
relationships that are activated in times of crisis, allowing them to
organize quickly and effectively. These relationships are not just
social but material, too: by building infrastructure that people actually need, they are slowly able to articulate a different vision of an
ecological, democratic economy and make it more real. Convivial
relationships are helped along by a kind of ecological glue between
people and nonhumans. That stickiness reclaims that twinkle in
our eyes. It is a stickiness that binds us together and stops us from
feeling alienated. It is motivated not by profit, narcissism, or short-
lived dopamine highs. It is motivated by *freedom*.[104]

In this chapter, we showed how a yearning for conviviality ani-
mates the sustainability class, who ultimately end up destroying
conviviality through branding and speculation, discarding anyone
and anything that doesn't fit with the brand. But being convivial,
as should be clear by now, isn't about individuals acting in isolation from each other—by buying a house and staring out large
windows or moving into a preexisting community to set up your

utopia–cum–investment strategy. It's about relational webs: connections with others, human and nonhuman, in ways that foster reciprocity and enhance conditions for life to thrive. They are the mangrove world, enacted and unfolding every second. It's about forging one's self-identity through collective belonging to the land and each other, in action that transforms the world.

We argued that the key to conviviality is solidarity. Solidarity means building ties based on trust and reciprocity. Standing with others in unity and knowing that they'll stand with you is very different from just donating to a charity. In a way, solidarity is about *being* convivial, rather than seeking to produce it, represent it, or show it off to others. And that means stepping outside of our class and exclusive enclaves to meet others where they are. We could go further: it means betraying our own class interests. In the next chapter, we'll see how conviviality becomes fertile ground for a politicized ecology, letting us imagine something different than impending ecological collapse.

8

TAKING BACK THE FUTURE

In Los Angeles, a feeling of disappointment, or perhaps uneasiness, ran through many of our conversations with those peddling "sustainability" solutions. We felt the uneasiness when we were sitting poolside across from Chuck at the Beverly Hills Hilton, talking about regenerative agriculture. We felt it when we interviewed Eduardo about flipping houses to make them greener, and when talking to Jessica on Abbot Kinney Boulevard about how veganism would save the world.

For one thing, all of them recognized that the solutions they were advocating didn't apply to low-income people, and they tried to propose ways around that. Eduardo believed that building more houses would make housing more affordable and get people off the street—a solution that does nothing to address the fact that housing has become a site of financial speculation. The fact is that while there are 36,000 unhoused people in Los Angeles, there are 93,000 housing units sitting empty, with 67 percent of all residential units controlled by corporate investors.[1] Jessica said she knew that high-end veganism was expensive, but that the first thing to do was to make it chic—that way it would eventually trickle down to everyone. She didn't sound too convinced. Chuck's idea was perhaps the most farcical: he believed that getting farmers to regenerate soil would miraculously result in migrant workers being treated more humanely.

They all seemed to have been working through the contradictions somehow—and, in some cases, even believed that "greening" was bogus. Eduardo was all for denser, more energy-efficient cities but was also personally thinking about places outside the city to escape to when climate change becomes unbearable. Jessica told us point blank that the lifestyle she was an ambassador for was in fact superficial and that plenty of people were really just in it for the vibes—she just thought this was the best we've got right now. Chuck was at pains to prove to us that he cared about global justice, for example by dropping mentions of Indigenous tribes in the Amazon. We very much felt that underneath the glossy green surface, there was a dissatisfaction with it all.

Creating vibes, donating, and branding green with labels like "LEED-certified" and "organic" has been going on for decades now. And yet we're going nowhere fast—the science is undeniable that we're careening past all the planetary boundaries faster and faster.[2] There's got to be something else that can be done. How can we bring our social metabolism back to what can be sustained within a single planet and not five? How do we build and reweave social and economic relationships that do not speculate on present and future lives (human and nonhuman)?

To begin to answer these questions, we need to accept that the answers will have personal implications for each of us. Before we can take ecological problems seriously, we've got to be honest with ourselves. Do we have the courage not to fall back on our class comforts? Do we feel that we need to be applauded or given a proof of purchase for taking active steps to care for the world? Do we have the commitment not just to follow fad after fad but to stew in the discomfort of purposeful action—not for anyone else, but because we are actually committed to change? Would our time and effort really be better placed moving to places like Hanoi's Ecopark, showing off how much we donated during the next Giving Tuesday (to alleviate our guilt from Black Friday), or awaiting carbon-neutral status to impress our neighbors? Simply put, as Swedish climate activist Greta Thunberg tells us:

We cannot live sustainably within today's economic system. Yet that is what we are constantly being told we can do. We can buy sustainable cars, travel on sustainable [highways], powered by sustainable petroleum. We can eat sustainable meat and drink sustainable soft drinks out of sustainable plastic bottles. We can buy sustainable fast fashion and fly on sustainable airplanes using sustainable fuels. And, of course, we are going to meet our short- and long-term sustainable climate targets, too, without making the slightest effort.[3]

Fortunately for us all, the future doesn't have to be net-zero floating islands and Martian colonies. The sustainable future doesn't have to be about synchronizing billions of human beings to a clock, from temporary migrant farm laborers to e-commerce employees and DoorDash drivers, all breaking their backs to produce cheap stuff delivered just in time with a click of a button by some self-proclaimed environmentalist sitting in an ergonomic chair in front of his screen thinking about his eco-friendly purchases. Emissions cuts don't need to be subsidized by oil and gas; renewables don't have to be a top-up to fossil-fuel-driven financial speculation that keeps shareholders in business class happy. Being ecological really isn't about guilt-tripped philanthropy that removes people from their homeland to make way for flammable carbon-offset forest plantations that allow the most polluting companies to go on as before. It's absurd that we've even come to this point.

We don't need to wait for fully automated, industrial vegan lifestyles, eating lab-grown, energy-intensive, and highly processed foodstuffs, stewing in our loneliness in glass condominium towers surrounded by soulless landscaped greenery and protected by a private militia to keep the unsavory out of our view. We don't need to have well-funded public relations and branding campaigns to cover up the fact that world crude oil production continues at a breakneck pace and climate-induced wildfires and disease continue to destroy trees as offsets for new development projects.[4] We don't need to experience the alienation and depression caused by constantly needing to virtue-signal to our peers or by continuously self-branding ourselves to be more employable—ending up with no one but a potted plant, or perhaps a real estate agent prowling our drought-resistant lawn to assess how much "nature" can add to our property value.

We might know very well that these are not desirable options. But that knowledge itself doesn't give us much to work with. Many of us experience climate anxiety especially in rich countries—feelings of grief, fear, powerlessness, anger, or guilt in response to a rapidly changing environment.[5] The inability to plan for the future or to even imagine a liveable and decent life has enormous psychological repercussions, particularly for Gen Z and Alpha youth.

A group of psychologists specializing in climate and mental health have found that there are actionable solutions to addressing climate anxiety—with collective organizing and activism against environmental injustice being key. In their peer-reviewed research, they found that while climate change anxiety was linked to higher symptoms of depression in students not engaged in collective action, this was not the case where students were actively organizing to combat climate.[6] That's the good news: we *do* have options.

There are others out there, like Greta Thunberg and other eloquent youth like Isra Hirsi and Sohanur Rahman, already showing us what it is like to step out of our comfort zone. They demonstrate what it looks like to be ecological without going green. Our individual efforts, when done in solidarity with others, *can* lead to change that we see every day—not just in our neighbors and communities but also in ourselves. That kind of connection is unlike any mindfulness course or yoga class you've ever taken.

Imagining the possible outside of the realm of the pragmatic isn't, in fact, idealistic dreaming. People do this all the time, to great effect. Concrete examples exist all around us. In fact, we can all get on board with supporting them where we live and work. There's no better way to combat climate anxiety.

In this chapter, we'll ask you to imagine alongside us what an alternative path could look like, one that isn't so inherently dissatisfying. We'll start by giving you a tour of a movement in the heart of Los Angeles, one that is reclaiming its *barrio* from real estate speculators and lifestyle environmentalists while offering a different kind of ecological vision. We then put forward that ecology is about reclaiming the imagination, making material relations political, weaving solidarity, and—above all—building power outside of, and against, the realm of the market.

Keep Beverly Hills out of Boyle Heights: The Union de Vecinos

Across town and seemingly a world away from the Beverly Hills Hilton, members of the Union de Vecinos (Union of Neighbors) from the largely Latino community of Boyle Heights are making sustainability happen for real.

Instead of showing off to their neighbors and staring blankly out large windows at manicured xeriscaped yards, tenants have been coming together block by block in Boyle Heights to stop police harassment and racial discrimination. In many buildings, they've stopped rent increases and won battles against abusive landlords and real estate developers. They distribute food for neighbors in need, fight for clean water and breathable air, clean the streets and sidewalks, install solar-powered lighting, grow food, fix potholes, organize to make street traffic safer, and, during the COVID-19 pandemic, protected and informed their neighbors. They do all this while generating an atmosphere of fun and refuge from the stress of everyday family life. Some of their activities include organizing regular outdoor movie nights, collective cooking events, and fiestas. What's so incredible about the

Union de Vecinos is how they seem to be everywhere in the area, engaged wherever there is injustice taking place or community to be built. They are taking back their environment from neglect and devastation and reconstructing it. And it is not a lifestyle choice. It is a livelihood choice.[7]

The roots of the Union de Vecinos date back to the 1990s, a time when Los Angeles police chief Daryl Gates initiated the War on Drugs. In Boyle Heights, police would often instigate conflict among rival gangs.[8] In response, mothers started a cop-monitoring program to protect their sons—which also reduced gang activity and violence in the area. It was these mothers who then started organizing in response to the demolition of public housing in Boyle Heights in 1996. At the time, the Department of Housing and Urban Development started a program to rebrand public housing as market-rate and mixed-income developments and call them "affordable."[9] The invariable outcome of this federal program was to green-light the eviction of long-standing lower-income residents—disproportionately impacting African Americans and Latinos. By 2003, the 1,262 public housing units in Boyle Heights were reduced to just 296 units. Only 25 percent of the almost two thousand displaced families were able to return to the neighborhood. In response, the Union de Vecinos was formed to ensure that contracts would allow residents to remain in the new mixed-income developments without an increase in rent.[10] Shortly afterward, they organized against a police station and the expansion of a new metro line (the Gold Line) that would encourage new forms of real estate speculation in their community. Twenty-five years later, they're still going strong.

One morning, we walked through the neighborhood with members of the Union de Vecinos: Leo Vilchis Sr., his son Leo Jr., Ofelia Platon, and Maria José. When we met up with them we knew we were at the right place because they were standing in front of a vivid mural loudly proclaiming "Boyle Heights se defiende" (Boyle Heights defends itself) and "Keep Beverly Hills out of Boyle Heights." On our walk we saw firsthand what an alternative vision of development looks like—a vision actually centered on the community.

They began by explaining to us that on this block, traffic would always go too fast. So they painted a crosswalk and put in benches to make it feel safer—which led to the elderly sitting on the benches, more people walking, and drivers slowing down. They painted the mural we were standing in front of and made signs telling people to pick up after their dogs. On telephone poles nearby were signs urging people to come to the next Union de Vecinos movie night.

How was this different from the bike lanes painted and trees planted as part of the city's official renewal plans, or even the building of a new metro line in the area that was advertised as green infrastructure? Well, when it came to trees, they had a very unique approach. The Union de Vecinos didn't allow trees to be planted unless they were accompanied by benches for the elderly to sit around them and where children could play. Tree planting that doesn't generate relationships with the community is tree planting that raises property values and kicks out the "wrong" type of residents. Nature isn't natural if it comes with destroying community.

Likewise, they weren't against green infrastructure, but their issue was with what kind of people bike lanes and the metro line were meant to benefit, and whether that would ultimately lead to gentrification. In the areas around Gold Line stations, for example, they saw many members of their community being evicted just as new market-rate housing was being built. Indeed, researchers have found that green infrastructure in Los Angeles has led to increased real estate values and came along with gentrification.[11] In response to this threat, they decided to take up space for the people living there—mostly working-class people of color—to build community. So they organized tenants' rights campaigns and anti-eviction protests, and brought people living around the new stations together by organizing block parties and regular community events. "We wanted to take control of our geography," Leo Sr. emphasized.

Another example of the strategy to take control of their geography was the coalition they started, called BHAAAD: Boyle Heights Alliance Against Artwashing and Displacement. This group came together to stop the spread of private art galleries whose "up-and-coming" aesthetic would lead to an influx of wealthy residents, real estate speculation, and rising rents for tenants. Around 2018, it became clear that the city wanted to designate an industrial area in Boyle Heights as a new arts district—just across the river from the existing Arts District, which, you will recall, is home to the "sustainable" Los Angeles Clean Tech Incubator.[12] The incoming people, well intentioned though they might be, were bringing in their class privileges, which so often align with the interests and aesthetics of white people, to a nonwhite working-class neighborhood. The Union de Vecinos saw how the so-called improvement of their neighborhood for the sake of art would become a recipe for their eviction, since members of the community themselves did not have ownership of the "beautification" process. So they organized protests in front of some of the new art galleries, showed up at city hall, graffitied the facades of galleries and chic businesses, and demanded that the galleries "leave Boyle Heights immediately." And that is what the galleries did. When the members of the Union de Vecinos walked us through the area, they showed us all the spaces where galleries had been that were now empty. Whatever businesses had decided to stay were very low-key.

When challenged by some observers asserting that BHAAAD was setting up an "us versus them" environment, they responded in a pamphlet: "The truth is, polarization is exactly what we are trying to fight. This is a polarization that was here long before us. Unfortunately, it's the basic geometry of capitalism. The uneven development of urban wealth and opportunity is as central to the brand of Los Angeles™, as it is central to the engine which drives the neoliberal economy."[13] And their tactics, even if feisty, helped change minds. Gallerist Robert Zin Stark, for example, initially dismissed the protests against his own gallery as misdirected but later ended up realizing that he had been wrong to be part of the artwashing of Boyle Heights. As he said in an interview, "It's made me question the gallery system itself."[14] Indeed, when the Los Angeles Police Department was called to investigate "a hate crime" when a wall on one of the new galleries was graffitied with "Fuck White Art," many local artists and white gentrifiers were quick to mobilize in support of the Union de Vecinos.[15] Confrontational? Yes. But it works. BHAAAD's strategy has led to ten galleries shutting their doors or relocating.[16]

Their approach is not limited to Boyle Heights. In the city of Maywood in southeast Los Angeles, the drinking water supply was found to be contaminated with lead, mercury, and manganese. While other environmental justice organizations wanted to start applying for grants to test the water supply, in order to prove to the city that they needed to do something about it, the Union de Vecinos organized residents to take over the Maywood city council, which then took charge over one of the water companies and changed bylaws to increase tenants' access to the company.[17] They also put pressure on state and city officials to force the private companies to decontaminate the water. Meanwhile, grant-funded nonprofits admonished them for acting too fast—even when those nonprofits had little to show for themselves.

The way the Union de Vecinos fights to reclaim local ecologies while paying attention to class is contagious. So contagious, in fact, that their model sparked a city-wide tenant movement. Inspired by the union and based largely on their organizing strategy, the Los Angeles Tenant's Union (LATU) was started by members of the Union de Vecinos in 2015 and by 2022 had 15 autonomous "locals" across the city.

LATU is an autonomous housing movement completely

funded by its members. Their mission is to "strengthen tenants' political power through education, advocacy, and direct action." They do this by building power from the community, for the community.[18] With much of real estate in Los Angeles owned by large corporate networks or having nebulous ownership, LATU's members research abusive large property owners and identify different buildings that they own. Then locals will reach out to residents of these buildings. Often, tenants will come to LATU with their concerns, such as when they face eviction or a drastic rent increase. LATU will then work with them to stop these abusive practices. But instead of just providing tenants with legal support—as many NGOs often do—they will support tenants to, themselves, organize their neighbors and, through collective power, pressure their landlords to stop the evictions, rent increase, or negligent maintenance of the building. LATU's power operates both as a kind of moral persuasion to landlords and, more importantly, as an investment risk that raises costs for landlords and actually draws in more resistance and publicity in a positive feedback loop. The beauty of LATU is that it is tenants themselves who organize, not some supporting organization or external nonprofit acting on their behalf.

On one Sunday afternoon, we attended one of LATU's rallies in the neighborhood of Highland Park, where we saw this strategy in action. Neighbors and members of the LATU local gathered in the front yard of Ana, a tenant whose landlord plans to evict her family so that their house can be demolished and the lot turned into a sleek new condo development. On the right and left of us the neighboring houses were already boarded up.

We were served tacos and juice while we sat around and chatted with neighbors who had shown up to support Ana. The tenants we talked to lamented being "boxed in" by developers using digital currencies to buy up land for luxury condos, decried the increasing number of power outages despite the new solar panel farm on the hills nearby ("Where is the electricity going to?" one man asked), and remarked that, even despite those outages, the new residents drove around in Teslas, increasing demand on the grid. The new unaffordable restaurants and bars on Figueroa Street were increasing the number of drunk-driving incidents in the area and putting upward pressure on rents. It all started, said one, when the new metro line was built nearby.

Soon the crowd of about fifty people fell silent as members of LATU introduced Ana and her family. Ana, a small woman in her fifties, then told us about her struggle to stay in her home and how much LATU's presence had given her the courage to fight. Speaking in Spanish while someone translated, she ended her speech on a rousing note:

> We have to fight for our homes and this land. The fight is long, but you gotta be strong. It's not a fight for the weak. They want to make you feel completely isolated and alienated when they come for your house. But our presence in this community is an act of resistance. We used to be afraid too, but now we're stronger thanks to LATU. We know they have our back.

The organizing ethic of LATU rejects the idea of a group of experts who have the answers to everyone's questions; instead, it is about facing dilemmas and acting on them together. It's about meeting people where they are—making the effort to learn different languages, bridging cultural divides in order to help each other to remake the world.

It's also a tentacle-like network that has had an impact at different scales. They have organized entire areas—like Flower Street near the University of Southern California, where tenants of two whole blocks were mobilizing to save their homes from being demolished for multi-story condos, and entire neighborhoods like Boyle Heights. In the summer of 2022, they hosted the first in-person meeting of the Autonomous Tenants Union Network, bringing together two hundred participants in twenty-five tenant unions—helping to kickstart a national movement, but also becoming an opportunity to create linkages with similar struggles across the world.

We don't want to make it seem as though organizations like LATU and Union de Vecinos are perfect. Like everywhere, there are strong personalities, internal tensions, burnout, and difficulties retaining membership. But despite the problems they face, their models were so clearly different from all the grift, boosterism, and woke consumption on display elsewhere. When we showed up at LATU's rally, we felt relief. It was the day after our stay in Venice, which had felt like an absurdist theater performance that we were worried would never end. This was such a contrast to the discomfort we felt walking down Abbot Kinney Boulevard and the awkwardness we felt emanating from the sustainability boosters we talked to. There was none of the uneasiness of Chuck sitting poolside at the Hilton trying to convince us that regenerative agriculture would lead to migrant farmers being paid better, or Jessica trying to apologize for the fact that she knew chic veganism was inaccessible to the unhoused people living around her. It wasn't alienating. Instead, we felt an easy comfort, a kind of happiness in purpose. What we felt was the difference between vibe and conviviality, hipster environmentalism and solidarity.

Reclaiming the Imagination

When we first met Ofelia, Maria José, Leo Sr., and Leo Jr. in Boyle Heights and they showed us how they transformed their block—starting with benches, a mural, and crosswalks—we were reminded of Lois at the Los Angeles Ecovillage just a few miles away, near Koreatown. Like the L.A. EcoVillage, they had a vision for their neighborhood, and, like the EcoVillage, they intervened in its ecology over time, slowly growing their vision into a flourishing community. As Leo Sr. explained:

Our work in developing our own initiatives to support our struggles is not just to meet our priorities, but also to build and make the social life here flourish. We want to support each other—*convivir* [live together] . . . create community. When we develop community relations, we will inevitably be involved in politics, sociology, and ecology. One has to act to start thinking, rather than thinking about acting. It is very important to be a part of acting rather than engaging in ideas. Ideas flourish through our actions and through our relations. It's very organic. It's an organic garden of ideology.

The "organic garden of ideology" complements the description of Colombian anthropologist Arturo Escobar's "mangrove-world" in the last chapter: conviviality, not dwelling in an experience, but actively creating and being created by it, building an abundance of life in the process. This is what ecology is about.

A sense of imagination and possibility is one of the most important ingredients for ecological action. The anthropologist David Graeber famously said that "the ultimate, hidden truth of the world is that it is something that we make, and could just as easily make differently." [19] We could pair this with another quote by the political thinker Murray Bookchin: "The assumption that what currently exists must *necessarily* exist is the acid that corrodes all visionary thinking." [20] Or yet another quote by science fiction author Ursula K. LeGuin: "We live in capitalism. Its power seems inescapable. So did the divine right of kings. Any human power can be resisted and changed by human beings." [21] For the Union de Vecinos, the L.A. EcoVillage, and Cooperation Jackson, being able to imagine a different world was the first step in acting to achieve it. They were not content with the assumption that the status quo was immutable, nor did they give in to the notion that organizing their community would have little impact on the world.

What does ecological imagination look like? Here we can think back to Robin Wall Kimmerer's story about her eutrophied pond, from Chapter 2. When she started clearing it of algae, she could see a future where the pond was clear, children could swim in it, and the biomass it had generated was taken up by her garden, allowing other life-forms to flourish. But she didn't know how long it would take her, nor did she know what she would learn about this ecosystem. Similarly, when people outside of Kolkata started using sewage water for fish production in the early twentieth century, they didn't know that they were going to be part of the largest fish-powered water treatment plant in the world.

Ecological imagination means building a vision based on understanding the present system and then intervening in that system—tinkering, really—to transform it. Each intervention leads to more possibilities, more opportunities for others to join in the vision. We may not know where we will end up; we won't know what we will learn along the way. When we build interventions that open possibilities for everyone, we may find many travelers (both human and nonhuman) who wish to take the journey with us.

There are different kinds of imagination out there. There can also be imagination to further alienate and deaden the world with new consumable vibes (if you can pay the price for entry), or to create networks of relationships based on greed, fear, calculability, predictability, and control. Think of speculative visions like Neom, BiodiverCity, carbon offsetting schemes, or NFTs for nature. Their (obscenely wealthy) promoters advertise that we can have our PIE (purity, innovation, and efficiency) and eat it, too—and then throw away the plates and cutlery that it's served on. We can continue economic growth indefinitely, stack the Jenga blocks forever. Year after year, we can host global meetings of jet-setting delegates staying in highly surveilled luxury enclave conference "resorts" to trade in new commodities like "green" bonds and climate risk insurance packages and then brag that such meetings are about addressing environmental problems. We can go on investing billions of dollars into energy-intensive projects that will presumably "decouple" us from environmental impacts—despite little evidence suggesting this ever happening. Ultimately, we can simply offset present-day unsustainability into a distant future. This is Ponzi scheme territory—and we are letting it happen by going along with this vision of "sustainability."

This type of imagination, promoted by the likes of the World Bank, tech billionaires, and the countless NGOs and ministries of foreign affairs who champion the United Nations Sustainable Development Goals, gives us a prepackaged solution. Forty-plus years of their PIE have not gotten us anywhere but deeper into a climate disaster. There are plenty of examples of their chicanery. For instance, the Middle East Green Initiative has involved billions of dollars being invested in renewables in countries like the United Arab Emirates and Saudi Arabia, which pledge to be domestically net zero by 2050 and 2060, respectively.[22] They aim to do this by planting 50 billion trees, becoming world exporters of green hydrogen, and building "climate-neutral" cities like Neom from scratch. Conveniently though, these countries continue to invest in oil and gas exploration for export—and since exported emissions don't count within net-zero targets, they still get the "green" credentials. The imagination employed for greenwashing is about "thinking outside the box" so that no one—least of all the sustainability class—has to question what's actually in the box.

Elsewhere, the Yale University Environmental Performance Index, together with World Bank Governance Indicators and the BP Statistical Review of World Energy, has concluded that "if your oil and gas came with a label, you would learn that Canada's oil and gas industry is a global leader in environmental and social standards."[23] It's worth noting that Canada, along with energy glut countries like Iceland, Norway, and Bahrain, has one of the highest rates of energy consumption per capita.[24]

These absurd indicators, indices, and credentials premised on an obsession with metrics are designed to bamboozle the public into accepting that nothing is supposed to change—that oil and gas extraction can be "sustainable." As James Altucher and Douglas R. Sease's "investment plan for the apocalypse" tells us, renewable energy and ESG (environmental, social, and governance) portfolios are really just part of what we referred to as the "fossil fuel plus" strategy—invest in alternatives while continuing to invest in fossil fuels themselves.[25] The creativity these people depend on is the imagination to deceive, to pretend to the world that continuing the charade of investment in and extraction of oil and gas can actually be "net zero."

We also need to be wary of how imaginative alternatives get preyed upon through branding and performative spectacle. You can hang out in Boyle Heights and consume the spectacle of resistance, post it to Instagram, then walk away and say you had good fun, showing it off to others.[26] You can become an Aurovillian, live in Hanoi's Ecopark, or make a down payment to live in The Line and convince yourself of your immediate and unadulterated access to some ambiguous notion of nature. You, perhaps inspired by Elon Musk selling off his mansion, might be living a minimalist lifestyle, but you have retreated into yourself—created a sparse life raft and left the rabble sinking with the *Titanic*.

These kinds of imaginative visions are not the kind of imagination we're talking about—if they are imaginative at all. Such visions reinforce class divisions rather than undo them. They are speculative—but not the kind of speculation that science fiction writers like Ursula K. Le Guin employ. They turn everything into a speculative investment that writes off the futures of billions of people, not just of those not even born, but also of those here and now—such as when Donald Trump's son-in-law, Jared Kushner, mused that Gaza's "waterfront property could be very valuable," and when Benjamin Netanyahu unveiled plans for Gaza to be turned into a "free trade zone" complete with a "new electric vehicle manufacturing city" and rail service to (wait for it . . .) Neom![27] We need the imagination to think outside of the (wellness) pills they want us to swallow, the war crime and ecocidal utopias they want us to normalize. We need the imagination so that we don't get wallowed down by constant outrage, and instead channel collective energy toward rebuilding and regenerating our neighborhoods, workplaces, energy systems, and food systems.

Making Material Relations Political

In our interview with the members of Union de Vecinos, Leo Sr. told us that he saw the fight for their neighborhood as very similar to the global movement against international development imposed by the West—often called *post-desarollo* in Latin America.[28] In his view, the ideology that imposed "sustainable development" on poor countries was mirrored in the discourse of elites who wanted to "renew" Boyle Heights and make it "green." All they want to do is turn neighborhoods and territories into amenities, services, raw materials, and labor for the rich: "We do not believe that *desarollismo* [developmentalism] is going to change the world: it's actually creating worse conditions for many." Leo Sr. was pointing to the material connection between his own struggle and that of people far away.

The Union de Vecinos' struggle against displacement through development is indeed a kind of urban analogue to what happens outside of cities. It parallels the way farmers' unions, peasants, and Indigenous people in the countryside organize to prevent their lands and territories from being sucked into speculative land grabs for things like monoculture palm oil, cash crops like nuts and açai berries, and soybeans for cattle. Food industry promoters claim that displacement of a few locals, biodiversity collapse, soil erosion, and eutrophication of waterways are the price we have to pay in order to "feed the world." But feeding the world with what? The food deserts in most working-class and migrant neighborhoods from New Orleans to Manchester and souped-up hypermarkets in places like Jakarta and Lima have aisles filled to the brim with processed and carcinogenic foodstuffs from instant noodles to bags of potato chips. People buy them because they're the only things that are affordable.[29] Healthy and affordable food is scant for many people. But the sustainability class, with their artisan-cut crackers and vegan nut butters, would have you think differently.

When we walked through Erewhon in Venice Beach, we saw how it made the real connection of its food to the world invisible. Lifestyle environmentalism depends on creating a "nowhere" that is disconnected from the actual material relations that tie all of us to the planet we live on. For their part, green modernists depend on the same kind of obfuscation: the proposals of the Breakthrough Institute, for instance, are really not so different from the absurd dreams of a decoupled green hydrogen-powered fossil-fuel-funded luxury resort in the desert—or on the Moon, for that matter. There is little grounding in the reality that there is only one known planet in the cosmos that allows life for our species and countless others.

As we've seen, material impacts have not diminished as a result of green lifestyles. At the same time, wages for the people who produce everything from widgets to oranges have not kept pace with rising costs of living, forcing workers to work harder than ever before to make ends meet. This is what material reality tells us. It's not PIE-in-the-sky pipe dreams for billionaire tourists; it's everyday reality for billions of ordinary people.

The dream of the sustainability class is the fantasy that you can have a squeaky-clean economy without changing its very foundation. But this type of green living just builds off of and adds on to raw material extraction and manufacturing taking place somewhere along the global supply chain. And then it tops up a whole lot of its own material and energy demands—everything from graphite to lithium to copper to rare earth minerals and pressure on already scarce groundwater to process these minerals. But this, as we explained in Chapter 3, is like thinking you could just keep playing Jenga forever without stopping—that the base of the tower doesn't matter, that physics isn't a real thing. You can keep taking blocks from the bottom, and you can try to place them on top with increasing precision, but eventually the whole thing is going to come crashing down. *That's* material.

So how do we make sure that remaking environments does not involve unmaking somewhere else? How do we make material relations political—and the basis of an ecology for everyone? In Chapter 6, we discussed how the movement for climate reparations is mobilizing poor countries to demand accountability for climate breakdown from rich countries, which overwhelmingly bear the responsibility for climate change. Here, being ecological means reversing centuries of unfair terms of trade and genocidal pillaging of people and resources. This is what it would mean to make material relations political on a global scale. Once we make material relations a political object, then they can't just be swept under the rug.

The climate protests that have been sweeping the globe over the last decade are another example of making material relations political. Focusing their demands on material limits (350 parts per million of carbon in the atmosphere, 1.5°C of global temperature rise, or simply stopping fossil fuel extraction—keeping coal in the hole, oil in the soil, etc.), climate activists can orchestrate global demonstrations that speak to a global audience.[31] As we'll discuss below, theirs is also an example of counterbranding: doing spectacular actions that can make their demands international news. What's important here is that they are finding ways to put material limits on the front pages.

And yet, making the material political isn't only about global trends of resource use, planetary boundaries, or social metabolism. While very much a concern, these things can often feel very distant from people's own lives. Concepts like "aggregate material and energetic throughputs" are measurable and real but can also feel very abstract and intangible.

Material relations don't have to be abstract. In fact, it turns out that people get involved with their community when they can see tangible material benefits in doing so. Here's an example. In the Indian state of Tamil Nadu, not too far from Auroville, a very different kind of ecological regeneration has occurred—one that puts class struggle at the center and has little to do with branding or exclusive lifestyles.

In Tamil Nadu, climate change has meant either unprecedented monsoon rains or extreme heat and drought, forcing farmers in the rice bowl of the Cauvery River delta to extract scarce groundwater. Traditionally, women of the Dalit caste (the lowest in the Hindu caste system and formerly known as "untouchables") have been excluded from owning land and holding political power. These women also struggle in the lowest class stratum, working as landless laborers, and are becoming increasingly vulnerable as they confront the "three-headed hydra of patriarchy, climate change, and caste oppression."[32]

Their strategy was to pool their skills and resources and then leasing property collectively for cultivation. Rather than growing rice using industrial production methods imposed on them by upper-caste men when they were landless laborers, these women used their own cultural and agricultural knowledge to sow a cultivar of *gram* (a pulse). Now they have financial security, have access to more nutritious food, and can provide for their families—what the international peasant organization La Via Campesina calls "food sovereignty." Not only did this strategy involve reclaiming their own knowledge about food production, but it was also better adapted to the dry soils and the increasingly hostile climate, and their produce is eaten locally rather than exported for urban consumers. These Dalit women have enriched their soils, worked to adapt to climate change, and chipped away at class, patriarchy, and caste subjugation. But it all started when they came together around a shared material basis: lack of access to land.

We could also see how material relations can bring people

together in the examples of the Union de Vecinos, LATU, and Cooperation Jackson. For instance, the Union de Vecinos helped organize residents to take over an entire water company in the Los Angeles suburb of Maywood. LATU provides on-the-ground support for tenants who are being intimidated by their landlords. Cooperation Jackson is growing food for neighbors in Jackson, Mississippi. Each of these groups based their community strategy on fighting for something people sorely needed (tenant power, water, and food) and, in the process, built convivial relations that transformed their environments, making them without unmaking them somewhere else. This isn't "outreach" or "capacity building" (as they would be called in nonprofit jargon); it's just being a good neighbor. Pretty basic stuff. No fancy language or expert knowledge needed. People get involved once they can see the real benefit of working together. The benefits are always both collective and individual, never just one or the other. As these groups show as well, this doesn't just have to be serious, Debbie Downer–type work. Conviviality is also about throwing parties and painting murals—in other words, living fully in the company of others.

The COVID-19 pandemic acutely demonstrated how structural inequality impacted some more than others. It also revealed cracks in the system, when national and local governments were entirely unequipped to coordinate access to food and hygienic supplies to much of the population. In almost every city in North America, mutual aid groups sprang up to support those who needed something: access to health care and information, paid sick leave, affordable food, rent freezes and suspension of debt payments, electricity, personal protective equipment and food for residents of tent encampments, housing for the unhoused in repurposed hotels and vacant speculative condominiums, translation, help in demanding unemployment support from employers, and support for standing up to their landlords.[33]

The student encampments against genocide in Gaza that spread across the world in 2024 are another example of what it looks like when the material is political. After seventy-six years of Israeli occupation, ethnic cleansing, and apartheid conditions that have caused generational trauma and taken an unthinkable toll on the Palestinian people, the sustained oppression took a turn for the worse on the morning of October 7, 2023, when Hamas organized a horrific attack killing 1,139 Israelis and kidnapping 252 people. By March 2024, six months later, the Israeli Defense Forces killed more than 30,000 Palestinians in Gaza and destroyed almost two-thirds of homes. After months of the genocide unfolding, frustrated students began encampments, spreading like wildfire from New York's Columbia University to universities across the country and the world. Students' demands are, among others, for their universities to disclose and divest from investments in companies complicit in Israel's slaughter of Palestinians. Students research and publish these relationships, vividly illustrating the ecosystem of research, investments, and power that funds weapons of war and surveillance. Despite every attempt to fracture the solidarity between Jewish and Muslim students against the occupation of Palestine, the students celebrate both Jewish and Muslim traditions with food and dance and often translate messages in Arabic and Hebrew. At the encampments, people bring food, tents, projector screens, and books—allowing them to organize teach-ins, resource libraries, movie nights, and community meals. In so many ways, they are making the material political. And they make a material difference. Universities in various parts of the world, from Spain, Norway, Ireland, and even a few across the United States, have disclosed their collaborations with Israeli weapons manufacturers and, in a growing number of cases, are vowing to end them. This is a start.

All of these actions involve pooling resources that can't be speculated on and do not depend on lavish and materially demanding lifestyles. This is what it means to make the material political where you live. This is what it means to imagine a different kind of world that isn't premised on divisions to justify the destruction of life on earth, but on solidarity across so much difference. And this is also what it means to be ecological.

Weaving Solidarity

When we walked through Boyle Heights with members of the Union de Vecinos, we were regularly stopped by passersby who wanted to talk with them about anything from problems with their landlords to church services. As we could see clearly, it was these connections with their neighbors that were the basis of their success. As Maria José told us, "Our projects are not just about meeting our priorities but also about building and making social life flourish here. We want to support each other—*convivir*, create community. When we create community, we resolve our own problems together. The power is in our organization." This same kind of conviviality is seen in Cooperation Jackson: personal connections are the threads that can be activated in times of crisis, such as being able to quickly mobilize hundreds of volunteers when the city's water plant fails.

As we argued in Chapter 7, these connections are essential for people to step out of their class position and act in solidarity with others. But how do these vital kinds of connections actually lead to real change?

One answer is that convivial relations have to reach across communities to achieve their transformative potential. Ofelia, Maria José, Leo Sr., and Leo Jr. stressed that much of the Union de Vecinos' work was grounded in the shared culture of the majority Latino community. "The threat we face is the removal of our culture here," said Ofelia. At the same time, they acknowledged that they needed to start creating links with other communities facing the same risks of displacement. For example, they had started to organize tenants in buildings that had mostly white gentrifier residents. While this was often more difficult, as the white new-comers didn't share the same culture of solidarity, they still managed to have some successes. This was also the reason they wanted to help start LATU (which they call the *sindicato*)—so that they could develop a network across neighborhoods, cultures, and people of different class backgrounds.

There are other illustrative examples of how convivial relationships can bring about large-scale transformative ecological change. In 2019, members of the Wet'suwet'en clan started blocking the Coastal GasLink Pipeline from being constructed on their ancestral land in what we now call British Columbia, Canada. In early 2020, a group of land defenders—mostly women—were violently arrested by the Royal Canadian Mounted Police. In response, Indigenous peoples started blocking railroads across Canada, in the countryside and in cities.[34] The rail system ground to a halt across the whole of Canada.

Actions such as these have a real impact. For example, one report calculated that in the United States and Canada, Indigenous resistance to fossil fuel infrastructure—such as the blockade by the Wet'suwet'en and the Dakota Access Pipeline protests by the Standing Rock tribe and its allies—has stopped or delayed 25 percent of emissions. This is the equivalent of 400 new coal-fired power plants.[35] Wet'suwet'en resistance, for instance, has cost the Coastal GasLink pipeline an extra C$11 billion, three more years of extra construction, and still, to date, oil is not flowing through the pipeline.[36] Indigenous organizers are among the hundreds of communities across the world blocking fossil fuel extraction. The Environmental Justice Atlas lists 697 such conflicts against fossil fuel infrastructure worldwide, only 78 of which are in the United States and Canada.[37]

When we see photos of these actions in the news, we often see the protestors facing off against police or military shooting water cannons and tear gas into the crowd. It looks confrontational and risky. But what we don't see is that protestors' resilience and tenacity is possible because of the many relationships that support them: legal systems that enshrine ethical relationships to the land, caring relationships with and generational wisdom from elders, and crucial support from non-Indigenous allies who will step up to cover legal fees, among others. As Métis and Cree writer Mike Gouldhawke explains:

> The strength behind Indigenous resistance flows from our community roots, and our sense of relationality, with each other and with all of our surroundings, living or otherwise. These already structured and long-held relations are what allow us to quickly respond to situations as they arise, with a strategic eye toward the future, toward securing a land and social base for generations to come. Such relations are the building blocks of the blockade, social as much as physical.[38]

Here, we are reminded again of the mangrove world, in which the trees propagate through a thick mesh of rhizomes, which then also holds the forest together. It's the stickiness of conviviality, to use Sara Ahmed's description of social connection, that brings about the mangrove world.[39] This relational meshwork of sticky connectivity is an invisible glue that can't easily be divided and conquered. Céline Chuang, an activist building community resistance against gentrification in Vancouver's Chinatown, has described networks of people collectively organizing to reclaim their communities as being "rhizomatic."[40] Rhizomes, those rootstalks that are sent out horizontally underneath the soil and then send shoots upward, eventually form a growing network of constantly budding life. Using examples from social movements in Greece, researcher and activist Angelos Varvarousis describes how the connectivity that drove social movements across Greece emerge, wane, and then re-emerge through loosely coordinated nodes of organization. He calls these spaces "liminal commons"—where, like the living and evolving mangrove world, they continuously unfold and evolve like a kaleidoscope, producing alternative ways to organize life. The glue that binds these movements spreads like mangrove rhizomes and seed pods from one site to another.[41] Over the past two decades, cities across North America and Europe have witnessed efforts to imagine and fight for different kinds of worlds, from Occupy Wall Street to Idle No More and Black Lives Matter, and the student encampments for Palestine. The sustainability class, enticed by the veneer of LEED-certified buildings and condo rooftop hydroponic gardens, may have no idea that in their very neighborhood, there is likely already a meshwork of intertwined roots of possible and lifegiving futures just waiting to break through that expensive rainwater-capturing permeable concrete surface.

You may be asking, "How could the professional and creative classes possibly be part of these rhizomatic networks?" One thing is for sure: they can't pretend to be different from who they are or where they are coming from. As Barbara Ehrenreich stressed in *Nickel and Dimed*, her middle-class readers can't and shouldn't pretend to be maids or truck drivers in their efforts to build solidarity.[42] Perhaps worse is when urban professionals think that they can just speak for those whose experiences are not their own—to think that they will be the white knights who will lift the poor out of poverty, that their learned expertise and book smarts override the lived experiences of people. Solidarity for middle-class urbanites requires a good dose of humility so that connections across class can be formed. That connection helps make the ecological possible—because we are always stronger together.

We can also be certain that for the sustainability class to take being ecological seriously would mean giving up on certain privileges, active betrayal of class position, ceding social and economic power, and even risking reputations in the face of fellow lifestyle environmentalists, their greenster peer group, or their social media bubble. But that's okay, because solidarity through people power means that someone's got your back, just as you have theirs—just like at LATU. Alienation begone! This can happen only by unraveling class privilege, being vulnerable to the discomfort of an uncertain future—a condition shared by the global majority.

We can't provide a blueprint for what exactly that kind of solidarity-building would look like here. It will be different in every setting, every context, and every moment in time. We can only point to some things it won't look like, and what people around the world are already doing to remake the world. It's up to each of us to find ourselves in those efforts, to figure out where we can fit in. We can't know if a floating seed pod of the mangrove will survive its journey across the ocean, to eventually be part of a new mangrove world on distant shores, spreading new rhizomes of abundant life where it travels. Likewise, we might all have a different path, carried by the currents of our own lives. But when we land somewhere, we'll have the option to send out our roots and join the tendrils of the rhizomes already around us, strengthening and reinforcing them. Or we can isolate ourselves in our exclusive "green" enclaves, all seed pods that never sprout and quickly die out.

Building Power

So far, we've gone through three crucial ingredients of ecological action: imagination, making the material political, and creating the conditions for solidarity. But it feels like something is missing. Shouldn't there be something that brings these three together, a kind of binding agent? Something solid enough to stand up to those driving this one-way train to a future of green apartheid?

That missing ingredient is *power*. What do we mean by power? In a way, power is another word for freedom. We have freedom, or agency, when we can make decisions and act on them. Right now, those in power have more freedom than us, in great part because they are the ones holding the purse strings. The sustainability class also has power, since they can decide what to do with their money—while most people in the world don't have that luxury.

To have power would mean being able to have a say in things that matter to us. It won't help to produce report after report about how these sustainability solutions still aren't working, or to make demands of our leaders by petitioning them. If you don't have power, those who do can just nod and smile and then turn around and do whatever they please—even if you voted for them.

What we need to figure out is how we can actually make demands and have them acted on. Or not to have to agree with the decisions imposed on us by political leaders and be able to stop them from being carried out. Or to make a decision about what we'd like the world to look like and have the capability to enact it. As Leo Sr. from the Union de Vecinos described it, "When the community is empowered and is allowed to make its own decisions, they can actually create different practices and different ways of seeing the world and organize to make sure that it is respected." That's what power is. Without community empowerment, we'll just be begging for change every four-year election cycle, choosing between the horrible and the abysmally unthinkable, while the world burns in front of our eyes.

The Union de Vecinos, small as it is, has built power. Mothers organized to keep the police out of their neighborhoods while keeping their children safe. When the Arts District arrived at their doorstep, they were able to organize and say no. When a community's water became too toxic to drink, they organized to turn the water system over to public ownership and democratize it. When landlords tried to evict tenants, they helped those tenants put a stop to it. And through the convivial connections they've built, they've had the people power to transform their neighborhood into a new vision, block by block. As Ofelia pointed out to us, "The police leave because they know that we as the community have the power. Our voice goes out. If we don't want the police, they won't be here. It's the same with the landowners! We have to build power."

But building power isn't simple. If you haven't seen it in action, it's hard to even know what it could look like, or to believe it could ever be possible. But it is. In the following, using a few more examples and referring to those we already discussed, we will argue that there are two kinds of power, each with its own strategies: the power to say no, and the power to say yes. Or, in other words, the power to fight, and the power to build.

The Power to Say No

The power to say no is paramount for a legitimately ecological transformation. As we've talked about throughout the book, we are up against not just an ideology that shuts out all other alternatives but also powerful elites who are very (literally) invested in maintaining that ideology. So what we need to be able to do is challenge the narratives that we're given and destabilize those investments. What kinds of strategies can we employ to subvert the appeal of lifestyle environmentalism? We suggest four (which are by no means exhaustive): an ecology of resistance, reconnaissance, counterbranding, and being the investment risk.

Here's an example of what all of this can look like. It is a conflict that has thus far resulted in the brutal slaying of an environmental defender—one of the first in recent U.S. history.[43] In the south of Atlanta, Georgia, lies the South River Forest. At 380 acres, it is one of the largest urban woodlands in the United States, and one of the city's last remaining forests, adjacent to a predominately Black and low-income part of the city. Also known as the Weelaunee Forest, it is sacred to the Muscogee (Creek) people, who once spanned much of Georgia, Alabama, Florida, and South Carolina. There are bobcats, snakes, turtles, mushrooms, birds, native grapes—a haven of permeable soil in a sea of concrete. The air is cooler here, and the forest has become a place for Atlanta residents to go on romantic walks, ride bikes, walk their dogs, forage, and even dance at mini-raves and DIY music and art events. In short, it is a place where life happens.

Unfortunately, the city's plan is to cut down the forest to make way for the world's largest police training facility and a mock police city that trains police in urban protest suppression tactics. It's worth mentioning that since 1992 the Atlanta Police Department has been learning about "community policing efforts" from none other than the Israeli Defense Forces—hardly a police force known for its community relations. This takes place through the Georgia International Law Enforcement Exchange (GILEE) nonprofit initiative that sends police officers to Israel for training.[44] The razed forest was also going to be the home for several massive new soundstages for Blackhall Studios, a major Hollywood studio, since 2022 renamed to Shadowbox Studios. Together, the film studio and police training facility are taking public land (which they are obtaining at $10 per year—essentially for free), deforesting it, polluting the South River (which crosses predominantly Black neighborhoods), and vastly increasing the likelihood of catastrophic floods in these same neighborhoods. Activists are calling it "Cop City": a megacheap lease of public land for the police and the movie industry. As activists opposing the project wrote, "The Blackhall development will exacerbate economic disparities and ecological collapse, while Cop City will equip the police to preserve them."[45]

The Cop City and studio developments were thrust upon the population despite overwhelming opposition to them. Public consultations were completely disregarded. Those arrested—some of whom just happened to show up to a festival that was raided by police—are now being accused of being domestic terrorists and are liable for a minimum jail sentence of five years. A forest defender named Manuel Esteban Paez Terán (nicknamed "Tortuguita") was shot by Atlanta police on the morning of January 18,

2023, while sitting in their tent. An independent autopsy found a total of fifty-seven gunshot wounds and determined that it was likely that Terán's hands were in the air at the time, even as police claimed they shot Terán in self-defense. There is still no substantial evidence to suggest that Tortuguita fired at officers.[46]

There are few limits to what the police, Hollywood, real estate, and Atlanta's city government are willing to do to rebrand, even "greenwash" the destruction of the South River Forest. For instance, project developers have proposed "community gardens" for youth at a nearby juvenile detention center—that is, children in detention would be tasked with building gardens for no pay. The police training facility would be called the Atlanta Institute of Social Justice—where new techniques will be developed to unleash untold cruelties against people fighting against systemic racism.[47] Gaslighting much? When the city started feeling the heat about this development, they offered to move Blackhall Studio's fifty-three-acre project to an already existing public park, while a chunk of the razed forest would be turned into—wait for it—Michelle Obama Park.[48] The liberal-sounding park name came with a $1.5 million pledge by Blackhall Studios for "community" initiatives, including film production internships for high school students and an "Americans-with-Disabilities-Act–compliant playground," all so that the studio can produce more dystopic blockbusters.

Resistance to Cop City has taken many forms—from tree sits and barricades to sabotage of construction equipment, teach-ins, community meals, and public festivals. As one forest defender we spoke with said: "We're not postponing imagining a different world until a revolution happens, we're making it happen right now in this place."[49] While the struggle remains far from over, the Atlanta forest defenders have shown how a small group of decentralized activists can generate an international-scale mobilization against climate change, anti-Black violence, Palestinian genocide, the prison system, and Indigenous land dispossession. As a collective of participants in the forest defense writes: "If the movement continues to grow, that will have been because of the dogged determination, flexibility, courage, creativity, and intelligence of a couple hundred people who pushed the envelope continuously from the beginning."[50]

This quote encapsulates the idea of an ecology of resistance as a first strategy in building power to say no to shallow lifestyle-oriented approaches to environmentalism. The longevity of the Defend Atlanta Forest movement has been credited to their use of "multiple grammars of struggle"—meaning many ways that people could participate. The movement has involved not just the front-line forest defenders like Terán, who camped in the forest, but also legal supporters, advocacy groups, teachers, students, and workers of all backgrounds and ages.[51] Despite differences in degrees of comfort with specific tactics, there has been a shared sense of objective in opposing the developments at all costs. Forest defenders are aware that there is an ecosystem of political organization required for the fight to stop ecological breakdown. They have developed a political strategy that was formed in practice and in reaction to opposing forces, locating weaknesses in the strategy of the proponents of the project and exploiting them. Autonomous and decentralized actions allowed forest defenders to participate in the movement as they saw fit, creating a plethora of actions all at once, confusing the police and their supporters. Like a biodiverse forest, with many species fulfilling a different niche, the forest defenders relied on many kinds of knowledge, even if there was some overlap of infrastructure and effort. In this way, when one person lost steam from organizing or was arrested by the police, others in the movement were there to pick up the slack. As participants in the forest defense state: "The different attitudes, aesthetics, and styles of organizing that comprise this movement are incommensurable, sometimes even mutually unintelligible, but this has made the movement stronger, like the proverbial many-headed hydra."[52] Once again, we are told about a "hydra," yet this time it represents not the forces of domination but those of resistance. That's what an ecology of resistance looks like.

This kind of ecology also made room for creative research. As we saw in the previous chapter, those responsible for the destruction caused by green development projects hide behind green-washed and whitewashed branding to avoid accountability for the harm they know they are causing. Obscuring the relationships between those who are truly responsible for ecological destruction is a classic way to avoid accountability. Deals between politicians, CEOs, and investors happen behind closed doors, and developers subcontract and sub-subcontract other companies to distance themselves from the project. The chains of accountability quickly become very difficult to trace when there are dozens of suppliers and logistics companies involved, and it becomes easy to just point the finger at someone else and wash your hands of the ecological destruction. And so a key tactic in resisting these development projects is to do creative investigative research into these connections.

The moment people caught wind of the Cop City project, they formed a number of groups to research the connections between different companies and politicians. The police training facility, for example, is largely funded by the philanthropic Atlanta Police Foundation—a slush fund that accepts money from a wide range of donors and to which the city of Atlanta has leased the land. But the foundation keeps itself at arm's distance from the contractors hired to demolish the forest. This makes it possible for individual companies that directly sponsor the foundation, like Coca-Cola, AT&T, Wells Fargo, and Bank of America, to say that they're not responsible for the project's outcomes on the ground. So just as the construction crews started digging up the forest, activists started digging into the murky connections between the different companies that were contracted, subcontracted, and sub-subcontracted to build the project. This reconnaissance is the second step in building the power to say no.

The third step is counterbranding. Branding, as we discussed in the previous chapter, is where a yearning for alternatives gets co-opted into speculative markets that ultimately sell out all of life for quick consumption. Counterbranding is kind of like using that same strategy, but to stop the deadening and to allow ecology to flourish again. It does so by interrupting the feedback loop in which every experience—even critique and resistance—is co-opted to create yet another in-crowd, something new to experience and consume. It's like using the mimetic capacity of branding against itself, to undermine the spectacle. Counterbranding makes the constant act of branding counterproductive—and redirects attention to real alternatives of hope, abundance, and thriving.

And so they co-opted Cop City's branding, rebranding it with plucky and impish actions. The first order of business, of course, was to turn the Institute for Social Justice back into what it truly was, Cop City. Initially, activists were able to delay a city council vote by protesting at the home of a city councilor, Joyce Shepherd, during the council meeting—which was held online due to COVID-19. Immediately after, and from the safety of a police precinct, Shepherd held a press conference about the project and the protests. As activists stated, "With this short statement, she catapulted the movement and its story into the mainstream . . . [transforming] the Cop City/Blackhall Developments from back-door agreements into public scandals."[53] Journalists became interested in the story, and politicians were forced to respond to questions about Cop City.

Following this success, activists focused on more specific targets. After it was uncovered that Coca-Cola funded the Atlanta Police Foundation, activists put public pressure on the company, which eventually stepped down from the board of the foundation. They also found that one construction company, Reeves Young Construction, was in charge of the demolition. So they protested at its headquarters, and this turned media attention onto the company. On April 25, 2022, Reeves Young announced that it was no longer involved with the project.[54]

As we write, the fight against Cop City and the Hollywood dystopia continues even as Atlanta's City Council approved funding for Cop City on June 6, 2023, and despite the fact that elected officials (many of them supposedly liberal Democrats) supporting the development blatantly contradict the public opinion they are meant to represent. Many might not agree with the protestors' tactics of intimidation, sabotage, and occupying forest land. But what is clear is that those involved were able to make the development a matter of public concern, rebrand the project in the eyes of the public, and bring attention to a variety of actors who were originally part of the project but then, under public pressure, withdrew their involvement. People used the media as a tool of counter-branding, with direct actions casting light on an initially nebulous development. By sabotaging the brand, they could disrupt the cycle of speculation and destruction. Despite the city's approval of funding for the project, the resistance is by no means over. One of the latest slogans is "If you build it, it's getting unbuilt."

This brings us to our fourth strategy of refusal: to be the investment risk.[55] We borrow this phrase from climate activists who, every year, have occupied large open-cast lignite coal mines in Germany, such as Tagebau, located on the site of the ancient Hambach Forest. Tagebau is owned by the German multinational energy company RWE, the world's second-largest offshore wind energy provider (and one of the key renewable-energy players behind Neom).[56] Calling themselves Ende Gelände—meaning "here and no further" in German—thousands of protestors dress in boiler suits and descend on the coal mine for a day, thrusting their way through private security and police lines. The image this creates is impressive, purposely designed to break through the media bubble and become a spectacle by itself. Not only is this a good example of counterbranding, but activists also are very aware of their wider goal: to discourage any further investment in coal by making it a financially unattractive asset. And so they have adopted the slogan "We are the investment risk."

Being the investment risk is one of the most powerful strategies available to us today. As we discussed in the previous chapter, the name of the game in the modern economy is speculation. With more and more wealth captured by a smaller and smaller group of elites, they need a place to park their money. Real estate is an especially stable asset, but resource extraction, IT, weapons manufacturing, and the creative and knowledge economies will do just as well. Because real estate is where *people* are—where we live and work—we actually have a lot of power to destabilize those assets. *We* can become the investment risk and make their assets less attractive.

The movement against Cop City has employed this same tactic, putting pressure on its investors by creating risk for them. This has involved sabotage of the machinery used to cut down trees, as well as protests at headquarters and media campaigns that expose the investors of the project. LATU has the same strategy. Often they organize tenants in buildings owned by a murky web of investors and shell companies. But a rent strike in one of those buildings isn't successful just because the companies don't get the rent. Actually, the monthly rent that low-income residents pay is peanuts to these big players. That's why they would prefer that the apartments sit vacant for years rather than have long-term, low-income tenants. It's more profitable for real estate investors to kick people out onto the street than to provide them a home at a livable rent. What *does* matter is the market value of their asset. A building where tenants are organized loses market value, simply because it's a riskier investment. Likewise, when tech workers at Amazon or Google or baristas at Starbucks organize to form a union, they are creating risk for those companies' investors, impacting the company's stock valuation—and forcing the company to come to the bargaining table.

When we become the investment risk, we connect with each

other. Just as the shadowy webs of real estate, tech investment, oil money, and the weapons industry are connected in a world-spanning network, blocking a coal mine or a forest from destruction connects protesters in Germany with tenants in Los Angeles, and the Muscogee Creek to Palestinians holding steadfast to the territory and their relationships with it. But it goes further: it is precisely when we become an investment risk that we have bargaining power. If we don't have chips in the game, we don't get to play. The power to deny profits is a chip, too, and that gives us a seat at the table.

So, we do have some strategies available to us to counter the ecological devastation caused by endless branding and speculation. We can be wacky and organize many different kinds of actions, always one step ahead of those responsible for ecocide. We can be sneaky and bring to light who we're up against. If elites can hoard wealth by squirreling away millions in offshore tax havens, and if corporations and governments can engage in under-the-table cash transfers, why shouldn't efforts to reclaim ecology thrive in the shadows, too? We can get frisky by creating counterspectacles that are jarring enough to intervene in the world of spectacles. And we can be risky, using our collective power to threaten profits and give us a seat at the bargaining table. Next time someone tells you that there's nothing that can be done, that the only power we have is our wallet, or that voting is the best way to get your voice heard, you can tell them with a smile that there is an alternative—being wacky, sneaky, frisky, and risky.

The Power to Say Yes

"Build and fight": that's how Cooperation Jackson summarizes its strategy.[57] We've talked about the fighting part, but what does building look like? For Cooperation Jackson, this means setting up land trusts, worker cooperatives, community gardens, mutual aid networks, and the People's Assembly. The Union de Vecinos builds community by making the neighborhood safer, holding events, organizing tenants, and setting up phone chains between neighbors and committees on each block. This ecosystem of relationships gives each of these organizations the power to say yes: to offer an alternative to the status quo, rather than just constantly fight it. Fighting fires that keep flaring up is exhausting, self-defeating, and can't be a strategy on its own.

There are two important strategies that we want to highlight here, both of which these organizations have employed. The first strategy is: *take it out of the market*. It's quite a simple solution, actually. When it comes to building housing, keeping green space in a city, or protecting trees from being torn down for development, we're constantly told that the only thing that can be done is to monetize it. If you want affordable housing, you need to sell off part of your neighborhood to the highest bidder and use those profits to build market-rate apartments for middle-income families. To get a park in your neighborhood, we're told that we need to pay a private company to run it—and their profit will come from leasing part of the park to boutique galleries. To save the forest, we're told we need to develop part of it, and set up carbon offsets, nature conservation payments, or crypto-based NFTs so that we can invest in it. But the high-end housing will just raise the market value of the affordable housing, quickly rendering it unaffordable, and eventually create a class of unworthy people to be discarded. The park will be so highly policed, boring, and sanitized that no one but trust-fund yuppies will feel comfortable there. And the forest, emptied of its original inhabitants, will become like a manicured lawn, a touristic version of itself, ready for Instagram stories and stock photography.

In contrast to all these Rube Goldberg machines, designed to gaslight us into thinking that selling something off will save it, the idea that it's possible *not to marketize it* can seem almost naive in its simplicity. But, in fact, taking wealth out of the market is quite common. In Vienna, Austria, half of the housing stock—housing 60 percent of the city's residents—is owned by the city or cooperatively owned.[58] In Singapore, nearly 80 percent of residents live in public housing.[59] In the United States, there is a growing movement for setting up community land trusts, which is a legal ownership model where land is taken out of the real estate market and owned and run by the community—often a cooperative.[60] Public parks are cleaner, safer, and more appealing than those managed by private companies.[61] When managed and owned by Indigenous communities, forests are far more biodiverse, hold more carbon, and are less in danger of forest fires.[62] The same holds for other basic needs: when utilities like electricity, water, and waste disposal are run by the municipality or owned by the public, they are less corrupt, more efficient, and more reliable—and less likely to screw their customers over with outlandish fees during heat waves or other extreme weather disasters.[63]

These days, the idea that you can just remove services from the market is taking hold under the concept of "universal basic services."[64] You might have heard of universal basic income: the idea that everyone could receive a monthly income that would allow them to meet their basic needs. Universal basic services is its lesser-known but perhaps more radical sibling. Basically, you can provide many of life's basic goods at very little cost to the public—simply because you offer them at scale.

How could we go about implementing this? We could start by turning those empty houses, condos, and ghost cities into cooperatives or public housing. Let's then put public transit everywhere, and make it on time and frequent, so you never feel like you can't do without a car—and no one complains about gas prices ever again. And why stop there? We could set up at-cost cafeterias in every neighborhood, where anyone could come eat and hang out. Sounds crazy? You might be surprised to learn that many countries have set these up throughout history, including Britain, which fed 600,000 people per day during the Second World

War.[65] This new economy could also be built on care: we could set up childcare collectives in every neighborhood, where each infant gets professional daycare at low cost to the parents. It's not really that outlandish; such a system already exists in the Canadian province of Quebec.[66] Or what about tool libraries, places where anyone could rent out a tool instead of buying a new one at Home Depot that they'll only use once? You could think of this as a "library economy"—where the library becomes the model not just for satisfying basic needs but for providing leisure as well—along with being a great place to meet people (in person, not on a screen or some pipe-dream Metaverse hologram).[67]

This economy would be far more ecological because it would reduce the need for everyone to buy their own version of the same thing—think frequent train and subway services instead of private (electric) cars, public swimming pools instead of private ones, air-conditioned community centers and cooperatives instead of single-family homes.[68] As sociologist Daniel Aldana Cohen points out in his study "Petro Gotham, People's Gotham," it is in working-class neighborhoods that you can find low-carbon lifestyles, precisely because it is there that you can find basic services available to all:

> This isn't to suggest celebrating the poorest New Yorkers' lack of income, their inability to consume. On the contrary, the thing to celebrate is what the radical urbanist Mike Davis in his essay "Who Will Build the Ark?" calls the "cornerstone of the low-carbon city . . . the priority given to public affluence over private wealth." Public housing, well-stocked libraries, accessible transit, gorgeous parks: these are democratic low-carbon amenities.[69]

By expanding public affluence, we would drastically reduce the social metabolism of the economy while improving well-being overall. A "sustainable" life would no longer be only for those who can afford it; it would be for everyone.

How would these services be paid for? The answer goes back to how the financial system works, as we explored in the last chapter. Currently, anyone who has assets can be given a loan by banks as long as they can show that they can maximize the return on their investment—"money begets money, lice beget lice," as that Arabic saying goes. However, projects like housing cooperatives are systematically at a disadvantage because, while they easily break even and are low-risk investments, they won't generate a profit. At a basic level, this is our financial system telling us that private wealth has more value than public wealth. But it doesn't have to be this way: we could easily reconfigure the monetary system so that it values public wealth instead.

On a local scale, municipalities can be pushed to build cooperative housing instead of so-called affordable market-rate housing, or to set up publicly owned companies to manage key services. On the national and even international levels, governments can use their central banks to, for example, buy out or nationalize fossil fuel companies or provide loans to cooperatives. Governments can also raise "windfall taxes" on corporations—like big oil—making scandalous profits during downturns, thereby also reducing their lobbying power. The possibilities are endless. We don't have the space to explore them here, but plenty of others already have.[70] What's important is that taking key services out of the market is one of the best strategies we have for putting a break on the endless train of co-optation, branding, and speculation that's leading us off the cliff.

A second strategy is to build collective agency. Ultimately, reverting the enormous power asymmetries between us and the billionaires will require building some kind of alternative power—and lots of it. We need to combat the overwhelming feeling of helplessness and hopelessness that becomes that little voice in our heads telling us that radical change is not possible anymore. We need what we could call dual power. Dual power means no longer depending on external representation; it's about representing our own interests, about being powerful enough to make decisions about our own future. Dual power means having agency about our collective future.[71]

The Union de Vecinos, for instance, has turned workers' and tenants' daily struggles into a power that authorities are forced to reckon with. The police won't even pick a fight with them— the public relations risks are too great. The Union de Vecinos has dual power: if they set their collective minds to stopping a speculative project like the gentrifying Arts District, they can. They have the power to make their neighborhoods safer by putting in benches and making signs, even as they reject green development projects and tree-planting initiatives that would increase property values and ultimately wind up displacing them in favor of wealthy creative types whose lifestyle demands are less ecological, not more. The protestors against Cop City also had this kind of power: they were able to build a different community, brought together by a positive vision for the forest, while using that momentum to force construction companies to leave the project. The L.A. EcoVillage and Cooperation Jackson have the power to use their collective resources to buy land, creating a buffer against gentrification.

For Ajamu Nangwaya and Kali Akuno of Cooperation Jackson, dual power is when autonomous, cooperative, and decentralized democratic structures exist in parallel with electoral politics but never need to depend on it.[72] Drawing from the Black liberation movement, dual power places economic self-determination as the very basis for building political power. Political legitimacy comes from democratic decision-making bodies of the cooperative rather than an electoral politics that adheres to gerrymandered jurisdictional boundaries. Dual power acts as a kind of counterpower to always ensure that communities have the autonomy to decide what's in their best interests.

Dual power doesn't have to be localized. The Democratic Confederation of Northeast Syria (previously known as Rojava) spans more than 250 miles along the Turkish border with Syria and is an example of this kind of dual power.[73] Democratic assemblies of between thirty and four hundred people make important community decisions and send delegates to assemblies at regional scales. Delegates can be recalled by the local assembly at any point. This is not representative democracy; it's *direct* democracy. It's true that Rojava has been able to experiment with this new government system by taking advantage of a geopolitical power struggle in the region—a fairly unique and precarious situation. Still, it's proof that it is possible to rethink our political system and develop a new one where women's empowerment, ecology, anti-racism, and direct democracy form core pillars of society.[74]

Building collective power is the most important ecological strategy we have. It's also something everyone can do, starting in their own neighborhoods—by supporting tenants against being evicted, growing food and distributing it through food cooperatives, organizing to stop fake "green" infrastructure that is out of reach for ordinary people, or ending your municipality or institution's investment in the military industrial complex. The ecological strategy here is about being part of the solution ourselves and feeling socially fulfilled in the process: being a part of an ecology, rather than detached and aloof consumers of it.

When the state and markets fail because of future financial crises, pandemics, and ecological disasters like floods or fires, it is the dual power of community assemblies, food and housing cooperatives, and mutual aid networks that will continue to serve as crucial lifelines. It is this collective power that will make attempting to profit from disaster "through the back door," as Wall Street investors Altucher and Sease suggest, socially impossible, risky, and ultimately too costly even for them. As the examples we have given show, restoring ecological abundance is about taking politics into our own hands—not depending on electoral political cycles, donor-driven NGOs, charity, technological innovation, or the obscene energy orgy that is the blockchain.

Building and fighting are intertwined strategies. Sometimes, fighting gives us the breathing room to build. At other times, we build community resources so that we have the power to pick our battles. There will be times when we'll be backed into a corner and we can only fight. But without building, we'll always be on the back foot, constantly outraged and putting out fires. Without setting up alternatives in the here and now, we won't know what we're fighting for.

At this point, you might be wondering whether there are in fact *any* hard and fast, quick-fix actions that one can do to build the kinds of solidarity needed to transform society in truly ecological ways. The short answer is there are plenty, but none of them can happen just by clicking a button. Donations can be useful, but we can't just transfer some money and call it a day. In Canada's cities of Vancouver, Toronto, and Montreal, a group called Resource Movement has been trying to build bridges between young people with inherited wealth and a desire and commitment for transformative social and ecological change. As described on their website:

> Our constituents' access to wealth and class varies, but the experience everyone shares is "having more than they need." Generally, members either come from families whose income or assets puts them in the top 20% of income earners or wealth holders; and/or our members' personal assets or income puts them in the top 20%.[75]

The strategy of Resource Movement has involved upfront and sometimes uncomfortable discussions about one's class privilege. The aim is to break the stigma among liberal- and progressive-minded people about the disposable wealth that cushions their lifestyle choices and even their thinking about the environment.

It involves tracing genealogies of wealth passed down across the generations or confronting wealth obtained through investments. These discussions do not stop there, lest they devolve into navel-gazing or "poor little rich kid" self-pity potlucks where mere discussion of wealth privilege absolves participants from taking any real action. Resource Movement's intention is to collectively call in members to participate in grassroots social movements, rather than opting for quick-fix donations.

Mobilizing resources that build dual power will not happen through philanthropic donations. It is about knowing how and when to provide meaningful inputs (monetary or otherwise) at specific moments of need in an active and ongoing struggle for change. This can happen only when those with privilege become participants in and allies to, not bystanders of, grassroots Indigenous and working-class movements, as we've described in this chapter. It can happen when we are emotionally and physically vested in the collective struggle, when not doing so becomes the bigger personal and collective risk.

Expect Co-optation

When we build real alternatives, people will start flocking to them, surprised that they haven't existed all along. But there will always be attempts to rebrand legitimate efforts into something that is more palatable and has less teeth. There will be efforts to join, then debilitate struggles through egotistical attention-seeking. There will be entrepreneurs who try to turn revolutionary messages into consumable spectacles, neutralizing the possibility for real change into a vapid aesthetic or vibe to soak one's personal brand in.

We should anticipate the co-optation of genuine strategies for change into cool buzzwords, product lines, academic article titles, or even slogans of political parties. Co-optation into meaninglessness is one of the things the sustainability class does best.

While some of the co-optation makes way for new product lines, in other cases, co-optation happens by far-right nationalists, who mix and match ideas as they suit them. William Callison and Quinn Slobodian call this co-optation *"diagonalism"*—a kind of mash-up of progressive demands repackaged into regressive politics, like when calls to shut down Big Tech are combined with banning "woke" curricula; or when the demand to guarantee jobs and a living wage is made in the same breath as the call to build the border wall and criminalize working-class immigrants. Diagonalism is hard to spot at first, and can deceive the unsuspecting into going down rabbit holes of conspiracy theories and false victimhood.

There is no reason to expect co-optation will not happen. This is how the word *sustainability*—which is ultimately about how to sustain ourselves on a single planet—has been co-opted to mean sustaining the lifestyles of an elite class. Words and ideas get twisted in perverse and insidious ways. We can expect all revolutionary words, thoughts, and art to be sucked up and become co-opted as weapons wielded back at us and all of life, plummeting us further into a downward spiral.

Social media has an unavoidable role to play in this aestheticizing process. Not all social media are created equal, of course. Some encrypted peer-to-peer messaging applications like Signal and Telegram can be vital to coordinate quick mobilization, while others like Instagram, TikTok, and X are exercises in self-branding that, as climate writer Matthew Haugen writes, "curate perfect ideological identities for clout" with the aim to "post our way to transforming society instead of investing in the slow and unglamorous work of building collective power with other people."[76] Still, between the brand promotion, otter videos, and wannabe influencers, they can also show people what's really happening on the ground—when interest-backed mainstream media sources continuously deny reality—and even offer avenues for cultural resurgence, liberation and freedom of expression from various forms of oppression.

Yet, on the whole, our (increasingly surveilled) digital personas reflect the imaginary gaze of transformation directed more toward ourselves and less on building collective power with others. Putting our energy into defining alternatives *through* digital tools, is to, more often than not, hand them over on a silver platter to tech billionaires and their green modernist fantasies. Something more is needed—especially since we are drowning in digital information overload within isolated bubbles, widespread disinformation sympathetic to powerful interests, and a general paralysis about how to respond to the onslaught of information about a collapsing world. Moving information out of social media and into people's hands has become an important tactic to rehumanize connection following the COVID-19 pandemic. The Indian farmers movement, or *Kisan Andolan*, that organized to repeal three farm bills in India that would disproportionately harm small-scale farmers, offers some clues on alternatives to social media. They provided regular updates from protest sites through a biweekly newspaper called *Trolley Times*.[77] The publication was published online, but also in print versions in multiple Indian languages, and was passed around like wildfire. Printed zines and newsletters are tried-and-true, easily accessible methods for sharing information collectively, often accompanied by dialogue and encounters with real people imagining and fighting for a better world.

As climate activist Andreas Malm says: "The revolution won't be televised, but the apocalypse certainly will be filmed, and is filmed."[78] The best way to combat disinformation and that sense of paralysis amidst digital information overload is real life face-to-face interactions. This not only reaffirms the centrality of lived experience, but also creates opportunities to process, debate, and discuss information. It's by meeting face-to-face that we can connect and bond with people, something increasingly missing in our very alienating existence. Offline interaction just works and feels better.

Final Words

This book doesn't have a recipe to save the world. Much of what we say has already been said before. But it's worth repeating.

So let's say it one more time. Being ecological is not about sitting around and waiting for engineered solutions that treat all of life's phenomena like mechanical puzzle pieces. It's not about consumer lifestyles, or self-branding exercises to keep us employable, or producing new content on X about a dying world while investors amass more wealth.

Being part of this system, many of us are inevitably caught up in lifestyle environmentalism. The point isn't to demonize each other's lifestyles. What we're asking is that we own up to it: to be honest with ourselves that these lifestyles aren't actually changing things, that deep down we know we're just as alienated as we were before we bought that Tesla or adaptogen-infused organic smoothie.

Those in power don't want you to engage in politics. They want you to remain in perpetual burnout mode, but they'll give you occasional mindfulness classes, therapy sessions, social media, and hot yoga to shut you up. They want to promise you PIE in the sky. They want to go to sleep at night knowing that their wealth is secure. A sustainability that is handed to us on a silver platter and that requires us to change nothing about our lives is nothing but a LEED-certified Trojan horse covered in hanging plants.

An ecological future, in contrast, has to be fought for if it is to be transformative. It's about redirecting our alienation and anxiety amid climate collapse toward meaning and purpose. It's about really changing the way we are living together. This is not without risk—risk to ourselves, our reputations, our community—but neither is doing nothing and continuing to eat from the hands of the ultra-rich. We say the latter is far riskier. The ultra-rich will head to their private militarized underground bunkers as soon as the shit hits the fan, and the rest of us will be left with nothing—and a lot of shit all over the place.

Being ecological is about having the imagination to transform our everyday physical environments, betraying our class comforts. It's about knowing that everything is political—from the food we eat to our relationships with our neighbors and with people in far-off places. It's about weaving a tapestry of solidarity across class, gender, ethnicity, and our nonhuman kin. It's about having the power to say "No!" to the constant gaslighting and "No!" to the absurd schemes cooked up by those who sell out the future. It's about building the power to have each other's backs in times of need, to have the agency to make decisions about our future together.

Unless we build collective institutions to break down class, the sustainability class will keep thriving off critique, new language, aesthetics, vibes, and forms of resistance. Class division worsens ecological crises, separating out the worthy from the unworthy, while the real perpetrators of ecological crimes use smooth language and aesthetics to become more powerful.

Solidarity—of the kind rooted in care and respect for all of life—can't be rationalized in words; it is felt in our hearts when we are connected in struggle. It is an interconnectedness that restores and replenishes ecological relations and transforms the physical environment. We are the only ones for each other.

If there's one actionable thing we want to leave you with, it's that stopping evictions, organizing a workplace, starting a co-op, calling out fake solutions with wacky and frisky protest campaigns, and building relationships of solidarity are ecological too. Our message is simple: *being ecological is about being in continuous and constant struggle against power.* When ecology becomes political, ecosystems of revolt will emerge and will thrive. The sustainability class won't know what hit them. They might even like it.

AFTERWORD

This book began when we watched a neighborhood called Park Extension in Montreal, Canada, get suddenly gentrified by a new so-called eco-friendly university campus (Université de Montréal). The neighborhood is among Canada's lowest-income neighborhoods and one of the most ethnically diverse, a first stop for many landed immigrants. They face a double whammy of deteriorating housing conditions and some of the city's fastest-rising rents. Landlords and real estate developers have bet on an influx of students and gentrifiers—drawn by the potential of bike lanes, urban agriculture, and ethnic vibes—to guarantee a return on their investments. The fertile backyard food gardens, managed through traditional knowledge from far-off places, and the tight-knit community relations among the earlier Greek and more recent South Asian immigrant communities are seen not as prosperity to protect but as vibes to extract rent from.

We both saw that this incredible neighborhood was worth protecting, and we became involved in tenant rights and anti-gentrification struggles, as well as organizing with the South Asian diaspora and mutual aid work. Vijay translated his frustration with the false green narrative that was contributing to the destruction of Park Extension into a 2019 article in Al Jazeera, "Why a hipster, vegan, green tech economy is not sustainable." It clearly hit a nerve, and Vijay was approached by Róisín Davis of Roam Agency to see if he was interested in turning it into a book. Vijay then asked Aaron, a longtime friend and collaborator at the time completing a PhD on green gentrification, if he wanted to join the project. The book was thus an expansion of our personal experience and has taken us to many corners of the world to witness and chronicle similar patterns as those we saw in our own community of Park Extension.

From the very beginning, we wanted to write a book that we could proudly give to anyone. We did not want to talk to people already "in the know." We wanted to write something that you could give to your grumpy conservative uncle and hippy-dippy aunt. We wanted a book that could encourage respectful dinner conversations as well as challenging introspection. We wanted a book that could speak to people across the world—because we could see the same patterns emerge in places as far-flung as Barcelona, Hanoi, Quito, Cape Town, Auckland, and Bengaluru. This is not the time, we felt, to always talk to the same people. We are all walking down the same "green" path—our fates are intertwined. And yet the solutions on offer are leading us further down the wrong path. Writing clearly and accessibly for a broad, global, audience is difficult, and we sincerely hope we did the task justice.

This is not to say that we have all the answers: we also wanted a book that would challenge us as authors. Writing from the heart, we felt, meant being open to addressing raw wounds in ourselves— by being brave enough to see ourselves as part of the problem. We write this book coming from an academic background in the social and environmental sciences, living in hip walkable cities, jetting around the globe occasionally for conferences. We write as avid cyclists and urban gardeners. We are both financially independent, but were also fortunate enough to have reached this current state with financial support from family at some point in our educational journeys—something that many do not have the luxury of. We are the sustainability class. We are of the class that we speak about in this book. And we share the desires and frustrations of many who seek significant environmental change and deep connection yet are skeptical of green consumerism.

Still, we didn't want to dwell in a pity party of privilege or paralyze ourselves into inaction. We are critical of our class position and want to take active steps by listening to, learning from, and allying with those outside of our class to reshape the system that is slowly killing our planet. There are countless ways to foster and support struggles for social and environmental justice in our neighborhoods and workplaces, such as joining a tenant union or mutual aid network, organizing your workplace, volunteering time for graphic design, writing press releases, translating, or growing food. We can only briefly point to the panoply of activities that can help dismantle the sustainability class and build real solutions. At times, we might come across as antagonistic to the sustainability class. But throughout, we tried to balance empathy with hard words and a dose of snarkiness that we felt are needed. We hope we succeeded in striking this balance.

Our problems also go beyond the sustainability class. Today, we urgently need to confront everything they won't teach you in school (or have outright banned from curricula). This includes collective healing to reconcile centuries of colonial violence inflicted on Indigenous peoples, on Africans brought to the Americas, on women who are under siege by an economic system that does not deem reproduction and care work to be of any worth, on working people who built the world we live in, yet continue to hear only promises but see very little of its rewards. Such a task is beyond the scope of this book, and we would like to direct readers to the work of writers like Leanne Betasamosake Simpson, Silvia Federici, Raj Patel, Mordecai Ogada, Amitav Ghosh, Angela Davis, Eduardo Galeano, Harsha Walia, Ursula K. LeGuin, Ruth Wilson Gilmore, and bell hooks—all of whom imagine a world of abolition, free from systems of oppression, patriarchy, and ecological harm.

We have not discussed strategy much in this book. Instead, we have chosen to focus our energy on the sustainability class since this group and their solutions are taking us further away from where we need to go. We wanted to clear the air, to avoid getting distracted so that we may better direct our energies. The next step is to begin strategizing about where exactly we need to go, how

we can begin building solidarity across deep social fragmenta-
tions. To these ends, we suggest readers explore the works of authors like Peter Gelderloos, Ashish Kothari, Kyle Powys White,
adrienne maree brown, Grace Lee Boggs, Esme Murdock, Jane
McAlevey, Andreas Malm, Glen Coulthard, Raúl Zibechi, Paolo
Freire, Stefania Barca, and Erik Olin Wright, who have written
about how to bring about alternative worlds and ecological visions
in the present, against all odds.

As a final warning, and as we've already emphasized at the end
of Chapter 8, we can't reiterate enough the unfortunate reality
that all our words, strategies, efforts and imaginations will almost
certainly be co-opted, reappropriated by corporate interests seeking to get hip and disruptive and innovative, then used against us
to gaslight us. This is to be expected! We should not be outraged
or surprised. Rather than wasting time constantly being outraged
by the next heinous idea tech bros concoct, it's going to be necessary to always be a step ahead of that tiring game.

It's important to remember that solidarity is a part of what it
means to be human—that we are social beings and not just selfish
individuals who would rather chop each other to bits than look
after each other. There's no evidence to suggest that the latter is
essential to our nature. Even in the worst of times, mutual aid and
support that breaks divisions of class and race have been pivotal
to our ongoing survival. That's something the solar-powered-
megayacht owners and tech bros will have to learn the hard way.

Before we close, we want to take some time to thank those who
have helped make this book happen. Thanks, first and foremost,
to Róisín Davis, our agent, without whom this book would never
have materialized. Her support and guidance in its early stages
were essential. We are truly indebted to her. We give thanks to
Ben Woodward and Gia Gonzales from The New Press for their
invaluable edits and accompaniment throughout this journey.
Our love and gratitude go to Ky Brooks and Diana Vela Almeida,
who were a part of this project in its inception, as well as Nicólas

Kosoy and Leah Temper for being there throughout. Thank you to Celia Robinovitch for the perceptive feedback, love, and support as the book was in its final stages. A big hug and thanks to Neal Rockwell for being present and for thinking and joking along with us. We couldn't have imagined a better co-conspirator to investigate the wild world of Los Angeles greensterism. Thank you to Kenneth Gould and Tammy Lewis for their helpful discussions at the start of this project and for their groundbreaking work on the sustainability class concept, which greatly informed our analysis.

None of this would have been possible without interest, enthusiasm, and endearing encouragement of our family, partners, and close friends—from long, intimate walks during pandemic days to insights from others' shared experiences and recognition of the sustainability class from around the world. Sending special wishes to Rama, Jeeva, and Preethy Kolinjivadi, Tom McFate, Simon Vansintjan, Cassie Anderson, Carine Gardin, Geert Vansintjan, Gert Van Hecken, Thomas Boucher, Danya Nadar, Ishan Kukreti, Sarah Katz-Lavigne, Sasha Plotnikova, Sigwan Thivierge, Max Ajl, Danji Buck-Moore, Kris De Decker, Ritwick Ghosh, Faiza Khan, Mahar Musleh, Tomaso Ferrando, Ann Lévesque, Justin Khan, Mouna Guidiri, Stephanie Collingwoode Williams, Katarina Hovden, Kiara Worth, Tallash Kantai, Jose Pinto-Bazurco, Guity Nadjafie, Matthias De Groof, Cherry Stoltenberg, Tejaswinee Jhunjhunwala, Burç Köstem, Hamza Hamouchene, Simon Chauvette, and Anastasia Kravtsova. Conversations with Elaine Lockwood, Martin Brooks, Susan Ross, the residents and friends of the Hungerfort, Anwesha Dutta, and Alejandra Zaga Mendez were crucial for the formation of the book. Big thanks to the folks at the Institute for Social Ecology, including Mason Herson Hord, Eleanor Finley, and Brian Tokar, members of Research & Degrowth, CICADA, Food Secure Canada, and the Barcelona Laboratory for Urban Environmental Justice, especially Isabelle Anguelovski and Melissa Garcia Lamarca. Without funding and support from the Leadership for the Ecozoic program, and the Flanders Fund for Scientific Research Grant number 12ZA921N, completion of this work would not have been possible.

We want to give a big thanks to the many people we talked to in Los Angeles and beyond, who took time out of their busy lives to spend it with us, and from whom we learned an enormous amount. A special shout-out to Ghassan Khoury, Ofelia Platon, Leonardo Vilchis, Leo Vilchis-Zarate, and Maria-José from Union de Vecinos, Hamid Khan from Stop LAPD Spying Coalition, Strategic Actions for a Just Economy, Yvonne Yen Liu from the Solidarity Research Center, Steve McFarland, Rayne Laborde Ruiz from UCLA's City Lab, CultivaLA with Jose Miguel, Isabelle Duvivier and Noel Johnston from Verdant Venice, Rose Lenehan, Tracy Rosenthal, Sam Alden, and Dont Rhine from the LA Tenants Union, Stephen Mejia and Tay Costa-Moura from Friends of the LA River, Steve Williams from Selva International, Joanna Swan and Kristina Meshelski from Streetwatch LA and the PowerUp Table, Lois Arkin from the LA EcoVillage, Rosie from the Stop Cop City Atlanta Forest Defenders, and Ashish Kothari, Gijs Spoor, Simran and Rahul Sureka (of Impprintz), Kristoff, Sandeep, Krishna, and Michelle from Auroville. Thanks as well to Nguyễn Phương Anh, Nguyễn Hồng Vân, and Hoàng Thị Thùy for their invaluable insight into Hanoi and its environs.

We also want to thank many of our friends and comrades in and around Park Extension in Montreal, whose tireless efforts to stop evictions from the joint efforts of greedy landlords and the Université de Montreal—who have failed to fulfill their promises to stop eco-gentrification and build affordable social housing—have inspired us to write this book. These people include activists, artists, writers, and community organizers around Tiotiá:ke (aka Montreal), including Simone Chen, Sasha Dyck, Alex Megelas, Shazma Abdullah, Rose Ndjel, Anna Pringle, Anna Kruzynski, Sharone Birapaka Daniel, Titas Banerjee, Stefan Christoff, Jonathan Durand Folco, Jenny Cartwright, Emanuel Guay,

Alessandra Renzi, Norma Rantisi, Bengi Akbulut, Tamara Vukov, Zahra Moloo, Sophie Toupin, Mostafa Henaway, Kasim Tirmizay, Faiz Abhuani, Amy Darwish, Jaggi Singh, and Rushdia Mehreen. There are many more people we haven't mentioned. You know who you are.

A huge thanks to editors and readers of chapters, including Tasha Goldberg, Felipe Ruiz, Daniel Horen Greenford, Nicólas Kosoy, Sam Bliss, Simon Vansintjan, Yuegenia Kleiner, and Kai Heron for their invaluable reflections and suggestions in editing and improving this book. We are extremely grateful! This book would simply not have been paw-sible without our furry friends Pan and Omkar to teach us daily about ecology and relations of deep connection across so much difference.

NOTES

Introduction

1. Names and affiliations have been anonymized.

2. G. Wozniacka, "Can Regenerative Agriculture Reverse Climate Change? Big Food Is Banking on It," NBC News, October 29, 2019, www.nbcnews.com/news /us-news/can-regenerative-agriculture-reverse-climate-change-big-food-banking -it-n1072941; J. Fassler, "Regenerative Agriculture Needs a Reckoning," The Counter, March 5, 2021, thecounter.org/regenerative-agriculture-racial-equity-climate -change-carbon-farming-environmental-issues; P. Newton, N. Civita, L. Frankel-Goldwater, K. Bartel, and C. Johns, "What Is Regenerative Agriculture? A Review of Scholar and Practitioner Definitions Based on Processes and Outcomes," *Frontiers in Sustainable Food Systems* 4 (2020): 194.

3. The Tongva are the Indigenous tribe in what is now the Los Angeles Basin. Starting in the eighteenth century, they were forcibly displaced, enslaved, and criminalized by both Spanish and American settlers.

4. Los Angeles Clean Tech Incubator website, laincubator.org.

5. T. Leary, *Flashbacks: A Personal and Cultural History of an Era: An Autobiography* (New York: Tarcher, 1990).

6. K. Sahota, "Meet Matthew Kenney: The Chef Behind Plant-Based Folia," *TimeOut Riyadh*, December 21, 2021, www.timeoutriyadh.com/food-drink/meet -matthew-kenney.

7. S. Blum, "Fear and Loathing at Erewhon, the High-Margin Grocery Store That Might Just Take Over the World," *Los Angeles Magazine*, August 19, 2019, www .lamag.com/citythinkblog/erewhon-shopping.

8. Blum, "Fear and Loathing at Erewhon."

9. Note that this was before Budweiser was cancelled for being too woke.

10. M. Berlinger, "How Erewon Became L.A.'s Hottest Hangout," *New York Times*, February 18, 2021.

11. F. Pearce, "Phantom Forests: Why Ambitious Tree Planting Projects Are Fail-

ing," Yale 360, October 6, 2022, e360.yale.edu/features/phantom-forests-tree-plant ing-climate-change; R. Nuwer, "Is Tree Planting a Get-Out-of-Jail-Free Card on Climate?," *Noema Magazine*, July 21, 2022; M. Gaworecki, "Is Planting Trees as Good for the Earth as Everyone Says?," Mongabay, May 13, 2021.

12. B. Martin, "How Garden Planters Became a Flashpoint in the Venice Gentrification Debate," *Los Angeles Magazine*, www.lamag.com/citythinkblog/venice -planters-controversy.

13. While Native Americans make up 1.5 percent of the population, they make up 2.8 percent of the U.S. unhoused population. E. Sherman, "Homelessness Has Racial, Gender, and Age Disparities," *Forbes*, December 29, 2018, www.forbes.com/sites /eriksherman/2018/12/29/homelessness-has-racial-gender-and-age-disparities.

14. A. Deener, *Venice: A Contested Bohemia in Los Angeles* (Chicago: University of Chicago Press, 2012).

15. See, for example, the California-based Breakthrough Institute (www.eco modernism.org), whose "Ecomodernist Manifesto" advertises intensive agriculture, dense urbanization, and nuclear energy, and argues that environmental impacts decrease as societies become wealthier.

16. M. Bergen and M. Day, "Big Tech Helps Big Oil Pump More, Belying Climate Pledges," Bloomberg, August 16, 2022, www.bloomberg.com/news/articles/2022 -08-16/microsoft-amazon-big-tech-help-big-oil-pump-more; T. Chiang, "Will AI Become the New McKinsey?," *New Yorker*, May 4, 2023, www.newyorker.com/sci ence/annals-of-artificial-intelligence/will-ai-become-the-new-mckinsey.

17. J. Guyer, "How Saudi Money Returned to Silicon Valley," Vox, May 1, 2023, www.vox.com/technology/2023/5/1/23702451/silicon-valley-saudi-money -khashoggi.

18. J. Blas, "ESG Is So, So, So Yesterday: Elements by Javier Blas," Bloomberg, August 5, 2022, www.bloomberg.com/opinion/articles/2022-08-05/esg-is-so-so -so-yesterday-elements-by-javier-blas.

19. G. H. Brundtland, "Our Common Future—Call for Action," *Environmental Conservation* 14, no. 4 (1987): 291–294.

20. U. Brand, "Green Economy—the Next Oxymoron? No Lessons Learned from Failures of Implementing Sustainable Development," *GAIA—Ecological Perspectives for Science and Society* 21, no. 1 (2012): 28–32.

21. D. Carrington, "Leak Reveals 'Touchy' Issues for UAE's Presidency of UN Climate Summit," *The Guardian*, August 1, 2023, www.theguardian.com/environ ment/2023/aug/01/leak-uae-presidency-un-climate-summit-oil-gas-emissions-yemen.

22. F. Harvey, "COP28 President: World Needs Business Mindset to Tackle Climate Crisis," *The Guardian*, April 7, 2023, www.theguardian.com/environment /2023/apr/07/cop28-president-world-needs-business-mindset-tackle-climate-crisis -sultan-al-jaber.

23. J. Kollewe, "BlackRock's Larry Fink: Climate Policies Are About Profits, Not Being 'Woke,'" *The Guardian*, January 18, 2022, www.theguardian.com/environ ment/2022/jan/18/blackrock-larry-fink-climate-policies-profits-woke.

24. Neom, "Changing the Future of Energy," 2022, www.neom.com/en-us/sec tors/energy; M. Thomas and V. Venema, "Neom: What's the Green Truth Behind a Planned Eco-City in the Saudi Desert?," BBC, February 22, 2022, www.bbc.com /news/blogs-trending-59601335; J. Scheck, R. Jones, and S. Said, "A Prince's $500 Billion Desert Dream: Flying Cars, Robot Dinosaurs and a Giant Artificial Moon," *Wall Street Journal*, July 25, 2019, www.wsj.com/articles/a-princes-500-billion-desert -dream-flying-cars-robot-dinosaurs-and-a-giant-artificial-moon-11564097568.

25. T. Buck, "RWE Aims to Be Carbon Neutral by 2040," *Financial Times*, September 30, 2019, www.ft.com/content/01e5a300-e36a-11e9-9743-db5a370481bc.

26. R. Michaelson, "'It's Being Built on Our Blood': The True Cost of Saudi Arabia's $500bn Megacity," *The Guardian*, May 4, 2020, www.theguardian.com /global-development/2020/may/04/its-being-built-on-our-blood-the-true-cost-of -saudi-arabia-5bn-mega-city-neom.

27. N. Barker, "Sustainability and Liveability Claims of Saudi 170-Kilometer City Are 'Naive' Say Experts," Dezeen, August 8, 2022, www.dezeen.com/2022 /08/08/sustainability-liveability-the-line-saudi-170km-city-naive.

28. US Geological Survey, "The Rare-Earth Elements—Vital to Modern Technologies and Lifestyles," 2014, pubs.usgs.gov/fs/2014/3078/pdf/fs2014-3078.pdf.

29. L. S. Teseletso and T. Adachi, "Future Availability of Mineral Resources: Ultimate Reserves and Total Material Requirement," *Mineral Economics* 36 (2023): 189–206; A. V. Bobin and V. Bobin, "Mining Lunar Hydrogen," *Room: Space Journal of Asgardia* 3, no. 29 (2021): 46–51.

30. M. Shaw et al., "Mineral Processing and Metal Extraction on the Lunar Surface—Challenges and Opportunities," *Mineral Processing and Extractive Metallurgy Review* 43, no. 7 (2022): 865–891.

31. R. Boyle, "A New Private Moon Race Kicks Off Soon," *Scientific American*, August 1, 2022, www.scientificamerican.com/article/a-new-private-moon-race -kicks-off-soon.

32. C. P. Mulder, C. G. Starling, and M. J. Massa, "A US Space Strategy for 2050:

Shaping a Domain on the Cusp," *Room: Space Journal of Asgardia* 3, no. 29 (202): 56–61.

33. R. Marsh, "Billionaires Are Funding a Massive Treasure Hunt in Greenland as Ice Vanishes," CNN, August 8, 2022, www.cnn.com/2022/08/08/world/greenland -melting-mineral-mining-climate/index.html.

34. O. Ellekrog, "Greenland Startup Begins Shipping Glacier Ice to Cocktail Bars in the UAE," *The Guardian*, January 9, 2024, www.theguardian.com/world/2024 /jan/09/greenland-startup-shipping-glacier-ice-cocktail-bars-uae-arctic-ice.

35. L. Cecco, "Exploring Deep Ocean Is 'Safer than an Elevator' Says James Cameron," *The Guardian*, July 22, 2023, www.theguardian.com/environment/2023 /jul/22/james-cameron-interview-titan-deep-sea-mining.

36. M. Costello, "The Ocean Floor Is Less Well Mapped than the Surface of Other Planets," Oceans of Biodiversity Research Group, March 23, 2019, www .oceansofbiodiversity.auckland.ac.nz/2019/03/23/the-ocean-floor-is-less-well -mapped-than-the-surface-of-other-planets.

37. V. Ramaswamy, *Nation of Victims: Identity Politics, the Death of Merit, and the Path Back to Excellence* (Nashville, TN: Center Street, 2022).

38. "Why 2C of Global Warming Is So Much Worse than 1.5C," World Economic Forum, July 28, 2021, www.weforum.org/agenda/2021/07/2c-global-warm ing-difference-explained; T. M. Lenton et al., "Quantifying the Human Cost of Global Warming," *Nature Sustainability* 6 (2023): 1–11.

39. "Copernicus: 2023 Is the Hottest Year on Record, with Global Temperatures Close to the 1.5°C Limit," Copernicus Climate Change Service, January 9, 2024, climate.copernicus.eu/copernicus-2023-hottest-year-record.

40. Institute for European Environmental Policy, "More than Half of All CO_2 Emissions Since 1751 Emitted in the Last 30 Years," April 29, 2020, ieep.eu/news /more-than-half-of-all-co2-emissions-since-1751-emitted-in-the-last-30-years.

41. C. Stager, "What Happens *After* Global Warming?," *Nature Education Knowledge* 3, no. 10 (2012): 7.

42. K. Jamie, "Stay Alive! Stay Alive!," *London Review of Books* 44, no. 16 (August 18, 2022), www.lrb.co.uk/the-paper/v44/n16/kathleen-jamie/diary.

43. K. Gould and T. Lewis, *Green Gentrification: Urban Sustainability and the Struggle for Environmental Justice* (New York: Routledge, 2016).

44. K. Bell. *Working-Class Environmentalism: An Agenda for a Just and Fair Transition to Sustainability*. Springer, Nature (2019).

45. K. Ummel, "Who Pollutes? A Household-Level Database of America's

Greenhouse Gas Footprint," CGD Working Paper 381, 2014, Center for Global Development, Washington, DC, http://www.cgdev.org/publication/who-pollutes-household-level-database-americas-greenhouse-gas-footprint-working-paper; D. A. Cohen, "Petro Gotham, People's Gotham," in *Nonstop Metropolis: A New York Atlas*, ed. R. Solnit and J. Jelly-Shapiro (Berkeley: University of California Press, 2016), 47–54.

46. J. L. Rice, D. A. Cohen, J. Long, and J. R. Jurjevich, "Contradictions of the Climate-Friendly City: New Perspectives on Eco-Gentrification and Housing Justice," *International Journal of Urban and Regional Research* 44, no. 1 (2020): 145–165.

47. D. H. Greenford, T. Crownshaw, C. Lesk, K. Stadler, and H. D. Matthews, "Shifting Economic Activity to Services Has Limited Potential to Reduce Global Environmental Impacts to the Household Consumption of Labour," *Ecological Economics* 34, no. 3 (2000): 409–423.

48. T. Piketty and L. Chancel, "Carbon and Inequality: From Kyoto to Paris: Trends in the Global Inequality of Carbon Emissions (1998–2013) and Prospects for an Equitable Adaptation Fund," 2015, Paris School of Economics, http://piketty.pse.ens.fr/files/ChancelPiketty2015.pdf.

49. A. Maitland, M. Lawson, H. Stroot, A. Poidatz, A. Khalfan, and N. Dabi, "Carbon Billionaires: The Investment Emissions of the World's Richest People," Oxfam, 2022.

1: The Rise of the Sustainability Class

1. A. Giridharadas, "The New Elite's Phoney Crusade to Save the World—Without Changing Anything," *The Guardian*, Jan. 22, 2019, www.theguardian.com/news/2019/jan/22/the-new-elites-phoney-crusade-to-save-the-world-without-changing-anything.

2. K. A. Gould and T. L. Lewis, "From Green Gentrification to Resilience Gentrification: An Example from Brooklyn," *City and Community* 17, no. 1 (2018): 12–15.

3. E. A. Harris, "In Brooklyn, Worrying About Not Only Flooding but Also What's in Water," *New York Times*, Nov. 5, 2012, www.nytimes.com/2012/11/06/nyregion/gowanus-canal-flooding-brings-contamination-concerns.html.

4. M. Cunningham, "Locals React to Plan to Add 15 ft. Tall seawall to Greenpoint Waterfront," Greenpointers, Mar. 3, 2023, greenpointers.com/2023/03/03/locals-react-to-plan-to-add-15-ft-tall-seawall-to-greenpoint-waterfront.

5. K. Gould and T. Lewis, *Green Gentrification: Urban Sustainability and the Struggle for Environmental Justice* (New York: Routledge, 2016).

6. Gould and Lewis, "From Green Gentrification to Resilience Gentrification."

7. R. Florida, *The New Urban Crisis: How Our Cities Are Increasing Inequality, Deepening Segregation, and Failing the Middle Class—and What We Can Do About It* (New York: Basic Books, 2017).

8. L. Lees, H. B. Shin, and E. López-Morales, *Planetary Gentrification* (Hoboken, NJ: John Wiley & Sons, 2016).

9. N. Smith, "Gentrification Generalized: From Local Anomaly to Urban 'Regeneration' as Global Urban Strategy," in *Frontiers of Capital: Ethnographic Reflections on the New Economy*, ed. M. S. Fisher and G. Downey (Durham, NC: Duke University Press, 2006), 191–208; T. Slater, "Planetary Rent Gaps," *Antipode* 49 (2017): 114–137.

10. S. Stein, *Capital City: Gentrification and the Real Estate State* (London: Verso Books, 2019).

11. X. Piao and S. Managi, "The International Role of Education in Sustainable Lifestyles and Economic Development," *Scientific Reports* 13, no. 1 (2023): 8733. Note that this doesn't mean that the sustainability class has less of an environmental impact, however. As we show later, environmental lifestyles and income are also associated with a higher environmental impact, paradoxically. We also know that environmental concerns and values are present throughout the population, and, in fact, people tend to underestimate the environmental concerns of visible minority groups. See, for example, A. R. Pearson, J. P. Schuldt, R. Romero-Canyas, M. T. Ballew, and D. Larson-Konar, "Diverse Segments of the US Public Underestimate the Environmental Concerns of Minority and Low-Income Americans," *Proceedings of the National Academy of Sciences* 115, no. 49 (2018): 12429–12434.

12. S. Frey, J. Bar Am, V. Doshi, A. Malik, and S. Noble, "Consumers Care About Sustainability—and Back It Up with Their Wallets," McKinsey and Nielsen IQ, 2023, www.mckinsey.com/industries/consumer-packaged-goods/our-insights/consumers-care-about-sustainability-and-back-it-up-with-their-wallets#; L. Yan, H. T. Keh, and J. Chen, "Assimilating and Differentiating: The Curvilinear Effect of Social Class on Green Consumption," *Journal of Consumer Research* 47, no. 6 (2021): 914–936.

13. M. Krishnan et al., "The Net-Zero Transition: What It Could Cost, What It Could Bring," McKinsey & Company, Jan. 2022, www.mckinsey.com/capabilities/sustainability/our-insights/the-net-zero-transition-what-it-would-cost-what-it-could-bring.

14. Krishnan et al., "The Net-Zero Transition."

15. D. P. McLaren and L. Carver, "Disentangling the 'Net' from the 'Offset':

Learning for Net-Zero Climate Policy from an Analysis of 'No-Net-Loss' in Biodiversity," *Frontiers in Climate* 5 (2023).

16. IFC, "Creating Markets for Climate Business: An IFC Climate Investment Opportunities Report," 2017.

17. C. Hicks-Webster, "To Sell Green Products, Target The Middle Class," NBS, Oct. 4, 2021, nbs.net/to-sell-green-products-target-the-middle-class.

18. T. Hardingham-Gill, "The 3D Printed Superyacht Concept Designed to Be 'Virtually Invisible,' " CNN, Mar. 21, 2023, edition.cnn.com/travel/article/virtually -invisible-superyacht-concept-pegasus/index.html.

19. D. Owen, *Green Metropolis: Why Living Smaller, Living Closer, and Driving Less Are the Keys to Sustainability* (New York: Riverhead Books, 2010).

20. B. Latour, *We Have Never Been Modern* (Cambridge, MA: Harvard University Press, 2012).

21. R. Boer, *Smooth City: Against Urban Perfection, Towards Collective Alternatives* (Amsterdam: Valiz, 2023).

22. E. Stamp, "Billionaire Bunkers: How the 1% Are Preparing for the Apocalypse," CNN, Aug. 7, 2019, www.cnn.com/style/article/doomsday-luxury-bunkers /index.html.

23. E. Jaffe, "How Are Those Cities of the Future Coming Along?," *City Lab*, Sept. 11, 2013, www.citylab.com/life/2013/09/how-are-those-cities-future-coming -along/6855; S. Goldenberg, "Masdar's Zero-Carbon Dream Could Become World's First Green Ghost Town," *The Guardian*, Feb. 16, 2016, www.theguardian.com/en vironment/2016/feb/16/masdars-zero-carbon-dream-could-become-worlds-first -green-ghost-town.

24. M. McArdle, "Is Masdar City a Ghost Town or a Green Lab?," *Popular Science*, Apr. 24, 2018, www.popsci.com/masdar-city-ghost-town-or-green-lab.

25. A. Chapman, "This Lily Pad Inspired Floating City Is Planned for Penang," *Urth Magazine*, Oct. 25, 2022, urth.co/magazine/emission-free-floating-city.

26. Note that 3D printing is by no means ecological. While it reduces the number of parts needed and thus shortens wasteful supply chains, the focus is only on making raw material use more efficient (more on that later). The electrical energy demand is 50 to 100 times greater than injection molding printers, and the plastic use is even more mind-numbing. H. Lipson and M. Kurman, "Is Eco-Friendly 3D Printing a Myth?," Live Science, July 20, 2013, www.livescience.com/38323-is-3d-printing -eco-friendly.html.

27. L. Grush, "Elon Musk Thinks the Best Government for Mars Is a Direct De-

mocracy," The Verge, June 2, 2016, www.theverge.com/2016/6/2/11837590/elon-musk-mars-government-direct-democracy-law-code-conference.

28. C. Sojit Pejcha. "Techno-Futurists Are Selling an Interplanetary Paradise for the Posthuman Generation—They Just Forgot about the Rest of Us," Document Journal, May 23, 2024, https://www.documentjournal.com/2024/05/the-myth-of-silicon-valley-messiahs-and-the-rise-of-tescrealism-longtermism-transhumanism-technology-ai/.

29. A. P. J. Mol, "Ecological Modernization and the Global Economy," *Global Environmental Politics* 2, no. 2 (2002): 92–115; G. Kallis and S. Bliss, "Post-Environmentalism: Origins and Evolution of a Strange Idea," *Journal of Political Ecology* 26, no. 1 (2019): 466–485.

30. C. Sojit Pejcha. "Techno-Futurists Are Selling an Interplanetary Paradise."

31. Earth Negotiations Bulletin MENA Climate Week Summary Bulletin, Oct. 15, 2023, 19, enb.iisd.org/middle-east-north-africa-mena-climate-week-2023-summary.

32. A. Cole, "Google and Amazon Are Now in the Oil Business," Vox, Jan. 3, 2020, www.vox.com/recode/2020/1/3/21030688/google-amazon-ai-oil-gas.

33. M. DiTrolio, "How Google Is Becoming More Eco-Friendly," *Marie Claire*, July 18, 2019, www.marieclaire.com/career-advice/a28428318/google-chief-sustainability-officer-kate-brandt-data-centers.

34. M. Michelson, "This Woman Is Turning Google into a Clean-Energy Power-house," Outside Online, July 5, 2018, www.outsideonline.com/2323696/kate-brandt-google-sustainability.

35. E. Glaeser, *Triumph of the City: How Our Greatest Invention Makes Us Richer, Smarter, Greener, Healthier, and Happier* (London: Penguin, 2011).

36. P. Krugman, "Slow Steaming and the Supposed Limits to Growth," *New York Times*, Oct. 7, 2014, krugman.blogs.nytimes.com/2014/10/07/slow-steaming-and-the-supposed-limits-to-growth.

37. A. McAfee, *More from Less: The Surprising Story of How We Learned to Prosper Using Fewer Resources—and What Happens Next* (New York: Simon & Schuster, 2019): 1

38. V. Jones, *The Green Collar Economy: How One Solution Can Fix Our Two Biggest Problems* (New York: HarperCollins, 2009).

39. "HRH Crown Prince Announces: 'The Saudi Green Initiative and The Middle East Green Initiative,' " Saudi Press Agency, Mar. 29, 2021, www.spa.gov.sa/w1532369.

40. S. Pinker, *Enlightenment Now: The Case for Reason, Science, Humanism, and Progress* (London: Penguin, 2018).

41. "Davos 2020: Trump Dismisses Environmental Concerns as 'Pessimism' at Climate-Focused WEF," Deutsche Welle, Jan. 21, 2020, www.dw.com/en/davos -2020-trump-rejects-prophets-of-doom-at-climate-focused-wef/a-52083749.

42. E. O. Wilson, *Half-Earth: Our Planet's Fight for Life* (New York: W. W. Norton, 2016); B. Büscher and R. Fletcher, "Why E.O. Wilson Is Wrong About How to Save the Earth," Aeon, Mar. 1, 2016, aeon.co/ideas/why-e-o-wilson-is-wrong-about -how-to-save-the-earth.

43. "Who Owns the World's Land? A Global Baseline of Formally Recognized Indigenous and Community Land Rights," Rights and Resources Initiative, Sept. 2015, http://rightsandresources.org/wp-content/uploads/GlobalBaseline_web.pdf.

44. "Summary for Policymakers," in *Climate Change and Land: An IPCC Special Report on Climate Change, Desertification, Land Degradation, Sustainable Land Management, Food Security, and Greenhouse Gas Fluxes in Terrestrial Ecosystems*, ed. V. Masson-Delmotte et al. (Geneva: Intergovernmental Panel on Climate Change, 2019), www.ipcc.ch/srccl/chapter/summary-for-policymakers; C. Ginsberg and S. Keene, "At a Crossroads: Consequential Trends in Recognition of Community-Based Forest Tenure from 2002–2017," Rights and Resources, 2018, rightsandresources.org/wp-content/uploads/2019/03/At-A-Crossroads_RRI_Nov -2018.pdf.

45. S. Engkilterra, "Armed, Vegan Troop of All-Women Bad Asses, Taking Down Poachers Along Africa's Zambezi Left and Right," Enviro News, Sept. 13, 2019, www.environews.tv/world-news/091319-armed-vegan-troop-of-all-women-bad -asses-taking-down-poachers-along-africas-zambezi-left-and-right.

46. W. J. Ripple et al., "World Scientists' Warning of a Climate Emergency 2021," *BioScience* 71, no. 9 (2021): 894–898.

47. Pinker, *Enlightenment Now*, 122; S. Pinker, "Is the World Really Getting Poorer? A Response by Steven Pinker," *Why Evolution Is True* (blog), Jan. 31, 2019, whyevolutionistrue.wordpress.com/2019/01/31/is-the-world-really-getting-poorer -a-response-to-that-claim-by-steve-pinker; N. J. Robinson, "The World's Most Annoying Man," *Current Affairs*, May 29, 2019, www.currentaffairs.org/2019/05 /the-worlds-most-annoying-man; G. Monbiot, "You Can Deny Environmental Calamity—Until You Check the Facts," *The Guardian*, Mar. 7, 2018, www.the guardian.com/commentisfree/2018/mar/07/environmental-calamity-facts-steven -pinker.

48. T. Chiang, "Will A.I. Become the New McKinsey?," *New Yorker*, May 4, 2023, www.newyorker.com/science/annals-of-artificial-intelligence/will-ai-become-the-new-mckinsey.

49. A. Ghosh, *The Great Derangement* (Chicago: University of Chicago Press, 2016), 155.

50. C. Spash, "The Shallow or the Deep Ecological Economics Movement?," *Ecological Economics* 93 (2013): 351–362.

51. C. Seagle, "Inverting the Impacts: Mining, Conservation and Sustainability Claims Near the Rio Tinto/QMM Ilmenite Mine in Southeast Madagascar," *Journal of Peasant Studies* 39, no. 2 (2012): 447–477.

52. C. Spash, "Bulldozing Biodiversity: The Economics of Offsets and Trading in Nature," *Biological Conservation* 192 (2015): 541–551.

53. Earth Negotiations Bulletin MENA Climate Week Summary Bulletin, Oct. 15, 2023, 16, enb.iisd.org/middle-east-north-africa-mena-climate-week-2023-summary.

54. Compare $182 billion to the $1.04 trillion pledged by the Biden administration for the Inflation Reduction Act. See J. Renshaw, "Analysis: Biden's IRA Climate Bill Won't Cut Deficit as Expected," Reuters, June 16, 2023, www.reuters.com/world/us/bidens-ira-climate-bill-wont-cut-deficit-expected-2023-06-16.

55. E. Rumney, I. Casado Sánchez, J. Dowdell, M. Nakayama, S. Murakami, and K. Takenaka, "Rich Nations Say They're Spending Billions to Fight Climate Change. Some Money Is Going to Strange Places," Reuters, June 1, 2023, www.reuters.com/investigates/special-report/climate-change-finance; P. Bigger and N. Millington, "Temporalities of the Climate Crisis: Maintenance, Green Finance and Racialized Austerity in New York City and Cape Town," in *Infrastructuring Urban Futures*, ed. A. Wiig, K. Ward, T. Enright, M. Hodson, H. Pearsall, and J. Silver (Bristol: Bristol University Press, 2023), 47.

56. M. Liboiron, "Firsting in Research," Civic Laboratory for Environmental Action Research, Jan. 18, 2021, https://civiclaboratory.nl/2021/01/18/firsting-in-research/.

57. E. Tuck and K. W. Yang, "R-Words: Refusing Research," in *Humanizing Research: Decolonizing Qualitative Inquiry with Youth and Communities*, ed. D. Paris and M. T. Winn (London: Sage, 2014), 223.

58. "Only an Expert," track 5 on Laurie Anderson, *Homeland,* Nonesuch Records, 2010.

59. D. E. Morrison and R. E. Dunlap, "Environmentalism and Elitism: A Conceptual and Empirical Analysis," *Environmental Management* 10 (1986): 581–589.

60. R. Fletcher, *Failing Forward: The Rise and Fall of Neoliberal Conservation* (Oakland: University of California Press, 2023).

58. C. Criddle, "Bitcoin Consumes 'More Electricity than Argentina,' " BBC, Feb. 10, 2021, www.bbc.com/news/technology-56012952; M. Clark, "NFTs, Explained," The Verge, June 6, 2022, www.theverge.com/22310188/nft-explainer-what-is-blockchain-crypto-art-faq.

62. Mora, R. L. Rollins, K. Taladay, M. B. Kantar, M. K. Chock, M. Shimada, and E. C. Franklin, "Bitcoin Emissions Alone Could Push Global Warming Above 2°C," *Nature Climate Change* 8 (2018): 931–933.

63. For a great breakdown of how exactly NFTs work and what is wrong with them, see the 2022 YouTube video by Dan Olson, "Line Goes Up: The Problem With NFTs," www.youtube.com/watch?v=YQ_xWvX1n9g&t=21s.

64. Regen Network, www.regen.network.

65. Regen Network, www.regen.network; KlimaDAO, www.klimadao.finance; Rewilder, rewilder.xyz; The Absurd Arboretum, opensea.io/collection/absurdarboretum.

65. D. Olson, "Line Goes Up: The Problem With NFTs."

68. R. Bunyan, "Who Would Shell Out for That? Designers Draw Up Outlandish Turtle-Shaped Floating City Concept That Would Cost £6.8 Billion to Build and Run on Solar Power," *Daily Mail*, Nov. 14, 2022, www.dailymail.co.uk/news/article-11425739/Designers-draw-Turtle-shaped-floating-city-concept-cost-6-8-billion-build.html. If you're lost in the lingo, a terayacht is a few orders of magnitude larger than a megayacht, as a terabyte is to a megabyte.

69. M. Sigalos, "These 23-Year-Old Texans Made $4 Million Last Year Mining Bitcoin off Flare Gas from Oil Drilling," CNBC, Feb. 12, 2022, www.cnbc.com/2022/02/12/23-year-old-texans-made-4-million-mining-bitcoin-off-flared-natural-gas.html.

70. N. Chestney, "Global Carbon Markets Value Surged to Record $851bln Last Year—Refinitiv," Reuters, Jan. 31, 2022.

71. N. Smith, "Nature as Accumulation Strategy," *Socialist Register* 43 (2007).

72. S. Ho, "The 'Spotify of Sustainability' Raises $5.7M to Scale Carbon Offset Subscription," Green Queen, July 9, 2021, www.greenqueen.com.hk/spotify-of-sustainability-carbon-offset-subscription.

73. O. Gordon. "Carbon offsets will weather the storm—Xpansiv," Energy Monitor, Feb. 2, 2023, https://www.energymonitor.ai/carbon-markets/carbon-offsets-will-weather-the-storm-xpansiv/.

74. "What Lies Beneath," Global Witness, Feb. 28, 2020, www.globalwitness.org/en/campaigns/forests/what-lies-beneath.

75. "Republic of the Congo: The Planting of More than One Million Trees Begins on the Batéké Plateaux," Total Energies, Nov. 8, 2021, totalenergies.com/media/news/press-releases/republic-congo-planting-more-one-million-trees-begins-bateke-plateaux.

76. T. Wells Lynch, "Your Fridge Uses More Electricity than the Average Tanzanian," *USA Today*, Oct. 2, 2014, reviewed.usatoday.com/refrigerators/features/your-fridge-uses-more-electricity-than-the-average-tanzanian.

77. P. Ditlevsen and S. Ditlevsen, "Warning of a Forthcoming Collapse of the Atlantic Meridional Overturning Circulation," *Nature Communications* 14, no. 4254 (2023), www.nature.com/articles/s41467-023-39810-w.

78. S. Meredith, "From Washington to Warsaw, a 'Greenlash' Is Picking Up Steam Despite Extreme Heat," CNBC, Aug. 1, 2023, www.cnbc.com/2023/08/01/extreme-heat-a-green-backlash-is-sweeping-across-the-us-and-europe.html.

79. V. Ramaswamy, *Woke, Inc.: Inside Corporate America's Social Justice Scam* (New York: Center Street, 2021).

2: What Is Ecology?

1. J. Manna, "Where Nature Ends and Settlements Begin," *e-flux journal* 113, Nov, 2020, https://www.e-flux.com/journal/113/360006/where-nature-ends-and-settlements-begin/.

2. L. Allsop, Open City Documentary Festival, London (April, 2024). https://opencitylondon.com/news/7273/.

3. D. Graeber and D. Wengrow, *The Dawn of Everything: A New History of Humanity* (London: Penguin 2021), 155.

4. U. K. Le Guin, "A Non-Euclidean View of California as a Cold Place to Be," 1982. Reprinted in U.K. Le Guin, *Dancing at the Edge of the World*. London: Gollancz, 1989.

5. A. Waldron et al., "Protecting 30% of the Planet for Nature: Costs, Benefits and Economic Implications," Campaign for Nature, 2020, www.conservation.cam.ac.uk/files/waldron_report_30_by_30_publish.pdf.

6. D. Harvey, "The Nature of Environment: Dialectics of Social and Environ-

mental Change," in *Real Problems, False Solutions: Socialist Register 1993*, ed. R. Miliband and L. Panitch (London: Merlin Press, 1993).

7. J. Mbaria and M. Ogada, *The Big Conservation Lie: The Untold Story of Wildlife Conservation in Kenya* (Auburn, WA: Lens & Pens, 2016).

8. C. Ross, "Tropical Nature in Trust: The Politics of Colonial Nature Conservation," in *Ecology and Power in the Age of Empire: Europe and the Transformation of the Tropical World* (Oxford: Oxford University Press, 2017).

9. L. Sutherland, "Tanzania, Siding with UAE Firm, Plans to Evict Maasai from Ancestral Lands," Mongabay, Feb. 18, 2022, news.mongabay.com/2022/02/tanzania-siding-with-uae-firm-plans-to-evict-maasai-from-ancestral-lands.

10. V. Rathore, "Can a Safari Park Outside Delhi Make Up for a Lost Nicobar Forest?," Scroll, Apr, 19, 2023, scroll.in/article/1047526/can-a-safari-park-outside-delhi-make-up-for-a-lost-nicobar-forest.

11. B. Webster, "Prince William Blames African Population Pressure for Wildlife Loss," *The Times*, Nov. 23, 2021, www.thetimes.co.uk/article/prince-william-blames-african-population-growth-for-wildlife-loss-d7rtjlp3d; N. Farhoud, "Royals' Bloody Trophy Hunting Past When Queen Posed with Tiger Shot by Prince Philip," *Daily Mirror*, Jan. 29, 2021, www.mirror.co.uk/news/uk-news/royals-bloody-trophy-hunting-past-23410242.

12. "Defending Territories of Life and Their Defenders: Policy of the ICCA Consortium," ICCA Consortium, Nov. 13, 2018, www.iccaconsortium.org/wp-content/uploads/2019/05/EN-Defending-Territories-of-Life-and-Their-Defenders-final.pdf.

13. "Territories and Areas Conserved by Indigenous Peoples and Local Communities," ICCA Consortium, Jan. 15, 2019, www.iccaconsortium.org/discover.

14. P. Greenfield, "Record $5bn Donation to Protect Nature Could Herald New Green Era of Giving," *The Guardian*, Sept. 29, 2021, www.theguardian.com/environment/2021/sep/29/record-5bn-donation-to-protect-nature-could-herald-new-green-era-of-giving-aoe.

15. C. Levis et al., "How People Domesticated Amazonian Forests," *Frontiers in Ecology and Evolution* 5 (2018): 171; D. R. Piperno, "The Origins of Plant Cultivation and Domestication in the New World Tropics: Patterns, Process, and New Developments," *Current Anthropology* 52, no. S4 (2011): S453–S470; J. R. Harlan, ed., *Origins of African Plant Domestication* (Berlin: De Gruyter, 2011); D. Q. Fuller, "Contrasting Patterns in Crop Domestication and Domestication Rates: Recent Archaeobotanical Insights from the Old World," *Annals of Botany* 100, no. 5 (2007): 903–924.

16. Graeber and Wengrow, *The Dawn of Everything*, ch. 7.

17. L. Abulu, " 'Pristine Wilderness' Without Human Presence Is a Flawed Construct, Study Says," Mongabay, Oct. 2021, news.mongabay.com/2021/10/pristine -wilderness-without-human-presence-is-a-flawed-construct-study-says/amp; C. Sobrevila, "The Role of Indigenous Peoples in Biodiversity Conservation: The Natural but Often Forgotten Partners," World Bank, 2008; W. S. Walker et al., "The Role of Forest Conversion, Degradation, and Disturbance in the Carbon Dynamics of Amazon Indigenous Territories and Protected Areas," *Proceedings of the National Academy of Sciences* 117, no. 6 (2020): 3015–3025; R. Schuster, R. R. Germain, J. R. Bennett, N. J. Reo, and P. Arcese, "Vertebrate Biodiversity on Indigenous-Managed Lands in Australia, Brazil, and Canada Equals That in Protected Areas," *Environmental Science and Policy* 101 (2019): 1–6.

18. P. Kropotkin, *Mutual Aid: An Illuminated Factor of Evolution* (Oakland, CA: PM Press, 2021).

19. E. Haeckel, *The History of Creation*, 6th ed. (New York: Appleton, 1914), 2:429.

20. D. Gasman, "*The Scientific Origins of National Socialism* (New York: Routledge, 2017); R. J. Richards, "Ernst Haeckel's Alleged Anti-Semitism and Contributions to Nazi Biology," *Biological Theory* 2 (2007): 97–103.

21. J. L. Graves Jr. and A. H. Goodman, *Racism, Not Race: Answers to Frequently Asked Questions* (New York: Columbia University Press, 2021).

22. R. C. Lewontin, S. Rose, and L. J. Kamin, *Not in Our Genes* (New York: Pantheon, 1984); R. Lewontin, "Biological Determinism as an Ideological Weapon," *Science for the People* 9, no. 6 (1977): 36–38; Sociobiology Study Group, "Review: Sociobiology—The Skewed Synthesis," *Science for the People* 8, no. 2 (1976): 7–9; S. Farina and M. Gibbons, " 'The Last Refuge of Scoundrels': New Evidence of E. O. Wilson's Intimacy with Scientific Racism," *Science for the People*, Feb. 1, 2022, maga zine.scienceforthepeople.org/online/the-last-refuge-of-scoundrels.

23. Southern Poverty Law Center, "Garrett Hardin," www.splcenter.org/fight ing-hate/extremist-files/individual/garrett-hardin.

24. E. G. Murdock. "Conserving dispossession? A genealogical account of the colonial roots of western conservation," *Ethics, Policy & Environment* 24.3 (2021): 235–249.

25. A. L. Sène, "Against Wildlife Republics," *The Republic*, Nov. 13, 2022, repub lic.com.ng/october-november-2022/conservation-and-imperialist-expansion-in-af rica; J. Geldmann, A. Manica, N. D. Burgess, L. Coad, and A. Balmford, "A Global-

Level Assessment of the Effectiveness of Protected Areas at Resisting Anthropogenic Pressures," *Proceedings of the National Academy of Sciences* 116, no. 46 (2019): 23209–23215; "In Numbers: Lethal Attacks Against Defenders Since 2012," Global Witness, 2023, www.globalwitness.org/en/campaigns/environmental-activists/num bers-lethal-attacks-against-defenders-2012.

26. M. Ogada (@m_ogada), "The quest for the 30x30 global conservation goal set by @UNEP will not result . . . ," Twitter, July 7, 2023, twitter.com/m_ogada /status/1677301832283222016.

27. M. Sharma, "Green and Saffron: Hindu Nationalism and Indian Environmental Politics," Permanent Black, Ranikhet, India, 2012.

28. C. Darwin, *The Formation of Vegetable Mould, Through the Action of Worms with Observation of their Habits* (1881; Chicago: University of Chicago Press, 1985).

29. G. T. Cushman, *Guano and the Opening of the Pacific World: A Global Ecological History* (Cambridge: Cambridge University Press, 2013*)*.

30. J. M. Gowdy and C. N. McDaniel, "The Physical Destruction of Nauru," *Land Economics* 75, no. 2 (1999): 333–338; A. Watanabe, "From Economic Haven to Refugee 'Hell,' " *Kyodo News*, Sept. 16, 2018.

31. C. Danielewitz, "Phosphate Mining and the Paradox of Abundance," *Edge Effects*, Sept. 17, 2019, edgeeffects.net/phosphate-mining.

32. F. Pearce, "Phosphate: A Critical Resource Misused and Now Running Low," Yale 360, July 7, 2011, e360.yale.edu/features/phosphate_a_critical_resource_mis used_and_now_running_out.

33. D. R. Montgomery, *Dirt: The Erosion of Civilizations* (Berkeley: University of California Press, 2012).

34. C. Ross, *Ecology and Power in the Age of Empire: Europe and the Transformation of the Tropical World* (Oxford: Oxford University Press, 2017).

35. For example, the Japanese economic historian K. Saito, after studying Karl Marx's notebooks, shows how Marx became interested in the newly emerging soil science and, through this study, came to the conclusion that there were real limits to economic expansion under capitalism. K. Saito, "The Emergence of Marx's Critique of Modern Agriculture: Ecological Insights from His Excerpt Notebooks," *Monthly Review* 66, no. 5 (2014): 25.

36. R. Lewontin and R. Levins, "Organism and Environment," *Capitalism Nature Socialism* 8, no. 2 (1997): 95–98.

37. Lewontin and Levins, "Organism and Environment," 97.

38. Lewontin and Levins, "Organism and Environment," 97.

39. M. G. Turner et al., "Climate Change, Ecosystems and Abrupt Change: Science Priorities," *Philosophical Transactions B of the Royal Society* 375 (2020): 10.1098/rstb.2019.0105.

40. E. Kirksey, *Emergent Ecologies* (Durham, NC: Duke University Press, 2015).

41. B. McKibben, *Eaarth: Making a Life on a Tough New Planet* (Toronto: Vintage Canada, 2015); B. Latour, "Love Your Monsters," *Breakthrough Journal* 2, no. 11 (2011): 21–28.

42. C. Koch, *The Feeling of Life Itself: Why Consciousness Is Widespread but Can't Be Computed* (Cambridge, MA: MIT Press, 2019); B. Kastrup, "The Universe in Consciousness," *Journal of Consciousness Studies* 25, nos. 5–6 (2018): 125–155; A. Vansintjan and G. Zlotnik, "Consciousness: An Extended Definition," unpublished manuscript, 2024.

43. H. Buch-Hansen and P. Nielsen. *Critical realism: Basics and beyond.* (Bloomsbury Publishing, 2020).

44. S. B. Klein, "Thoughts on the Scientific Study of Phenomenal Consciousness," *Psychology of Consciousness: Theory, Research, and Practice 8*, no. 1 (2021): 74–80; H. Buch-Hansen and P. Nielsen, *Critical Realism: Basics and Beyond* (London: Red Globe Press, 2020).

45. K. Barad, *Meeting the Universe Halfway: Quantum Physics and the Entanglement of Matter and Meaning* (Durham, NC: Duke University Press, 2007).

46. A. Loewenstein, *The Palestine Laboratory: How Israel Exports the Technology of Occupation Around the World* (London: Verso, 2023).

47. "China's Electric Car Capital Has Lessons for the Rest of the World," Bloomberg, June 27, 2021, www.bloomberg.com/news/features/2021-06-26/china-s-electric-car-capital-has-lessons-for-the-rest-of-world.

48. K. Arora, S. Prandi, F. Cicculli, and C. Aagaard, "Behind the Sweetness of Italy's Kiwi Fruit Lie the Trafficking and Exploitation of Indian Workers," The Wire, Apr. 14, 2023, thewire.in/rights/italy-kiwi-farms-indian-workers.

49. "#7CheapThings: Raj Patel on World Ecology and More," UC Press Blog, Oct. 20, 2017, www.ucpress.edu/book.php?isbn=9780520293137.

50. D. Renfrew and T. W. Pearson. " 'The Social Life of the "Forever Chemical': PFAS Pollution Legacies and Toxic Events," *Environment and Society* 12, 1 (2021): 146-163, accessed May 27, 2024, https://doi.org/10.3167/ares.2021.120109.

51. "The State of World Fisheries and Aquaculture 2018—Meeting the Sustainable Development Goals," Food and Agriculture Organization, 2018.

52. R. Wallace, *Big Farms Make Big Flu: Dispatches on Influenza, Agribusiness,*

and the Nature of Science (New York: New York University Press, 2016); R. Wallace and R. G. Wallace, "Blowback: New Formal Perspectives on Agriculturally Driven Pathogen Evolution and Spread," *Epidemiology and Infection* 143, no. 10 (2015): 2068–2080.

53. M. Widgren, "Precolonial Landesque Capital: A Global Perspective," in *Rethinking Environmental History: World-System History and Global Environmental Change*, ed. A. Hornborg, J. R. McNeill, and J. Martinez-Alier (Lanham, MD: AltaMira Press, 2007), 61–77.

54. E. Livingstone, "Mud and Guts: Europe's Forgotten Environmental Crisis," *Politico*, Apr. 3, 2019, www.politico.eu/article/europe-forgotten-environmental -crisis-soil.

55. B. Strafford, "Cheat Neutral," YouTube, posted by GreenTV, Mar. 8, 2012, www.youtube.com/watch?v=I6zpnVW134k.

56. E. J. Sobo, M. Lambert, and V. Lambert, "Land Acknowledgments Meant to Honor Indigenous People Too Often Do the Opposite—Erasing American Indians and Sanitizing History Instead," *The Conversation*, Oct. 7, 2021, https://theconver sation.com/land-acknowledgments-meant-to-honor-indigenous-people-too-often -do-the-opposite-erasing-american-indians-and-sanitizing-history-instead-163787.

57. Ross, *Ecology and Power in the Age of Empire*.

58. R. V. Kumar, "Green Colonialism and Forest Policies in South India, 1800– 1900," *Global Environment* 5 (2010): 101–125, www.environmentandsociety.org /mml/green-colonialism-and-forest-policies-south-india-1800-1900.

59. D. Lascaris. "Vijay Prashad and Dimitri Lascaris Discuss the Rise of Neo-Fascism in the West." YouTube (2024) https://www.youtube.com/watch?v=wnfP4 x4DDmw. See also S. Lindqvist, *Exterminate all the Brutes* (Granta Books, 2021) and A. Ghosh, *The Nutmeg's Curse* (Penguin Random House India, 2021).

60. Ross, *Ecology and Power in the Age of Empire*, 252.

61. Ross, *Ecology and Power in the Age of Empire*, 253.

62. Lindqvist, *Exterminate all the Brutes*.

63. G. V. Jacks and R. O. Whyte, *The Rape of the Earth: A World Survey of Soil Erosion* (London: Faber & Faber, 1939), 69–70, cited in Ross, *Ecology and Power in the Age of Empire*, 261.

64. N. Sundar, "When Victors Claim Victimhood: Majoritarian Resentment and the Inversion of Reparations Claims." *Development and Change* (2024), 1–23.

65. M. B. Qumsiyeh and M. A. Abusarhan, "An Environmental Nakba: The Palestinian Environment Under Israeli Colonization," *Science for the People* 23, no. 1

(2020), magazine.scienceforthepeople.org/vol23-1/an-environmental-nakba-the
-palestinian-environment-under-israeli-colonization; I. Braverman, "Planting the
Promised Landscape: Zionism, Nature, and Resistance in Israel/Palestine," *Natural
Resources Journal* 49 (2009): 317.

66. Visualizing Palestine, Nov. 2023, visualizingpalestine.org/visual/gaza-water
-2023; "Water in Gaza: Scarce, Polluted, and Mostly Unfit for Use," B'Tselem, the
Israeli Information Center for Human Rights in the Occupied Territories, Aug. 18,
2020, www.btselem.org/gaza_strip/20200818_gaza_water_scarce_polluted_most
ly_unfit_for_use.

67. K. Ahmed, D. Gayle, and A. Mousa, " 'Ecocide in Gaza': Does Scale of Environmental Destruction Amount to a War Crime?," *The Guardian*, Mar. 29, 2024,
www.theguardian.com/environment/2024/mar/29/gaza-israel-palestinian-war
-ecocide-environmental-destruction-pollution-rome-statute-war-crimes-aoe.

68. S. C. Molavi, *Environmental Warfare in Gaza* (London: Pluto Press, 2024).

69. I. Braverman, *Settling Nature: The Conservation Regime in Palestine-Israel*
(Minneapolis: University of Minnesota Press, 2023).

70. A. Dilawar, "How Israel Weaponizes Tree Planting to Displace Palestinians,"
Jacobin, Mar. 15, 2024, jacobin.com/2024/03/israel-afforestation-jnf-naqab-dis
placement; M. Shqair, "No, Israel Is Not Making the Desert Bloom," *Jacobin*, Oct. 21,
2023, jacobin.com/2023/10/israel-setrler-colonialism-greenwashing-eco-normal
ization-water-energy.

71. H. Ritchie, M. Roser and P. Rosado, "Energy," *Our World In Data*, 2022,
https://ourworldindata.org/energy.

72. N. Lakhani, "Emissions from Israel's War in Gaza Have 'Immense' Effect on
Climate Catastrophe," *The Guardian*, Jan. 9, 2024, www.theguardian.com/world
/2024/jan/09/emissions-gaza-israel-hamas-war-climate-change.

73. R. W. Kimmerer, "A Mother's Work," in *Braiding Sweetgrass: Indigenous Wisdom, Scientific Knowledge and the Teachings of Plants* (Minneapolis, MN: Milkweed
Editions, 2013).

74. J. Mukherjee, *Blue Infrastructures* (Singapore: Springer, 2020).

75. S. Banerjee and D. Dey, "Eco-System Complementarities and Urban En-
croachment: A SWOT Analysis of the East Kolkata Wetlands, India," *Cities and the
Environment* 10, no. 1 (2017): 2.

76. D. Mara, *Domestic Wastewater Treatment in Developing Countries* (London:
Routledge, 2013); S. J. Cointreau, "Aquaculture with Treated Wastewater: A Status
Report on Studies Conducted in Lima, Peru," Applied Research and Technology

(WUDAT), Technical Note No. 3, World Bank—Water Supply and Urban Development Department, 1987.

77. A. Vansintjan, "Urban Fish Ponds: Low-Tech Sewage Treatment for Towns and Cities," *Low-Tech Magazine*, March 2021, solar.lowtechmagazine.com/2021/03/urban-fish-ponds-low-tech-sewage-treatment-for-towns-and-cities.

78. Calculated using the Indian rupee to US dollar exchange rate in 2000, adjusted by the authors for inflation of USD in 2021 from data provided by B. B. Jana, J. Heeb, and S. Das, "Ecosystem Resilient Driven Remediation for Safe and Sustainable Reuse of Municipal Wastewater," in *Wastewater Management Through Aquaculture*, ed. B. B. Jana, R. N. Mandal, and P. Jayasankar (Singapore: Springer, 2018), 163–183.

79. Mukherjee, *Blue Infrastructures*.

80. F. H. King, *Farmers of Forty Centuries: Organic Farming in China, Korea, and Japan* (1911; Project Gutenberg, 2004); M. Fukuoka, *The One-Straw Revolution: An Introduction to Natural Farming* (New York: New York Review of Books, 2010).

81. S. A. S. R. Senarathna, G. A. S. Ginigaddara, A. N. Kodithuwakku, and V. Vimaladhas, "Homegardening for Food Security and Income Generation of War Affected Women-Headed Families: A Case Study in Cheddikulam, Northern Province of Sri Lanka," *Sri Lankan Journal of Agriculture and Ecosystems* 1, no. 1 (2019): 73–86.

82. M. Rodrigo, "Amid Lockdown, Sri Lankans Nurture Their Own Oases Through Home Gardening," Mongabay, May 15, 2020, news.mongabay.com/2020/05/amid-lockdown-sri-lankans-nurture-their-own-oases-through-home-gardening.

83. K. M. Son, "Từ 'Tắc đất' đến 'Nông nghiệp Việt Nam': Báo Tắc đất - Tắc vàng" [From 'tac dat' to 'Vietnamese agriculture': Tac Dat Tac Vang Newspaper], Nong Nghiep, nongnghiep.vn/tu-tac-dat-den-nong-nghiep-viet-nam-bao-tac-dat-tac-vang-post152392.html. Translated by Tran True Minh.

84. S. Gupta, "A Mekong Island Too Tiny for Industrial Farming Now Points to Vietnam's Future," Mongabay, Jan. 11, 2024, news.mongabay.com/2024/01/a-mekong-island-too-tiny-for-industrial-farming-now-points-to-vietnams-future; D. K. Nhan, L. T. Duong, N. V. Sanh, and M. C. Verdegem, "Development of 'VAC' Integrated Farming Systems in the Mekong Delta, Vietnam—A View of a System and a Participatory Approach," in *Development of Integrated Agriculture Farming Systems in the Mekong Delta, Tuoitre*, ed. R. Yamada (Ho Chi Minh City: Tre, 2005), 101–125.

85. S. R. Gliessman, *Agroecología: procesos ecológicos en agricultura sostenible* (Turrialba, Costa Rica CATIE, 2002), 13, biowit.wordpress.com/wp-content/uploads /2010/11/agroecologia-procesos-ecolc3b3gicos-en-agricultura-sostenible-stephen -r-gliessman.pdf; R. Patel, "Agroecology Is the Solution to World Hunger," *Scientific American*, Sept. 22, 2021, www.scientificamerican.com/article/agroecology-is-the -solution-to-world-hunger.

86. M. J. Haugen, "Raj Patel on Agroecology, Reparative Approaches, and Land Reform," *Terrain*, July 13, 2022, www.terrain.news/p/interview-raj-patel-on-agro ecology.

87. "An Ecomodernist Manifesto," www.ecomodernism.org.

3: Purity

1. S. Blum, "Fear and Loathing at Erewhon, the High-Margin Grocery Store That Might Just Take Over the World," *Los Angeles Magazine*, Aug. 19, 2019.

2. C. Beavan, *No Impact Man: The Adventures of a Guilty Liberal Who Attempts to Save the Planet, and the Discoveries He Makes About Himself and Our Way of Life in the Process* (New York: Farrar, Straus and Giroux, 2009).

3. E. Kolbert, "Green Like Me: Living Without a Fridge, and Other Experiments in Environmentalism," *New Yorker*, Aug. 31, 2009, www.newyorker.com/magazine /2009/08/31/green-like-me.

4. V. Kolinjivadi, "Of Jenga Towers and Environmental Offsets," Truthout, Sept. 17, 2014, truthout.org/articles/of-jenga-towers-and-environmental-offsets.

5. F. Harvey, "Atlantic Ocean Circulation at Weakest in a Millennium, Say Scientists," *The Guardian*, Feb. 26, 2021, www.theguardian.com/environment/2021 /feb/25/atlantic-ocean-circulation-at-weakest-in-a-millennium-say-scientists.

6. A. Ford, "Groundwater: The World's Neglected Defence Against Climate Change," WaterAid India, 2022, www.wateraid.org/in/publications/groundwater -the-worlds-neglected-defence-against-climate-change.

7. M. Weisberger, "Humans Pump So Much Groundwater That Earth's Axis Has Shifted, Study Finds," CNN, June 26, 2023, www.cnn.com/2023/06/26/world /pumping-groundwater-earth-axis-shifting-scn/index.html.

8. C. Lecher, "American Trash: How an E-Waste Sting Uncovered a Shocking Betrayal," The Verge, Dec. 4, 2019, www.theverge.com/2019/12/4/20992240/e -waste-recycling-electronic-basel-convention-crime-total-reclaim-fraud.

9. B. Kerr, "The People Who Think Air Is Food," *GQ*, Sept. 7, 2017, www.gq .com/story/breatharians-the-people-who-think-air-is-food; "Immortality Work-

shop," Breatharian Institute of America, Mar. 4, 2016, web.archive.org/web/2016 0304062436/http://www.breatharian.com/immortalityworkshop.html.

10. T. Hardingham-Gill, "The 3D Printed Superyacht Concept Designed to Be 'Virtually Invisible,' " CNN, Mar. 21, 2023, edition.cnn.com/travel/article/virtual ly-invisible-superyacht-concept-pegasus/index.html.

11. See, for example, S. Pinker, *Enlightenment Now: The Case for Reason, Science, Humanism, and Progress* (London: Penguin, 2018); A. McAfee, *More from Less: The Surprising Story of How We Learned to Prosper Using Fewer Resources—and What Happens Next* (New York: Simon & Schuster, 2019).

12. S. Moser and S. Kleinhückelkotten, "Good Intents, but Low Impacts: Diverging Importance of Motivational and Socioeconomic Determinants Explaining Pro-Environmental Behavior, Energy Use, and Carbon Footprint," *Environment and Behavior* 50, no. 6: (2018): 15, 20.

13. E. L. Glaeser, "Triumph of the City: How Our Greatest Invention Makes Us Richer, Smarter, Greener, Healthier, and Happier (an Excerpt)," *Journal of Economic Sociology* 14, no. 4 (2013): 75–94; J. Speck, *Walkable City: How Downtown Can Save America, One Step at a Time* (New York: North Point Press, 2012).

14. J. L. Rice, D. A. Cohen, J. Long, and J. R. Jurjevich, "Contradictions of the Climate-Friendly City: New Perspectives on Eco-Gentrification and Housing Justice," *International Journal of Urban and Regional Research* 44, no. 1 (2020): 145, 152.

15. Rice et al., "Contradictions of the Climate-Friendly City," 145, 152.

16. Rice et al., "Contradictions of the Climate-Friendly City," 153.

17. M. Jacobs, *The Green Economy: Environment, Sustainable Development, and the Politics of the Future* (London: Pluto Press, 1991); A. Omri, "Entrepreneurship, Sectoral Outputs and Environmental Improvement: International Evidence," *Technological Forecasting and Social Change* 128 (2018): 46–55.

18. D. Horen Greenford, T. Crownshaw, C. Lesk, K. Stadler, and H. D. Matthews, "Shifting Economic Activity to Services Has Limited Potential to Reduce Global Environmental Impacts Due to the Household Consumption of Labour," *Environmental Research Letters* 15, no. 6 (2020): 064019, doi.org/10.1088/1748-9326/ab7f63.

19. D. Horen Greenford and C. Lesk, "Can We Save the Planet by Growing the Service Sector?," Al-Jazeera, Aug. 19, 2020, www.aljazeera.com/opinions/2020/8 /19/can-we-save-the-planet-by-growing-the-service-sector.

20. J. Watts, "Richest 1% Account for More Carbon Emissions than Poorest 66%, Report Says," *The Guardian*, Nov. 20, 2023, www.theguardian.com/environ

ment/2023/nov/20/richest-1-account-for-more-carbon-emissions-than-poorest
-66-report-says.

21. D. Carrington, "Revealed: The Huge Climate Impact of the Middle Classes," *The Guardian*, Nov. 20, 2023, www.theguardian.com/environment/2023/nov/20/revealed-huge-climate-impact-of-the-middle-classes-carbon-divide.

22. L. Chancel, "Global Carbon Inequality over 1990–2019," *Nature Sustainability* 5, no. 11 (2022): 931–938.

23. T. Wiedmann et al., "Scientists' Warning on Affluence," *Nature Communications* 11, no. 1 (2020): 1–10.

24. J. Hickel, "Quantifying National Responsibility for Climate Breakdown: An Equality-Based Attribution Approach for Carbon Dioxide Emissions in Excess of the Planetary Boundary," *The Lancet Planetary Health* 4, no. 9 (2020): e399–e404.

25. O. Milman, "Elon Musk Was Once an Environmental Hero: Is He Still a Rare Green Billionaire?," *The Guardian*, Nov. 20, 2023, www.theguardian.com/environment/2023/nov/20/elon-musk-green-credentials-clean-energy-climate-deniers.

26. Calculated from numbers provided by https://nyseg.chooseev.com/carbon/ and https://co2.myclimate.org/, and the Federal Highway Administration.

27. Milman, "Elon Musk Was Once an Environmental Hero."

28. L. Miall, "Canada's Carbon Tax Is Hurting Working People," *Jacobin*, Aug. 8, 2022, jacobin.com/2022/08/canada-carbon-tax-working-class-environment-climate-change-policy.

29. L. Bergmann, "Bound by Chains of Carbon: Ecological-Economic Geographies of Globalization," *Annals of the Association of American Geographers* 103, no. 6 (2013): 1348–1370.

30. A. Maitland, M. Lawson, H. Stroot, A. Poidatz, A. Khalfan, and N. Dabi, "Carbon Billionaires: The Investment Emissions of the World's Richest People," Oxfam, 2022.

31. M. Kotz, A. Levermann, and L. Wenz, "The economic commitment of climate change," *Nature* 628 (2024): 551–557.

32. S. Gössling and A. Humpe, "Millionaire Spending Incompatible with 1.5°C Ambitions," *Cleaner Production Letters* 4 (2023), doi.org/10.1016/j.clpl.2022.100027.

33. M. Kotz, A. Levermann, and L. Wenz. The economic commitment of climate change. *Nature* 628 (2024), 551–557. https://doi.org/10.1038/s41586-024-07219-0.

34. R. Harrabin, "Google Says Its Carbon Footprint Is Now Zero," BBC, Sept. 14, 2020, www.bbc.com/news/technology-54141899.

35. B. McKibben, "Could Google's Carbon Emissions Have Effectively Doubled Overnight?," *New Yorker*, May 20, 2022, www.newyorker.com/news/daily-comment/could-googles-carbon-emissions-have-effectively-doubled-overnight.

36. J. Guyer, "How Saudi Money Returned to Silicon Valley," Vox, May 1, 2023, www.vox.com/technology/2023/5/1/23702451/silicon-valley-saudi-money-khashoggi; A. Lucente, "Saudi Public Investment Fund Acquires Shares in Amazon, Google, Uber," Al-Monitor, www.al-monitor.com/originals/2022/08/saudi-public-investment-fund-acquires-shares-amazon-google-uber.

37. D. H. Meadows, D. L. Meadows, J. Randers, and W. W. Behrens III, "The Limits to Growth," Club of Rome, 1972; D. Meadows and J. Randers, The Limits to Growth: The 30-Year Update (London: Routledge, 2012); Wiedmann et al., "Scientists' Warning on Affluence"; T. Jackson, *Prosperity Without Growth: Foundations for the Economy of Tomorrow* (London: Routledge, 2016).

38. S. Samuel, "How to Slash Carbon Emissions While Growing the Economy, in One Chart," Vox, Nov. 13, 2022, www.vox.com/future-perfect/23447414/degrowth-decoupling-carbon-emissions-economic-growth.

39. "Emissions Gap Report, 2022: The Closing Window: Climate Crisis Calls for Rapid Transformation of Societies," UN Environment Programme, 2022, www.unep.org/emissions-gap-report-2022.

40. T. Parrique, J. Barth, F. Briens, C. Kerschner, A. Kraus-Polk, A. Kuokkanen, and J. H. Spangenberg, "Decoupling Debunked: Evidence and Arguments Against Green Growth as a Sole Strategy for Sustainability," European Environment Bureau, Brussels, 2019; H. Haberl et al., "A Systematic Review of the Evidence on Decoupling of GDP, Resource Use and GHG Emissions, Part II: Synthesizing the Insights," *Environmental Research Letters* 15, no. 6 (2020): 065003; "Summary for Policymakers of the Global Assessment Report on Biodiversity and Ecosystem Services of the Intergovernmental Science-Policy Platform on Biodiversity and Ecosystem Services," IPBES, Bonn, 2019.

41. J. Vogel and J. Hickel, "Is Green Growth Happening? An Empirical Analysis of Achieved Versus Paris-Compliant CO_2-GDP Decoupling in High-Income Countries," *Lancet Planetary Health* 7, no. 9 (2023): e759–e769.

42. Haberl et al., "A Systematic Review of the Evidence on Decoupling."

43. J. Horowitz, "Degrowth: A dangerous idea or the answer to the world's biggest crisis?" CNN Business, Nov. 2022, https://www.cnn.com/2022/11/13/econo

my/degrowth-climate-cop27/index.html. J. Hickel, "Gesprek Jason Hickel en Barbara Baarsma over degrowth" (in Dutch), YouTube, Mar. 2023, www.youtube.com/watch?v=mKO5m3_7hHY&t=6s.

44. L. C. King, I. Savin, and S. Drews, "Shades of Green Growth Scepticism Among Climate Policy Researchers," *Nature Sustainability* 6 (2023): 1–5.

45. W. Steffen, K. Richardson, J. Rockström, S. E. Cornell, I. Fetzer, E. M. Bennett, R. Biggs, S. R. Carpenter, W. De Vries, C. A. De Wit, and C. Folke, "Planetary Boundaries: Guiding Human Development on a Changing Planet," *Science* 347, no. 6223 (2015):1259855; P. N. Owens, "Soil Erosion and Sediment Dynamics in the Anthropocene: A Review of Human Impacts During a Period of Rapid Global Environmental Change," *Journal of Soils and Sediments* 20 (2020): 4115–4143.

46. British Antarctic Survey, "Larsen C Ice Shelf," Natural Environment Research Council, 2024, www.bas.ac.uk/data/our-data/publication/larsen-c-ice-shelf.

47. G. Kallis, *Limits: Why Malthus Was Wrong and Why Environmentalists Should Care* (Stanford, CA: Stanford University Press, 2019).

48. Haberl et al., "A Systematic Review of the Evidence on Decoupling."

49. S. Osaka, "These 'Nuclear Bros' Say They Know How to Solve Climate Change," *Washington Post*, Sept. 30, 2022, www.washingtonpost.com/climate-environment/2022/09/30/nuclear-bros-power-activists; A. Stein, J. Messinger, S. Wang, J. Lloyd, J. McBride, and R. Franovich, "Advancing Nuclear Energy: Evaluating Deployment, Investment, and Impact in America's Green Energy Future," Breakthrough Institute, 2022, thebreakthrough.org/articles/advancing-nuclear-energy-report; T. Nordhaus and M. Shellenberger, *Break Through: From the Death of Environmentalism to the Politics of Possibility* (New York: Houghton Mifflin Harcourt, 2007); M. Shellenberger, R. Watson, and C. Follett, "Apocalypse Never: Why Environmental Alarmism Hurts Us," Cato Institute, 2020; Pinker, *Enlightenment Now*.

50. D. Thorpe, "Extracting a Disaster," *The Guardian*, Dec. 5, 2008, www.theguardian.com/commentisfree/2008/dec/05/nuclear-greenpolitics.

51. V. Jack, "French-Russian Nuclear Relations Turn Radioactive," *Politico*, Apr. 20, 2023, www.politico.eu/article/french-russian-nuclear-relations-radioactive-rosatom-sanctions.

52. G. Leali, "Niger coup sparks concerns about French, EU uranium dependency", *Politico*, Jul. 31, 2023, https://www.politico.eu/article/niger-coup-spark-concerns-france-uranium-dependency.

53. F. De Beaupuy and T. Gillespie, "France Cuts Nuclear Output as Heat Triggers Water Restrictions," Bloomberg News, Jul. 13, 2023, https://www.bloomberg

.com/news/articles/2023-07-13/france-cuts-nuclear-output-as-heat-triggers-water -restrictions. J. Kollewe, "EDF cuts output at nuclear power plants as French rivers get too warm," *The Guardian,* Aug. 3, 2022, https://www.theguardian.com/busi ness/2022/aug/03/edf-to-reduce-nuclear-power-output-as-french-river-tempera tures-rise.

54. The importance of the Zaporizhzhia nuclear power plant during Russia's war on Ukraine is one example of the kind of instability that will likely increase as climate change accelerates. For a sober assessment of the potential of nuclear energy for addressing climate change, see M. V. Ramana, *Nuclear is Not the Solution: The Folly of Atomic Power in the Age of Climate Change* (London: Verso Books, 2024) and S. M. McDonald, "Is Nuclear Power Our Best Bet Against Climate Change?," *Boston Review*, Oct. 12, 2021, bos tonreview.net/science-nature/samuel-miller-mcdonald-nuclear-power-our-best-bet -against-climate-change.

55. M. Iyoda, "Nuclear Energy Cannot Lead the Global Energy Transition," Al-Jazeera, Apr. 3, 2024, www.aljazeera.com/opinions/2024/4/3/nuclear-energy-can not-lead-the-global-energy-transition.

56. P. Achakulwisut, P. Calles Almeida, and E. Arond, "It's Time to Move Beyond 'Carbon Tunnel Vision,' " SEI, 2022.

57. E. Elhacham, L. Ben-Uri, J. Grozovski, Y. M. Bar-On, and R. Milo, "Global Human-Made Mass Exceeds All Living Biomass," *Nature* 588, no. 7838 (2020): 442–444.

58. Steffen et al., "Planetary Boundaries."

59. W. Steffen, W. Broadgate, L. Deutsch, O. Gaffney, and C. Ludwig, "The Trajectory of the Anthropocene: The Great Acceleration," *Anthropocene Review* 2, no. 1 (2015): 81–98.

60. McAfee, *More from Less.*

61. H. Schandl et al., "Global Material Flows and Resource Productivity: Forty Years of Evidence," *Journal of Industrial Ecology* 22, no. 4 (2018): 827–838.

62. T. O. Wiedmann, H. Schandl, M. Lenzen, D. Moran, S. Suh, J. West, and K. Kanemoto, "The Material Footprint of Nations," *Proceedings of the National Academy of Sciences* 112, no. 20 (2015): 6271–6276.

63. Schandl et al., "Global Material Flows and Resource Productivity."

64. J. K. Steinberger, F. Krausman, M. Getzner, H. Schandl, and J. West, "Development and Dematerialization: An International Study," *PloS One* 8, no. 10 (2013): e70385.

65. "Cities and the Circular Economy," Ellen MacArthur Foundation, 2022, archive.ellenmacarthurfoundation.org/explore/cities-and-the-circular-economy.

66. T. Kantai, "Multiple-Use Plastics Only Delaying Menace of Pollution," *Business Daily Africa*, Apr. 27, 2022, www.businessdailyafrica.com/bd/opinion-analysis/columnists/multiple-use-plastics-idea-only-delaying-menace-of-pollution-3796486.

67. T. Kantai, "Multiple-Use Plastics Only Delaying Menace of Pollution."

68. K. De Decker, "How Circular Is the Circular Economy?," *Low-Tech Magazine*, Nov. 2018, solar.lowtechmagazine.com/2018/11/how-circular-is-the-circular-economy.html.

69. M. A. Reuter, A. van Schaik, and M. Ballester, "Limits of the Circular Economy: Fairphone Modular Design Pushing the Limits," *World of Metallurgy—ERZMETALL* 71, no. 2 (2018): 68–79.

70. B. Geueke, D. W. Phelps, L. V. Parkinson, and J. Muncke, "Hazardous Chemicals in Recycled and Reusable Plastic Food Packaging," *Plastics* 1 (2023): e7, doi: 10.1017/plc.2023.7.

71. P. Boisacq, M. De Keuster, E. Prinsen, Y. Jeong, L. Bervoets, M. Eens, A. Covaci, T. Willems, and T. Groffen, "Assessment of Poly- and Perfluoroalkyl Substances (PFAS) in Commercially Available Drinking Straws Using Targeted and Suspect Screening Approaches," *Food Additives and Contaminants: Part A* 40, no. 9 (2023): 1–12.

72. E. A. Crunden, "How Useful Is Recycling, Really?," *The Atlantic*, Jan. 28, 2021, www.theatlantic.com/science/archive/2021/01/recycling-wont-solve-climate-change/617851.

73. Associated Press, "Malaysia to Ship Back Tonnes of Plastic Waste to Canada and Other Nations," Global News Canada, May 28, 2019, globalnews.ca/news/5324429/malaysia-ship-back-plastic-waste-canada; H. Ellis-Petersen, "Philippines Ships 69 Containers of Rubbish Back to Canada," *The Guardian*, May 30, 2019, www.theguardian.com/world/2019/may/31/philippines-puts-69-containers-of-rubbish-on-boat-back-to-canada; C. Katz, "Piling Up: How China's Ban on Importing Waste Has Stalled Global Recycling," Yale E360, Mar. 7, 2019, e360.yale.edu/features/piling-up-how-chinas-ban-on-importing-waste-has-stalled-global-recycling.

74. "Earth Negotiations Bulletin MENA Climate Week Summary Bulletin," Oct. 15, 2023, 12, enb.iisd.org/middle-east-north-africa-mena-climate-week-2023-summary.

75. Kerr, "The People Who Think Air Is Food."

4: Innovation

1. J. P. Smith, P. Baker, R. Mathisen, A. Long, N. Rollins, & M. Waring. A proposal to recognize investment in breastfeeding as a carbon offset. *Bulletin of the World Health Organization*, 102(5), 336-343.

2. "Massive Expansion of Renewable Power Opens Door to Achieving Global Tripling Goal Set at COP28," International Energy Agency, Jan. 11, 2024, www.iea .org/news/massive-expansion-of-renewable-power-opens-door-to-achieving-glob al-tripling-goal-set-at-cop28.

3. R. York, "Do Alternative Energy Sources Displace Fossil Fuels?," *Nature Climate Change* 2 (2012): 441–443.

4. O. Milman, " 'Monster profits' for energy giants reveal a self-destructive fossil fuel resurgence," *The Guardian*, Feb. 9 2023, https://www.theguardian.com/envi ronment/2023/feb/09/profits-energy-fossil-fuel-resurgence-climate-crisis-shell -exxon-bp-chevron-totalenergies.

5. B. Johnson, *Carbon Nation: Fossil Fuels in the Making of American Culture* (Lawrence: University Press of Kansas, 2019).

6. A. Dunlap, "End the 'Green' Delusions: Industrial-Scale Renewable Energy Is Fossil Fuel+," *Verso Blog*, May 10, 2018, www.versobooks.com/en-ca/blogs/news /3797-end-the-green-delusions-industrial-scale-renewable-energy-is-fossil-fuel.

7. "Biden-Harris Administration Announces $4.9 Billion to Deploy Infrastructure Necessary to Manage and Store Carbon Pollution," press release, U.S. Department of Energy, Sept. 23, 2022, www.energy.gov/articles/biden-harris-admi nistration-announces-49-billion-deploy-infrastructure-necessary-manage; "Canada Opens Call for Carbon Capture Research, Development and Demonstration Projects," Jul. 7, 2022, press release, Natural Resources Canada, www.canada.ca/en/natu ral-resources-canada/news/2022/07/canada-opens-call-for-carbon-capture-re search-development-and-demonstration-projects.html.

8. C. Farand and J. Lo, " 'Oil and Gas Trade Show' Promotes Carbon Capture at COP27," Climate Home News, Nov. 13, 2022, www.climatechangenews.com /2022/11/13/oil-and-gas-trade-show-promotes-carbon-capture-at-cop27.

9. K. Joshi, "New Global CCS Report Shows Up Silliness of Clean Coal Predictions in News Corp," Renew Economy: Clean Energy News and Analysis, Dec. 7, 2020, reneweconomy.com.au/new-global-ccs-report-shows-up-silliness-of-clean -coal-predictions-in-news-corp-81413.

10. K. Joshi, "CCS Causes the Problem It Fails to Solve," Nov. 15, 2022, ketanjo shi.co/2022/11/15/ccs-causes-the-problem-it-fails-to-solve.

11. Joshi, "CCS Causes the Problem It Fails to Solve."

12. P. Radtke, " 'Ukraine Is a False Justification': America's Destructive New Rush for Natural Gas," *The Guardian*, Mar. 20, 2023, www.theguardian.com/environ ment/2023/mar/20/ukraine-is-a-false-justification-americas-destructive-new-rush

-for-natural-gas; "World's Biggest Fossil Fuel Firms Projected to Spend Almost a Trillion Dollars on New Oil and Gas Fields by 2030," press release, Global Witness, Apr. 12, 2022, www.globalwitness.org/en/press-releases/worlds-biggest-fossil-fuel-firms-projected-to-spend-almost-a-trillion-dollars-on-new-oil-and-gas-fields-by-2030.

13. "Crisis Year 2022 Brought $134 Billion in Excess Profit to the West's Five Largest Oil and Gas Companies," Global Witness, Feb. 9, 2023, www.globalwitness.org/en/campaigns/fossil-gas/crisis-year-2022-brought-134-billion-in-excess-profit-to-the-wests-five-largest-oil-and-gas-companies.

14. Joshi, "CCS Causes the Problem It Fails to Solve."

15. "Oxagon: A Blueprint for Advanced and Clean Industries," Neom, 2022, www.neom.com/en-us/regions/oxagon.

16. "Saudi Neom to Start Producing Green Hydrogen in 2026—Oxagon's CEO," Zawya Projects, Sept. 14, 2022, www.zawya.com/en/projects/industry/saudi-neom-to-start-producing-green-hydrogen-in-2026-oxagons-ceo-ygq0p905.

17. R. W. Howard and M. Z. Jacobson, "How Green Is Blue Hydrogen?," *Earth Science and Engineering* 9 (2021): 1676–1687.

18. Joshi, "CCS Causes the Problem It Fails to Solve."

19. T. Hiscox and J. Heinemann, "Chasing Future Biotech Solutions to Climate Change Risks Delaying Action in the Present—It May Even Make Things Worse," The Conversation, Nov. 28, 2022, theconversation.com/chasing-future-biotech-solutions-to-climate-change-risks-delaying-action-in-the-present-it-may-even-make-things-worse-194147.

20. T. R. Sinclair, T. W. Rufty, and R. S. Lewis, "Increasing Photosynthesis: Unlikely Solution for World Food Problem," *Trends in Plant Science* 24, no. 11 (2019): 1032–1039.

21. M. Ajl and R. Wallace, "Red Vegans Against Green Peasants," *New Socialist*, Oct. 16, 2021, newsocialist.org.uk/red-vegans-against-green-peasants.

22. G. Walton, "Shared Solutions Are Our Greatest Hope and Strength," in *Not Too Late: Changing the Climate Story from Despair to Possibility*, ed. R. Solnit and T. Young Lutunatabua (Chicago: Haymarket, 2023).

23. A. Vetter, "The Matrix of Convivial Technology: Assessing Technologies for Degrowth," *Journal of Cleaner Production* 197 (2018): 1778–1786.

24. N. S. Kabunga, T. Dubois, and M. Qaim, "Impact of Tissue Culture Banana Technology on Farm Household Income and Food Security in Kenya," *Food Policy* 45 (2014): 25–34.

25. M. A. Schnurr, *Africa's Gene Revolution: Genetically Modified Crops and the Future of African Agriculture* (Montreal: McGill-Queen's University Press, 2019).

26. "The Bill and Melinda Gates Foundation Invests $1.4 Billion in Climate Adaptation," Gates Foundation, Nov. 2022, docs.gatesfoundation.org/documents /bill_and_melinda_gates_foundation_invests_1.4_billion_in_climate_adaptation _fact_sheet_november_2022.pdf.

27. J. Hickel, "On Technology and Degrowth," *Monthly Review* 75, no. 3 (2023): 44–50.

5: Efficiency

1. M. Ross, "Celebrity Resorts Threaten Isolated Tribes," Survival International, June 15, 2009, www.survivalinternational.org/news/4663.

2. E. Shove, "What Is Wrong with Energy Efficiency?," *Building Research and Information* 46, no. 7 (2018): 779–789.

3. S. Bliss, "Jevons Paradox," Uneven Earth, June 16, 2020, unevenearth .org/2020/06/jevons-paradox.

4. R. McKie, "Child Labour, Toxic Leaks: The Price We Could Pay for a Greener Future," *The Guardian*, Jan. 3, 2021.

5. G. Kallis, *In defense of degrowth: Opinions and minifestos* (Montreal: Uneven Earth Press, Montreal, 2018).

6. M. Goldman, *Imperial Nature: The World Bank and Struggles for Social Justice in the Age of Globalization* (New Haven, CT: Yale University Press, 2005).

7. S. Safdie, "Global Food Waste in 2023," Greenly Institute, Mar. 23, 2023, greenly.earth/en-us/blog/ecology-news/global-food-waste-in-2022; "Global Food Crisis Putting Millions of Young Lives at Risk," UN News, Jan. 12, 2023, news.un .org/en/story/2023/01/1132407.

8. Bliss, "Jevons Paradox."

9. H. Rosa, *Social Acceleration* (New York: Columbia University Press, 2013).

10. J. Loos, D. J. Abson, M. J. Chappell, J. Hanspach, F. Mikulcak, M. Tichit, and J. Fischer, "Putting Meaning Back into 'Sustainable Intensification,'" *Frontiers in Ecology and the Environment* 12, no. 6 (2014): 356–361; L. Blomqvist, "Do High Agricultural Yields Spare Land for Conservation?," Breakthrough Institute, Aug. 29, 2016, thebreakthrough.org/issues/conservation/do-high-agricultural-yields-spare -land-for-conservation.

11. A. Calo, "Land Sparers Feel Their Oats," *Land Food Nexus*, Aug, 2, 2022, adamcalo.substack.com/archive.

12. Calo, "Land Sparers Feel Their Oats."

13. F. F. Goulart, M. J. Chappell, F. Mertens, and B. Soares-Filho, "Sparing or Expanding? The Effects of Agricultural Yields on Farm Expansion and Deforestation in the Tropics," *Biodiversity and Conservation* 32, no. 3 (2023): 1089–1104.

14. A. Calo et al., "Achieving Food System Resilience Requires Challenging Dominant Land Property Regimes," *Frontiers in Sustainable Food Systems* 5 (2021): 683544.

15. "Land Reform," La Via Campesina, Oct. 6, 2000, viacampesina.org/en/land-reform.

16. Calo, "Land Sparers Feel Their Oats."

17. G. Kallis and S. Bliss, "Post-Environmentalism: Origins and Evolution of a Strange Idea," *Journal of Political Ecology* 26, no. 1 (2019): 466–485.

18. R. Patel and J. W. Moore, *A History of the World in Seven Cheap Things: A Guide to Capitalism, Nature, and the Future of the Planet* (Berkeley: University of California Press, 2017).

19. For further reading on this question, check out J. Delisle, "Decolonizing Ecology," *Briarpatch Magazine*, July 2, 2020, briarpatchmagazine.com/articles/view/decolonizing-ecology; A. Chaillou, L. Roblin, and M. Ferdinand, "Why We Need a Decolonial Ecology: A Conversation with Malcolm Ferdinand," *Green European Journal*, June 4, 2020, www.greeneuropeanjournal.eu/why-we-need-a-decolonial-ecology; H. Alberro, "Humanity and Nature Are Not Separate—We Must See Them as One to Fix the Climate Crisis," The Conversation, Sept. 17, 2019, theconversation.com/humanity-and-nature-are-not-separate-we-must-see-them-as-one-to-fix-the-climate-crisis-122110.

20. I. Perfecto, J. Vandermeer, and A. Wright, *Nature's Matrix: Linking Agriculture, Biodiversity Conservation and Food Sovereignty* (London: Routledge, 2019); R. B. Kerr et al., "Agroecology as a Transformative Approach to Tackle Climatic, Food, and Ecosystemic Crises," *Current Opinion in Environmental Sustainability* 62 (2023): 101275; M. J. Chappell and L. A. LaValle, "Food Security and Biodiversity: Can We Have Both? An Agroecological Analysis," *Agriculture and Human Values* 28 (2011): 3–26.

21. A. Waldron et al., "Protecting 30% of the Planet for Nature: Costs, Benefits and Economic Implications," Campaign for Nature, 2021, www.campaignfornature.org/protecting-30-of-the-planet-for-nature-economic-analysis; "#DearHumanity," Survival International, 2022, www.survivalinternational.org/about/dearhumanity; "Le Grand Mensonge Vert," Survival International, 2022, www.survivalinternation

al.fr/campagnes/mensongevert; S. Corry, "Why the New Deal for Nature Is a Disaster for People and Planet," Survival International, Feb. 21, 2020, survivalinternation al.medium.com/why-the-new-deal-for-nature-is-a-disaster-for-people-and-planet -5148108d2768; F. Longo, "Why 30x30 Would Be the Worst Possible Outcome of COP15," African Arguments, Dec. 8, 2020, africanarguments.org/2022/12/why -30x30-would-be-the-worst-possible-outcome-of-cop15.

22. M. Birnbaum and T. Root, "The U.S. Army Has Released Its First-Ever Climate Strategy. Here's What That Means," *Washington Post*, Feb. 10, 2022, www .washingtonpost.com/climate-solutions/2022/02/10/army-military-green-climate -strategy; S. Salazar Hughes, S. Velednitsky, and A. Arden Green, "Greenwashing in Palestine/Israel: Settler Colonialism and Environmental Injustice in the Age of Climate Catastrophe," *Environment and Planning E: Nature and Space* 6, no. 1 (2023): 495–513. C. Holland, "Israeli Army to Offer Vegan Meals and Leather-Free Boots," *VegNews*, Dec. 29, 2014, https://vegnews.com/2014/12/israeli-army-to-offer-vegan -meals-and-leather-free-boots.

6: The PIE in the Sky

1. W. K. Kapp, *The Social Costs of Private Enterprise*, 1st ed, 1950, New York: Shocken H. Healy, J. Martínez-Alier, L. Temper, M. Walter, and J. F. Gerber, eds., *Ecological Economics from the Ground Up* (New York: Routledge, 2013).

2. C. L. Spash, "The Contested Conceptualisation of Pollution in Economics: Market Failure or Cost Shifting Success?" *Cahiers d'economie politique* 1 (2021): 85–122.

3. S. Lerner, *Sacrifice Zones: The Front Lines of Toxic Chemical Exposure in the United States* (Cambridge, MA: MIT Press, 2012); R. Bullard, "Environmental Justice in the 21st Century," in *Debating the Earth: The Environmental Politics Reader*, 2nd ed., ed. J. S. Dryzek and D. Schlosberg (Oxford: Oxford University Press, 2005), 431–449; R. Salvidge, "Explainer: 'Forever Chemicals': What Are PFAS and What Risk Do They Pose?," *The Guardian*, Feb. 8, 2022, www.theguardian.com/environ ment/2022/feb/08/what-are-pfas-forever-chemicals-what-risk-toxicity; C. Gillam, " 'A Worldwide Public Health Threat': Rob Bilott on His 20-Year Fight Against Forever Chemicals," *The Guardian*, May 1, 2022, twww.theguardian.com/environ ment/2022/may/01/pfas-forever-chemicals-rob-bilott-lawyer-interview; D. E. Taylor, *Toxic Communities: Environmental Racism, Industrial Pollution, and Residential Mobility* (New York: New York University Press, 2014). F. Demaria, "Can the Poor Resist Capital? Conflicts over 'Accumulation by Contamination' at the Ship Breaking Yard of Alang (India)," in *Nature, Economy and Society: Understanding the Link-*

ages, ed. N. Ghosh, P. Mukhopadhyay, A. Shah, and M. Panda (New Delhi: Springer, 2016), 273–304.

4. "Carrying the environmental burdens," in K. Bell. *Working-Class Environmentalism*.

5. H. Lyons, "New BNP Paribas Fortis Headquarters Wins Award at Cannes Property Fair," *Brussels Times*, Mar. 18, 2022, www.brusselstimes.com/211335/new-bnp-paribas-fortis-headquarters-wins-award-at-cannes-property-fair.

6. N. Nunn, "The Long-Term Effects of Africa's Slave Trades," *Quarterly Journal of Economics* 123, no. 1 (2008): 139–176.

7. Patel and Moore, *A History of the World in Seven Cheap Things*.

8. T. Piketty, Twitter post, Apr. 18, 2024, https://twitter.com/PikettyWIL/status/1780943104649920951.

9. J. Hickel, "Imperialist Appropriation in the World Economy: Drain from the Global South Through Unequal Exchange, 1990–2015," *Global Environmental Change* 73 (2022): 102467.

10. A. Olla, "Why Is SNL Giving Elon Musk Yet Another Platform?," *The Guardian*, May 8, 2021, www.theguardian.com/commentisfree/2021/may/08/elon-musk-snl-saturday-night-live-hosting-politics.

11. Price, C. C. Price , and K. A. Edwards, K.A. Sep, 2020. "Trends in Income from 1975 to 2018," RAND Corporation Working Paper WR-A156, Sept. 2020, www.rand.org/pubs/working_papers/WRA516-1.html.

12. Hickel, "Imperialist Appropriation in the World Economy."

13. V. Prashad, *The Darker Nations: A Biography of the Short-Lived Third World* (New Delhi: Leftword Books, 2007).

14. Bergmann, "Bound by Chains of Carbon."

15. A. Dewan, "A UAE Company Has Secured African Land the Size of the UK for Controversial Carbon Offset Projects," CNN, Nov. 23, 2023, www.cnn.com/2023/11/22/climate/uae-cop28-adnoc-fossil-fuels-expansion-climate-intl/index.html.

16. M. Specter, "Extreme City," *New Yorker*, May 25, 2015, www.newyorker.com/magazine/2015/06/01/extreme-city-specter.

17. Hickel, "Imperialist Appropriation in the World Economy."

18. C. McGreal, "Big Oil and Gas Kept a Dirty Secret for Decades. Now They May Pay the Price," *The Guardian*, June 30, 2021, www.theguardian.com/environment/2021/jun/30/climate-crimes-oil-and-gas-environment.

19. O. Milman, "Criticism Intensifies After Big Oil Admits 'Gaslighting' Public

over Green Aims," *The Guardian*, Sept. 17, 2022, www.theguardian.com/environ ment/2022/sep/17/oil-companies-exxonmobil-chevron-shell-bp-climate-crisis.

20. A. Bhadani, "What Are Climate Reparations?," *Yes Magazine*, Nov. 29, 2021, www.yesmagazine.org/environment/2021/11/29/climate-reparations.

21. "People's Agreement of Cochabamba," World People's Conference on Climate Change and the Rights of Mother Earth, Apr. 10, 2010.

22. R. Kelley, *Freedom Dreams: The Black Radical Imagination* (Boston: Beacon Press, 2022); A. Mitchell and A. Chaudhury, "Worlding Beyond 'the' 'End' of 'the World': White Apocalyptic Visions and BIPOC Futurisms," *International Relations* 34, no. 3 (2020): 309–332.

23. O. O. Táíwò, *Reconsidering Reparations* (Oxford: Oxford University Press, 2022), 140.

24. Táíwò, *Reconsidering Reparations*, 135.

25. S. Sen, "Why the West Hesitates to Condemn Racism," Al-Jazeera, Nov. 29, 2022, www.aljazeera.com/opinions/2022/11/29/why-the-west-hesitates-to-con demn-racism.

26. R. French, "Speech: UN Human Rights Council 51: UK Explanation of Vote on Racism Resolution," Foreign, Commonwealth and Development Office, Oct. 7, 2022, www.gov.uk/government/speeches/un-human-rights-council-51-uk-explana tion-of-vote-on-racism-resolution.

27. L. Lohmann, "Reparations, Time and Struggle," discussion paper for the Global Working Group Beyond Development, Sept. 2023, The Corner House, UK.

28. "Historic 'Loss and Damage' Fund Adopted at COP27 Climate Summit," Al Jazeera, Nov. 20, 2022, www.aljazeera.com/news/2022/11/20/historic-loss-and-dam age-fund-adopted-at-cop27-climate-talks. Reuters, "World Bank to Host Climate Damages Fund Despite Opposition from Developing Nations," CNN, Nov. 5, 2023, www.cnn.com/world-bank-loss-damage-climate-cop28-intl/index.html. N. Lakhani, "$700m pledged to loss and damage fund at Cop28 covers less than 0.2% needed," *The Guardian*, Dec. 6, 2023, https://www.theguardian.com/environment/2023/dec/06 /700m-pledged-to-loss-and-damage-fund-cop28-covers-less-than-02-percent-needed. B. Rich, "The World Bank's Legacy of Environmental Destruction: A Case Study," Open Democracy, Apr. 12, 2019, www.opendemocracy.net/en/oureconomy/the -world-banks-legacy-of-environmental-destruction-a-case-study.

29. N. Chomsky, *Hegemony or Survival: America's Quest for Global Dominance* (New York: Macmillan, 2003); V. Bevins, *The Jakarta Method: Washington's Anti-*

communist Crusade and the Mass Murder Program That Shaped Our World (New York: PublicAffairs, 2020).

30. P. Bigger and S. Webber, "Green Structural Adjustment in the World Bank's Resilient City," *Annals of the American Association of Geographers* 111, no. 1 (2021): 36–51.

31. A. L. Fanning and J. Hickel, "Compensation for Atmospheric Appropriation," *Nature Sustainability* 6 (2023): 1077–1083, www.nature.com/articles/s418 93-023-01130-8.

32. A. Salleh, "Listening to Ecological Voices from the Global South," *Journal of Environmental Thought and Education* 8 (2015): 64–71; M. Lang, C. D. König, and A. C. Regelmann, *Alternatives in a World of Crisis* (Bruselas: Universidad Andina Simón Bolívar, 2019); M. Deveaux, "Poor-Led Social Movements and Global Justice," *Political Theory* 46, no. 5 (2018): 698–725; M. Ajl, *A People's Green New Deal* (London: Pluto Press, 2021); K. Kinninburgh, "Climate Politics After the Yellow Vests," *Dissent*, Spring 2019, www.dissentmagazine.org/article/the-yellow-vests-un certain-future; S. Van Outryve, "Realising direct democracy through representative democracy: From the Yellow Vests to a libertarian municipalist strategy in Commercy," Urban Studies 60, no. 11 (2023): 2214-2230. To learn more about these movements, see the work of organizations like Focus on the Global South (www.fo cusweb.org), Food First (www.foodfirst.org), Global Footprint Network (www .footprintnetwork.org), GRAIN (grain.org), Landless People's Movement (www .mst.br), Lucha Indigena (www.luchaindigena.com), Shack Dwellers International, (www.sdinet.org), Survival International (www.survivalinternational.org), Third World Network (www.twnside.org.sg), and the Transnational Institute (www.tni .org). Thanks to Ariel Salleh for this list.

7: Exclusively Green

1. R. Rathore and R. Conway, "The Road to Utopia Is Not Smooth," *Disegno*, Jan. 9, 2021, disegnojournal.com/newsfeed/road-to-utopia-auroville-india-crown -road-controversy.

2. Rathore and Conway, "The Road to Utopia Is Not Smooth."

3. J. L. Namakkal, "European Dreams, Tamil Land: Auroville and the Paradox of a Postcolonial Utopia," *Journal for the Study of Radicalism* 6, no. 1 (2012): 59–88.

4. J. L. Namakkal, "Transgressing the Boundaries of the Nation: Decolonization, Migration, and Identity in France/India, 1910–1972" (PhD diss., University of Minnesota, 2013), 239, conservancy.umn.edu/bitstream/handle/11299/154035 /Namakkal_umn_0130E_13579.pdf.

5. J. L. Namakkal, *Unsettling Utopia: The Making and Unmaking of French India* (New York: Columbia University Press, 2021), 195.

6. A. Kothari, "Bulldozing a Dream?," Meer, Jan. 9, 2022, www.meer.com/en /68234-bulldozing-a-dream.

7. I. Illich, "Health as One's Own Responsibility—No, Thank You!," speech given in Hannover, Germany, Sept. 14, 1990, translated by Jutta Mason, edited by Lee Hoinacki.

8. A. Escobar, *Designs for the Pluriverse: Radical Interdependence, Autonomy, and the Making of Worlds* (Durham, NC: Duke University Press, 2018), 70.

9. Namakkal, "Transgressing the Boundaries of the Nation," 225–226.

10. A. Deener, *Venice: A Contested Bohemia in Los Angeles* (Chicago: University of Chicago Press, 2012), 130.

11. G. Lizarralde, *Unnatural Disasters: Why Most Responses to Risk and Climate Change Fail but Some Succeed* (New York: Columbia University Press, 2021), 105.

12. "This Vertical Forest in Vietnam Is Setting a New Standard in Eco-Architecture," *Travel and Leisure Asia*, Nov. 11, 2020, travelandleisureasia.com /this-vertical-forest-in-vietnam-is-setting-a-new-standard-in-eco-architecture.

13. C. Provost and M. Kennard, "Inside Hanoi's Gated Communities: Elite En-claves Where Even the Air Is Cleaner," *The Guardian*, Jan. 21, 2016, www.theguardian .com/cities/2016/jan/21/inside-hanoi-gated-communities-elite-enclaves-air-cleaner.

14. Ecopark, 2015, ecopark.com.vn/ecopark-overviewen.html.

15. T. Kumari, "Matrimandir: Construction Features of a Unique Temple," The Constructor, 2020, theconstructor.org/architecture/matrimandir-construction-fea tures/60491.

16. Deener, *Venice*, 125–158.

17. Deener, *Venice*, 125–158.

18. Deener, *Venice*, 125–158.

19. Deener, *Venice*, 125.

20. L. Poon, "Sleepy in Songdo, Korea's Smartest City," Bloomberg, June 22, 2018, www.bloomberg.com/news/articles/2018-06-22/songdo-south-korea-s-smart est-city-is-lonely.

21. R. Bunyan, "Who Would Shell Out for That? Designers Draw Up Outland-ish Turtle-Shaped Floating City Concept That Would Cost £6.8 billion to Build and Run on Solar Power," *Daily Mail*, Nov. 14, 2022, www.dailymail.co.uk/news/arti cle-11425739/Designers-draw-Turtle-shaped-floating-city-concept-cost-6-8billion -build.html.

22. G. Debord, *La société du spectacle* (Paris: Buchet-Chastel, 1967), 2–4. Translated by Ken Knabb.

23. K. Wagner, "A Seamless Dystopia," *The Nation*, Mar. 12, 2024, https://www .thenation.com/article/culture/what-happened-to-21st-century-city/.

24. B. Shecter, "Canadian Pension Funds Inconsistent on Climate Policy, Watchdog Group Says," *Financial Post*, Jan. 18, 2023, financialpost.com/fp-finance/canadi an-pension-funds-inconsistent-climate-policy-watchdog-group; N. Rockwell, " 'They Try to Build Their Money from Our Weakness': Tenants Fight Rent Increases, Maintenance Issues at Apartment Complex Owned by Federal Pension Fund," *National Observer*, Apr. 26, 2023, www.nationalobserver.com/2023/04/26/news/they -try-build-their-money-our-weakness-tenants-fight-rent-increases. M. Kawas, "Canada's Scotiabank Is Funding Israeli War Crimes,"*Mondoweiss*, June 10, 2023, https:// mondoweiss.net/2023/06/canadas-scotiabank-is-funding-israeli-war-crimes/. K. Chaudhary, "Canadian Pension Funds Invested $1.6 Billion in Companies Tied to Israeli Apartheid," *The Breach*, Jan. 16, 2024, https://breachmedia.ca/canadian -pension-funds-invested-israeli-apartheid/.

25. Neom, 2022, www.neom.com/en-us.

26. R. Michaelson, "COP27 Protestors Will Be Corralled in Desert Away from Climate Conference," *The Guardian*, Oct. 31, 2022, www.theguardian.com/environ ment/2022/oct/31/egypt-cop27-showcase-charms-sharm-el-sheikh-protest-mall.

27. A. A. Omar, "Saudi Arabia Making $1 Billion from Oil Exports Every Day," Bloomberg, May 26, 2022, www.bloomberg.com/news/articles/2022-05-26/saudi -arabia-s-oil-exports-hit-the-highest-level-since-2016; I. Kottasová, "Here's Where Saudi Arabia Has Invested Around the World," CNN, Oct. 17, 2018, www.cnn .com/2018/10/15/investing/saudi-arabia-global-investments.

28. N. Tandon Sharma, "Worth 5 Times More than Elon Musk and Bill Gates Combined, the Saudi Royal Family Leads a Life So Luxurious That Even Billionaires Cannot Imagine—Their Megayacht Has a $450M Painting, They Drive Gold Plated Supercars and Their Palaces Have Thousands of Rooms." *Luxury Launches*, Apr. 9, 2023, https://luxurylaunches.com/celebrities/lifestyle-and-networth-of-the-saudi -royal-family.php.

29. R. Umoh, "This Royal Family's Wealth Could Be More than $1 Trillion," CNBC, Aug. 18, 2018, www.cnbc.com/2018/08/18/this-royal-familys-wealth -could-be-more-than-1-trillion.html.

30. D. Kirkpatrick and K. Kelly, "Before Giving Billions to Jared Kushner, Saudi

Investment Fund Had Big Doubts," *New York Times*, Aug. 10, 2022, www.nytimes
.com/2022/04/10/us/jared-kushner-saudi-investment-fund.html.

31. P. Doherty, "A $2 Trillion Object Lesson in Sustainability from Saudi Ara-
bia," Marsh McLennan Brink News, Mar. 17, 2017, www.brinknews.com/a-2
-trillion-object-lesson-in-sustainability-from-saudi-arabia.

32. P. Beaumont, "End of the Line? Saudi Arabia 'Forced to Scale Back' Plans for
Desert Megacity," *The Guardian*, Apr. 10, 2024, https://www.theguardian.com
/world/2024/apr/10/the-line-saudi-arabia-scaling-back-plans-105-mile-long-des
ert-megacity-crown-prince.

33. J. Spencer Jones, "Toyota's Woven City—A Future Smart City Prototype,"
Smart Energy International, June 11, 2021, www.smart-energy.com/industry-sectors
/smart-cities/toyotas-woven-city-a-future-smart-city-prototype; Junto Group LLC,
"Telosa," 2022, cityoftelosa.com; E. Maulia, "Nusantara, Indonesia's Future Capital on
Borneo Gets Underway," Nikkei Asia, Feb. 13, 2022, asia.nikkei.com/Politics/Nusan
tara-Indonesia-s-future-capital-on-Borneo-gets-underway; EkoAtlantic, 2022, www
.ekoatlantic.com/about-us; L. Crook, "BIG Reveals Masterplan for 'Urban Lilypads'
off Coast of Penang Island," Dezeen, Aug. 21, 2020, www.dezeen.com/2020/08/21
/biodivercity-big-masterplan-penang-island-architecture; M. Descalsota, "Malaysia's
$100 Billion Luxury Estate Was Supposed to Be a 'Living Paradise.' Instead, 6 Years
into Development, It's a Ghost Town Full of Empty Skyscrapers and Deserted Roads,"
Insider, June 8, 2022, www.insider.com/ghost-town-malaysia-forest-city-china-devel
oper-estate-photos-2022-6; A. Mendívil, "Bicentenary City: Peru Decides to Invest in
Sustainable Urban Planning," GreenCitizen, 2021, greencitizen.com/news/bicentena
ry-city-peru-decides-to-invest-in-sustainable-urban-planning; Masdar City, 2022,
masdarcity.ae; "Sidewalk Toronto," Google Sidewalk Labs, 2022, www.sidewalklabs
.com/toronto; Fosters + Partners, "Amaravati Master Plan," 2022, www.fosterandpart
ners.com/projects/amaravati-masterplan. "New futuristic $400bn US city to give
tough competition to Saudi Arabia's Neom," *The News International*, May 13, 2024,
https://www.thenews.com.pk/latest/1188503-new-futuristic-400bn-us-city-to-give
-tough-competition-to-saudi-arabias-neom.

34. EkoAtlantic, 2022, www.ekoatlantic.com/about-us.

35. J. Brustein, "The Diapers.com Guy Wants to Build a Utopian Megalopolis,"
Bloomberg, Sep. 1, 2021.

36. J. K. Galbraith, *Money: Whence It Came, Where It Went* (Princeton, NJ: Princeton University Press, 1975), 29; D. Graeber, "The Truth Is Out: Money Is Just an IOU,

and the Banks Are Rolling in It," *The Guardian*, Mar. 18, 2014, www.theguardian.com /commentisfree/2014/mar/18/truth-money-iou-bank-of-england-austerity.

37. T. Wilkes, "Emerging Markets Drive Global Debt to Record $303 Trillion— IIF," Reuters, Feb. 23, 2022, www.reuters.com/markets/europe/emerging-markets -drive-global-debt-record-303-trillion-iif-2022-02-23.

38. A. Jackson and B. Dyson, *Modernising Money: Why Our Monetary System Is Broken and How It Can Be Fixed* (London: Positive Money, 2012).

39. J. E. Stiglitz, "Inequality, Living Standards and Economic Growth," in *Rethinking Capitalism: Economics and Policy for Sustainable and Inclusive Growth*, ed. M. Jacobs and M. Mazzacato (West Sussex: Wiley Blackwell, 2016), 134–155; L. Chancel, T. Piketty, E. Saez, and G. Zucman, "World Inequality Report 2022," wir2022.wid.world/www-site/uploads/2022/01/Summary_WorldInequalityRe port2022_English.pdf.

40. A. Benanav, *Automation and the Future of Work* (London: Verso, 2020); R. J. Gordon, *Rise and Fall of American Growth: The U.S. Standard of Living Since the Civil War* (Princeton, NJ: Princeton University Press, 2016).

41. A. Altstedter and K. Orland, "The Housing Boom That Never Ends Already Wiped Out All the Short-Sellers," Bloomberg, Mar. 15, 2021, www.bloomberg .com/news/articles/2021-03-15/the-housing-sales-boom-that-never-ends-already -wiped-out-all-the-short-sellers; M. Lundy, "Canada Bet Big on Real Estate. Now, It's an Economic Drag," *Globe and Mail*, Sept. 6, 2021, www.theglobeandmail.com /business/article-canada-bet-big-on-real-estate-now-its-an-economic-drag; J. Kirby, "Eight Charts That Provide Insight into the Housing Market for the Year Ahead," *Globe and Mail*, Jan. 1, 2022, www.theglobeandmail.com/business/article-charts -household-finances.

42. S. Stein, *Capital City: Gentrification and the Real Estate State* (London: Verso, 2019).

43. M. Fairbairn, *Fields of Gold: Financing the Global Land Rush* (Ithaca, NY: Cornell University Press, 2020).

44. N. Estes, "Bill Gates Is the Biggest Private Owner of Farmland in the United States. Why?," *The Guardian*, Apr. 5, 2021, www.theguardian.com/commentis free/2021/apr/05/bill-gates-climate-crisis-farmland.

45. M. Ajl, *A People's Green New Deal* (London: Pluto Press, 2021), 119.

46. L. Adkins, M. Cooper, and M. Konings, "Class in the 21st Century: Asset Inflation and the New Logic of Inequality," *Environment and Planning A: Economy and Space* 53, no. 3 (2021): 548–572.

47. S. Stephens-Davidowitz, "The Rich Are Not Who We Think They Are. And Happiness Is Not What We Think It Is Either," *New York Times*, May 14, 2022, www .nytimes.com/2022/05/14/opinion/sunday/rich-happiness-big-data.html.

48. المال رُجَي المال و القَمل رُجَي السّيبان.

49. H. Angelo, *How Green Became Good: Urbanized Nature and the Making of Cities and Citizens* (Chicago: University of Chicago Press, 2021).

50. "About Matrimandir," 2022. www.auroville.com/about-matrimandir.

51. S. Lotfallah, "Auroville, the Fulfilment of a Dream," *UNESCO Courier* 1 (1993): 46–49, sri-aurobindo.co.in/workings/other/soliman_lotfallah-auroville _the_fulfilment_of_a_dream.htm.

52. Namakkal, *Unsettling Utopia*, 193.

53. Namakkal, *Unsettling Utopia*, 192.

54. Namakkal, *Unsettling Utopia*, 193.

55. Namakkal, *Unsettling Utopia*, 193.

56. Namakkal, *Unsettling Utopia*, 194.

57. Namakkal, *Unsettling Utopia*, 194.

58. Namakkal, *Unsettling Utopia*, 195.

59. Inspired by Brazilian Amazonian activist Chico Mendes, who stated, "Ecology without class struggle is just gardening"—warning against an environmentalism that treated nature as entirely separate from human activity and human social relations.

60. Kothari, "Bulldozing a Dream?"

61. "Auroville Residents Protest Uprooting of Trees for Contentious Crown Project," *The Hindu*, Dec. 4, 2021, www.thehindu.com/news/national/tamil-nadu /auroville-residents-protest-uprooting-of-trees-for-contentious-crown-project/arti cle37835625.ece.

62. S. Namasivayam, "Auroville Doesn't Give Foreigners Right to Undermine India's Laws. Govt Must Step In," *The Print*, Feb. 22, 2022, theprint.in/opinion/auro ville-doesnt-give-foreigners-right-to-undermine-indias-laws-govt-must-step -in/840895.

63. Kothari, "Bulldozing a Dream?"

64. M. Sharma, *Green and Saffron: Hindu Nationalism and Indian Environmental Politics* (New Delhi: Permanent Black, 2012).

65. Ghosh, *The Nutmeg's Curse*, 225.

66. *Gazette Aurovilienne*, Aug. 19, 1966.

67. "Vietnam Land Clash: Arrests After Police Evict Hundreds," BBC, Apr. 25, 2012, www.bbc.com/news/world-asia-17844198.

68. "Vietnamese Farmers Demand Tough Action Against Land-Grabbing 'Thugs,' " Radio Free Asia, Mar. 7, 2014, www.rfa.org/english/news/vietnam/van -giang-03072014153929.html.

69. "EcoPark Satellite City Project, Hanoi, Vietnam," Environmental Justice Atlas, June 19, 2015, ejatlas.org/conflict/ecopark-satellite-city-project-hanoi-vietnam.

70. N. Osman and M. A. Sneineh, "Saudi Activist's Killing Exposes Local Tensions over Neom Construction," Middle East Eye, Apr. 16, 2020, www.middleeast eye.net/news/tribal-activist-reportedly-killed-protesting-saudi-neom-megacity -project.

71. M. Rasool, "Saudi Arabia Sentences 3 Men to Death for Refusing to Vacate NEOM Development Site," Vice, Oct. 11, 2022, www.vice.com/en/article/5d3kkd /neom-saudi-arabia-howeitat-tribe.

72. Rasool, "Saudi Arabia Sentences 3 Men to Death"; "Timeline of the Murder of Journalist Jamal Khashoggi," Al-Jazeera, Feb. 26, 2021, www.aljazeera.com /news/2021/2/26/timeline-of-the-murder-of-journalist-jamal-khashoggi.

73. R. F. Worth, "The Dark Reality Behind Saudi Arabia's Utopian Dreams," *New York Times*, Jan. 28, 2021, www.nytimes.com/2021/01/28/magazine/saudi-arabia -neom-the-line.html.

74. R. Stock, "Power to the Plantationocene: Solar Parks as the Colonial Form of an Energy Plantation," *Journal of Peasant Studies* 50, no. 1 (2022), doi: 10.1080/03066150.2022.2120812.

75. Stock, "Power to the Plantationocene," 5.

76. Environmental Justice Atlas, 2022, ejatlas.org.

77. C. Zografos and P. Robbins, "Green Sacrifice Zones, or Why a Green New Deal Cannot Ignore the Cost Shifts of Just Transitions," *One Earth* 3, no. 5 (2020): 543–546.

78. E. Zhao, "Unilever and Nestlé Are Burning Indonesia. Is 'Sustainable Palm Oil' a Con?," Medium, Nov. 10, 2019, medium.com/the-climate-reporter/unilever -and-nestl%C3%A9-are-burning-indonesia-is-sustainable-palm-oil-a-con-4a15e 3110d1a.

79. A. Dunlap and M. Correa-Arce, " 'Murderous energy' in Oaxaca, Mexico: Wind Factories, Territorial Struggle and Social Warfare," *The Journal of Peasant Studies* 49, no 2. (2022): 455480.

80. Dunlap and Correa-Arce, " 'Murderous energy' in Oaxaca, Mexico: Wind Factories, Territorial Struggle and Social Warfare," 2022.

81. "Nonprofit Compensation Packages of $1 Million or More," Charity Watch, 2022, www.charitywatch.org/nonprofit-compensation-packages-of-1-million-or -more.

82. L. Kern, 2022. "It's Not All Coffee Shops and Hipsters: What We Get Wrong About Gentrification," *The Guardian*, Sept. 4, 2022, www.theguardian.com/com mentisfree/2022/sep/04/coffee-shops-hipsters-gentrification-communities.

83. W. Staley, "When Gentrification Isn't About Housing," *New York Times Magazine*, Jan. 23, 2018, www.nytimes.com/2018/01/23/magazine/when-gentrifi cation-isnt-about-housing.html.

84. B. Ehrenreich, *Nickel and Dimed: On (Not) Getting By in America* (New York: Metropolitan Books, 2010).

85. G. Winant, "On Barbara Ehrenreich: Look at Yourself, She Always Asks the Reader; What Do You See There?," *n+1*, Sept. 9, 2022, www.nplusonemag.com /online-only/online-only/on-barbara-ehrenreich.

86. Winant, "On Barbara Ehrenreich,"

87. E. Newburger, "Mississippi Governor Declares Emergency After Jackson's Main Water Plant Fails," CNBC, Aug. 30, 2022, www.cnbc.com/2022/08/30/mis sissippi-governor-declares-emergency-amid-jackson-water-crisis.html.

88. A. Umoja, "The People Must Decide: Chokwe Lumumba, New Black Power, and the Potential for Participatory Democracy in Mississippi," *Black Scholar* 48, no. 2 (2018): 7–19.

89. Cooperation Jackson, 2022, cooperationjackson.org/intro.

90. P. Dolack, "Reversing Past Oppression, Cooperation Jackson Builds a Better Future," Cooperation Jackson, Apr. 18, 2018, cooperationjackson.org/blog/2018/7/13 /reversing-past-oppression-cooperation-jackson-builds-a-better-future.

91. E. Forman, E. Gran, and S. van Outryve, "The Municipalist Moment," *Dissent*, Winter 2020, www.dissentmagazine.org/article/the-municipalist-moment.

92. Dolack, "Reversing Past Oppression."

93. Ghosh, *The Nutmeg's Curse: Parables for a Planet in Crisis* (Chicago: University of Chicago Press, 2021).

94. K. Akuno, "Justice4Jackon. Help Us Fix Jackson's Water System and Build More Autonomy and People Power in the City," Cooperation Jackson, Sept. 5, 2022, cooperationjackson.org/announcementsblog/justice4jackson.

95. Atlanta Black Star, "Build and Fight: The Program and Strategy of Cooperation Jackson," Cooperation Jackson, May 21, 2017, cooperationjackson.org

/blog/2017/8/19/build-and-fight-the-program-and-strategy-of-cooperation
-jackson.

96. J. L. Namakkal, *Unsetting Utopia*, 2021

97. D. Spade, "Solidarity Not Charity: Mutual Aid for Mobilization and Survival," *Social Text* 38, no. 1 (2020): 131–151.

98. "Solidarity and Tenderness for the Zapatista Communities," Chiapas Support Committee, Dec. 21, 2013, chiapas-support.org/2013/12/21/solidarity-tenderness-for-the-zapatista-communities.

99. For a critique of electoral politics and what a more democratic alternative can look like, see D. Van Reybrouck, *Against Elections: The Case for Democracy* (New York: Seven Stories Press, 2018).

100. A. Weaver, " 'Electoral Pursuits Have Veered Us Away': Kali Akuno on Movement Lessons from Jackson," Black Rose Anarchist Federation, Apr. 18, 2018, blackrosefed.org/electoral-pursuits-have-veered-us-away-kali-akuno-on-movement-lessons-from-jackson.

101. M. M. Francis, "The Price of Civil Rights: Black Lives, White Funding, and Movement Capture," *Law and Society Review* 53, no. 1 (2019): 275–309.

102. E. Tuck and K. W. Yang, "R-Words: Refusing Research," in *Humanizing Research: Decolonizing Qualitative Inquiry with Youth and Communities*, ed. D. Paris and M. T. Winn (Thousand Oaks, CA: Sage, 2014), 248.

103. A. Choudry and E. Shragge, "Disciplining Dissent: NGOs and Community Organizations," in *Situating Global Resistance*, ed. L. M.Coleman and K. Tucker (London: Routledge, 2013), 117–132.

104. On stickiness, see S. Ahmed, "Affective Economies," *Social Text* 22, no. 2 (2004): 117–139. Building on the words of science fiction writer Ursula K. Le Guin, who, at the National Book Awards on Nov. 19, 2014, spoke in defense of the art of writing books over the business of publishing books. She said: "The name of our beautiful reward is not profit, its name is freedom."

8: Taking Back the Future

1. A. Ferrer, T. Graziani, J. Woocher, and Z. Frederick, "The Vacancy Report: How Los Angeles Leaves Homes Empty and People Unhoused," Strategic Actions for a Just Economy, 2022, www.acceinstitute.org/thevacancyreport.

2. C. J. A. Bradshaw et al., "Underestimating the Challenges of Avoiding a Ghastly Future," *Frontiers in Conservation Science* 1 (2020), doi: 10.3389/fcosc.2020.615419; S. L. Boehm et al., "State of Climate Action 2022," World

Resources Institute, 2022, doi.org/10.46830/wrirpt.22.00028; W. Steffen, W. Broadgate, L. Deutsch, O. Gaffney, and C. Ludwig, "The Trajectory of the Anthropocene: The Great Acceleration," *Anthropocene Review* 2, no. 1 (2015): 81–98; D. Carrington, "World Close to 'Irreversible' Climate Breakdown, Warn Major Studies," *The Guardian*, Oct. 27, 2022, www.theguardian.com/environment/2022/oct/27/world-close-to-irreversible-climate-breakdown-warn-major-studies; C. Einhorn, "Researchers Report a Staggering Decline in Wildlife. Here's How to Understand It," *New York Times*, Oct. 12, 2022, www.nytimes.com/2022/10/12/climate/living-planet-index-wildlife-declines.html.

3. G. Thunberg, "Greta Thunberg on the Climate Delusion: 'We've Been Greenwashed out of Our Senses. It's Time to Stand Our Ground," *The Guardian*, Oct. 8, 2022, www.theguardian.com/environment/2022/oct/08/greta-thunberg-climate-delusion-greenwashed-out-of-our-senses.

4. G. Tverberg, "Is Global Oil Production Growing Fast Enough?," OilPrice.com, Apr. 25, 2022, oilprice.com/Energy/Crude-Oil/Is-Global-Oil-Production-Growing-Fast-Enough.html; M. Taft, " 'High-Tech' Reforestation Company Starts Wildfire in Spain," Gizmodo, July 21, 2022, gizmodo.com/high-tech-reforestation-company-starts-wildfire-in-spai-1849314518.

5. A. Matei, "Climate anxious? Here's how you can turn apprehension into action," Nov. 16, 2023. *The Guardian*. https://www.theguardian.com/wellness/2023/nov/16/climate-anxiety-tips.

6. S.E.O. Schwartz, L. Benoit, S. Clayton, M.F. Parnes, L. Swenson, and S.R. Lowe, "Climate change anxiety and mental health: Environmental activism as buffer," *Current Psychology* 42 (2022): p. 16708–16721.

7. See also K. Bell. *Working-Class Environmentalism.*

8. J. Woocher, "Union de Vecinos: 25 Years of Impact on LA's Tenants Movement," KnockLA, Aug. 23, 2021, knock-la.com/union-de-vecinos-25-years-los-angeles-tenants-movement.

9. M. Davis, "Gentrifying Disaster," *Mother Jones*, Oct. 25, 2005, www.motherjones.com/politics/2005/10/gentrifying-disaster.

10. Woocher, "Union de Vecinos."

11. A. Rigolon, T. Collins, J. Kim, M. Stuhlmacher, and J. Christensen. "Does gentrification precede and follow greening? Evidence about the green gentrification cycle in Los Angeles and Chicago," *Landscape and Urban Planning* 248 (2024): 105095.

12. Los Angeles Cleantech Incubator, "Los Angeles Cleantech Incubator Offi-

cially Launches," press release, Oct. 10, 2011, www.prnewswire.com/news-releases /los-angeles-cleantech-incubator-officially-launches-131441048.html.

13. Boyle Heights Alliance Against Artwashing and Displacement, "The Short History of a Long Struggle," 2012, southwarknotes.files.wordpress.com/2012/03 /bhaaad-pamphlet.pdf.

14. C. A. Miranda, "Must Reads: The Art Gallery Exodus from Boyle Heights and Why More Anti-Gentrification Battles Loom on the Horizon," *Los Angeles Times*, Aug. 8, 2018, www.latimes.com/entertainment/arts/miranda/la-et-cam-gen trification-protests-future-of-boyle-heights-20180808-story.html.

15. M. Stromberg, "Boyle Heights Activists Question LAPD's Hate Crime Charge," *Hyperallergic*, Dec. 2, 2016. hyperallergic.com/342364/boyle-heights-ac tivists-question-lapds-hate-crime-charge; A. Nazaryan, "The 'Artwashing' of America: The Battle for the Soul of Los Angeles Against Gentrification," *Newsweek*, May 21, 2017, www.newsweek.com/2017/06/02/los-angeles-gentrification-california-de velopers-art-galleries-la-art-scene-608558.html.

16. Boyle Heights Alliance Against Artwashing and Displacement, "Contra-Against the Artwashing of Boyle Heights," Anti-Eviction Mapping Project, artwash ing.antievictionmap.com.

17. C. Smith, "Justice Fund Stories: Democracy in Action with Union de Vecinos," Center for Environmental Health, Nov. 28, 2012, ceh.org/justice-fund-stories-democ racy-in-action-with-union-de-vecinos; Union de Vecinos/Sindicato de Inquilinos, "Environmental Justice," 2022, www.uniondevecinos.org/index.php/what-we-do-3 /environmental-justice; K. Alcocer, E. Blaney, and L. Vilchis, " 'Where the Most in Need Direct the Work': Lessons from Union de Vecinos' First 25 Years," University of the Poor, 2021, universityofthepoor.org/union-de-vecinos-first-25-years.

18. Los Angeles Tenants Union, 2022, latenantsunion.org/en.

19. G. Graeber, *The Utopia of Rules: On Technology, Stupidity, and the Secret Joys of Bureaucracy* (Brooklyn, NY: Melville House, 2015), 79.

20. M. Bookchin, "The Meaning of Confederalism," *Green Perspectives* 20 (1990).

21. "Ursula K. LeGuin on the Art of Words vs. the Business of Books," The Tyee, Feb. 14, 2018, thetyee.ca/Video/2018/02/14/Ursula-Le-Guin-Art-Words-Busi ness-Books.

22. E. Gibney, "The Middle East Is Going Green—While Supplying Oil to Others," *Nature* 611 (2022): 216–217.

23. "Explore the Label," Made the Canadian Way, 2022, madethecanadianway .ca/explore-the-label.

24. "Energy Use per Person, 2021," Our World in Data, 2021, ourworldindata.org/grapher/per-capita-energy-use.

25. T. Corcoran, "Terence Corcoran: More Fossil Fuels—Plus Net Zero?," *Financial Post*, Mar. 25, 2022, financialpost.com/opinion/terence-corcoran-more-fossil-fuels-plus-net-zero.

26. See, for example, the episode "Protest Tacos" of the Netflix show *Gentefied*.

27. P. Wintour, "Jared Kushner says Gaza's 'waterfront property could be very valuable,' " Mar. 19, 2024. *The Guardian*. https://www.theguardian.com/us-news/2024/mar/19/jared-kushner-gaza-waterfront-property-israel-negev; D. Roche, "Israel Prime Minister Benjamin Netanyahu unveils regional plan to build a 'massive free trade zone' with rail service to NEOM," May 21, 2024, *The Architect's Newspaper*, https://www.archpaper.com/2024/05/benjamin-netanyahu-unveils-regional-plan-free-trade-zone-rail-service-neom/.

28. F. Demaria and A. Kothari, "The Post-Development Dictionary Agenda: Paths to the Pluriverse," *Third World Quarterly* 38, no. 12 (2017): 2588–2599.

29. R. Patel and J. W. Moore, "How the Chicken Nugget Became the True Symbol of Our Era," *The Guardian*, May 8, 2018, www.theguardian.com/news/2018/may/08/how-the-chicken-nugget-became-the-true-symbol-of-our-era.

30. P. Greenfield, "Brazil, Indonesia and DRC in Talks to Form 'OPEC of Rainforests,' " *The Guardian*, Nov. 5, 2022, www.theguardian.com/environment/2022/nov/05/brazil-indonesia-drc-cop27-conservation-opec-rainforests-aoe; L. Sommer, "Do Wealthy Countries Owe Poorer Ones for Climate Change? One Country Wrote Up a Bill," NPR, Nov. 7 2022, https://www.npr.org/2022/11/07/1133270753/climate-change-loss-damage-cop27.

31. H. Healy, J. Martinez-Alier, L. Temper, M. Walter, and J. F. Gerber, *Ecological Economics from the Ground Up* (London: Routledge, 2013).

32. N. Kolachalam, "Caste, the Patriarchy, and Climate Change," *Slate*, Feb. 15, 2019, slate.com/news-and-politics/2019/02/india-dalit-tamil-nadu-caste-climate-change-farming.html.

33. E. Finley and A. Vansintjan, "The Lay of the Land: Radical Municipalism in the US and Canada," Minim, Nov. 16, 2021, minim-municipalism.org/reports/the-lay-of-the-land-radical-municipalism-in-the-us-and-canada.

34. "Timeline of Wet'suwet'en Solidarity Protests and the Dispute That Sparked Them," Global News Canada, Feb. 17, 2020, globalnews.ca/news/6560125/timeline-wetsuweten-pipeline-protests.

35. D. Goldtooth, A. Saldamando, K. Gracey, T. Goldtooth, C. Rees, and J. Fal-

con, "Indigenous Resistance Against Carbon," Indigenous Environmental Network and Oil Change International, 2021, www.ienearth.org/wp-content/uploads/2021/09/Indigenous-Resistance-Against-Carbon-2021.pdf.

36. Zia and Jenny, "From the Yintah to Palestine: A Talk by Wet'suwet'en Resistance Leaders at the UBC Encampment," *Spring Magazine*, May 17, 2024, https://springmag.ca/from-the-yintah-to-palestine-a-talk-by-wetsuweten-resistance-leaders-at-the-ubc-encampment.

37. Environmental Justice Atlas, 2022, ejatlas.org.

38. M. Gouldhawke, "Building Blocks," *Midnight Sun*, June 6, 2021, www.midnightsunmag.ca/building-blocks.

39. S. Ahmed, "Affective Economies," *Social Text* 22, no. 2 (2004): 117–139.

40. C. Chuang, "Resistance Is Rhizomatic: Towards an Anti-Colonial Praxis Against Gentrification in Chinatown Vancouver," *The Funambulist* 31 (2020), the funambulist.net/magazine/politics-of-food/resistance-is-rhizomatic-towards-an-anti-colonial-praxis-against-gentrification-in-chinatown-vancouver-by-celine-chuang.

41. A. Varvarousis, *Liminal Commons: Modern Rituals of Transition in Greece* (London: Bloomsbury Publishing, 2022).

42. B. Ehrenreich, *Nickel and Dimed: On (Not) Getting By in America* (New York: Metropolitan Books, 2010).

43. O. Milnan and N. Lakhani, "Atlanta Shooting Part of Alarming US Crackdown on Environmental Defenders," *The Guardian*, Feb. 2, 2023, https://www.theguardian.com/environment/2023/feb/02/atlanta-shooting-manuel-teran-crackdown-environmental-defenders.

44. A. Bennett and T. Kosloski, "Israel and the Militarization of Atlanta's Police," *The Signal*, Sept. 28, 2021, georgiastatesignal.com/israel-and-the-militarization-of-atlantas-police; T. Pratt, " 'Our Struggles Are Connected': Atlanta Protestors Link Cop City to Gaza War," *The Guardian*, May 13, 2024, https://www.theguardian.com/us-news/article/2024/may/13/cop-city-emory-atlanta-israel.

45. "The City in the Forest : Reinventing Resistance for an Age of Climate Crisis and Police Militarization," CrimethInc., Apr. 11, 2022, crimethinc.com/2022/04/11/the-city-in-the-forest-reinventing-resistance-for-an-age-of-ecological-collapse-and-police-militarization.

46. A. A. Akbar, "The Fight Against Cop City," *Dissent*, Spring 2023, www.dissentmagazine.org/article/the-fight-against-cop-city; "The Forest in the City: Two Years of Forest Defense in Atlanta, Georgia," CrimethInc., Feb. 22, 2023, crime-

thinc.com/2023/02/22/the-forest-in-the-city-two-years-of-forest-defense-in-at lanta-georgia; Associated Press, "Activist Killed in 'Cop City' Protest Had Hands in the Air When Shot, Family Say," *The Guardian*, Mar. 14, 2023, www.theguard ian.com/environment/2023/mar/14/cop-city-georgia-activist-autopsy-results -manuel-paez-teran.

47. E. Fassler, "Activists Are Occupying the Woods of Atlanta to Block a New Police Facility," Vice, Feb. 17, 2022, www.vice.com/en/article/4aw7xn/activists-are -occupying-the-woods-of-atlanta-to-block-a-new-police-facility.

48. J. Fuster. "Atlanta Studio Sparks Protests for Plan to Clearcut 200-Acre Forest for More Soundstages," Yahoo, July 7, 2021, ca.sports.yahoo.com/news/atlanta-stu dio-sparks-protests-plan-130000587.html.

49. Personal communication, Atlanta Forest Defender, July 2022.

50. "The Forest in the City."

51. Akbar, "The Fight Against Cop City."

52. Akbar, "The Fight Against Cop City."

53. "The Forest in the City."

54. Stop Reeves Young, 2022, stopreevesyoung.com.

55. Ende Gelände, "Mass Action for Climate Justice Launched in Brunsbüttel. Thousands Set Out to Initiate Immediate Gas Phase-out," press release, Jul. 31, 2021, www.ende-gelaende.org/en/press-release/press-release-on-31-07-2021-at-9-a-m.

56. C. Carpenter, "Saudi Arabia's Future City NEOM Plans Hydrogen-Based Ecosystem," S&P Global Commodity Insights, Feb. 9, 2021, www.spglobal.com /commodityinsights/en/market-insights/latest-news/electric-power/020921-saudi -arabias-future-city-neom-plans-hydrogen-based-ecosystem.

57. "The Build and Fight Formula," Cooperation Jackson, June 24, 2020, coop erationjackson.org/announcementsblog/2020/6/24/the-build-and-fight-formula.

58. J. Ball, "Housing as a Basic Human Right: The Vienna Model of Social Hous ing," *New Statesman*, Sept. 3, 2019, www.newstatesman.com/spotlight/2019/09 /housing-basic-human-right-vienna-model-social-housing.

59. "Why 80% of Singaporeans Live in Government-Built Flats," *The Economist*, July 6, 2017, www.economist.com/asia/2017/07/06/why-80-of-singaporeans-live -in-government-built-flats.

60. "Community Land Trusts," Grounded Solutions Network, 2022, grounded solutions.org/strengthening-neighborhoods/community-land-trusts.

61. C. De Magalhaes and S. F. Trigo, "Contracting out Publicness: The Private Management of the Urban Public Realm and Its Implications," *Progress in Planning*

115 (2017): 1–28; A. Vansintjan, "Open Public Spaces and the Private Sector: A Toolkit for Overcoming Barriers and Best Practices," Healthbridge Canada, 2021.

62. W. S. Walker et al., "The Role of Forest Conversion, Degradation, and Disturbance in the Carbon Dynamics of Amazon Indigenous Territories and Protected Areas," *Proceedings of the National Academy of Sciences* 117, no. 6 (2020): 3015–3025; Indigenous Environmental Network, "Indigenous Resistance Against Carbon," Oil Change International, 2021; R. Schuster et al., "Vertebrate Biodiversity on Indigenous-Managed Lands in Australia, Brazil, and Canada Equals That in Protected Areas," *Environmental Science and Policy* 101 (2019): 1–6.

63. O. Hoedeman, S. Kishimoto, and M. Pigeon, "Remunicipalisation: Putting Water Back into Public Hands," Transnational Institute, Mar. 15, 2013, www.tni.org /en/publication/remunicipalisation; S. Kishimoto, L. Steinfort, and O. Petitjean, eds., *The Future Is Public: Towards Democratic Ownership of Public Services* (Amsterdam: Transnational Institute, 2020).

64. D. Roberts, "The Coronavirus Crisis Has Revealed What Americans Need Most: Universal Basic Services," Vox, June 3, 2020, www.vox.com/2020/6/3/212 75755/coronavirus-us-stimulus-economy-universal-basic-services; UCL Institute for Global Prosperity, "Social Prosperity for the Future: A Proposal for Universal Basic Services," 2017, www.ucl.ac.uk/bartlett/igp/sites/bartlett/files/universal_ba sic_services_-_the_institute_for_global_prosperity_.pdf.

65. P. J. Atkins, "Communal Feeding in War-Time: British Restaurants, 1940–1947," in *Food and War in Twentieth Century Europe*, ed. I. Zweiniger-Bargielowska et al. (London: Routledge, 2011).

66. K. Hurley, "In Quebec, Child Care Is Infrastructure," Bloomberg, Apr. 29, 2021, www.bloomberg.com/news/articles/2021-04-29/lessons-from-quebec-on -universal-child-care.

67. A. Vansintjan, "Public Abundance is the Secret to the Green New Deal," *Green European Journal*, May 27, 2020, www.greeneuropeanjournal.eu/public -abundance-is-the-secret-to-the-green-new-deal. Also see "We Need a Library Economy," YouTube, posted by Andrewism, Oct. 5, 2022, www.youtube.com/watch ?v=NOYa3YzVtyk.

68. UCL Institute for Global Prosperity, "Social Prosperity for the Future"; C. Felber, *Change Everything: Creating an Economy for the Common Good* (London: Zed Books, 2019); M. Kelly and T. Howard, *The Making of a Democratic Economy: How to Build Prosperity for the Many, Not the Few* (Oakland, CA: Berrett-Koehler, 2019).

69. D. A. Cohen, "Petro Gotham, People's Gotham," in *Nonstop Metropolis: A New York Atlas*, ed. R. Solnit and J. Jelly-Shapiro (Berkeley: University of California Press, 2016), 47–54.

70. C. Cattaneo and A. Vansintjan, "A Wealth of Possibilities: Alternatives to Growth," Green European Foundation, Brussels, 2016; J. B. Schor, *Plenitude: The New Economics of True Wealth* (Melbourne: Scribe, 2010); S. Cox, *The Green New Deal and Beyond: Ending the Climate Emergency While We Still Can* (San Francisco: City Lights Books, 2020); Felber, *Change Everything*; Kelly and Howard, *The Making of a Democratic Economy*; W. Bello, *Deglobalization: Ideas for a New World Economy* (Dhaka: Zed Books, 2005).

71. ROAR Collective, "A Dual Power Reading List," *ROAR*, Dec. 22, 2019, roar mag.org/magazine/a-dual-power-reading-list.

72. A. Nangwaya and K. Akuno, *Jackson Rising: The Struggle for Economic Democracy and Black Self-Determination in Jackson, Mississippi* (Wakefield, PQ: Daraja Press, 2017).

73. "The Main Principles of Democratic Confederalism," Komun Academy for Democratic Modernity, Nov. 22, 2018, komun-academy.com/2018/11/22/the -main-principles-of-democratic-confederalism.

74. D. Dirik, *The Kurdish Women's Movement: History, Theory, Practice* (London: Pluto Press, 2022); Internationalist Commune of Rojava, *Make Rojava Green Again* (n.p.: Dog Section Press, 2020).

75. "What Is Resource Movement?," Resource Movement, 2023, www.resource movement.org/about.

76. M. J. Haugen, "Dark Mirrors: Projection, Palestine, and Progress," Terrain, Nov, 8, 2023, https://www.terrain.news/p/dark-mirrors.

77. Shah, and K. Sandwell, "*Lessons from the Indian Farmers' Movement: Emerging solidarities in the Kisan Andolan*," Transnational Institute (TNI), May 2023.

78. Malm, interviewed in "*The Society of the Spectacle*," a film by R. Farhat and G. H. Olsson, 2023, https://story.se/film/the-society-of-the-spectacle/.

INDEX

Absurd Arboretum, 51
The Abyss (1989 film), 17
Adivasis (Indigenous people in India), 69
agriculture. *See* climate-smart agriculture; industrial agriculture; sustainable agriculture
agroecology, 98–99, 146, 154
agroforestry, 146
Ahmed, Sara, 241
Ajl, Max, 144
akkoub *(Gundelia tournefortii)*, 61
Akuno, Kali, 258
Alfassa, Mirra ("The Mother"), 172–74, 194–99, 210
Alibaba, 38
Alphabet (Google), 11, 38, 117
Altucher, James, 52–53, 144, 232, 259
Amaravati (India), 187
Amazon, 38, 117, 252
Amazon (rainforest), 50, 158, 218
Andaman and Nicobar Islands (Bay of Bengal), 147, 155
Anderson, Laurie, 48
Andreessen, Marc, 37
Anger, Roger, 172, 174, 196, 197
Angola, 162–63
Anooni, Fahad, 65
Antarctica's Larsen C ice shelf, 123
anthropogenic mass, 127–28
Apple, 11
Arctic Ice (Greenland start-up), 16
Arkin, Lois, 99–102, 228

artificial intelligence (AI) technology, 11, 38, 76, 79, 80, 185
asset economy, 191–92
Atlanta, Georgia
    Defend the Atlanta Forest movement (Stop Cop City), 245–49, 250–51, 252, 258
    greenwashing, 247
    police killing of forest defender, 246–47
Atlanta Police Department, 246–47
Atlanta Police Foundation, 249, 250
Atlantic Council's Scowcroft Center for Strategy and Security, 15–16
Atlantic Institute of Social Justice, 247, 250
Aurobindo, Sri, 172, 174, 198
Auroville (Tamil Nadu), 171–77, 178–79, 193–99, 205, 210
    colonial roots, 172, 194–97, 210
    exclusion of local Tamils, 173–74, 193–99
    founding as utopian project, 172–73, 194, 210
    the Matrimandir and rituals of purity, 178–79, 193
    "The Mother," 172–74, 194–99, 210
Auroville Foundation, 173–74
Autonomous Tenants Union Network, 227–28

back door investment strategy (Altucher and Sease), 52–53, 144, 259
Baka people of the Republic of Congo, 202

banana tissue culture (matooke), 145–46
Barca, Stefania, 270
Barefoot Resorts (India), 147–48
Basmair, Tariq, 133
Bayer, 151–52
Beavan, Colin, 103–4
Belgium, 86, 107, 158, 167
Belli, Giaconda, 211
Belt and Road Initiative (China), 160
Bernard, Robert, 38
Bezos, Jeff, 16
BHAAAD: Boyle Heights Alliance
    Against Artwashing and
    Displacement, 224–25
Bharatiya Janata Party (BJP), 174, 197–99,
    205
Bicentenary City (Peru), 187
BIG (architectural firm), 36
The Big Conservation Lie (Mbaria and
    Ogada), 64–65
BiodiverCity (Malaysia), 35–36, 187, 230
biomass, 91, 128, 131, 137, 230
biotech sector, 143–44
Bitcoin, 50, 52, 88
Black freedom movement in the United
    States, 207–8, 210, 258
Black Lives Matter, 242
Blackhall Studios, 246–47
BlackRock, 12, 29
blended finance, 146
Bliss, Sam, 148–50
blockchain, 50–51, 56, 137, 259
Bloomberg, Michael, 16
Blue Carbon (Dubai-based company), 162
blue hydrogen (fossil hydrogen), 143
blue infrastructure, 95
Blum, Steve, 7
BMW, 5
BNP Paribas Fortis, 46, 158
Boggs, Grace Lee, 270
Bolivia, 159, 165
Bookchin, Murray, 229
Bou Craa (Western Sahara mine), 73

Boyle Heights neighborhood (Los Angeles),
    221–29, 233, 239
BP (British Petroleum), 14, 164
BP Statistical Review of World Energy,
    231
branding, 178–84, 188–89, 204, 232, 250
    counterbranding, 235, 245, 250–51
    green lifestyle branding, 84
    and performative spectacle, 179, 182–83,
        188, 203, 232, 250, 253, 261
    self-branding, 220, 262, 264
Brandt, Kate, 38–39
Brazil, 112, 126, 158, 169
The Breakthrough Institute, 37, 125, 234
Breatharian Institute of America, 107
breatharianism, 107–8, 133, 163
British colonialism, 65, 74, 85–87,
    166–67
Brooklyn, New York, 25–26. *See also* New
    York City
Brooks, Wiley, 107, 133
brown, adrienne maree, 270
Brundtland Commission (1987 report), 11
Butler, Samuel, 7

Callison, William, 262
Calo, Adam, 151–53
Cameron, James, 3, 6, 16–17
Canada
    carbon tax policy, 115
    CCS technology, 139
    land ownership and effect on
        independent farmers, 152–53
    oil and gas industry, 231
    Park Extension in Montreal, 267–68
    Quebec childcare collectives, 256
    real estate investment and GDP,
        190–91
    Resource Movement's strategies,
        260–61
    Toronto's Sidewalk City, 187
    Wet'suwet'en clan's blockade of Coastal
        GasLink Pipeline, 240

cancer cell ecology, 79–82
carbon capture and storage (CCS), 16, 37,
  102, 139–44
carbon emissions, 109–21
  and CCS technology, 16, 37, 102,
    139–44
  climate change and current rates of CO_2
    increase, 19
  consumption-based accounting,
    109–15
  decoupling CO_2 from GDP growth,
    117–21, 132–33, 231, 234
  and GDP, 118–20
  global carbon budgets, 112–13, 116–17
  Global North/Global South, 112–13,
    124, 168
  investment-based accounting, 115–17
  net zero targets, 29, 47, 103–4, 127, 136,
    141, 231–32
  Paris Agreement, 119–20
  of polluter elite (the richest 1 percent),
    20–21, 111–12, 114–15, 116–17
  territory-based accounting, 109–15
  and uneven trade, 161
  See also carbon footprints; carbon
    markets
carbon footprints, 20–21, 109–17
  cities and, 20, 110–11
  consumption-based accounting,
    109–15
  income and, 20–21, 111–12
  investment-based accounting, 115–17
  territory-based accounting, 109–15
carbon markets, 53–56, 135–36
  carbon credits, 9, 53–56, 136–37, 162
  carbon offsets, 8–9, 54–56, 82–84, 117,
    135–37, 162, 230
  carbon verifiers, 54–55
  voluntary carbon market (VCM), 54
carbon offsets, 8–9, 54–56, 82–84, 117,
  135–37, 162, 230
carbon taxes, 114–15, 169
carbon tunnel vision, 127

Cargill, 158
charities, 204–5, 210–11
Cheat Neutral, 82
Chevron, 139, 164
Chiang, Ted, 44
childcare collectives, 256
China, 79, 112, 160, 161
chlorofluorocarbons (CFCs), 150
Chuang, Céline, 241
circular economy, 130–33
Circular Economy Company, 133
cities, 39, 108, 110–11
  carbon footprints/environmental
    impacts, 20, 110–11
  green urbanism, 39, 108, 110
  inequality, 26–27
  waste recycling, 132
  See also cities, planned
cities, planned, 21, 35–36, 171–78, 182–83,
  185–88
  Amaravati, 187
  Auroville, 171–77, 178–79, 193–99,
    205, 210
  Bicentenary City, 187
  BiodiverCity, 35–36, 187, 230
  Ecopark, 177–78, 182, 187, 199–200
  Eko Atlantic, 187, 188
  Forest City, 187
  Masdar City, 35, 187
  Neom, 13–15, 41, 117, 142–43, 185–87,
    200–201, 230, 231, 232
  Nusuranta, 187
  Sidewalk City, 187
  Songdo City, 182–83
  Telosa, 187
  Toyota's Woven City, 187
climate adaptation, 17, 45
climate anxiety, 220–21
climate protests, 164, 218–19, 235, 251
climate reparations, 165–68, 235
climate-smart agriculture, 37, 145, 150,
  151–53
cloud seeding, 37, 137

coal power, 14, 73, 79, 143, 149, 187, 240, 251–52
Coastal GasLink Pipeline (British Columbia, Canada), 240
Coca-Cola, 154, 249, 250
Cohen, Daniel Aldana, 256
colonialism
    Auroville's roots, 172, 194–97, 210
    and big game conservation for sport hunting, 64–66, 85–86, 135
    British Raj in India, 85
    and climate reparations, 165–68
    and conservationists, 65–67, 71, 85–88
    European powers in Africa, 64–65, 74, 85–88, 162
    green gaslighting, 85–88
    history of soil science, 73–74
    legacy of ecological debt, 161–63
    and racist history of ecology, 71
    and the tsetse fly and sleeping sickness in Africa, 86–88, 135
    and uneven trade, 160
Community Healing Gardens (Venice Beach), 3
community land trusts, 255
Congo, Democratic Republic of (DRC), 57, 106
Congo, Republic of, 55–56, 202
conservationists
    and European colonialism, 65–67, 71, 85–88
    hunting lobby and big game reserves in Africa, 64–67, 85–88, 135
conspicuous consumption, 27, 30
consumption-based accounting, 109–15
convivial technology, 144–46
conviviality, 175–78, 214–15, 229, 237, 239–40
    convivial technology, 144–46
    Cooperation Jackson, 214, 237, 239
    and interconnectedness (living with), 175–78, 229
    stickiness, 214, 241

turned into a product (branding), 179–83, 188–89
    Union de Vecinos, 229, 239, 244–45
    See also solidarity
Cooperation Jackson, 207–14, 229, 237, 253, 258
cooperative housing, 100, 254–55, 257, 259
co-optation, 250, 261–64, 270
    diagonalism, 262
    and social media, 262–63
    and the word "sustainability," 62, 262
Cop City (Atlanta, Georgia), 246–49, 250–51, 252, 258
copper mining, 148–49, 158, 201–2
cost-shifting successes, 157–58
counterbranding, 235, 245, 250–51
COVID-19 pandemic, 15, 77, 209, 221, 237, 263
creative class, 20, 26–27, 28, 242
crop rotation, 81, 146
cryptocurrency, 50–51, 79

Dakota Access Pipeline protests, 240
Dalit women of Tamil Nadu, 236
Darwin, Charles, 70, 72
DeBeers, 154
Debord, Guy, 183
decentralized autonomous organizations (DAOs), 51
decoupling CO2 from GDP growth, 117–21, 132–33, 231, 234
Deener, Andrew, 177, 180–82
deep-sea mining, 17
Defend the Atlanta Forest (Stop Cop City), 245–49, 250–51, 252, 258
dematerialization, 128–30, 132–33, 157
Democratic Confederation of Northeast Syria (Rojava), 258–59
diagonalism, 262
DiCaprio, Leonardo, 6
Dolack, Pete, 208–9
DoorDash, 117, 218

dual power, 257–61. *See also* power, building

Dunlap, Riley, 30, 48

easyJet, 55

eco-fascism, 71–72

Ecologi, 54

ecological debt, 161–63, 169

ecological economics, 106–7

ecological imagination, 99–102, 228–33, 265

ecological modernization, 37. *See also* green modernists

ecology, 61–102
  as always transforming, 76–77
  collaborative, 69–70
  defining, 62, 68–70, 74–79
  the ecological imagination, 99–102, 228–33, 265
  history of, 68–74
  key features (what it means to be ecological), 74–79
  large-scale industrial production and, 79–82
  and meaning of nature, 63–68, 77–78
  neutrality of, 78–79
  racist and eco-fascist applications, 70–72
  revealing relationships, 90–99, 102
  as site of conflict, 72–74, 80
  social nature of, 75–76

ecology of resistance, 245, 248–49

ecomodernists, 37, 102. *See also* green modernists

Ecopark (Vietnam), 177–78, 182, 187, 199–200, 218

eco-pessimism, 41–42

eco-tourism, 64–66, 83–84

Ecovillage. *See* L.A. EcoVillage

efficiency, 52–56, 129, 147–56
  and back door investing, 52–53
  and carbon markets, 53–56
  fallacy of thinking efficiency is inherently good, 148–53

Jevons paradox, 149

land sparing, 151–53

problem of efficiency gains, 148–52

and sufficiency, 155–56

See also PIE (purity, innovation, and efficiency)

Ehrenreich, Barbara, 205–6, 242

Eko Atlantic (Nigeria), 187, 188

El Paso, Texas shooting (2019), 71

electric vehicles (electric cars), 16, 25, 28–29, 35, 39, 48, 79, 155–56, 159, 163, 232, 256

electronic e-waste, 106, 164

elitism, environmental, 30, 48–49

Ellenbogen, Maryann, 33–34, 35

Ellenbogen, Richard, 33–34, 35

emissions. *See* carbon emissions

empowerment. *See* power, building

Ende Gelände, 251–52

Enlightenment Now: The Case for Reason, Science, Humanism, and Progress (Pinker), 41

environment, social, and governance (ESG) criteria, 46, 58, 140, 232

Environmental Justice Atlas, 201–2, 240

environmental NGOs, 64, 154, 202, 213

Erewhon (luxury supermarket), 7–8, 103–4, 138, 234

Escobar, Arturo, 175–76, 229

European Academies' Science Advisory Council, 17

European Commission, 202

European Union, 112–13, 168

eutrophication, 91–93, 94–95, 123, 230, 233

evolution, theory of, 70

exclusion, 22, 193–203
  Auroville and local Tamils, 173–74, 193–99
  Ecopark in Vietnam, 199–200
  green sacrifice zones, 202
  large-scale solar parks in India, 201
  Neom and Howeitat tribal people, 200–201

externalities (cost-shifting successes),
  157–58
Extinction Rebellion, 32
ExxonMobil, 11, 139, 164

Faherty (Venice Beach clothing store),
  4–5, 9
Fair Phone, 131
Farm Rio (fashion brand), 4, 8–9
fertilizers, synthetic, 73, 81, 98, 122, 123,
  154
finance. *See* speculative finance
Fink, Larry, 12–13
fishing, industrial, 81
fishpond sewage treatment systems, 93–96,
  230
Flashbacks (Leary), 5–6
Florida, Richard, 20, 26
food deserts, 233–34
food sovereignty, 236
food systems, 150, 151–54, 233–34
  debate over land sparing, 151–53
  forest gardens of South Asia, 96–97,
    196
  home gardens of Sri Lanka, 96–98
  land ownership and land reform, 152–53,
    168–69, 236
  satoyama landscapes of Japan, 96–97,
    98, 102
  and sustainable agriculture, 151–54
  tissue culture technology and food
    security, 145–46
  vườn ao chuồng (VAC) system, 97–98
food waste, 150
Foragers (2022 film), 61–62, 75
foraging, 61–63
Forest City (Malaysia), 187
forest defenders. *See* Defend the Atlanta
  Forest (Stop Cop City)
forest gardens, 96–97, 196
forever chemicals (PFAS), 132, 158
Fosters and Partners (architectural firm),
  35

France
  colonialism, 86, 97, 194
  nuclear power industry, 126
  Yellow Vest movement, 169
Friedman, Thomas, 111

game reserves, 64–67, 85–88, 135
gaslighting. *See* green gaslighting
Gates, Bill, 11, 16, 18, 38, 41, 42, 102, 166,
  191
Gates Foundation, 145
gene-editing technologies, 38, 143–45
General Motors (GM), 39, 154, 186
Georgia International Law Enforcement
  Exchange (GILEE), 246
Germany
  colonialism, 87
  Nazi regime, 70
  protests against coal mines in the
    Hambach Forest, 251–52
  study of green lifestyles and carbon
    footprints, 109–10
Ghosh, Amitav, 45, 198, 209, 269
Gilmore, Ruth Wilson, 269
Giridharadas, Anand, 25
Glaeser, Edward, 39
Glasgow Finance Alliance for Net-Zero,
  29
Global North/Global South
  carbon emissions, 112–13, 124, 168
  and climate reparations, 165–68
  material footprints, 130
  uneven trade and unfair labor
    arrangements, 159–61
global warming and the 1.5°C threshold,
  18–19, 116, 120–21, 156, 168, 235
Gold Standard (carbon verifier), 54–55
Goldsmith, Ben, 67–68
Google, 5, 38–39, 252
  Alphabet, 11, 38, 117
  carbon offsetting, 117, 136
Gould, Kenneth, 20, 26
Gouldhawke, Mike, 241

Gowanus waterfront and sea-level rise
(Brooklyn), 25–26
GQ, 107
Graeber, David, 63, 229
great acceleration, 128
Great Nicobar Island (Bay of Bengal), 66
Greece
ancient, 68–69
social movements in, 241–42
green administrators, 31, 44–49
academics and, 48–49
green finance, 46–47
and impact elitism, 48–49
"there is no alternative" logic, 46
green finance, 46–47, 140
green gaslighting, 41, 82–90, 164
and carbon offsets, 82–84
charge of eco-pessimism, 41–42
charge of Luddism, 41, 43–44, 85
by colonial empires, 85–88
decoupling and, 124–25
by oil and gas companies, 164
green hydrogen, 13–14, 15, 143, 231, 234
green modernists, 31, 37–44, 49, 57,
108–10, 125, 164, 174, 234, 263
The Breakthrough Institute, 37, 125,
234
cities and green urbanism, 39, 108,
110
Ecomodernist Manifesto, 102
economic growth, 40–42, 119–21
land sparing, 151–53
nuclear energy, 125–27
Pinker's "enlightened
environmentalism," 41–42, 44
Wilson's "Half Earth" concept, 42–43,
70–71, 154
green sacrifice zones, 202
green transition and world conflicts,
201–2
green urbanism. *See* cities
greenhouse gas emissions. *See* carbon
emissions

Greenland, 16
greenlash (green backlash), 57–59
GreenLeaf Café (Venice Beach, California),
3, 6
greensters (green hipsters), 10–11, 18,
19–21, 31–36, 205, 242–43. *See also*
lifestyle environmentalists
greenwashing, 7, 9, 55, 58–59, 154, 186–87,
188, 212, 231, 247, 249
groundwater, 48, 66, 105, 158, 172, 197,
202, 234, 236
Groundwork Coffee (Venice Beach), 3–4
guano, 72–73
Guardian, 67–68

Haber-Bosch process, 122
Haeckel, Ernst, 70, 71
Half Earth, 42–43, 70–71, 154
Hamas, 89, 238
Hardin, Garrett, 71
Harvey, David, 64
Haugen, Matthew, 262
Herodotus, 68, 69
Hickel, Jason, 121
Highland Park neighborhood (Los
Angeles), 226–27
Hindu nationalism, 71–72, 174, 197–98,
205
Hirsi, Isra, 220
Ho Chi Minh, 97
home gardens, 96–97
hooks, bell, 269
housing cooperatives. *See* cooperative
housing
Human Development Index, 163
Humboldt, Alexander von, 72
Hurricane Katrina (2005), 208
Hurricane Sandy (2012), 26
al-Huwaiti, Abdul Rahim, 200–201
hydrogen energy, 13, 33, 138, 143
blue hydrogen, 143
emissions from renewable hydrogen,
143

hydrogen energy (*cont.*)
  gray hydrogen, 143
  green hydrogen, 13–14, 15, 143, 231,
    234

ICCA Consortium, 67
Idle No More, 242
Illich, Ivan, 175
India
  Amaravati, 187
  Auroville in Tamil Nadu, 171–77,
    178–79, 193–99, 205, 210
  Barefoot Resorts, 147–48
  British colonialism, 85
  Hindu nationalism and the BJP, 174,
    197–99, 205
  Kisan Andolan (Indian farmers
    movement), 169, 263
  Kolkata's fishpond sewage treatment
    system, 93–96, 230
  luxury safari park, 65–66
  Puducherry, 173, 194
  solar power farms and economic
    exclusion, 201
  Tamil people, 173–74, 193–99
Indian Farmers' Movement (*Kisan
  Andolan*), 169, 263
Indonesia, 187, 202
industrial agriculture, 73–74, 81, 122, 124,
  150, 151, 154, 162, 169
information technology (IT) industry, 111
Ingels, Bjarke, 36
innovation, 49–52, 129, 135–46
  CCS technology, 16, 37, 102, 139–44
  and convivial technology, 144–46
  and hubris about human-made solutions,
    136–37
  and renewables, 11, 137–39, 143, 231,
    232
  See also carbon offsets; PIE (purity,
    innovation, and efficiency)
Instagram, 8, 64, 103, 262
Institute of International Finance, 189

intercropping, 146, 154
International Energy Agency, 137, 141
International Finance Corporation, 29
International Panel on Climate Change
  (IPCC), 120
International Property Awards, 177, 200
investment risk, being the, 251–53
investment-based accounting, 115–17.
    See also decoupling CO2 from GDP
    growth
Iroquois of Turtle Island (North America),
  69
Irwin, Elaine, 10
Iseman, Luke, 137
Israel, 79, 89–90, 246
  assault on Gaza, 89, 237–38
  ban on Palestinian akkoub foraging, 62
  carbon emissions, 90
  creation of, 62, 89
Israel Nature and Parks Authority, 62, 64
Israeli Defense Forces, 89, 155, 238, 246
Italy, 79
Iyoda, Masayoshi, 126–27

Al Jaber, Sultan Ahmed, 12–13
Jackson, Mississippi, 207–10
  Cooperation Jackson, 207–14, 229, 237,
    253, 258
  Jackson People's Assembly, 208, 211–12,
    253
  Justice for Jackson, 209–10
  the 2007 water crisis, 207, 209, 214
Jamie, Kathleen, 19
Japan
  agricultural industrialization and loss of
    forest gardens, 96
  satoyama landscapes, 96
  Toyota's Woven City, 187
Jarawa territory on the Andaman Islands,
  147
Jay-Z, 6
Jevons, William Stanley, 149
Jevons paradox, 149

Jones, Van, 40–41, 111
Joshi, Ketan, 139–41, 143
Joven, Mark, 47
JPMorgan Chase, 5

Kantai, Tallash, 131
Kapp, Karl William, 157–58
Kenney, Matthew, 6–7, 18
Kenya, 74, 145
Kerr, Breena, 107, 133
Khashoggi, Jamal, 201
Kikuyu people, 74
Kimmerer, Robin Wall, 90–93, 95, 230
Klein, Naomi, 41
KlimaDAO, 51
knowledge economy, 111
Kolbert, Elizabeth, 104
Kolkata, India, 93–96, 230
Kothari, Ashish, 197, 270
Kropotkin, Peter, 70
Krugman, Paul, 40
Kumar, V. M. Ravi, 85
Kushner, Jared, 186, 232
Kuznets, Simon, 108
Kuznets curve, 108–9, 157, 163

L.A. EcoVillage, 99–102, 228, 229, 258
lab meat replacements (lab-grown meat),
    41, 42–43, 46, 143–44
land ownership, unequal, 152–53, 155, 191
land reform, 152–53, 168–69, 236
land sparing (sustainable intensification),
    151–53
land trusts, 255
Landless Workers' Movement (Movimento
    dos Trabalhadores Rurais sem Terra),
    169
Le Guin, Ursula K., 63, 229, 232, 269
Leary, Timothy, 1, 2–3, 5–6
LEED certification, 33, 35, 39, 109, 182,
    218
LEED-brain, 33
Levins, Richard, 75–76

Lewis, Tammy, 20, 26
Lewontin, Richard, 75–76
lifestyle environmentalists, 23, 31–36, 49,
    209, 234, 264
    consumption-oriented beliefs (individual
        actions), 31–35
    greensters (green hipsters), 10–11, 18,
        19–21, 31–36, 205, 242–43
    LEED-brain, 33
    purity mindset, 32–36, 107–8
The Line, 13–15, 17, 187. See also Neom
    (Saudi Arabia)
lithium, 93, 158, 159, 201–2
livelihood environmentalism, 209, 210
Liwa al-Quds (East Jerusalem), 61–62
Lockheed Martin, 35
Los Angeles, 2, 21, 217, 221–29
    Arts District, 5, 224, 258
    Boyle Heights neighborhood, 221–29,
        233, 239
    Clean Tech Incubator (LACI), 5, 10, 224
    EcoVillage, 99–102, 228, 229, 258
    green infrastructure and gentrification,
        223–24
    Highland Park neighborhood, 226–27
    house-flipping in gentrifying
        neighborhoods, 179–80
    Maywood water crisis, 225, 237
    Oakwood neighborhood, 9–10, 35
    Tenant's Union (LATU), 225–28, 237,
        240, 252
    unhoused people, 9–10, 217
    the Union de Vecinos, 221–29, 233, 237,
        239–40, 244–45, 253–54, 258
    Venice Canals neighborhood, 177,
        180–82
    War on Drugs (1990s), 222
    See also Venice Beach, California
Los Angeles Clean Tech Incubator (LACI),
    5, 10, 224
Los Angeles Police Department, 225
Los Angeles Tenant's Union (LATU),
    225–28, 237, 240, 252

Luddism, 41, 43–44, 85
Lugard, Frederick, 86
Lumumba, Chokwe, 207–8
Lumumba, Chokwe Antar, 207, 208
luxury safari tourism, 64–67, 87
Lyft, 186

Maasai people, 65, 86
Make Sunsets, 137
making the material political, 164–69,
    233–39, 265
  climate protests and climate activists,
    164, 218–19, 235, 251
  climate reparations, 165–68, 235
  Cooperation Jackson, 237
  Dalit women's food sovereignty
    movement, 236
  land reform and shareholder movements,
    153, 168–69, 236
  student encampments against genocide
    in Gaza, 237–38, 242
  Union de Vecinos, 233
Malaysia, 35–36, 187, 230
Malm, Andreas, 263, 270
Malthusianism, 123–24
Mander, Damien, 43
mangroves, 175, 243
  mangrove-world (Escobar), 176, 215,
    229, 241–42, 243
Manhattan, New York, 104, 108, 110–11.
    See also New York City
Manna, Jumana, 61–62, 75
Mapuche people, 69
Marinetti, Filippo Tomasso, 37
Mars colonization, 36
Masdar City (UAE), 35, 187
material extraction, 129–30, 158, 234
material footprints, 118, 129–30, 131, 133,
    149
material relations. See making the material
    political
matooke (plantain bananas), 145–46
Maywood, California, 225, 237

Mbaria, John, 64–65
McAfee, Andrew, 40, 111, 128–29
McGill University, 188
McKinsey & Company, 28–29
McMansions, 183
Meta (Facebook), 38, 117
Microsoft, 11, 38
Middle East Green Initiative, 231
Mill, John Stuart, 85
Mississippi Disaster Relief Coalition, 208
Modi, Narendra, 174
Montreal, Canada, 132, 260, 267–68
Morrison, Denton, 30, 48
Moser, Sarah, 188
"A Mother's Work" (Kimmerer), 90–93
Mukherjee, Jenia, 95
Murdock, Esme, 270
Muscogee (Creek) people, 245
Musk, Elon, 11, 36, 102, 114, 116, 117–18,
    159, 186, 232

Namakkal, Jessica, 173, 176–77, 193, 194
Namasivayam, Satheesh, 197
Nangwaya, Ajamu, 258
The Nation, 183–84
National Geographic, 64
nature, 63–68, 77–78. See also ecology
Nauru, island of, 73
Nazi Germany, 70
Neom (Saudi Arabia), 13–15, 41, 117, 142–43,
    185–87, 200–201, 230, 231, 232
  The Line, 13–15, 17, 187
  Oxagon, 142–43
Nestlé, 154
Net Zero (zero waste or emissions), 29, 47,
    103–4, 127, 136, 141, 231–32
Netanyahu, Benjamin, 232
Network for Business Sustainability, 29
New Age spirituality, 2
New York City
  Brooklyn, 25–26
  Gowanus waterfront and sea-level rise,
    25–26

Manhattan, 104, 108, 110–11
research on carbon footprints/
    environmental impacts, 20, 110–11
New York Times, 8, 41
New York Times Magazine, 201, 204
New Yorker, 44, 104
Nickel and Dimed (Ehrenreich), 205–6,
    242
NielsenIQ, 28
Niger, 126
Nigeria, 164, 187, 188
No Impact Man (Beavan), 103–4
no-impact living, fantasy of, 103–5, 108,
    157, 163
non-fungible tokens (NFTs), 50–51, 54,
    230
Norhaus, Ted, 125
nuclear energy, 108, 125–27, 138
Nusuranta (Indonesia), 187

Oakwood neighborhood (Los Angeles),
    9–10, 35
Oakwood Recreation Center, 9–10
Oaxaca, Mexico, 202
Occupy Wall Street, 242
oceans
    deep-sea mining, 17
    and Half Earth, 42
    and mangrove dispersal, 243
    nitrogen runoff, 151
    ocean acidification, 18, 105, 122, 123,
        128
    plastic pollution, 131
    and salmon lifecycles, 76
    and sewage treatment plants, 94
Oculus VR, 5
Ogada, Mordecai, 64–65, 71, 269
oil and gas companies (big oil), 11–12, 14,
    55–56, 138, 231–32
    CCS technology, 139–41
    green gaslighting by, 164
    and the Russia-Ukraine war, 140–41
Oldfield, Philip, 14–15

"Our Common Future—Call for Action"
    (1987 Brundtland Commission
    report), 11
Outer Space Treaty (1967), 15
Owen, David, 33
Oxagon, 142–43. *See also* Neom (Saudi
    Arabia)
Oxygenate, 38

Palestine, 61–62, 79, 89–90, 237–38
    Gaza, 89, 232, 237–38
    Hamas, 89, 238
    history of foraging akkoub, 61–62
    Israel's displacement and ecological
        destruction, 62, 89–90
    the Nakba (1948), 62
    and student encampments against
        genocide, 237–38, 242
Pangeos (floating city "terayacht"), 51
Paris Agreement, 119–20
Park Extension neighborhood (Montreal,
    Canada), 267–68
parks, public, 247, 254–55
Patel, Raj, 98, 269
Pearce, Fred, 8–9
Pearl, Mike, 103
Pearl Jam, 55
Pegasus (3D-printed superyacht), 32–33,
    143
Penske, Jay, 10
Peru, 72, 187
PFAS ("forever chemicals"), 132, 158
phosphate mining, 73, 80
PIE (purity, innovation, and efficiency),
    49–56, 107, 129, 157–69, 230–31
    and cost-shifting successes, 157–58
    and ecological debt, 161–63, 169
    efficiency, 52–56, 129, 147–56
    innovation, 49–52, 129, 135–46
    no-impact living fantasy, 103–5, 108,
        157, 163
    and uneven trade, 159–61
    See also purity

Pinker, Steven, 41–42, 44, 102, 111, 125
pipeline protests, 240–41
planetary boundaries, 121–25, 127, 151,
    218, 235
Plant Food and Wine (Venice Beach), 3,
    6–7, 16–17
plastic production and recycling, 131–32
Pondicherry. See Puducherry, India
post-desarollo, 232
Pouyanné, Patrick, 11
power, building, 243–61
    being the investment risk, 245, 251–53
    counterbranding, 245, 250–51
    dual power and collective agency,
        257–61
    ecology of resistance, 245, 248–49
    reconnaissance, 245, 249
    strategies for saying "no," 245–53, 265
    strategies for saying "yes," 253–61
    taking key services out of the market,
        254–57
pragmatists. See green administrators
prana (Hindu philosophy), 107
Prashad, Vijay, 85
precision agriculture, 151
Puducherry, India, 173, 194
Pure Food and Wine (New York), 6
purity, 32–36, 103–33
    breatharianism, 107–8, 133, 163
    eco-fascist ideas of order and, 71–72
    fantasy of no-impact living, 103–5, 108,
        157, 163
    rituals of Auroville's Matrimandir,
        178–79, 193
    See also lifestyle environmentalists; PIE
        (purity, innovation, and efficiency)

Quebec, Canada, 256

racism and the history of ecology, 70–71
Rahman, Sohanur, 220
Rainforest Alliance, 31
Rasmussen, Malik V., 16

raw food veganism, 6–7
reconnaissance (as strategy in building
    power to say no), 249
recycling, 130–33. See also renewables
Reddit, 117
Regen Network, 51
regenerative agriculture, 1–2, 217, 228
regenerative finance (ReFi), 51
regenerative revolution, 2–3, 10, 21, 28
regolith (lunar soil), 15
renewables, 11, 137–39, 143, 231, 232
    as "fossil fuel plus," 139, 232
    solar energy, 13–14, 51, 137–39, 201,
        226–27
    wind energy, 13–14, 137–39, 202
    See also hydrogen energy
reparations. See climate reparations
Resource Movement, 260–61
Reuters, 47
Rewilder ("green" cryptocurrency), 50, 54
rhizomatic networks, 176, 241–42, 243
Richman, Jonathan, 2, 7
right-wing movements
    BJP and Hindu nationalism, 174,
        197–99, 205
    and the greenlash, 58–59
Riot Games, 5
The Rise of the Creative Class (Florida), 20
Robinson, Kim Stanley, 36
Rojava. See Democratic Confederation of
    Northeast Syria (Rojava)
Rosa, Hartmut, 150
Ross, Corey, 86
Royal Dutch Shell, 14
Ruder Finn (public relations firm), 201
Russia
    enriched uranium supplies, 126
    invasion of Ukraine, 59, 126, 140
RWE (German energy company), 14, 251

SARS-CoV-2. See COVID-19 pandemic
satoyama landscapes, 96–97, 98, 102
Al Saud, Khaled bin Alwaleed, 7, 18, 20

Al Saud, Mohammad bin Salman (MBS), 13–14, 41, 186–87, 201
Saudi Arabia, 5–7, 13–14, 17, 33, 41, 51, 117, 142–44, 185–87, 192, 200–201
greenwashing, 13–14, 186–87, 231
House of Saud, 7, 13–4, 186–87
net zero pledge, 231
See also Neom (Saudi Arabia)
Saudi Aramco, 186
Schandl, Heinz, 129–30
Sease, Douglas R., 52–53, 144, 232, 259
Seminole people, 69
Senegal, 73
service sector industry, 111
sewage treatment systems, 93–96, 230
Shack Dwellers International, 169
Shadowbox Studios. See Blackhall Studios
Sharjah Safari Park (Dubai), 65
Sharma, Mukul, 71–72
Sharm-el-Sheikh, Egypt, 167, 185–86
Shell, 55, 139, 164
Shellenberger, Michael, 125
Shuar people, 69
Sidewalk City (Toronto), 187
Signal, 262
Silicon Valley, 11, 107, 111
Singapore, 255
Slack, 117
slavery, 12, 41, 73–74, 79, 85, 159, 194
and reparations, 166–67
sleeping sickness in sub-Saharan Africa, 86–88, 135
Slobodian, Quinn, 262
smallholder farmer movements, 153, 168–69, 236
Snapchat, 5, 186
social acceleration, 150–51
The Social Costs of Private Enterprise (Kapp), 157
social media, 262–63
social metabolism, 106–7, 133, 164–65, 169, 218, 235, 256
soil science, 72–74, 80, 81

solar energy, 137–39, 201
and Neom, 13–14, 51
solar financing, 201
solar power farms and parks, 201, 226–27
solidarity, 22, 59, 169, 175, 206–13, 215, 239–43, 260, 265–66, 270
Cooperation Jackson, 207–14, 239, 253
defining, 210–13
Indigenous resistance to fossil fuel infrastructure, 240–41
as not a career, 212–13
as not political representation, 212
as not the same as voting, 211–12
as reciprocal, 210–11
Union de Vecinos, 239–40, 253–54
weaving a network and creating conditions for, 239–43
See also conviviality
Songdo City (South Korea), 182–83, 187
South Korea, 182–83, 187
South River Forest (Weelaunee Forest) (Atlanta, Georgia), 245–49, 250–51
Southern Poverty Law Center, 71
space colonization, 36
space race, 15–16
Spain, 79
Spash, Clive, 45–46
speculative finance, 184–93, 204, 232, 252
the asset economy, 191–92
the role of concentrated wealth and wealth inequality, 190–91
the role of money and the world's debt, 189–90
and the workings of the global financial system, 189–93, 257
See also cities, planned
Sri Lanka, 96–97
Staley, Willy, 204
Standing Rock protests, 240
Star Trek, 108, 127

Starbucks, 252
Stephenson, Neal, 137
Stockholm Environment Institute, 127
stratospheric aerosol injection, 137
student encampments against genocide in
    Gaza, 237–38, 242
sufficiency, 155–56. *See also* efficiency
Sunrise Movement, 164
Survival International, 154
sustainability
    co-optation of the word, 62, 262
    defining, 11–12, 31, 62–63, 262
sustainability class, 19–23, 25–59
    term and definitions, 19–23, 26–31
    See also green administrators;
        green modernists; lifestyle
        environmentalists; PIE (purity,
        innovation, and efficiency)
sustainable agriculture, 151–54
sustainable intensification (land sparing),
    151–53
Sweden, 124
Syria. *See* Democratic Confederation of
    Northeast Syria (Rojava)

Tagebu (open-cast lignite coal mine in
    Germany's Hambach Forest),
    251–52
Táíwò, Olúfẹ́mi, 165–66
Talatona (Luanda, Angola), 162–63
Tamil Nadu, India
    Auroville's exclusion of local Tamils,
        173–74, 193–99
    Dalit women's food sovereignty
        movement, 236
    See also Auroville (Tamil Nadu)
Tanzania, 65
tech-industry workers
    and consumption-based accounting,
        111
    union organizing, 252
technology companies (big tech)
    carbon emissions, 117

green modernism, 38–39
greensters, 11
Silicon Beach, 5, 11
Silicon Valley, 11, 107, 111
Venice Beach, 5
Telegram, 150, 262
Telosa (future city in Nevada), 187
Terán, Manuel Esteban Paez
    ("Tortuguita"), 246–47, 248
Terium, Peter, 14
Terminator Shock (Stephenson), 137
territory-based accounting, 110
Tesla, 48, 114, 118, 186, 227
Themba-Nixon, Makani, 208
The Theory of the Leisure Class (Veblen),
    27
Thorpe, David, 126
Three-Body Problem (novel/television
    series), 30
Thunberg, Greta, 218–19, 220
TikTok, 139, 262
TimeOut, 7
Tinder, 5
tissue culture technology, 145–46
tool libraries, 256
Toronto, Canada, 187, 260
TotalEnergies SE (French oil company),
    11, 55–56
tourism, 64. *See also* eco-tourism
Toyota's Woven City (Japan), 187
"Tragedy of the Commons" (Hardin), 71
transatlantic slave trade, 159
tree planting projects, 8–9, 42, 135, 177,
    223, 231
trees, 3D-printed, 51
Trolley Times (Indian Farmers' Movement),
    263
trophy hunting, 64–65, 87–88, 135
Trudeau, Justin, 115, 139
Trump, Donald, 4, 15, 41–42, 232
tsetse fly, 86–88
12 Monkeys (film), 30
Twitter, 186. *See also* X (formerly Twitter)

Uber, 39, 117, 186
Uganda, 145
Ukraine, 59, 126, 140
UN Biodiversity Conference in Montreal (2022), 43, 154
UN Climate Change Conference in Dubai (2023) (COP28), 12, 46, 167
UN Climate Change Conference in Glasgow (2021) (COP26), 201
UN Climate Change Conference in Sharm-el-Sheikh (2022) (COP27), 167
UN Development Programme, 202
UN Environment Program's 30x30 Global Biodiversity Framework (2022), 43, 154
UN Global Environment Facility, 45, 202
UN Human Rights Council's draft resolution on reparations (2022), 166–67
UN Paris Agreement for Climate Change, 119–20
UN Sustainable Development Goals, 101, 214, 231
UNESCO, 194, 210
uneven trade, 159–61
unhoused people (homeless), 9, 10, 21, 57, 67, 99, 217, 228, 237
Union de Vecinos (Los Angeles), 221–29, 233, 237, 239–40, 244–45, 253–54, 258
    BHAAAD coalition against artwashing, 224–25
    building power, 244–45, 258
    creation of, 222
    tenants' rights and anti-eviction campaigns, 223–24, 225–28, 239–40
United Airlines, 5
United Arab Emirates
    carbon offsetting schemes, 162
    COP28, 12

luxury safari tourism, 65
Masdar City, 35, 187
net zero pledge, 231
United Kingdom
    carbon emissions, 168
    conservation game reserves in Africa, 66–67, 87
    rejecting notion of reparations, 166–67
    See also British colonialism
United States
    carbon emissions, 112–13, 168
    and climate reparations, 167–68
    community land trusts, 255
    material footprint, 129–30
    uneven trade, 160
universal basic income, 255
universal basic services, 255–57
Université de Montréal, 267
uranium mining, 125–26
Urban Alchemy, 10
Urth Caffé, 5
U.S. Department of Housing and Urban Development, 222
U.S. military, 155

Vancouver, Canada, 260
Varvarousis, Angelos, 241–42
Veblen, Thorstein, 27, 30
veganism, 3, 6–7, 203, 217, 228
Venice Beach, California, 2–9, 181
    Abbot Kinney Boulevard, 3, 9, 44, 217, 228
    Erewhon luxury supermarket, 7–8, 103–4, 138, 234
    Silicon Beach, 5, 11
    unhoused people, 9, 21
Venice Canals neighborhood (Los Angeles), 177, 180–82
Verra (carbon verifier), 54–55
vertical farming, 151, 177
La Via Campesina, 153, 168–69, 236
Vienna (Austria), 254–55

Vietnam
  Ecopark in Hanoi, 177–77, 182, 187,
    199–200, 218
  vườn ao chuồng (VAC) system, 97–98
virtue signaling, 22, 84, 205, 206, 220
voluntary carbon market (VCM), 54
Vonnegut, Kurt, 147
voting, 211
vườn ao chuồng (VAC) system, 97–98

wage disparities, 160–61
Wagner, Kate, 183–84
Walia, Harsha, 269
*The Wall Street Journal Guide to Investing
  in the Apocalypse* (Altucher and Sease),
    52–53
Wallace, Rob, 144
Walmart, 202
water crises (drinking water)
  Gaza, 89
  Jackson, Mississippi, 207, 209, 214
  Maywood, California, 225, 237
Watts, Alan, 1, 3
wealth inequality, 21, 111–12, 190–91
Wells Fargo, 5
Wengrow, David, 63
Wet'suwet'en clan, 240
Whatsapp, 150
William, Crown Prince, 66–67, 87
Wilson, E. O., 42, 70–71, 154

wind energy, 13–14, 137–39, 202
  and Neom, 13–14
  turbines and green sacrifice zones, 202
windfall taxes, 257
Winslet, Kate, 147
wokeness, 5, 10, 12, 21, 58, 205, 262
World Bank, 29, 45, 149, 167, 231
World Bank Governance Indicators, 231
World Conservation Society (WCS),
    154
world ecology, 79–80
World Economic Forum in Davos (2020),
    41–42
World People's Conference on Climate
    Change and the Rights of Mother
    Earth in Cocahbamba, Bolivia
    (2010), 165
World Wildlife Fund for Nature (WWF),
    64, 154, 202

X (formerly Twitter), 117, 139, 262
X, Malcolm, 57
Xpansiv, 54

Yale University Environmental
    Performance Index, 231
Yanomami people, 69
Yellow Vest movement (France), 169

Zimbabwe, 162

ABOUT THE AUTHORS

Vijay Kolinjivadi is an assistant professor at the School for Community and Public Affairs, Concordia University in Montreal, Canada. He is also a co-editor of the website Uneven Earth. He has been published in *Al Jazeera*, *New Internationalist*, *Truthout*, and *The Conversation*. He lives in Montreal.

Aaron Vansintjan is the founder and co-editor of Uneven Earth and co-author of *The Future Is Degrowth*. He has been published in *The Guardian*, *Truthout*, *openDemocracy*, and *The Ecologist*. He lives in Montreal.

PUBLISHING IN THE PUBLIC INTEREST

Thank you for reading this book published by The New Press. The New Press is a nonprofit, public interest publisher. New Press books and authors play a crucial role in sparking conversations about the key political and social issues of our day.

We hope you enjoyed this book and that you will stay in touch with The New Press. Here are a few ways to stay up to date with our books, events, and the issues we cover:

- Sign up at www.thenewpress.com/subscribe to receive updates on New Press authors and issues and to be notified about local events
- Like us on Facebook: www.facebook.com /newpressbooks
- Follow us on Twitter: www.twitter.com/thenewpress

Please consider buying New Press books for yourself; for friends and family; or to donate to schools, libraries, community centers, prison libraries, and other organizations involved with the issues our authors write about.

The New Press is a 501(c)(3) nonprofit organization. You can also support our work with a tax-deductible gift by visiting www.thenewpress.com/donate.